William Palmer

William Palmer (1811– 1879)

William Palmer

The Oxford Movement and a Quest for Orthodoxy

by Robin Wheeler

Holy Trinity Publications
Holy Trinity Seminary Press
Holy Trinity Monastery
Jordanville, New York

Printed with the blessing of His Eminence,
Metropolitan Hilarion, First Hierarch
of the Russian Orthodox Church Outside of Russia

HTSP
HOLY TRINITY
SEMINARY PRESS

An imprint of

HOLY TRINITY PUBLICATIONS
Holy Trinity Monastery
Jordanville, New York 13361-0036
www.holytrinitypublications.com

ISBN: 978-1-942699-37-8

Cover images: "The Alexander Nevsky Cathedral in Tallinn, Estonia" by jcg_oida. Source: stock.adobe.com. 118617809; "The Gothic Cathedral in Lincoln, Lincolnshire, England" by kilhan. Source: stock.adobe.com. 241308486; "Map of the World 1882" THEPALMER. Source: istockphoto.com. 241308486.

Engraving on page *ii* from: *Notes of a Visit to the Russian Church* by William Palmer (London: Kegan Paul Trench, 1882). Digital Image Source: Internet Archive, archive.org.

Bibliographic information published by Die Deutsche Bibliothek Die Deutsche Bibliothek lists this publication in the Deutsche National- bibliografie; detailed bibliographic data is available on the Internet at<http://dnb.ddb.de>.

British Library and Library of Congress Cataloguing-in-Publication Data: A catalogue record for this book is available from The British Library, Great Britain, and from The Library of Congress, USA

Contents

Introduction

If William Palmer is known at all today, it is as a strange Anglican obsessive on the margins of the Tractarian movement, a man who for all his considerable learning was entirely lacking in common sense and judgement. Little wonder perhaps, when in books such as P. E. Shaw's *The Early Tractarians and the Eastern Church* Palmer is described as 'sincere but eccentric and misguided',[1] or in John Lawrence's centenary tribute in *Sobornost*[2] as 'a vintage Oxford eccentric'. Nor is this view a retrospective one. It is entirely of a piece with the way that Palmer was regarded in his day. A friend, Canon Frederick Meyrick,[3] described him as 'an ecclesiastical Don Quixote',[4] a description that Palmer applied to himself with grim humour in his correspondence,[5] as he did the sobriquet of 'monomaniac'[6] accorded him by Bishop Terrot of the Scottish Episcopal Church. When James Barmby went to St. Petersburg in 1849, he found that the British living or trading there remembered Palmer only as 'a fool', 'a Madman', 'an ass', or 'a strange enthusiast'.[7] But Palmer was far from being a blinkered fool. Meyrick saw that this Don Quixote was also 'a man of noble soul, unselfish, honest, true, lovable'. In his preface to *Notes of a Russian Visit* Cardinal Newman paid tribute to Palmer's 'many and winning virtues; to his simplicity, to his unselfishness, to his gentleness and patience, to his singular meekness, to his zeal for the Truth, and his honesty whether in seeking or defending it; and to his calmness and cheerfulness in pain, perplexity and disappointment'.[8] He too characterised Palmer as 'a true and loyal friend' whose memory was 'very dear' to him.[9]

To understand this man who provoked both exasperation and affection in equal measure, this book draws on Roundell Palmer Lord Selborne's[10] *Memorials Family and Personal*, Palmer's own weighty publications such as the *Appeal to the Scottish Church*, his extensive correspondence, and his diaries and journals. The latter reveal a soul tormented by consciousness of sin, a sufferer from depression and a Victorian aspiring to the monastic asceticism of the Middle Ages.

His writings reveal the price he paid for his idiosyncratic quest for truth, not just in his stoical renunciation of a successful academic or legal career, but in his growing isolation, and a frequently awkward and angry relationship with his father. They show the dignity with which he dealt with humiliation and rejection in Scotland, and what amounted to betrayal by his own Church, in the character in which he presented it in France and later in Russia. Palmer had it seems only to make an assertion about the Anglican Church for some member of its hierarchy, often at the very highest level, to subvert it by act or word, and by so doing expose him to ridicule and contempt.

Elsewhere in his journals we find another Palmer, the evocative travel writer. These journals present a piquant contrast to the sedate life of an Oxford don for which he appeared to be destined. In them Palmer the Imperial adventurer braves the privations of a ship's hold to reach Mount Athos, is held up at spearpoint by an Arab tribesman, and struggles back to his Roman palazzo through the revolutionary troops of Garibaldi. A more esoteric and mystical side of his character is shown in Palmer's interest in dreams and their meaning, which he saw throughout his life as highly significant.

Light is also shed on episodes that remained unpublished in his lifetime. These include his treatment by the bishops of the Scottish Episcopal Church, his contest with the volatile Princess Galitsin, and his unsuccessful attempts to take his *Appeal* to the Episcopal Church of America, which unlike the Scottish Church recognised his qualities and treated him with courtesy. The book charts the course of his disillusionment with Anglicanism, and the subsequent tension between his intellectual conviction of the truth of Orthodox doctrine and his natural preference for the Roman Catholic Church. To follow this process is to understand how 'a man "of highest ability and learning, singleness of heart and noble purpose [...] one of the very ablest and best men the College had"'[11] could nonetheless fail to achieve any kind of worldly success, and end his days in the obscurity of exile in Rome.

1 Childhood, Rugby and Oxford

William Palmer was born on 12 July 1811 at Mixbury in Oxfordshire. William displayed from his infancy 'uncommon signs of ability, and a marked individuality of character'.[1] He 'was the favourite at Gledstone', the home of his maternal grandparents. A letter from his Aunt 'EAP' (presumably his Aunt Elizabeth) from Gledstone,[2] has a note at the top by Roundell Palmer which confirms this favourite status 'WP there – worshipped by Grandparents – EAP to take him back to Mixbury or Beachampton'.[3] His Aunt said of the three-year- old William:

> He is *certainly a very uncommon child in understanding*: & it is this consciousness of superiority, I suppose, that makes him dislike so much the company of other children of his own age: [...] W. has another quality of a very dangerous tendency, if not early noticed & guarded against; a very fertile invention; so much so, that he will tell a long history about a bear, horse, or anything else without the slightest foundation: and when you tax him with it, & say this is not true, he very readily answers, *It is only Willy's imagination*! But I must leave talking of this dear & interesting child. Pray God he may grow up a good and religious character! – or else I think he will be removed from this world, before he can be responsible for his own notions![4]

Apart from its charming aspect, the letter ironically foreshadows the many times that those who heard him on the Anglican Church would ascribe what they heard to his 'very fertile invention'.

His family was a distinguished one, that included a seventeenth- century member of parliament, Archdale Palmer, and merchants in the City of London, Thomas and William Palmer, William Palmer's great-grandfather and grandfather respectively, who began a connection with the Mercers' Company that extended to include William. On his mother's side there was Bishop Samuel Horsley, the leading prelate in the Church of England in his time, and 'a distinguished mathematician, editor of Newton's works, and secretary to the Royal Society' as well as 'a learned theologian'.[5] His uncle Edward was a Royal Naval Commander who was lost when his ship, HMS *Nautilus*, was wrecked in the Dardanelles in 1807.

Palmer's father, William Jocelyn Palmer, was educated at Charterhouse and Brasenose College, Oxford. At Oxford he both hunted and shot, but gave up field sports on ordination. Lord Selborne remarks that 'there were no honour examinations in those days', and he has no reason to suppose that his father 'received from his college any strong intellectual impulse'.[6] However his later correspondence with William, particularly as he saw him moving inexorably towards Rome, displayed a strong intelligence and a capacity for logical argument that would have made him an impressive figure in any court of law, had he chosen the Bar over the Church. More than once he had the best of the argument, sometimes displaying an unexpected talent for a sardonic and sarcastic turn of phrase that reduced William to evasion or silence.

William Palmer senior was ordained deacon in 1801, and priest in February 1802.[7] He was presented to the Rectory of Mixbury by his uncle Samuel Horsley,[8] then Bishop of Rochester, the same year. He was clearly a conscientious Rector, taking a personal interest in the 'five or six hundred poor people at Mixbury and Finmere' in his charge, and so generous to them as to make some of his parishioners speculate that he must have had some funds for the purpose, rather than his own money, although the latter was the case.[9] His preaching was 'thoughtful but not ambitious', with 'no thought of self; no aim at display'.[10] His churchmanship appears to have been Broad rather than High, as we would now understand High Church Anglicanism, although he subscribed whole-heartedly to the proposition that the Anglican Church belonged to the 'one Catholic and Apostolic Church', the credal proposition on which William was to rely so heavily in Russia. He had no sympathy, emotional or intellectual, for the Roman Catholic Church. Above all he had none of William's restlessness. He was entirely content to discharge the duties he had been given, although as Roundell Palmer says 'There was no position in the Church which he could not (in my belief) have worthily filled, and which he might not have ennobled and adorned'.[11] He also sat as a magistrate, and in the 1830s at the time of the 'Captain Swing' disturbances displayed both presence of mind and strength of character in confronting and calming a possibly dangerous mob.[12]

William's mother, Dorothea Roundell, was herself the daughter of a clergyman, the inheritor of an estate near Skipton. Except as the occasional addressee of his letters, she seems to have played hardly any rôle in William's life. In 1832 she was struck by a mysterious illness that began, so Lord Selborne tells us, with the 'loss of power' in one foot, 'the foot gradually turning round'.[13] This illness failed to respond to surgical treatment, and indeed went on to deprive her of movement, speech, hearing and sight. 'An eminent Oxford surgeon', Mr. Tuckwell,[14] diagnosed 'the nervous system as the seat of the disorder',[15] and advised that only time would be the cure, as was the case. There may be some connection between the illness and the tragic loss of Dorothea's son Tom[16] after an accident in 1823; but the gap in time is large. At any rate, it 'continued for years'.[17] In February 1834 Palmer's father wrote that she '[...] has certainly been gaining ground [...] tho' she does not yet speak, and we are occasionally troubled with distressing states of inquietude'.[18] And again in March the same year:

> Certainly her case is an extraordinary one of a very strange and extraordinary complaint. Her want of speech is attended with a difference of affection from any that has occurred before. She has the use of the organs of voice so far as the throat is concerned but the mouth and the tongue refuse to act in concert.[19]

Her condition made her less than easy to live with. In his journal for 1840, Palmer noted 'Resolutions: [. . .] Patentius cum matre (her bodily ails causing her to be often very excitable)'.[20]

Lord Selborne recalls how he and William were taken by their father on walks or on horseback on his visits to parishioners, or on fishing expeditions, and how they learned from him to 'find a pleasure in the observation of nature'. This extended from the habits of birds and animals to amateur astrology, chemistry and mineralogy. The boys spontaneously developed an interest in botany and entomology, helped by their Aunt Mary, and created a 'museum' in their schoolroom 'for insects, fossils, and other objects of natural history'.[21] This became something of a trial for their father when they went away to Rugby. He wrote to William in October 1823 'I like the specimens of stuffed birds for the Museum far better than the living ones which are troublesome unprofitable things for those who have anything else to do'[22] and later in the same month 'I am pleased that you have parted with the linnets'.[23] Their interest in nature led them to invent their own names for butterflies and wild plants, and this 'faculty of imagination increased in power. It coloured all our childish pleasures; it accompanied us upon the ice and into the woods; it mixed dreams of the supernatural with the most ordinary things'. They fancied themselves, in the middle of a frozen pool, on 'the islands discovered by Columbus or Cook', and had an early sense of the magical, or miraculous:

> We carved out of cleft sticks what passed with us for images of humanity, and stuck them into the damp ground at night, hoping [. . .] that we might find them endowed with life when we came to look for them in the morning.[24]

However, their childhood was by no means all a bucolic idyll of walks and butterfly collecting. They were schooled at home by their father 'with great assiduity, and admirable regularity, patience and judgement'.[25] It was no easy programme.

> We rose early, and began every day by reading with him the Psalms for that morning. We began Latin at five years old and Greek at six [...] by the time we were nine years old, we were fairly well grounded in Virgil and Horace, and not unpractised in verse translation, and had begun the Greek Testament. Pope's Homer and Dryden's Virgil were familiar to us, and before we went to school we had made some progress in the original of Homer, and had read though the *Prometheus* of Aeschylus. Nor were we ignorant of Shakespeare, Milton, and some other English classics.[26]

Their father was 'not technically an exact scholar, but, in a practical sense [. . .] a good one'. Lord Selborne concludes 'I do not think we could have been better prepared for a public school by any teacher then living in England'.[27]

This encomium has, however, to be balanced against the explanation he gives for the difficulties he faced at Rugby, that led to his being removed and sent to Winchester. 'Our parents,' Selborne says, 'managed us upon a regular and methodical system, and we sometimes chafed at it. I had to be taught the government of my tongue and my hands by correction, more severe on some occasions than my conscience acknowledged to be just',[28] presumably caning on the hand or the backside. Although he piously expresses himself 'thankful' that 'those aberrations were effectually checked', this was 'at some cost to the openness and unreserve which is so important between parents and children',[29] and possibly by 'openness and unreserve' he may mean natural love and trust. When Palmer's younger brothers were also educated at home, 'the strictness of the original method may have been somewhat softened'.[30] In dealing with his parishioners Palmer's father was 'not demonstrative, nor a man of many words; he kept his feelings, which were naturally warm and strong, quite under command'.[31] That their father's feelings were warm, and that he was affectionate, emerges convincingly enough from his correspondence with William, even when relationships between them were at their most strained; but he appears to have been a demanding and stern figure. Resentment of the strictness of this early upbringing may have contributed to William Palmer's stubborn insistence on following his own course at the cost of a successful conventional career.

RUGBY SCHOOL

The brothers' home education ended in the summer of 1823 when they were both sent to Rugby. Rugby was the nearest public school to Mixbury, and the nephew of a family friend was already a pupil there.[32] Founded in 1567 by Laurence Sheriff as a local charity, by the second half of the eighteenth century Rugby had ceased to serve the needs of the local population and the children of the poor, becoming instead the provider of a classical education to the children of the higher ranks of society.[33] The school had fallen into dilapidation in 1750, but thanks to the initiative of the trustees ('twelve gentlemen of Warwickshire') in moving the school to a new site, it prospered and 'achieved national reputation under the headmastership of Dr. Thomas James, (1778-94), under whom the number of pupils rose to nearly three hundred'.[34] However in 1797, the next headmaster, Dr. Henry Ingles, faced a rebellion during which 'desks and other furniture were burned in the Close, the headmaster's door was blown off its hinges, and troops (in the guise of a recruiting party) were brought to the scene'.[35] Fortunately under the next headmaster, Dr. John Wooll, 'Rugby's reputation was fully restored';[36] he was headmaster when Roundell and William Palmer went there in 1823.

Contemporary public schools were frequently anarchic places. Drunkenness was rife at Rugby and elsewhere; in 1814 two boys, Fisher (the grandfather of Geoffrey Fisher, Archbishop of Canterbury 1945–61) and Cook were in trouble for persistent drunkenness. Fisher was flogged, and Cook ran away from the school, the headmaster refusing to take him back again. J. H. Macaulay wrote home that the boys had got into a scrape 'for drinking which has lately got into the school very much'.[37] Fighting was equally commonplace, not in the form of some momentary scuffle, but in gladiatorial contests designed to test the combatants' powers of endurance of pain and fatigue.[38] Roundell Palmer records his 'first and only pugilistic encounter with a Manx boy of about my own size, in which neither can be said to have come off victorious, for our backers made us go on till we were both fairly exhausted'.[39]

The Rev. Lucas Collins, who was at Rugby in 1833, found that 'there was a terrible amount of flogging'.[40] Lord Selborne writes that he 'had a taste of the birch-rod, compared to which the Winchester instrument of castigation was child's play'. Bullying was a feature of life at Rugby, although allegedly 'the worst excesses of bullying, "buffeting",[41] "chairing",[42] "clodding",[43] were put down in 1815'.[44] Nonetheless, 'civilisation had not yet found its way into our great public schools. I was sensitive to bullying, and was (no doubt for that reason) a great deal bullied'.[45] Roundell's father 'thought it prudent' to remove him from Rugby after two years; Roundell later wrote that 'it was certainly best for me to be removed, though I did not like it at the time'. He thought that 'my brother derived from Rugby more benefit than I did, and was fitter, morally and physically, to hold his own there. It might perhaps have been better for him to have remained there longer than he did [...] '.[46] What William made of Rugby can be seen from what he wrote to the Roman Catholic convert George Spencer[47] in 1840, when Spencer had raised with him the question of

> the horrible state of English Public Schools & Universities in respect of morals: I said that I could find no simile to express the difference between my early education at home and the new world I found myself in at School better than that of a transplantation from Paradise to Pandemonium & yet I have reason to think that Rugby was considerably less vicious than some other Public Schools.[48]

His 'first letter after reaching school,' as it is annotated, dated August 1823, reflected his shock:

> Dear Papa and Mama,
>
> I find my expectation more than realised for surely I never saw such a complication of wickedness since I was born. Out of 19 boys whom I know there are only two who have not in my presence done or said something which ought alone to be sufficient to prevent my associating with them [...]. [49]

His next letter, written in September, gave examples, as well as indicating the extraordinary freedom that public schoolboys of the time enjoyed, despite the official rules:

> Dear Mama,
>
> There has been a great commotion here: two boys have been expelled one for refusing to do a punishment set him, the other for stealing money from my drawer [...] I go out of bounds every day, for there is not one boy in the whole school who does not, sometimes to fish and sometimes to walk or get flowers and insects.[50]

Their father wrote to Roundell in November

> I am extremely concerned to hear of the repeated rows and expulsions that have taken place this half-year at Rugby in all of which the master seems to have conducted himself with great propriety while his scholars have equally disgraced themselves.
>
> It is well for them that I am not their master. I think they might find my hand somewhat heavier than the Doctor's.[51]

In the mention of the 'hand' that might be 'somewhat heavier than the Doctor's' is a possible indication of the 'correction' administered in the Mixbury schoolroom.

Roundell Palmer says that when letters home mentioned 'anything disagreeable', their father 'advised us to bear silently what we could not help, unless it were of a corrupting as well as a tormenting kind,' in which case they were to seek the help of 'the elder boy to whom we had been recommended',[52] presumably the nephew of the family friend. He also urged them to remember what they had gone through so that when they were older and bigger, they would not do the same again to the younger boys. When faced with immorality of whatever kind they should hate the sin and love the sinner. In September 1824 he wrote to William

> No doubt what you allude to is wrong, very wrong, and I pray God you may ever be sensible of it and ever able to keep yourselves from it. But [...] when you see others speak and act as they ought not and shock you even perhaps by indecency and profaneness, while you cannot but hate the thing you should regard the person [...] at least with pity and compassion.[53]

It might be, after all, that they had reason for self-examination. In the same letter he wrote:

> My Dear Willy [...] remember also that no place will bring satisfaction with it unless you are liked as well as respected by your schoolfellows; therefore be kind and considerate and beware of a forward carriage or presumptuous manner, which are sure to make one disliked and often deprive us of the credit we otherwise deserve. But the remedy against this is a lowly opinion of oneself therefore remember always what a poor helpless boy you yourself are, and have regard to the merit of another.[54]

Most likely this was precautionary advice after an academic success that might have led to over-confidence. Mr. Moor, one of the masters, wrote to their father: 'Your elder son was removed a few weeks since into Mr. Birch's form, who speaks very well of him, though he complains that he takes it for granted that he understands things, without always ascertaining that fact with sufficient care'.[55]

Both William and Roundell were made vividly aware by their father of the importance of not incurring debt. On one occasion William brought home some stuffed birds as presents for his sisters. On examination by his father he confessed that he had not yet paid for them, but proposed to do so the next term, as the tradesman concerned was willing to wait. His father despatched him with the birds back to Rugby ('a three days' journey, there and back') in the gig, to return them to the dealer. He also carried a letter to the headmaster, requesting him to instruct the Rugby tradesmen not to supply his sons, unless for ready money. 'This,' wrote Emily Palmer, 'was a lesson the boys never forgot'.[56]

There was no repetition, during William's time at Rugby, of the riots of 1797, but there were certainly what he describes in letters to his father as 'commotions'. On 15 March 1825 he wrote that somebody had thrown stones at the house of 'the Supervisor or Master Exciseman' whose house was just across the Dunchurch road from the school playground. The Supervisor, understandably furious, 'collared the first Rugby boy [...] who passed by, and with very gross language told him that he would break his head'. The tables were turned however when the boy 'roared out' for help 'to his schoolfellows in the Playground', who 'immediately came and rescued the boy, and well licked the Supervisor, who went off muttering vengeance in which however the boys anticipated him, for the next evening they assembled to the number of 50 or 60 and utterly demolished all his windows'! 'I rather think,' William remarked drily in closing, 'the Supervisor will be attacked again'.[57] His father, having suggested appropriate punishment for the damage done, rather surprisingly took the side of the boys: 'I do not pity the man the licking he got in the first instance at all', and thanked William very much for giving him an account of 'these commotions'.[58] In June the same year there were other excitements: 'the other day Wombwell's caravan of wild beasts came here, and in it there was the great lion [Nero?] which is to fight 6 mastiffs on Warwick race course in August'.[59]

MAGDALEN

On 27 July 1826, at the age of 15, William Palmer matriculated at Magdalen College, Oxford. This was by any standards a remarkably young age at which to do so:[60] 'it was a disadvantage to him [...] to be a boy among men', and 'at each step of the race, during his undergraduate course, he felt himself thrown back by having to work, as it were, against time'.[61] It was particularly galling when with 'a powerful intellect, strong will, and ambitious temperament' he knew himself to be 'superior in natural abilities, and in the desire of distinction, to those around him'.[62] The practical effect of his comparative youth was to delay the success of which he knew himself capable; he was beaten for the Ireland Scholarship by 'Shrewsbury men, well "crammed", but not otherwise remarkable',[63] and failed to win the Chancellor's prize for Latin verse until just before he took his degree. However, he did win that prize with a poem on Tyre in 1830, taking a First class in Classics the same year; and in 1833 he won the University Latin Essay Prize. 'He did everything very well, but nothing without the discipline of previous disappointments'.[64]

Initially, Palmer swung between anxiety and intellectual self- confidence. When the Porter brought him a note reminding him of a lecture on Herodotus, he was 'terribly frightened', indeed 'in the utmost consternation', for he 'did not know what sort of thing Ellerton's lecture was'. But after frantic study of 'the History grammatical construction Chronology Geography and the like', leaving no time to look at the text itself, he 'found it was "Montes parturiunt, nascetur ridiculus mus"', for the whole lecture consisted of a shabby loose construe of a chapter of Herodotus apiece and as I had the luck to be on last I had plenty of time to look over my part'. The lecture was 'a perfect farce and my hour completely thrown away – for I knew about as much when I came out as I did when I went in as not one question or observation of any sort passed during the whole time'.[65]

His domestic arrangements, too, failed to come up to the mark: 'the Scouts are never stirring before a quarter past seven so that before that I am obliged to sit in my bedroom and their cleaning my sitting room occupies till at least 8 o' clock'. Worse, 'All my linen comes so damp from the laundress that I am obliged to air at my own fire every article I put on'.[66] There was however some light relief. In January 1827, 'during the vacation after Christmas [...] a Dancing Master came to give us lessons, and amused us a good deal by the importance he attached to [his] art and the pomposity with which he harangued us on it'.[67]

In 1829 he tried for the Ireland Scholarship but 'had the honour of being *third*, when two men of *junior standing* to myself, (though how much older it is needless to say) were first and second', he wrote furiously to his father. 'I hope *Roundell*, at least, will be spared so much a mortification [...] the whole of this next year [...] I shall employ in working to wipe off some of my disgrace'. His frustration at being so much younger than his contemporaries, already hinted at, burst out: 'I will not recur to a sore subject, but [...] this would never have happened if I had come to the University, at the same age that other men do. You cannot conceive how vexed I am, nor how tormented with the *congratulations*! of my illiterate acquaintances'.[68] He even berated himself for having headaches and being so unwell during the papers he knew best and was most secure in that he 'could do nothing, except what I should have been flogged for in the upper fourth at Rugby'.[69]

His father in reply confessed that his early entry to Oxford was a matter of financial necessity. Family expenses had already entailed making 'some inroads more or less upon the capital':

> It is clear [...] that the earlier the period at which we may be relieved from the charges of maintenance and education for the older brothers, the freer will be our means of doing the same part for the younger. Hence the beneficial influence is apparent, which your early entrance at the University your conduct there, which is deserving of all praise, and your prospects, may have upon those who are to follow.[70]

He reassured him:

> You have stood forward even with the very first, and you are not disgraced. Nay, you have pressed them hard who had every advantage over you. What patient and persevering industry may achieve, we have still to see. But no matter. I care not for this crown: Yet you will certainly attain.[71]

He felt it necessary to add a cautionary note, about some 'fears' which may be 'ridiculous': 'Do not neglect society - do not grow formal and precise in speech; but be cheerful and easy and confident without sauciness or presumption'. To some Palmer could appear aloof and 'formal'. The writer[72] of a waggish and anonymous article in *The Rock* related that he

> occupied in my undergraduate days rooms almost close to those of Mr. Palmer [...] he was very studious, very dry, and very cold. I do not think I ever heard him laugh! One morning I was startled by a merry peal from Magdalen tower at an unwonted time, and on asking "the reason why", was informed that "Mr. Palmer had won the Chancellor's Prize for Latin verse", so

> I hastened to congratulate, and found him as happy as his impassive nature would permit. This was repeated next year[73] when the prize for the best Latin essay was adjudged to him.[74]

Others took a more jaundiced view. His friend Edward Whately[75] asked teasingly: 'You want to know the V-P's private opinion of you?' and after some prevarication described a meeting with the Vice- President at Whately's house, at which the Vice-President affected, when asked, not to know who Palmer was: 'Palmer – Palmer – do you mean a young man who has won a prize or something of that sort?' Whately retorted that not only had he got '*some prize* but that by his degree he had established a reputation which reached beyond the walls of his college and that he might be known by name at least to one of its officers, for I was somewhat nettled at this commonplace affectation'. The Vice-President then admitted, 'as if it was extorted from him,' that he did know Palmer. '"He is no favourite of yours?" "No, nor of anybody else"'. Whately suggested that he was mistaken, told him 'that you were a favourite of *mine*,' and pressed him to explain his remark:

> He then proceeded to say that an overweening confidence in your own abilities produced an insufferable conceit which made you despise the acquirements of everybody else. That to the Tutors etc. of your College in particular you used a most contemptuous manner, and the care and advice they were willing to bestow, you rejected or perhaps ridiculed.

He instanced an occasion on which Palmer allegedly cut short a tutor's recommendation to read Livy with the languid observation that '"One takes up Livy, sir, as a *post-chaise* companion but you cannot expect to see him on my *study table*"'.[76] Whately said that he expressed his surprise at this, and the stories like it that followed. Palmer could be blunt in his assessment of what he perceived as second-rate ('a shabby loose construe,' for example) but this sort of studied insolence was not in his style. It is certainly conceivable, however, that his confidence in his very evident ability may have given others the impression of conceit – others who knew they could not match him, perhaps. It is unlikely that the President of Magdalen, Dr. Routh[77], could have been fond of Palmer had Palmer been as conceited and contemptuous as the Vice-President allegedly thought him.

As a corrective to the view of Palmer as remote and 'cold' there is the testimony of his brother to his close friendships, most notably with Charles Wordsworth of Christ Church[78] and Thomas Legh Claughton[79] ('the glory of Rugby, and of my own College').[80] Palmer's diary describes a wider circle, 'the Club': 'dined with Wordsworth at the Club till 12 (present W'worth, Hamilton, Claughton, Twiss, Dudding, Grant, Walker, Hillyard, Wilson)'.[81] The 'Club' in question appears to have been 'the Bachelors' Club', referred to more than once with nostalgia by

Claughton in his letters to Palmer after leaving Oxford: 'I could not have remained in Oxford "ultimus Romanorum" [...] Romanorum signifying here the Bachelors' Club',[82] and 'I do not repent of having left Oxford – only excepting those desolate moments when I sigh for the jolly Bachelors – for the clerical Wordsworth, for the philosophical Palmer, for the vivacious Jeffreys – even for the garrulous Twiss!'[83]

Claughton, according to Roundell Palmer, 'had a great charm of countenance and manner, and a disposition which nobody could help loving [...] a quick sense of humour, and an inexhaustible command of playful irony, which only enhanced his affectionateness'.[84] This appears in his letters to Palmer, not least in his penchant for peculiar nicknames. He urged Palmer in July 1833, 'Do not delay to write to me, my dear Loo Choo – on any account', and in November that year 'I hear you *Loo-Chooed* them a little'. Perhaps at a dinner of the Bachelors' Club the 'philosophical Palmer' had alluded pompously to the Chinese philosopher Lao-Tzu, and this was Claughton's way of teasing him about it. In 1835, apropos of a projected visit by Palmer to Ireland, where Claughton was tutoring the children of Lord and Lady Ely, he wrote (rather startlingly): 'What shall I say of *you*, who fall in love with Children of 4 years old – you setter at nought of all ordinary rules and proprieties, you inexplicable old Sphinx – What are you coming into this horrid country for at Easter? To floor some Jesuits?'[85] and elsewhere, apropos of nothing in particular, 'for it is to be allowed that you are a most profound old Monster'[86] before going on to speak of receiving a letter from an Oxford friend of Roundell's, John Thomas: 'He told me that you and Roundell were two excellent fellows – but ascribed to *you* this singular superiority – that you were *great fun* into the bargain. I hope you have had no more gout, Old Gentleman'.[87] He rebutted Palmer's accusation of 'profligate facility' in passing a student – 'a very serious accusation, coming from *some* people – but from *you* I don't mind it – because you are a most tyrannical old monster'.[88] Sometimes nicknames were forsworn in favour of absurd 'Franglais': 'Dites-moi, je vous prie, que faites vous avec vous même? Combien de fois avez vous diné chez le Docteur Pusey?'[89] Palmer was no bloodless, dusty academic. He was capable of inspiring and reciprocating friendship, to the extent of being described as 'great fun'. His capacity for extreme seriousness (which Claughton's teasing probably reflects, to some degree) was the other side of this coin.

Palmer's father hoped that his son would follow him into the Church: 'It is indeed my desire and my prayer that you may be found worthy of the Ministry. But things may not appear to you as they appear to me [...]'[90] Palmer responded 'What you seem to wish [...] that I should not even think of Politics [...] is impossible – I should lose every spur to exertion every hope of success by exertion – and should be like a ship without any destination, a labourer without an object'.[91]

Despite this surprising declaration he must, by 1831, have raised again the question of ordination with his father, who, possibly as a ploy to stimulate his son's decision, refused to be drawn:

> You no longer possess that elastic mind, which might receive any impression from me and I cannot, therefore, choose your profession. I dare not to choose for you the Church as a profession, unless [...] you choose it for yourself. If that may not be, I see no alternative but the Law.[92]

In December Palmer confessed 'that, though I feel the superiority of the Church, I never felt any preference for the species of life which a clergyman is obliged to lead'.[93] Nine days later the Church was *not* ruled out, although Medicine and the Law were: 'Of Law or Physic I do not even *dream*, but if *circumstances do* in any way *drive* I would rather be *driven* anywhither than into the Church, though perhaps I had rather *choose* the Church than any thing else'.[94] The series of underlinings may indicate a consciousness on Palmer's part of pressure on him to choose a profession. In the same letter he remarked 'I feel that I am unfit to decide for myself and hope for advice from you and direction from above'.

2 France and Durham

On 9 December 1831, a prospectus had appeared for 'The University of Durham, Durham College', which it was intended should open in October 1832. One of the proposed posts was 'Junior Tutor and Censor'. The first Warden of Durham, Archdeacon Thorp,[1] wrote to Palmer's grandfather, the Reverend W. D. Roundell: 'I attended the Chapter on Saturday to put down Mr [...] Palmer's name as a Candidate for the Junior Tutorship'.[2]

Palmer's father dismissed other possibilities: 'Would you be a man of the world, a diplomatist? I think not. Would you make letters a profession? I advise it not'[3] (wise advice, given the struggle Palmer had to make a living as a historical writer during the last twenty-four years of his life). On the other hand 'the Durham appointment, if they will have you, promises [. . .] to one of your standing who does not object to work, a year or two of useful pastime' in particular because

> We (of the Church I mean) stand in need of all the learning and all the talent we can enlist [...] nor need you fear [. . .] the least necessity or inducement to confine your energies hereafter to the care of a parish, or even accept of such a cure.[4]

He still considered that

> If you do not ultimately take Orders, the Law must be your lot [...] I do not agree [...] that the Durham appointment is incompatible with the future profession of the Law. There is one branch of the Law to eminence in which some ten or twelve years of active employment in a University has been no impediment and may be none again.

Strangely, he even appears to have begun to favour his son's idea of a political career:

> I think there are other circumstances which might lead you to consider the Commons as more eligible in your case than the Inns of Court – And with such a view as this a previous

> connexion with a University and with a Church especially such a Church as Durham promises much advantage [...][5]

This last observation seems rather at odds with his earlier pronouncement that 'Nothing [. . .] that is of this world is, or ought to be considered as separate, distinct, opposed to the service of God; – except worldly ambition [...]'.[6] He also encouraged him: '[...] have more confidence in yourself: nothing more is wanting. The power is in you'.[7]

Meanwhile his son entertained himself by compiling lists in his diary:

> Pack up making a list of *Clothes*: Linen etc. as follows:
> 12 Shirts
> 11 pr cotton stockings
> 7 silk pocket handkerchiefs
> 6 black silk neckcloths
> 3 coloured ditto
> 6 pair calico drawers
> 4 buff waistcoats
> 3 cotton neckcloths
> 4 cotton night caps
> 1 Black coat
> 1 Invisible Green do
> 1 pair rough trousers
> 1 Black waistcoat
> 1 Flannel dressing gown
> 4 satin stocks
> 1 silk waistcoat
> 2 cambric pocket handkerchiefs
> 1 Black cloth waistcoat
> 1 Black coat
> 1 Green ditto
> 1 Black frock
> 1 pair buff trousers
> 1 pair black trousers
> 1 pair Plaid Trowsers
> 2 pair washleather gloves
> 7 pair silk socks
> 3 pair white gloves
> 3 pair white gloves
> 1 Petersham.[8]

Another was no doubt attributable to the voyage of his brother Henry to India and China in 1832, as a midshipman in the naval service of the East India Company:

> Write out list of things that may be procured from China - or India
> + Betel-nut tooothpowder
> + Nankin trowsers
> White silk Trowsers
> Thin shoes
> + Ricepaper paintings
> Bows & arrows
> Manila hats
> Wafer stamps
> White Nankin trowsers
> China Duck Trowsers
> White silk P. handkerchiefs
> Set of chess men
> Backgammon board
> Corals & shells
> Edible swallow nests
> Mother of pearl pens or ivory Writing desks.[9]

In 1832 he was making resolutions. The first, 'Resolve to write in a flashy style next year and learn some of Cicero's orations by heart',[10] so far as we know came to nothing. However, he also recorded that he was seeking information about a French master 'the first indication [...] of a wish or plan for going abroad'. He also explained the logic that led him, as one who had until now been concerned with the study of Classics, to form:

> an intention of specially cultivating acquaintance with the clergy whether Protestant or Catholic, which I took up while reading an article, I think, on Boswell's Life of Johnson in the Quarterly. Dr. J. gave Boswell this advice as the Clergy, he said, commonly think more about subjects of importance and know more about them than the Laity. And I generalising from the few opportunities I had had of observing English Squires and Parsons in conversation together, fancied that I had come to the same conclusion.[11]

To Charles Wordsworth he described how he had 'been more engaged with hunting antediluvian Elephants & excavating gravel-pits than with my books'.[12] He was also reaping the rewards of his undergraduate achievements. In July 1833 he was 'admitted [...] actual Fellow of Magdalen, and attended as such the College Meeting afterwards'.[13] On 2 October there were 'letters from Durham announcing my appointment to the Junior Tutorship and I resolve to accept it, and write the next day to the Warden and to RP'.[14]

Palmer moved up to Durham on 22 October 1833, and lodged 'at first for a few days in the house of the Archdeacon Prebendary Mr. Thorp Warden of the new University, and afterwards in Mr. Gisburne's house in the College'. Roundell warned his brother that:

> In spite of this smoothness of manner and other pleasing qualities, every one who has had experience of the reverend Archdeacon finishes his encomium upon them with a – "but" – [...] so you must not be off your guard – particularly after the experience we have had of him ourselves.[15]

Palmer's first impressions of Durham organisation were mixed:

> On my arrival I found no such preparations made as I expected; no rooms ready for tutors, no houses for Professors, no places for Lectores, in short nothing. There were a good many workmen employed in separating three private houses which belong to the Chapter into as many minute sections as possible just large enough to hold a huge clumsy French bed and a chest of drawers – each of the students has *one* of these and no sitting room!

His own position was not much better: 'I am to have a house to myself in time: this sounds very fine, doesn't it? But I can tell you that you are a good deal better off in your rooms in Trinity. This house is a sort of cottage consisting of four rooms – each of which is a most curious shape'. He nonetheless concluded: 'My opinion of the whole is good'.[16] His friend Claughton expressed his sympathy in ribald terms:

> I must say, my dear Palmer, I cannot forgive the Durhamites their behaviour to you – tho' there is something in what you say of your age. Nobody could imagine that such a stiff steady old Cock as you are, covered with laurels, could be found of one and twenty [...] That is your time of life, is it not? But however you are quite wise to bury all this in oblivion, and shew them what a fine animal you are.[17]

Claughton wrote again in December, perhaps influenced by his own experience of tutoring, with the brittle comment that: 'The backwardness of the boys must be a great bore – one's soul does not expand in drumming rudiments into their dense little craniums'.[18]

The Durham students were indeed dense, a consequence of the Warden's lowering of standards in the interests of business. Palmer, who it was agreed should lecture 'in Aeschylus [...] and Virgil', was infuriated by Thorp's resolution 'to admit bad (vile) scholars saying he will examine them himself'.[19] Two days later Palmer agreed with a fellow tutor 'to admit no more incapables whatever'.[20] The Warden was equally frustrating when it came to drawing up statutes and a constitution for the new university, initially both a university and a college after the model of Trinity College, Dublin, and governed by the Dean and Chapter of the cathedral. In May he blocked the grant of a veto to Convocation on legislation affecting the University, which in Palmer's view left Durham 'the mere temporary creation of the Dean & Chapter of Durham & liable to be remade and remade and have all its statutes changed from time to time by the same Dean & Chapter'.[21] In October the Warden pronounced that 'the Dean and Chapter and the Warden *were* the University';[22] but by November he was coming under pressure:

> The Warden is regularly at bay for he can find nobody to speak of the University as founded and the Chapter are all beginning to find that something must be done – but nobody knows what – it is impossible to say what the Warden's thoughts are upon the subject – his mind seems to be something like a quicksand.
>
> Whoever heard of a University governed by a Warden [...] or of tutors and Professors members at once of a University and a College in one? [23]

Statutes were at last drawn up by one of the prebendaries, Dr. Smith, put before the Chapter on 21 November 1834, and passed.[24] There was likewise a struggle to obtain recognition of Durham degrees, but by January 1834 'The 2 Archbishops of Canterbury & York' had 'distinctly recognised the BA degrees of the University of Durham as carrying all the privileges of an Oxford or a Cambridge degree'.[25]

Discipline was a pressing concern. Palmer had to institute a system of 'sconcing' or fining in Hall 'in consequence of some rude noises in Hall yesterday during dinner.' 'Two Seniors' were made responsible to the Censors, of whom Palmer was one, for 'any unseemly noise, or any breach of gentlemanly manners & decorum

[…] perceived by the High Table'.[26] In addition 'the Butler wishes to know what *things* and Persons are to be permitted to enter the gates (in consequence of a noisy party last night)' – very likely those responsible for the rude noises earlier in Hall. By 'things' the Butler perhaps referred to musical instruments rather than drunken undergraduates: 'Put up a notice that no Key Bugle or other loud instrument be played in College except between the hours of 2 & 4 (3 & 5 in Winter)'.[27] A confrontation between Palmer and a freshman called Curwen ('Mr. Curwen *declined* giving me the names of his friends') led to the observation that 'some regulations are wanting also with respect to hours of Parties, and continuance of strangers in college after the gates are locked'.[28] Curwen's Durham career appears to have been enjoyable but short. Palmer noted in his journal 'Curwen left much in debt'.[29] On this question too, the Warden was less than helpful. Palmer reminded him that 'every Freshman on being matriculated at Oxford received a Book of the Statutes which he promised to obey', only to receive the bland retort 'Yes – & great Humbug — for nobody reads them'.[30]

In June Palmer was again having to draw attention to the effects of the haphazard University discipline: 'During the last week there has been no Watchman – The gate has sometimes been open, sometimes the men have got over the gate. There was a drunken rowing Party on the river a few nights ago'.[31] The question of gates and hours had become a pressing one, since the presence of students had created a stir in the town, and the fascination was mutual:

> The people are quite wild, the ladies especially about the gown. There being few young men in Durham, they declare that they will begin to dance at one in the day if necessary; but Academical beaux they *will* have! On the other hand the students are no less enchanted.[32]

A 9 o'clock curfew, imposed in February 1834, was consequently a relief to 'the young gentlemen of the town,' who were 'very glad of the new regulations as the ladies would scarcely notice them in the presence of the student'.[33] The students' keenness to make the acquaintance of the local females sometimes took a rather disturbing form. Some of the undergraduates were reported to Palmer as having been seen 'following women of the town in the streets'.[34] Other amusements were of a robust kind: 'There is boxing and wrestling with two or three fiddlers, Watson, Stephenson and Moorhouse Thompson',[35] while student eccentricity in 1834 was potentially lethal: –'Maddison is looked upon as mad, and has madness in his family – He threatened to shoot Wright and actually cocked his pistol the other day – he walks six miles every week to get his linen washed a penny cheaper […] '.[36]

Palmer was alive to the beauty of Durham and the countryside around it. In April 1834 he 'launched a skiff which I had procured from Oxford on the Wear; and kept it moored at the foot of the Old Mill now the Reading Room and Museum in the Walks'.[37] He told Christopher Wordsworth 'If you have never spent any *time* here – you will be surprised to hear that no place, I should think in England has more interesting walks in the environs – besides "the Banks" which are well known'.[38] Despite this, and despite encouragement from his father and brother to look on the positive side of life at Durham, Palmer had begun to chafe at his life as a Durham Tutor as early as March 1834. 'You seem to use' wrote his father 'rather strong expressions with regard to the occupation of your time – "perfect slavery" – "great nuisance" – but you do well to consider the length of the vacations also'.[39] Nonetheless by November 1834 Palmer was writing to Roundell: 'pray inquire and let me know what the *rule* is at Magdalen with respect to taking orders as a Fellow – and also what indulgence is customary as to the time'.[40]

TRAVELS AND RELIGIOUS DISPUTATION IN FRANCE

It was astute of Palmer's father to highlight the advantages of long vacations, for Palmer had formed the habit of spending the long summer holidays in France. His first taste of life abroad was in August 1833, when he 'crossed from Southampton to Havre' with his cousins. Although for Palmer it was 'as if we had dropped or disembarked into another world [...] everything in short was more or less different from what we had been used to in England', [41] his father had taken pains to ensure that his son's churchgoing at least should remain the same. For preference it should be 'a service of our own [...] i.e. an English chaplain', otherwise 'the Protestant Church for the prayers or ordinary worship, but not perhaps [...] the Communion as their Pasteurs [sic] were not episcopally ordained'.[42] This was in accordance with Palmer's disposition 'to favour the Foreign Protestant'; but his 'prejudices against the Foreign Churches' were soon 'reversed by my personal acquaintance with both'.[43] From a bookstall in the Place de la Pucelle Palmer purchased three Catholic books, a 'Parisien' (i.e. a Missal of the local use), "L'Ange Conducteur", and a one volume History of the Church. 'I underlined everything "new or contrary to my own Anglicanism"'.[44]

He returned to France the following year, accompanied by Charles Wordsorth.[45] He again bought a History of the Church, in which he 'afterwards underlined some statements, e.g. that in the Council of the Apostles at Jerusalem S. Peter *presided*'.[46] In Paris he saw two people who were to play significant parts in his life in the 1840s. The first was Benjamin Harrison,[47] shortly to be engaged in controversy in the columns of *L'Univers* with the abbé Jager,[48] and later chaplain to the Archbishop of Canterbury, Archbishop Howley.[49] Harrison had come to Paris 'to learn Arabic under a pupil of De Sacy'. The second was 'Bp. Luscombe, who is Chaplain to our Embassy',[50] with whom he had dined in England in April of 1834.[51] In Paris

Palmer attended the Comic Opera, and found the English an occasion for French hilarity: 'The jest of the evening was a Milord Anglais who made false concords & talked of coaches, to the great amusement of the Company'.[52] This was by no means necessarily affectionate laughter. Palmer recorded a conversation with his French hosts about English boorishness and xenophobia:

> They said to me the English cannot laugh like the French. They are less cheerful, and freeze society instead of enlivening it. The Abp has often heard himself called in London and elsewhere in England "French dog" and "d[...].d Frenchman"; and when he spoke English imperfectly, he was often laughed at most insultingly, even by people of the higher classes, a thing which would never happen to an Englishman in France.[53]

From Paris, Palmer went to Tours, where he agreed to live with a French priest, the abbé Robert,[54] 'en pension paying 130 francs a month'.[55] Lord Selborne describes the abbé as a man 'of much *bonhomie* and simplicity, but not otherwise remarkable',[56] although he had been a Professor at the College Royal for a year, 'when he lost his place by refusing to take the oath to Louis Phillipe'.[57] Palmer 'was installed with M. Robert' and his sister on 4 August. Palmer's theory of the Church, which made it simply a question 'of history and of human reason' as to the 'true opinion about the definition of the Church, and [...] the limits of her power', met with no sympathy from his host: 'There are not here two opinions equally matter for private judgement [. . .] that indeed of the Protestants is, like all their religion, a mere opinion, and a very shallow one'. He cynically dismissed Palmer's assertion that despite the Reformation the Anglican Church had preserved essential Catholic doctrine: 'if the Anglican Church has always preserved the same doctrine, it is only because its priests [ministers] are well paid to preserve it: and when once its revenues shall be taken away, your Church will dissolve of itself, and give place to the Catholics who are already making great progress in England'.[58] The abbé disliked Palmer's penchant for argument, rebuking him in terms that must have stung, given Palmer's voracious appetite for theological and ecclesiological reading: 'You love to discuss, while I detest it, because I find it useless to argue against ignorance & prejudice. You ought to read more'.[59]

Palmer found a more patient audience in M. Robert's sister. To her he rehearsed the view of the Reformation that he was to propound later in Russia, that it was at least as much the fault of the Pope as of Henry VIII, involving only the rejection of 'some doctrines [. . .] contrary to the Scriptures (and to primitive usage)', and 'certain customs' which were found to be 'inexpedient'. 'Their conscience, (not their reason alone) justified resistance', but in 'other indifferent matters' not contrary to their consciences they did not wish to reject the authority of the Pope. From this Palmer deduced that there was in the Church of England 'a true authority: but in a case which touches one's conscience one may be justified in resisting the authority, because the authority is not absolute nor infallible; but always with the prospect of having to give an account of our conscience to God'.[60] In ascribing all to the exercise of individual conscience and/or expediency this principle comes close, if it does not altogether conform, to M. Robert's description of 'a mere opinion'.

Despite these views, Palmer did not appear to others as a conventional Protestant Englishman. Monsieur de Martigny, out shooting with Palmer's friend Charles Whateley,[61] described him as 'Moitié Jesuite'.[62] Palmer wrote in his journal: 'Today being meagre day a fast day rather [the Vigil of the Assumption] I dined as a Catholic though I had breakfasted as an heretic'.[63] If this was written partly tongue in cheek there is no doubt that he did very soon begin to practise fasting and rigorous self-examination. M. Robert 'said often "You will be Catholic: your heart has not been entirely corrupted by Protestantism"',[64]and '"I hope you will be a Catholic, and a Catholic priest"'.[65] It is moving to read that when Palmer requested a letter of introduction to the Prefêt des Etudes at the College Stanislas in Paris (which in the event was never used) 'the old priest' wrote of him as

> a young Englishman who is seeking the true faith [...] I have taken the liberty of addressing him to you in the persuasion that you will do all you can to gain a soul to God, and withdraw it from error. He likes nothing so well as conversing about religion. If I were ever to hear of his return to the Catholic Church, I should be happy beyond expression.[66]

His parting with Palmer was evidently an affectionate one, with an embrace in the French manner. Palmer had obviously described it to his friend Edward Whateley as 'affecting,' and in reply Whateley suggested mockingly that he would have been 'titillated' to observe the scene: 'had he, as I wonder he did not, fallen on your neck without invitation I should have laughed out right – It would have been no joke [...] the effect of which added to the weekly beard and shirt must have certainly killed you – you who faint at the smell of *Beer* and turn pale at metal buttons on a waistcoat'.[67] It would seem that Palmer had established a reputation for fastidiousness among his friends.

Palmer was back in France in March 1835, in Paris with Bishop Luscombe. The Bishop bewailed the lack of zeal of the English for the evangelisation of France.[68] He had spent £7000 of his own money in building a chapel in the Rue Aguesseau, while the English had only given enough to pay for the organ. Whilst 'il voudrait surtout avoir une service en Français', the French themselves and their habits were another matter. 'Il ne juge pas apropos d'admettre une congregation Française dans sa Chapelle pour cracher sur le nave etc.'.[69] Palmer was also the guest of M. Monod,[70] Moderator of the French Calvinist Consistory, and expressed an intention, apparently not acted on, to spend his Long Vacation between Paris and Geneva as there was a Jubilee meeting of Pastors in Geneva at that time.[71]

The question of Palmer's future had not ceased to occupy his father, who it seems had come round to his son's view that Durham had served its purpose: 'I think,' he wrote, 'you will have the satisfaction of knowing you have been of use in the formation of the University and in giving it a name and an efficiency exceeding those of ephemeral quackeries of the age'.[72] Palmer's contribution to Durham was recognised in March, when he was asked by the Warden to be an examiner for the AB and AM degrees.[73] To these academic honours was added a family distinction dating from 1469, when Gilbert Palmer became a member of the Mercers' Company. Palmer's father wrote to him in May 1835 that his Uncle George was anxious for him to 'put on his gown [...] at Guildhall',[74] which entailed first taking up the Freedom of the City.

Palmer's father thought the Durham post might nonetheless be retained 'for a short time, two or three terms [. . .] Perhaps it would be best to defer your return to Oxford for another year [...] you will not be so rich a man at Oxford perhaps as you are at Durham'.[75] Roundell, however, hoped his brother would leave Durham 'this very Summer,' giving as reason

> the care and vexation and responsibility of your present employment. Nobody would bear the labour and annoyance of working hard for an inadequate remuneration, and being thwarted in his attempts to do good and even regarded with personal jealousy, (for such your letters lead me to think must be the case) by narrow-minded co-adjutors; unless for some solid prospect of future advantage [...].

This was unlikely to be had at Durham. 'It will never be a University; for you will never have degrees like those of Oxford and Cambridge'. Stalls would not be annexed to the Professorships, indeed the Professorships themselves would never be filled up. Without a beneficial foundation they could not hope to attract 'a constant succession of students,' which made likely 'a sudden evacuation of the university whenever your original set of undergraduates leave; for the numbers appear marvellously stationary'. Oxford, on the other hand, held out the prospect of 'a very large and extensive field for doing good', with 'a sure prospect of rising to an eminence and independence proportionate to the free enjoyment of literary society in general, and especially of the society of your dearest friends'. Should money be a problem, he could match his Durham salary by taking private pupils. In time succession to a College tutorship might add to his income, or a post as resident tutor 'to some nobleman or man of fortune'.[76] He cited as example their mutual friend Claughton, then making £500 a year from his tutoring in Ireland.

In February Palmer's father related a conversation with Dr. Routh, in which the President of Magdalen 'observed you must be thinking of offering so[on] for Holy Orders, presuming such to be your intention and he desired me to suggest to you that the time was come or soon would be'. Having sown the seed he tactfully left the decision to his son: 'Nothing on that subject has passed between us for some time – and you have not expressly acquainted me with the conclusion you may have arrived at – you know I leave the matter of your profession wholly to divine providence and yourself'.[77]

In the meantime, Palmer was vacillating. He had called on Dr. Routh at Oxford, and noted the hints dropped by the President that 'I must not suffer myself to become a stranger in my own College at Oxford – and that he did not see things at Durham, which should make it worthwhile to lose that connexion with Oxford which I had before';[78] but felt that he 'should be unwilling to give up my situation here, before things are a little more settled and the University established upon a fixed basis; especially after having taken part in its first Institution'.[79] He was part of a group that went on a reconnaissance of the Castle ('much as if we were come to take possession') and was impressed by the Hall which he thought 'would be inferior to few either at Oxford or Cambridge', and some of the rooms which struck him as 'very handsome', although he believed the Castle to be 'very cold'. But he felt that rooms in the Castle would be a poor exchange for the '3 tolerable ones' he currently occupied; and besides he did not think he would 'remain at Durham long enough to see the Castle in full occupation by the University' but looked forward 'to a return to Magdalen about this time next year'.[80]

Certainly he seems from his diary for April 1836 to be in need of change and stimulation: 'My thoughts are wandering and incoherent, hands and feet cold, two thirds of my time escapes me – I am lazy in the morning, too late at night, take no exercise, live on pills, have little memory, cannot compose, nor write straight – cannot readily express my thoughts in words'.[81] This listlessness extended to his spiritual life. 'Lazy – thoughts wandering at Church; irritable or spiteful: broke two resolutions, one not to waste time in reading the newspaper, the other to fast'.[82] This drifting emboldened his father to press him to leave Durham and start making decisions:

> I would press upon you the necessity of coming to some certainty of decision in your own mind on these three points; 1. The time of entering into Holy Orders; 2. taking your leave of Durham; and 3. The new course of study and employment to be entered upon when you return to the University. [...] These considerations … seem to involve the necessity of leaving Durham at the end of this term [...].

He mentioned as reason for returning to Oxford 'the duties you owe your College', which had recently appointed him to 'an Office requiring to a certain extent your presence and attention',[83] likely Palmer's appointment to a Lectureship in Moral Philosophy.[84] He ended bluntly: 'I have given you my opinion that it is advisable to quit Durham *now*'.[85] Roundell reiterated that 'Durham cannot be much longer a place for you', not least because Lord John Russell had made government funding for Durham conditional on the admission of Dissenters: 'Surely this is insuperable'.[86] Apart from the prospect of Durham becoming 'a liberal establishment,' the Durham appointment 'was never meant to go further than what might be compatible with a first connexion [...] Oxford and Magdalen must not be neglected'.[87] By summer 1836 Palmer had taken leave of Durham.[88] A letter to his father of '28 Aout' from the 'Cité d'Aosta', assumes approval of 'my removal from Durham'.[89]

In 1836 Palmer travelled to Switzerland to meet the Vaudois and renew his friendship with M. Monod. He found the Vaudois pastors 'desirous of cultivating the Anglican connection', and 'all more or less Episcopalians, and were finding their way towards the adoption of our Liturgy'. On his return to England he sought to be placed on a committee to help the Vaudois congregations.[90] In June 1836 he returned to France. There is a different tone in his journals for this period, introspective and gloomy, almost at times hysterical. At the end of his diary for 1835 he had written: 'Lapsus graviores XX, ignavia, vitiositates etc. innumerabiles deploro'[91] ('20 serious failures, idleness, I bewail innumerable vices'), and at the start of his 1836 diary is the observation 'In the diary of this year there are frequent observations about myself as distrait – triste – mismanaged time, idle & irritable etc.'. But the entry for 'Dimanche Juin 26 a Dieppe', written in unaccented French, is a frenzy of self-disgust: 'Si je savais que la vie d'aucun de mes amis avait ete telle que la mienne, que penserai j'en? Mon estime ne serait-il pas changé en horreur et en aversion?' he asked at the start, going on to describe how 'chacque fois que je me trouve priant ou lisant a peu pres mechanicalement, je suis porté a penser, ou je suis le plus insensible, le plus endurci, le plus sensuel des êtres [...] je pense quelquefois m'etre déjà si entierement corrompu, que je suis ruiné'. He continued bleakly:

> La vie même m'est ennuyeuse. J'aime ma famille, mes amis. Et mon coeur et mon esprit se portent exclusivement a des choses bonnes et importantes. Cependant ma vie est un mensonge contre tous les deux. – Si je me repent quelque jour, si je prie, et crois etre pardonné je revolte plus dangereusement que jamais le jour suivant.

He expatiated on his feeling that his life was an exercise in hypocrisy:

> Avec de telles pensées, continuellement dans mon âme.. cependant je porte toujours la meme visage, je parais interessér [sic] seulement aux choses vraiment importants et edificants, je

> remplie mes devoirs externels d'une maniere satisfaisante a mes amis et a mes voisins – je jouis d'une reputation élevée.... je me sens etre aimé. Ceci est-il supportable?

This hymn of self-hate concluded by wondering whether the better course would not be to

> confesser le bassesse, la depravitée, l'impiété de ma vie, de m'humilier, en acceptant le deshonneur et la honte que me sont dues et de me retirer quelque part en cherchant quelqu'autre chemin pour mener une vie nouvelle dans la penitence et dans l'obscurité?[92]

Some indication of the occasions for his self reproach emerge from his description of a 'voyage sans prieres a peu pres mais fortuitement sans crime', and 'les tentations au moment meme d'entrer a Lausanne les Catholiques pieuses a Pontarlier – Les dereglements du matin et du soir au Lion d'Or – especialement au moment meme ou je faisais une prière'; later, his going to 'la Chapelle sans m'y etre preparé [...] l'interet intellectuel que je prenais neamoins', as well as 'les belles choses que j'ai dits a Mr. Robert (belles si elles avaient venues d'un coeur droit – les regards pas merites que la pensé intellectuelle peut s'attenir meme quand elle n'est pas fondée'.[93]

Palmer was astute in identifying the 'interet [sic] intellectuel' which often seems to have the upper hand over genuine spiritual feeling in his religious enquiries. In his approach to church doctrine and history he can appear more a religious archaeologist, and in controversy more a barrister manqué, than a humble seeker after truth. A week later he bemoaned 'les vains efforts que j'ai faits [sic] de fixer quelque epoque d'amendment', and wondered whether he should confess and seek absolution before his ordination ('ma consecration' [sic]), and whether he should be ordained at all 'etant dans l'etat que je suis'.[94] His self-analysis was unsparing:

> What is my real position? [...] I am not worthy of the communion of the faithful: when I speak as a member of the Church I am an impostor, when I meet with interest, friendship, love, respect or praise from others, I ought to be in torture at it: It is true that from my cold heart I wish as I have always wished to walk in the Commandments of God; but I am at once, cold & corrupted. I pray from time to time & sometimes with fervency; but the evil habit of sin has the mastery over me, and is for ever returning: rebellion gets stronger, and my state worse and worse [...].[95]

He reviewed his attempts to pray more fervently, powerfully and continually, but concluded hopelessly 'I have already tried, but such as I am myself, such will be my prayers. There is no health nor power towards safety & salvation in me. I am slipping down rapidly towards destruction'. All this when 'there are now only four months & the time will come for me to be Ordained'.[96]

There follows in the original French passage a series of passionate appeals to his relatives alive and dead, which will strike the reader as either heart-rending or absurd:

> O mon frere Thomas .. mon cher frere Henri... O mon cher frere R - O mes soeurs et mes freres innocents – O mon bon pere qui [...] ne me faisais jamais de reproches [...] qui m'as toléré patiemment qui m'as aimé et meme as été fier de moi – O ma mere dont j'ai reproché avec impieté ta maladie forte et doloreuse – O vous tous mes amis bons dont je suis indigne - de la profondeur de mon ame je me jette je me roule a vos pieds [...].[97]

As Palmer's cast of mind was naturally objective, logical and analytical, this orgy of chest-beating is rare, although the theatrical style resurfaces in his initial draft of a Memorial to Archbishop Howley over the Jerusalem Bishopric.

His father reassured him that he possessed the qualities 'requisite for successful enquiry [...] you are kind patient and persevering and not conceited'[98] but to no avail: 'How weak we are! [...] I need tears of repentance, a discipline more severe, more constant & sincere prayers, a more lively charity, a more true repentance, a stronger faith, and above all more confirmed habits of virtue'.[99] If such remarks put us in mind of a monastic standard of asceticism, it is the less surprising to read that Palmer told 'M. Hilaire, a Jesuit from Lyons' that he was 'a sort of Protestant monk or member of a Protestant monastery; which it surprised him much to hear'[100] (as no doubt it would have surprised the other members of Magdalen) who had 'come here to study the present state of religion & of the Church'. He made similar assertions in September at Turin, when he went to see 'les Oblati' – 'j'ai parlé avec le Père Raymondi et deux autres d'abord de mon College ou Monastère scholastique sans vaux à Oxford'.[101] The startled Jesuit predicted, as had M. Robert, that 'going so far as I did, & having such principles, I would find it impossible to persist in denying the Pope's authority, when I should have studied more the writings of the Early Fathers'. Palmer denied that he would ever leave the Anglican Church, but when they parted M. Hilaire told him that he was on the high road towards the truth, a view shared by the convert to Roman Catholicism, Miss Trelawney,[102] who had engineered the visit. Palmer's misgivings about the state of his own soul did not prevent him from telling Miss Trelawney confidently that 'she had simply become a schismatic by separating from the Church of her country to follow her own imagination'.[103]

As with M. Robert, his claims for the Anglican Church were met with scepticism or contempt, although often combined with respect or affection for Palmer himself. In a discussion at Aosta on the Apostolic Succession in the Church of England, for example, his question 'Qu'est-ce qu'on en pense ici?' met the dismissive reply 'On n'a aucun motif pour l'examiner'; and the verdict of a priest on the Church of England was that 'Une armée tout composée de Généraux ne serait que confusion'.[104] Likewise at the Jesuit College in Aosta he was told 'Je ne comprends point vôtre idée de Catholicité. Vous détruitez de fond au comble l'Eglise visible. Souvenez vous de la promesse, Tu es Petrus &c.', to which he gave the elliptical reply that while the promise would doubtless be fulfilled, it was a promise and not a doctrine.[105] Later he was frankly told 'L'Eglise Anglican tombera sans doute: elle n'a point de racine: comme d'autre eglises, quoique tenantes à l'unité, sont tombés'.[106] By the end of September and beginning of October M. Robert was tiring of endless argument: 'ces discussions n'ont point de fin, ni de conclusion'.[107] He mellowed enough to tell Palmer 'souvent' 'Ah, vous êtes Catholiques jusqu'au Pape', and 'vous êtes libre; nous sommes esclavés. Je voudrais être comme vous, pour être libre';[108] but this was 'en plaisantant, dans un moment d'abandon'.

The Archbishop of Tours paid Palmer 'des compliments exaggerés, et se plait à croire que Dieu operera un miracle en ma faveur pour me convertir', although when Palmer described the Church of England as 'ma mère', he was less polite. 'Votre mère est bâtarde; nous ne sommes pas d'accord sur les choses essentielles'. He urged him solemnly to pray to be led into the truth, and even to reject and condemn the Church of England '"parce que" dit-il, "vous êtes grand Docteur, et non pas un petit enfant"'.[109]

At Paris Palmer was driven to see the Bishop of Pignerol, whose face and manner he instinctively disliked, a view not altered by the Bishop's description of the Church of England as 'a sect calling themselves Episcopalian'.[110] The abbé Jager, the epistolary opponent of Benjamin Harrison and then Newman in *L'Univers*, felt that 'si tous les Anglais étaient comme moi, on pourrait facilement faire un reconciliation', saying of Palmer 'Il est Gallican lui-même'. This was a reasonable description of Palmer's view of the Church of England as a national Church that was part of the Catholic and Apostolic Church, and so far as the Reformation was concerned, at least as much sinned against as sinning; but it draws attention to a sort of ecclesiological schizophrenia on Palmer's part at this time. He wrote in his diary while at Aosta in September: 'Je defends les Reformateurs et les Protestans [sic] [continentaux]. J'admire leur vertu, leur courage, leur zèle, [leur pieté], leur *savoir*. Je les regarde comme des Chrétiens échappés à leur Mère cruelle et corrompue'.[111] However, he was to find, to his surprise, that his natural sympathies were with the Roman Catholics and not (however much he might sympathise with the Vaudois) with the Protestants, as he confessed to a Mr. O' Ryan in 1838.[112]

He also found that the behaviour of the Anglican clergy on the Continent undermined his defence of the Church of England: 'I most heartily regret that there should be so little disposition among our stray clergy to act together in unity under that form of discipline they profess to recognise'.[113] He wrote to Roundell; 'Bp. Luscombe & the Bp. of London are on bad terms & some congregations invite the one of them and some the other'.[114] Human frailty and the fissiparous nature of Anglicanism combined to subvert the ideal picture that he wished to present.

3 Return to Oxford

On his return to Oxford in autumn 1836 Palmer was struck by the 'very great change' in public opinion during his three year absence, in particular the emergence of what he called the 'High Church party',[1] later known as the Tractarian Movement after the *Tracts for the Times.* He was initially baffled by the 'party language' he heard, 'especially against the "Oxford opinions"', which failed to mention any specific doctrine but was 'always of a trimming-Latitudinarian kind full of such expressions as "going too far", "verging towards Popery"', with "sect, party, exclusiveness, formality" in abundance'.[2] He felt that with 'only a general idea of *what it is* that Newman and Pusey[3] teach', his best course was 'to abstain carefully from reading the Oxford *Tracts,* or attending any of Pusey's lectures', until he had had the chance to discuss the matter with those concerned, when at last 'something tangible' might emerge.[4] For the time being the only differences he could discern were 'of disposition & tendency, but not of doctrine. It seems to me they are all essentially Anglican'.[5]

One thing that had not changed was the behaviour of the undergraduates, apparently 'a very bad set', who reminded him 'much of the time when I first came up myself by the noises which they make nightly. Faber[6] has been treating them with excessive indulgence – which they have repaid, as might have been expected, with all kinds of riot'.[7]

On Sunday 18 September 1836, Palmer finally took the step over which he had so much agonised, and was ordained deacon by Bishop Bagot of Oxford. Finding that it was customary to issue a Licence to Preach to all newly-ordained deacons with their Letters of Orders, with characteristic contrariness he wrote to the authorities requesting 'that none be made out for me, as I had no intention of applying for any such permission'.[8] It was not until two years later, at a time when his father was seriously ill, that he wrote to the Bishop to obtain the Licence, preaching his first sermon on 9 December 1838.[9] As deacon he assisted his father at both

Mixbury and Finmere 'by reading the Morning & Evening Services with one of the printed Homilies instead of a Sermon, Catechising the children & occasionally Baptising'.[10] He was initially reluctant to carry out baptisms, apparently on two grounds, first, the mode of administration and secondly, the standing with the Church of the sponsors. His father wrote to him: 'It will be well if you can overcome your reluctance to take an infant in your arms [...] But if you really have a scruple about the mode of administering, you shall decline the office till you have satisfied yourself, or have had licence and opportunity to instruct the people in the reason of the thing', and 'if a stranger offers himself as sponsor I conclude without particular enquiry that all is right, and that he is as well acquainted with what ought to be, as they for whom he appears'. His father's approach foreshadowed, in terms, the difference between Palmer and the Anglican hierarchy over Passive Communion, and by extension the question of authority in the Church, that largely determined his decision to leave the Church of England. His father evidently thought him over-scrupulous:

> Conscience I know must be satisfied, but then discretion should be used. And there is some danger of doing serious injury for want of it by insisting stiffly on a form which may be more correct in opposition to one that is established, tho' it be less so, in matters not essential. [11]

By March Palmer had overcome his scruples sufficiently to carry out his first christening, although he was 'not a little nervous for fear I should not hold it [the child] properly'.[12]

His family's predictions that a wider and more successful career lay open to him at Oxford were vindicated by a sequence of appointments. He was already Praelector of Moral Philosophy, and gave his first lecture in the ante-chapel at the end of the Michaelmas term 1836. In early 1837 he became Junior Bursar, went as Examiner to Durham and to Rugby, and was appointed Public Examiner in Litteris Humanioribus in the Schools of the University.[13] His duties as Bursar meant that he could expect to spend little time at home, as he was 'obliged to be in almost constant residence'. One chance to escape lay in performing the duties of 'what they call the riding Bursar whose business it is to go to those places of which the College hold[s] the Manors and hold Courts' – a prospect he looked forward to if 'it happened to be the year for giving the Lincolnshire Progress as it is termed, for I have some curiosity to see a little more of that county'.[14]

Busy as he was with his new duties, he did not abandon his attempts at self-improvement, although he met with a disturbing lack of success. This is perhaps unsurprising, given the very ambitious goals he set himself. His resolutions for 1837 were.

> To attend to Moral Philosophy & Chronology; Then 1 To rise at 4 am if possible: 2 To say the Morning & Evening Prayer of the Church according to the Rubric [...] 3 Hoc agere i.e. to be intent on the business in hand avoiding idle thoughts & interruptions: 4 To fast on fast-days 5 To keep diary & accounts regularly: 6 To keep away from the fire: 7 To answer letters immediately: 8 To walk for exercise regularly: 9 To leave the Common Room at 7 pm: 10 To drink no wine 11 To read original authors by preference; & to make some short analyses of what I read 12 To read some Hebrew daily 13 To read Classics in preparation for the Schools from 10 am to 1 pm daily 14 To write an analysis of the same from 7 pm to 8 pm 15 To read German: 16 To read Italian & 17 To read French.

Alas he was soon writing that he had been 'late in rising, too long in dressing', had wasted much time avoiding 'Hoc Agere', followed Resolution 2 ('saying the Office Morning & Evening daily') 'carelessly, unprofitably & impatiently', had read no Classics, broken his resolutions to fast ('no distinct rule for the manner of doing it laid down') and to keep away from the fire, and had taken no exercise.[15] His diary for early 1837 is filled with entries such as this one:

> Headache: no circulation: sit listlessly over the fire: always up too late in the morning: near 10 am before I am at work: scarce set down to it when called to early dinner, nor well at it again when called to Tea, after which there is nothing to be done. Even in going to bed I frequently waste an hour. Do not even take a healthy walk partly from habit, partly from the weather: inside gouty: head confused, and I feel my body beginning to give way already: no energy for work; no relish of life: think of past opportunities wasted, and faults contracted: think of those that are gone and the certainty of all following: dream on in this state: Prayers & reading make me feel how I have blunted my mind for both: that it is not now for me to cultivate, develop, improve, strengthen, build, but to labour listlessly & apparently with little effect for the extirpation of vicious habits of soul, intellect, feeling & body. How the time flies! How is all past, and passing![16]

In March he returned to the theme of withdrawal from the world in which he moved: 'When shall I see my real position? Humility & penitence are my real business for life. Neither conversations, nor publishing, no thinking, nor books can be without great danger for me'.[17] He still felt himself to have 'no energetic motive', with an intellect that was 'dissipated, enfeebled, & nerveless; my will for work is so too'. His mind was 'very corrupt', in fact delighted in 'vanity & corruption'; his body was 'governed by love of ease & softness'. Spiritually he veered between indifference and 'a deep degree of rebellion'. However much he might spend his time 'in formal efforts & right-minded conversation, yet a practical rebellion breaks out on the slightest occasions'. The cold-heartedness mentioned in the French diaries of the previous Summer was still evident: 'In the world I take little interest; only just mechanically mention in my prayers even my nearest relations; much less have I any warm charity for strangers, and for all men'.[18] He noted that 'Bad thoughts are perpetually recurring', that he seemed to have gained no benefit from Lent, on the contrary his attempts at fasting had produced only 'a growing discontent'. His readings of Morning and Evening Prayer (described in Tractarian style as 'the Breviary') had become 'irregular, formal with distractions almost a profanation; it begins to be irksome'. With this disinclination to pray went a drift to the secular, to 'lose myself in intellectual questions & interests'. He even shrank 'from professional duty'. 'Sloth' overcame him: 'feel numbed: sit with my legs before the fire; waste time especially in reading the newspapers: feel an aversion for good practical thoughts, and for all energy: have no spirit to work or write, but sit dawdling, & unable to satisfy myself'.[19] He made the strange observation 'In mind I am still young, in body ageing rapidly', with 'time [...] lost – evil ingrained – practical professional habits unacquired' and even worse 'new evils (hypocrisy & false principle) in prospect'.[20] This may well refer to his increasingly uneasy attempt to be 'a Catholic & a Protestant at once'[21] mentioned in his journal in the context of his visit to the Vaudois.

Wanting to relieve his conscience by confessing these failings, Palmer asked his father to hear his Confession. His father refused, unless, in accordance with the first Exhortation in the Communion Service in the Book of Common Prayer,[22] Palmer told him he would not or could not go to Communion without it. Palmer deferred to his father's decision ('partly from timidity, & partly from not liking to seem to dictate my own opinion to him'), taking the refusal as satisfying his own conscience, and removing any difficulty over taking Communion. However either from stubbornness or the genuine need to unburden himself he continued to look for a Confessor, finding one in the other father-figure in his life, the President of Magdalen, Dr. Routh, who 'made no difficulty' and absolved him 'by the same form as is prescribed in the Office for the Visitation of the Sick'.[23] Thereafter if he was unable to confess to Dr. Routh he simply asked the nearest available priest, regardless of churchmanship; he 'only in two or three cases failed of my object [...] I used to say simply I cannot otherwise satisfy my conscience'.[24] He may also have found consolation in a letter from his friend Claughton, who wrote that he had asked '*young* Whitley' (presumably an undergraduate) 'whether they understood *you* [...] W. said "Oh yes – they understood Palmer and liked him very much"'.[25]

Summer 1837 found him back with M. Robert at Abbeville. The priest used Palmer's love of religious debate to disconcert a friend, one M. Duquin, who, he told Palmer 'aime la discussion'. Sure enough the Frenchman found that he had met his match, exclaiming in dismay 'Mais il va toujours en devant: il m'anticipe à chacque pas!' Palm er noted with amusement that 'M. Robert a été très content de l'embarras de son ami'.[26] M. Robert was not, however, persuaded that his guest's idiosyncratic views about Anglicanism were shared by other Englishmen. He told Palmer: 'J'ai vecu longtemps avec les Anglais à Tours: ils ne partagent point *vos* principes'. A Mr. Hughes, asked if all the English thought as Palmer did, had described Palmer's ideas as 'beaucoup exagerées'. '(Ce Mr. Hughes était Radical et Latitudinaire)' wrote Palmer dismissively by way of explanation.[27] M. Robert returned to his theme the following day: 'Je sais bien les faits de votre Histoire; car j'ai connu beaucoup d'Anglais: mais vous avez corrompu l'Histoire'.[28] Nonetheless, he repeated that his guest deserved 'être Catholique, et prêtre Catholique [...] qu'on me trouvera une [sic] Curé en France', and that he would pray for him; 'Il faut prier le bon Dieu six mois; ... et nous prierons que Dieu fasse un miracle en votre faveur. Pour cela il faut un miracle de grace'. His sister recommended saying the Rosary, which could be 'efficace'.[29] Palmer was quite prepared to admit that the state of England was not favourable to the Anglican (or perhaps any other) Church: 'La Nation va commettre une suicide politique et religieuse [...] nous sommes arrivés au dernier developpement des erreurs contraire de la Reformation. Le mystère de trois siècles commence à se denouer'.[30]

At the seminary 'de M. Haffreingue,' Palmer's views were scornfully rebuffed, first by Saint Augustine's argument against the Donatists – 'securus iudicat orbis terrarum' – that had such a powerful effect in converting Newman; secondly, and more humiliatingly, by the contention that at the end of the day the Church of England was completely insignificant. 'Vous avez tout le monde contre vous: il nous faut une microscope pour voir L'Eglise Anglicane: toute l'Antiquité aussi; et les Grecs sont avec nous pour condamner les Protestans [sic]'. When Palmer responded that it was for God to judge between the two Churches, he met with more French sarcasm: 'Ah! Il faut donc d'abord mettre cette petite Eglise Microscopique à côté en égale avec l'Eglise de tout le Monde, et puis attendre!' But for Palmer the Branch Theory of the Church meant that 'il n'y a aucune absurdité en supposant que pas seulement les Eglises Anglicans mais aussi les Eglises Grecques et Russes fassent part à la véritable Eglise Catholique avec les Eglises Latines qui recoivent le Concile de Trent'.[31]

It was a meeting in Autumn 1837 that led Palmer, in Lord Selborne's view at any rate,32 to begin to take an interest in the Easter Churches. A librarian in the British Museum told him of 'a Syrian priest from Mount Lebanon' who wished to examine some Manuscripts in the Bodleian. This turned out not to be a priest, but a Mr. Christian Rassam of Mosul ('the ancient Nineveh, on the banks of the Tigris'),[33] a member of the Nestorian Church of Chaldea and Kurdistan. Palmer offered him 'any civility in my power if he came to Oxford', with the result that he stayed a fortnight in Magdalen, and visited Mixbury.[34] After leaving for Mosul he wrote to Palmer asking him to write whenever he had an opportunity 'but *with clear hand*' – an occupational hazard of corresponding with Palmer, whose handwriting was often indecipherable. It was typical of Palmer's romantic and impulsive nature to reply that so far as fostering close ties between the Nestorian Church and the Church of England was concerned, there was nothing

> which I would not willingly do to contribute any thing however little to so good an end whether by undertaking the education of Chaldeans here or going to Mesopotamia, if I could render any service by so doing, & was sent by my superiors.[35]

In the event the service that Palmer rendered was to look after Christian Rassam's younger brother Hormuzd, who came to England to complete his education in 1848. Lord Selborne, recalling that Hormuzd 'spent a considerable amount of time at Mixbury', remarked on one of his brother's most engaging characteristics, witnessed by his many letters: 'Constancy and fidelity were qualities in which William resembled my Father; he never neglected or dropped a friend'.[36]

The same Autumn Palmer caused a storm in the Oxford teacup by wearing a stole over his surplice, and over his left shoulder. This is the custom for deacons in the Orthodox Church, although Palmer seems never to have relied on this fact as a reason for doing so. The President, Dr. Routh, was asked to speak to him about it, but chose not to.[37] Dr. Pusey, on the other hand, sent for Palmer and advised him to stop the practice, 'as you are one of us, and must be careful not to give offence in unimportant matters'. Palmer 'thanked him for his kind intentions' but went on 'As I did not ask your advice, I shall hold myself at liberty to do as I think best'. 'What business was it of his? He is not the President of Magdalen' he later remarked to his family.[38] He was more polite to Newman who had had remarks made to him about the stole 'and suggested that it might be better to discontinue it'. Palmer apologised to him for having been bothered about it, reassured him that the idea had certainly not come from Newman, 'but told him what reasons I saw for doing it; and he seemed to feel that they had force'.[39] Palmer's father was less easily persuaded. He confessed himself 'a good deal annoyed by the feeling with which your adoption of a certain singularity in the use of the clerical costume appears to be regarded in College'.[40] This was partly because of the potential damage to 'the cause we have at heart' (presumably the vindication of the Church of England as part of the Catholic Church worldwide) by Palmer's being described in print as 'affecting the rags of Popery',[41] and partly because of the injury he might be doing to his prospects at Magdalen. 'For', he said, 'I am persuaded, if it please God, that you have not only a mind, but a power and talent also, to profit much in the society where you have been cast – and I would not have such promise so marred'.[42] He wondered that his son could not see that in itself 'the width of a scarf, and the manner in which it is worn' were matters 'of very great indifference', but that after a change in practice had occurred, 'a return to the ancient mode in an individual by its singularity [...] seems only to provoke animadversion on himself'. He asked his son to 'note down, chapter and verse, his authority' for what he was doing; but Palmer 'continued his own practice, without, as far as I know, alleging for it any Anglican authority'.[43]

Lord Selborne sees the episode as emblematic of his brother's character and approach to life. His virtues he describes as 'alloyed with some combativeness, perhaps with excessive tenacity' – citing as corroboration Claughton's description of him as as ὁ μέγας, ὁ πολεμικός, ὁ λογομάχος – 'the great, the polemical, the disputatious'. While young men of great mental ability are often combative, they generally find out that their 'ideal of abstract and absolute perfection' must yield to the 'disturbing forces' that operate everywhere. 'My brother William,' he wrote, 'had not that flexibility; and, for want of it, he was always more or less out of his element, and leading forlorn hopes in the battle of life'.[44] His sister Emily remarked of his response to Pusey, 'William was never really of any one party, he was his own party!'[45]

Nor were his sartorial idiosyncrasies the only matter causing his father concern. He also warned him against introducing 'extraneous matter' into a College Meeting, particularly those regarding 'your own strict views of duty to the Foundation' which he guessed had probably already created some alarm.[46] Palmer explained that this referred to a sort of monastic and charitable rule that he had romantically proposed for the residents of Magdalen:

> I used to say that we ought all to reside under discipline and obedience, and work for the good of the foundation: that being fed & clothed & having a reasonable allowance of money for our statutable vacation of two months in the year, we ought not to divide amongst ourselves any surplus revenues; but rather employ them in feeding poor scholars, or as times are now, in founding affiliated Colleges with estates & farms & benefices dependent on them in the Colonies[47]

This went in tandem with a scheme for a sort of University scriptorium in which 'scholars should be trained & afterwards associated together in preparing a re-edition of the Fathers'.[48] He was evidently enamoured of the idea of reviving monasticism, if not in Oxford, then in Chaldea. Having urged Christian Rassam to 'practise devotion as strictly as if you were a hermit in the first ages, and [...] study theology as carefully as if you were to be Bishop or Patriarch to have the charge of all the churches', he exhorted him to turn his entire attention as soon as possible to making 'a School and College'

> for the study of Divinity and [...] the practice of Devotion. For this purpose you will want 1st a kind of Monastery or College in which the Brethren can live at little expense under a rule of holy discipline & perhaps also supporting themselves by their own labour in cultivating the

ground. I should think perhaps the rule of St. Basil which the Greeks profess to follow in their Monasteries would do very well.[49]

No wonder Claughton dubbed him 'the Monk of Magdalen'.[50]

None of these eccentricities seem to have affected his career. In early 1838 he became Tutor in his College.[51] The prospect of this appointment had caused him 'considerable anxiety' because he feared that he would 'lose for an indefinite period that leisure for study which I hoped to obtain when I left Durham'. As it was he had been

completely occupied, I might almost say night and day with the business of the Schools [...] it is the hardest work I have ever had [...] we are obliged to sit examining in Public from ten o'clock in the morning every day to five at night – and besides this to read over carefully and compare with each other about 1500 closely written foolscap pages in every variety of hand – and this for the Honours alone.[52]

The tutorship gave him 'more work than is convenient at present considering the number of things wh. I ought to read for the Schools. I have 3 Lectures a week in Aristotle's Ethics, 2 in Sophocles 2 in Logic and one on Sunday in St. John's Gospel. Besides this a great deal of time is taken up in interruptions consequent on the business'.[53] Reminded teasingly by his father of the undergraduate lecture on Herodotus, he replied ruefully that 'I am afraid a College Lecture is very apt to be a shabby Construe – but of course I mean to do my best to make it otherwise'.[54] He was more taxed than ever before, and still plagued by the 'disinclination to shave, walk or in fact do anything requiring exertion, also especially to write letters'.[55] Nor did his professional advance bring him any inner contentment: 'What a diseased chaos of vanity, regret, envy, jealousy, is now in my mind through my perverse obstinacy'.[56] He was still attempting to keep a rule of discipline; he records in hieroglyphics, later translated by himself, that he had a 'Fast headache', and goes on to mention 'several strokes of a whip'.[57]

On 21 May 1839 the Grand Duke Alexander of Russia, later the Emperor Alexander II, visited Oxford, and Palmer, as one of the Public Examiners, was invited to meet him 'at dinner in the Hall'.[58] Palmer decided to seize the chance to present to the Grand Duke a petition in French, which he took to Dr. Routh for approval. The passage in *Notes of a Visit to the Russian Church* describing the conversation that ensued is one of the most comic in the book. Palmer proposed first that 'some Russian ecclesiastic' should come to Oxford to be taught English by Palmer himself while living in Magdalen College, so as to be equipped to make known to the Czar and the Eastern Bishops the best books of Anglican theology. Conversely Palmer sought the protection of the Grand Duke should he go to Russia 'to study there the theology and ritual of the Russian Church' – the first time that this is mentioned as a concrete possibility. The aim was that unity to which the whole Catholic Church ought to aspire.[59] Palmer described Dr. Routh's reaction to his draft:

> "While the Catholic Church of England"–
>
> "Leave out the word 'Catholic', sir; it will not be understood."
>
> "While the Church of England constantly defends the rights of Christian Sovereigns, invaded equally by the ambition of the Roman Pontiff and by democratical licentiousness, she is herself at present in great danger, isolated in a corner of the West, unsupported by the Civil Government and"–
>
> "I would leave that out, sir."
>
> "In a corner of the West, and threatened by the hatred of all the Protestant sects"–
>
> "Leave out the word 'Protestant'"–
>
> "Of all the sects, which have leagued with schismatical Papists to overthrow her [...]
>
> May God bless the throne of the Emperor of Russia, and may all the peoples committed to him obey him as a father. May he never see the anarchical principles of heretical Protestantism coming to disturb his Empire and its churches; and may it be given to him, on the occurrence of some just opportunity, to deliver the East from the yoke of the Infidels."
>
> "I would leave out this last sentence, sir," said Dr. Routh; "the first clause will not be understood, and the second will seem un-English".[60]

The proposals emerge in distorted form in an article written by another alumnus of Magdalen, Goldwin Smith:[61] 'Palmer had, or was supposed to have, a scheme for his great object ['bringing the Anglican and Greek Churches into communion with each other'] by an interchange of monks between Magdalen and a Russian monastery. To this Magdalen demurred, having heard that the monks [...] oiled themselves instead of washing'.[62] This sort of speculative facetiousness neatly illustrates the apocryphal stories that were told of Palmer.

On the other hand, the encouragement given to Palmer by the President, and the care he took to curb Palmer's romantic excesses, indicate his affection and respect for him. Lord Selborne describes him as

> always his friend, admiring the strength, simplicity, and disinterestedness of his character, sympathising with his pursuits, and agreeing to a large extent (though not wholly) with his disposition [...] to try all theological questions, which might reasonably be considered open, from a Catholic and Primitive rather than a merely Anglican standard.[63]

Dr. Routh would have been 'glad to see him devote himself to College work sufficiently to acquire a position and influence worthy of his abilities'. Perhaps swayed too far by fraternal loyalty, he adds 'I believe there was no one whom he would have been better pleased to see qualifying himself for that succession than William, who certainly excelled all the other members of the Society in learning and intellectual power, and was not excelled by any of them in virtue'.[64] Routh's loyalty to Palmer, and his willingness to protect him in his absence, were to be amply demonstrated during the 1840s.

Although the East was beginning to call Palmer, he had not yet done with travelling in France, returning there in summer 1839 accompanied by his brother Horsley,[65] and going 'to Rennes, Nantes, Angers, and Tours, and remaining for some time with M. Robert at Abbeville',[66] where Roundell and their younger brother Edwin[67] joined them for a night. The nervousness with which Palmer's opinions and churchmanship were regarded within the family is shown by the stern warning Horsley was given by his father (Palmer's Uncle George) before he left: 'Now when you are abroad with your brother William if he tries to take you into any Church or monastery or to see Priests leave him at once, and come straight back to England'.[68] Palmer engaged in the usual arguments with sceptical French protagonists. Again and again he was taxed with being a man on his own. M. de Gesvrolles 'said all the English he had known had spoke [sic] very differently – He did not think Mr. Oxenham the "Ministre" would agree with me [...]',[69] and "some English persons" objected to Palmer's views of the doctrine of the real presence 'that I must hold very singular notions [...] nobody else spoke so'.[70] Madame de Montesquieu told him '[...] if I were to talk of this to the English who I meet in Society not one in a hundred would speak as you do [. . .]'.[71] Another 'French gentleman' was 'exceedingly astonished' at what Palmer told him of the English Church, as the other English people he had spoken to, whilst admitting that 'the Prayer Book contained many relics of Popery', had said 'that nobody thought of following them – and whenever there was an opportunity we should have a new Prayer Book'.[72]

The response of the Archbishop of Angers to Palmer's assertion that the Church of England had all the 'days of abstinence & fasting; the ember days – Lent &c vigils' was forthright: 'Bah! Bah! He said I lived at Oxford many years & remember how they eat & drank & gave dinners & parties all the same on all of them. I said I can only speak for myself – I know that common practice is very bad'.[73] At dinner with the Curé de Tabori on 17 September he was 'asked how the doctrine of the Church of England was ascertainable – whether there might not be as many opinions as men and what right I had to suppose that what I thought was the doctrine of the Church'.[74] He did not record his response; but his position can hardly have been helped by the testimony of a 'Mrs. C', a Catholic convert, who before her conversion from Anglicanism 'had the instruction of four Bishops at least & none of them agreed with one another'.[75] He contended as before that 'the Church of England no more pretends to be the whole Catholic Church than the Church of France does – [. . .] we say this Church consists of the Greek & Russian Communion the Continental Latin & the English'.[76] He spoke of 'the moral evidence afforded by Charles' [the First's] conduct that the English Episcopate was not the mere creation of the State',[77] and again 'blamed Henry VIII in violence against the Pope and the Pope against Elizabeth equally'.[78] He denied that the Oxford Movement was introducing new doctrines, but maintained that its object was solely 'to make people learn & follow & obey better the true, & old & constant doctrine both of the University & of the Church of England & indeed of the whole Catholic Church'.[79] However, his admission to the Archbishop that 'common practice is very bad' was typical of a much greater readiness to admit openly the faults both of the Anglican Church and the English Government. To a M. Gesvrolles he 'admitted that the surface of English society presented every appearance of Heretical Protestantism',[80] and that

> Ever since the Revolution of 1688 & the rebellious introduction of a Presbyterian King – the Government of Great Britain has been essentially Philosophe having either no religious conviction or one made out of its two establishments & agreeing with neither [...] it is evident that the whole influence of the Civil Power in matters of religion must have gone during the last 140 years to the recommendation of a latitudinarian compromise.[81]

He even identified a peculiarly English heresy, 'the Gentleman heresy [...] for in truth it is rare to meet any person of the Higher classes with anything like humility or simplicity marked on their countenance & yet though God has instituted divers ranks, yet the mind of the King should be as humble as that of a slave'.[82] He hoped, with naïve optimism, that the Executive by their actions were without knowing it 'unloosing one by one & removing all the chains & shackles which Henry VIII & his successors bound upon the Church' and 'untying the hands of the Bps which will one day or other lance the thunder of an anathema against them & against their principles'.[83]

The behaviour of the English congregations, 'sitting through the Doxology and even the Nicene Creed',[84] and even more that of the English clergy abroad, had made an ineradicably bad impression upon the French with whom he spoke. M. de Gesvrolles 'had seen a great many English clergymen but had no idea that any of them received orders except for the sake of a provision'. Those whom he had seen in England he had nothing against: they 'were very good fellows quite Gentlemen', although 'they all drank enormously'. But they were 'anything rather than Priests – he mentioned one man by name who was at a party when a dying man sent for him, but said he could not come'. On the Continent he had seen a great number, one of whom had been in the army but 'was ordained for preferment – now holds two livings in England, where he goes 3 or 4 times a year – residing here on pretence of ill-health. He was dressed like a Gamekeeper and his cards are inscribed *Mr.* &c. He was not long ago Steward of a ball here'. Another young clergyman 'was distinguished for his love of gaiety and for his vanity & impudence. Another was remarkable for his voracity – several he had seen intoxicated – of one or two he mentioned still worse faults [...]'. This was not French prejudice talking. Palmer notes that what he heard from other English people 'went far to bear him out in his assertions'.[85] Still he dared to think that one day unity would come – perhaps

> When the Pope & his Church see our Communion extending itself – united with the Orientals purified from all false differences & heretical ἦθος & praying for him night & day & willing to concede everything lawful for peace's sake to the dignity of his See – perhaps he will be brought to admit that he has erred on some secondary points which now divide us [...].

Small wonder that a M. Dupont 'cried out "Quel rêve!"'[86]

However bad a face the Anglican Church might show abroad, Palmer was still loyal to it, and impatient with the Roman Catholic expectation of unquestioning obedience to authority. He noted with irritation that the Abbé Dupont des Loges 'brought in the eternal "Il faut" as usual'.[87] When a M. Blancart said to him that Palmer had to admit there were great presumptions in their [the Roman Catholics'] favour, and that he 'seemed to him to be in a most unhappy position – fixed blindly in one idea', Palmer replied 'I cannot force my understanding. My understanding is with my Church'.[88] Even so on his return he again raised with his father the question of confession, claiming to have sins 'worthy of excommunication' to confess. When pressed, Palmer replied that they were those sins whose perpetrators St. Paul had advised Christians to avoid, in his own case 'deliberate lying, theft, drunkenness a certain sin of uncleanness'.[89] With the possible exception of the last, which might perhaps refer to occasional masturbation, this seems remarkably unlikely. An Oxford Tutor and Junior Bursar could hardly hope to perform his duties while leading the Jekyll and Hyde existence entailed by habitual lying, theft, and drunkenness. His father was sceptical: 'I cannot believe that you ever lived in the allowance or practice habitual of any of those sins which you enumerate, and I have a good hope you never will'. On the broader question of confession, he reiterated the Anglican position: 'In the exercise of our functions we are restrained by the order and discipline of the Church whose servants we are. That Church discourages the use of private confession [...]'.[90] He was suspicious both of his son's motives in asking for confession – 'I fear that you are moved now by a notion of the propriety and usefulness of this sort of

confession, the comfort to be derived from a particular and special absolution, more than by the sense of sin itself'[91] and of his glib use of the formula in the Exhortation:

> I intreat of you to search & examine, & deceive neither yourself nor me. In any other case than that of your being unable to satisfy your own conscience not as to the use of Confession, but as to sin itself & the pardon of it, I feel that I ought not to comply with your request.

Despite all his reservations he still expressed himself ready

> to hear you, to give you counsel & advice, & the sentence of absolution, which for our Lord's sake is promised to the penitent & believing. And I desire in so doing my feelings may not be considered.[92]

Palmer confessed to Dr. Routh instead: 'I felt a very great moral relief and happiness at having at length done this'.[93]

Soon after his return to England he was drawn into controversial but friendly disputation with George Spencer,[94] a convert to Roman Catholicism 'at a time when such conversions were rare'.[95] A female relative, thinking Palmer a possible convert, had caused Spencer to write a 'long and very pleasing letter'[96] to Palmer; in reply Palmer gave 'Romanists,' credit for the good motives which had carried them into the Roman Church, conceding that 'the Society itself has all the organisation of a Church though I think a schismatical one'.[97] He felt himself bound to ensure that he had done all he could to live up to what was good in the Church of his Baptism before quitting it. Otherwise the fault if any would lie not with his Church but with him[98] – no doubt referring more to Spencer's decision to leave the Church of England than to any future move by Palmer. He then set out the arguments for his belief that the Church of England was the true Church, rehearsed and refined by endless debates in France. He described his recognition of continental Catholics as 'Brethren & of one and the same the same religion',[99] and conversely how he had found that he 'had no community of sentiment or principle' with the Protestants of France and Switzerland. The Reformation might have brought a change in 'certain accidents & ornaments as well as of some errors & abuses & corruption of religion', but not of anything essential, 'and held on Ecumenical authority to be essential in 1500 AD. You say that you have returned to 1500. I say that I have never departed from 1500'.[100]

He also refuted Spencer's assumption that he was an integral part of the Oxford Movement. 'You take it for granted that I belong to a body of Divines here with whom I have never had any sort of connection,[101] not having so much as read their writings'. That Palmer's understanding of 'the clear and undoubted inheritance of the Church' and the views of the Oxford Movement were in fact extremely close was illustrated by Palmer's *Introduction to the 39 Articles*. This work, approved and corrected by Dr. Routh, took 'as the governing rule for their [the Articles'] interpretation, the principle of "agreement with the known sense of the Fathers and of the Church" laid down in the Canon (which never had legal authority) of A. D. 1571', and explained the Articles 'according to what he understood as the sense of the Fathers "even if in any places they might be suspiciously or ambiguously worded"'.[102] Newman was not to read the *Introduction* until after Palmer's death, but said of it that 'its spirit and drift is the same as that of *Tract 90* of the *Tracts for the Times*'[103] although it was written a year before *Tract 90*. Although Palmer wrote the *Introduction* for his pupils at Magdalen, he took it to Russia with him to show in what sense he took the Thirty Nine Articles, and thought they might fairly be explained. 'The Russians, however, thought the Introduction was more orthodox than the Articles themselves'.[104]

By coincidence it was about this time that Palmer described the preaching of two of the greatest figures of the Oxford Movement, Pusey and Newman, and its effect. He began with Pusey preaching the University Sermon at Christchurch:

> When Dr. P preached the Cathedral was always crowded, and though the greater part had to stand and his sermons were always very long, and his style perplexed and anything but easy to follow, he was heard in breathless silence. The same indeed was true of Newman's sermons also [...] but Newman is the only one whose peculiar monotone and long pauses, and rapid utterances & falls of voice between them, and risings of voice again to an emphasis which were all very natural & impressive in him but by no means fit for general imitation, were actually mimicked (unconsciously I suppose) by numbers; as were also certain habitual phrases and divisions and introductions of his which adhere still to the style written or spoken by some even of those who were never willing to be thought his followers.[105]

Invitations were extended by Palmer and Spencer to Oxford and Oscott respectively. Palmer, 'with more regard to prudential considerations than was usual with him',[106] declined to go to Oscott, 'for it would look to other people as if I either fancied I could convert the whole Community or was inclined to be converted myself'.[107]

Spencer came instead to Magdalen during the Christmas vacation of 1839. Of the visit Palmer wrote in his diary: 'I myself had no scruple, nor fear of being compromised, no more than I had had when I invited the Bp. and the professors of Ushaw College to dine with us in Hall at Durham; as I was simply desirous to benefit them & to reconvert Mr. Spencer'.[108] Spencer's reaction to Palmer's arguments was that, as he put it to Palmer, his metaphorical masts and rigging had been carried away by Palmer's shot. He frankly admitted that Palmer had gained the advantage over him, suggesting that as an unlearned man, he was no match for Palmer's erudition. Palmer was nettled: 'I did not attempt then to examine with you or prove any point by learning',[109] later adding 'You cannot hurt me more than by talking about my Learning & ingenuity in such matters'.[110] In conceding defeat, Spencer echoed M. Robert:

> I do not think there are many of us, whom at a first encounter, you would not considerably puzzle: because you make out a case for the Anglican Church, which I never dreamed of [...] I would tell others as I tell you, that I was greatly surprized and extremely baffled by your conversation [. . .] [111]

Spencer's Parthian shot was to warn Palmer of over-confidence: 'I do not think you are yet in the way to be convinced by any one. I may be judging you too hard, but I think you want more diffidence in your own judgement, than you have gained'. He accurately prophesied a lonely future for him:

> I will tell you the impression which your conversation makes upon me about you: It is that you have admirable Catholic principles in your mind, that in a great many things you apply them to practice beautifully, but when I look at the whole exposition and defence which you make of your position, as a Churchman I see [you] most plainly to be standing *almost alone*. If you have the success which I formerly would have wished to have, when I was following my own ideas, you may have followers soon & not be quite alone. Others may take your explanation of the foundation of the Church of England & of her doctrines; but if you are as I trust you are incapable of being settled into a Party leader, you will have I am convinced no real associates until you come to that communion which, notwithstanding your clever & learned reasoning I still must say most confidently & clearly, our fathers *chose to leave*, thinking, but presumptuously, to reform what could not be reformed. [112]

The feline quality of this assessment is reflected in Newman's impression of Spencer: 'a gentlemanlike, mild, pleasing man, but sadly smooth'.[113] Spencer declared that despite his defeat there was no prospect of Palmer's converting him back to the Church of England; if he found himself 'perplexed,' he would do 'as a child will do, fly to his mother for refuge and comfort'.[114] When he did so, he was forbidden by his superiors to read any more of Palmer's letters, and the correspondence ceased.

Responding to Spencer's criticisms, Palmer set out two of his main objections to Roman Catholic attitudes and doctrine:

> I have generally found myself that they attempt first to beg & assume the whole question. Then if all is not conceded at once to browbeat and bully simple people into calling them Catholics & themselves by implication Heretics [. . .] I really believe that this is one great reason why the whole question between our church and Rome has seldom if ever yet been fairly worked out. It has always been taken for granted.[115]

He also objected to the 'most dangerous and Anticatholic doctrine' of 'blind and unreasonable submission [. . .] to the self-asserted absolute supremacy of the Roman Bishop and the new definition of the Church itself & its doctrine [. . .]

which follows upon the assumption of that Monarchy'.[116] He admitted that Roman Catholics were given an insuperable prejudice *in limine* against the Anglican Church by its 'weak, divided, ignorant & corrupt state'. If the Church of England had clergy who were 'good and holy' rather than 'ignorant and worldly', many a Dissenter might be converted rather than rail or even preach against them.[117] He even confessed that 'all my first prejudices (since I have been used to study Theology) in every question lean very much against my own Church, and in favour of Rome'.[118] Palmer admitted too that he had 'too great confidence' in his own judgement, and was 'deficient in humility and docility'; he assured Spencer that he prayed constantly for improvement in those respects.

In private he indulged in further self-flagellation at resolutions made and broken. Having resolved '1. Surgere statim 2. Hoc agere[119] 3. Avoid useless & idle self reflection whether by dwelling on the past or anticipating the future 4. Patientius cum matre[120] (her bodily ails causing her to be often very excitable)',[121] by 6 March he was writing:

> I lay in bed till as near 6am as I could 2. I was indisposed to begin 3. Wasted time more or less between 7 & 10 am 4. Had wandering thoughts in Chapel 5. Again indisposed to work: 6. Impatient of the cold 7. Stayed too long, wasting time, in the Common Room; 8. Talked in a bad tone.

Having broken all but one of his original resolutions, he reiterated them and added: 'Not to sit by the fire: Not to stay after half past 6 or (if there are strangers with us) after 7pm in the Common Room'.[122] But the very next day he wrote: '1. Nequeo surgere mane; 2 totum fere diem tero nihil agendo; 3. Je lis les journaux; 4. Minimi "*hoc* ago"; 5. Frigoris impatiens ad focum sedeo'.[123] Just over a week later he reviewed his continuing laxness – 'I have lately wasted my time– lain in bed – neglected my Prayers – said my private Prayers, with distractions and & by rote' – and concluded 'I am full of pride, vanity, laziness, hypocrisy sensuality & all this in Lent '.[124]

THE SPCK

Lord Selborne described 1840 for William and himself as 'an epoch of transition from the privacy of domestic and collegiate or professional to larger and more public spheres of activity'.[125] A series of public controversies were to bring Palmer to general notice, the first over the general function and control of the Society for Promoting Christian Knowledge. William Palmer senior had written of the Society for the Propagation of the Gospel: 'I feel no confidence in the usefulness of societies, *per se*, to to effect objects truly and properly ecclesiastical where a Church exists'.[126] Palmer agreed, and in April 1840 proposed to put to the SPCK a Resolution that it renounce its 'usurpation of episcopal powers'. He was spurred to do so by unedifying squabbles, in the absence of episcopal authority, between Evangelical and High Church clergymen over publications approved by the Tract Committee. Archbishop Howley, chairing one meeting, had to intervene with the words 'the wrath of man worketh not the righteousnesss of God'.[127] Roundell Palmer 'with some misgiving [...] consented to act the part of Sancho Panza to his Don Quixote'[128] by giving notice in Palmer's name of a motion to be put to a meeting of the Society. The reaction was as he had feared: 'I have done your bidding today – not without some tremor of nerve, I assure you. To my apprehension, the members of the [...] Society received your notice much in the same way that they might have received a thunderbolt if it had fallen among them. Some were disposed to laugh at what evidently seemed to them to be the extravagance of the proposition [...]'.[129] He remonstrated with his brother for not giving him notice that would have allowed him time to voice objections, and without which he felt bound to act for fear of appearing cowardly. He asked, though he must have known the answer, if William had 'consulted Dr. Pusey and Mr. Newman, before venturing upon so decided a step'. To this Palmer typically replied, 'I have not mentioned my intention to anybody, nor do I intend to trouble myself about anybody's vote or opinion', seeing it as a matter of 'discharging my own private duty and conscience [...] having placed myself from the first, in a false position by becoming a member of the Society at all, which I did without due consideration'.[130] Pusey was later consulted, and wanted the notice withdrawn, but Palmer 'was not the man to give such a notice and afterwards withdraw it, at Dr. Pusey's or any other man's bidding'.[131]

Roundell was concerned that his brother should 'in speaking upon the motion, use the most guarded temperance and calmness and discretion of language [...] nothing but the most exemplary discretion on your part can prevent the discussion from assuming a very strong and perhaps personal and disgraceful character. Whatever happens, do not let us be agitators, or adopt anything in the least resembling their tone'.[132] A postscript to the letter revealed an unexpected side to Palmer: 'P.S. It would be no surprise to me if the adversaries should scout up and [...] bring forward to your prejudice stories of your indiscretion (as I must call it) in France &c. Such as playing at cards on Sunday &c. &c.'.[133] Palmer replied reassuringly that he intended 'to do my best to observe the caution and temper which you recommend'.[134]

The Resolution proposed that the Society should rid itself of any function or responsibility, 'which belongs of right to the Bishops of the Church'. In particular it should not 'pronounce any decision upon doctrine', nor choose books or tracts for churches at home and abroad. It was to confine itself instead to the raising of money, whose expenditure was to be determined by the archbishops and bishops.

Palmer put forward the motion on 6 May to a full meeting, at which 257 voted, though more were present. The Chairman, Dr. Russell,[135] 'obtained for him a very fair and patient hearing',[136] although himself opposed to the motion. He read the motion 'with a suppressed smile',[137] stopping 'some attempt from a few members to make confusion'.[138] Roundell had anticipated that the obvious question would be whether the bishops themselves been consulted about the motion, which would otherwise be disrespectful. This was indeed put by the celebrated Evangelical vicar of Harrow, Mr. Cunningham,[139] but Palmer 'parried' it by saying that the question would be answered in his speech. Palmer then began to read the speech, which was itself objected to as being out of order, but again this was overruled by Dr. Russell. The speech 'was long, and occupied about an hour in reading'[140] and 'was much more religious in its tone than [...] usual at these meetings, scarcely less so than a sermon'.[141]

Although it 'went very much into detail, and, in parts, without sufficient care to make the relevancy of the detail apparent'[142] it 'was listened to with much respect and attention'. 'Upon the whole' wrote Roundell to his father afterwards, 'I must praise our opponents for their forbearance [...] I think (to say nothing of the *reading* it) it was a speech which no other man in the room would have made [...] It might have been framed more skilfully, and better and more concisely expressed in many parts. It was delivered, on the whole, calmly and without excitement [...] the temper with which he took interruption was perfect [...]'.[143] This was no doubt a huge relief both to Roundell and his father. A motion 'that the question be not put' was carried by a majority of only 27, 'a virtual triumph' for the Palmers, given the numbers they had expected to support them.[144] Satisfied, Palmer published the speech and then resigned from the Society. Lord Selborne commented that 'many others besides my father and myself thought he had done good service',[145] although these sentiments were not, apparently, shared by Bishop Bagot of Oxford:[146]

> I entirely sanction (as it is more satisfactory to yourself to have that sanction) your publication of your late speech at the monthly meeting of the SPCK, and much regret the course which has led to the letter, and to the necessity of the step you feel it right to take by withdrawing from the Society – a step I am sure you would not have taken without very strong grounds.[147]

It is pleasing to read that in the same month the abbé Robert, so often Palmer's host in France, was entertained by the family at Mixbury. He 'equipped himself, along with other habiliments which he supposed to be appropriate to such an occasion, in a blue coat with bright brass buttons', and was driven about in an elderly family gig which had descended 'from prehistoric times' and was consequently 'not too elastic in its springs'. The abbé on his return wrote up his experiences 'not without some embellishments' for French readers, 'horses of all work' appearing as 'mettlesome steeds', and 'the ancient vehicles transformed into "*beaux charabancs*"'.[148]

PREPARATION FOR RUSSIA

In summer 1840 Palmer began an acquaintance that was to last for the rest of his life, with R. W. Blackmore,[149] the chaplain to the English Russia Company, stationed at Cronstadt.[150] He laid out to Blackmore a plan to visit Russia:

> for the purpose of studying the Oriental Church and learning the Russian language [...] I am firmly convinced that Communication and better knowledge of each other would unite the English and Oriental Communions [. . .] My present idea is to procure letters under the seal of the Society, sending me as it were on a mission by their authority to study the Russian Theology, and recommending me to the charitable assistance of the Authorities of the Russian Church, requesting them both to examine into the orthodoxy of my belief and to countenance and assist study of their Church & doctrine with a view ultimately [. . .] of working towards a restoration of unity to the visible Church.[151]

He raised for the first time the idea of living in the Spiritual Academy, 'following all the rules of the society' or of being 'placed in attendance upon some Bishop or Archbishop till I should have both learned the language and the whole system both of their doctrines and ceremonies'. He also proposed in all seriousness that: 'if I found it possible I should very likely seek to be admitted into Priest's Orders [. . .] by some Russian Bishop', although he realised that he would need 'the consent and approbation of my superiors at home', and agreement by the Russian spiritual authority in his interpretation of the 'Filioque'.[152] 'I do not see myself,' he wrote naively, 'how there could be any other obstacle to my admission to their Communion'.[153] He agreed that 'no solid union between Churches is to be gained by *straining points* nor by "*explaining away*" on either side' but only by 'clear and ascertained agreement or honest admission of error on Conviction and amendment'. Then latitude might be given in matters of secondary importance relating to discipline or tradition, as distinguished from those articles essential to 'the saving Faith'.[154]

Palmer discussed in the letter the correspondence between the Non-Juring bishops of Scotland and England and the Russian and Greek Churches. Palmer suspected that the correspondence, begun in the early 1700s with a view to union, had been 'mismanaged on both sides, and that if there had been a little more communication and a better understanding before they began it would have had a very different result.' Palmer could, however, have anticipated his own reception in Russia by studying the words of the Patriarch Chrysanthus to the Non-Jurors in July 1718, namely that the Orthodox Faith was 'the only true, religious and right Faith',[155] and that there was 'no room for adjustment or dispensation in matters of doctrine – complete agreement with the Orthodox faith [was] absolutely indispensable'.[156]

The significant difference between Palmer and the Non-Jurors was that Palmer did not seek reunion with the Eastern Church, believing as he did that communion between the two churches had never been lost. Relying on the 'Branch theory', he could demand admission to Communion as of right, and seek ordination at the hands of a Russian bishop. Palmer considered the Church

> to exist in three main branches, or rather in a triple presence, the Latin, the Greek, and the Anglican, these three being one and the same Church, distinguishable from each other only by secondary, fortuitous and local, though important, characteristics [...] it followed that Christians generally, wherever they were, were bound to recognize, and had a claim to be recognized by, that one, ceasing to belong to the Anglican Church, as Anglican, when they were at Rome, and ignoring Rome as Rome, when they found themselves at Moscow.

This, Newman said,

> is what Mr. Palmer intensely believed and energetically acted on when he went to Russia. It was his motive cause for going there; for he hoped to obtain from the Imperial Synod such a recognition of his right to the Greco-Russian Sacraments, as would be an irrefragible proof that the doctrine of Anglican divines was no mere theory, and that an Anglican Christian was *ipso facto* an Oriental Orthodox also.[157]

Hence the importance of the letters Palmer sought from his College, and his mention of examination into the orthodoxy of his belief. In this he sought to conform to the letter of the Church of England Canon XXIII 'of those called Apostolical', which stated:

> Let no stranger Bishop or Priest or Deacon be received without Letters Communicatory; and when such Letters are brought, let the parties be nevertheless first *examined*, and if they be found professors of godly doctrine, let them be received.[158]

As a first step in the process of obtaining the letters, Palmer asked Dr. Routh, whether he 'ought voluntarily to separate myself from the Russian Church, or rather seek the Communion from the local Bishop'. Routh approved of the latter course, but recognised the realities of the situation: 'It will lead to nothing, I fear, sir, for a separation there unhappily is; but it will show that there are some among us who wish it were otherwise'.[159] He confirmed that the English Church had never by any public or synodical act renounced the communion of the Eastern Church, nor had those Churches excommunicated the English Church by name.

Palmer therefore drafted a letter of recommendation, which was corrected by Dr. Routh, and engrossed on parchment. This was read to a College meeting on 27

July 1840, and the President proposed that the College seal be affixed to it. However Richard Waldo Sibthorp, a Fellow of Magdalen,[160] who was himself received into the Roman Church the following year, objected excitedly to 'giving encouragement to the idea of intercommunion with the *idolatrous* Greek Church', at which others including the Vice-President also objected. Dr. Routh remarked urbanely 'Unity, gentlemen, is very desirable' and moved on to other business. A compromise in the form of a Certificate of leave of absence from the College for study was proposed and accepted. The next day Dr. Routh sent for Palmer and observed 'I should be sorry, sir, that you should go to Russia with only that meagre document', pointing out that 'there is nothing to prevent *my* giving you, in my own name, any letter I please'. He returned the parchment abbreviated and altered, saying that he could find precedents for what he was doing, 'but that in strictness such letters ought to be from a Bishop'.[161] This was true, and was later to present Palmer with problems in Russia. The body of the letter reflected Palmer's aims as stated to Blackmore, requesting 'the Russian Bishops' and 'especially the Most Holy Spiritual Synod' that by their 'favour and protection' Palmer might 'become acquainted with the doctrines, rites, and ceremonies of the Russian Church, and may learn the Russian language, either in the Spiritual Academy or elsewhere'. A request for admission to communion followed, couched in archaic and dramatic terms:

> Further, I ask, and even adjure in the name of Christ, all the most holy Archbishops and Bishops, and especially the Synod itself, that they will examine him as to the orthodoxy of his faith with a charitable mind, and, if they find in him all that is necessary to the integrity of the true and saving faith [...] will [...] admit him to communion in the Sacraments.[162]

The President's seal was affixed under the closing wish that Palmer might 'submit and conform himself in all things to the injunctions and admonitions of the Russian Bishops', always providing that he neither affirmed nor did anything 'contrary to the faith and doctrine of the British Churches'.[163] Routh approved Palmer's proposal to ask the Archbishop of Canterbury to countersign or authorise the letter, and urged him to take up introductions to the English residents in St. Petersburg, including the Ambassador, Lord Clanricarde,[164] that Palmer had declined 'as making nothing to my purpose'.[165] The letters of introduction Palmer received from Lord Clanricarde were to Count Pratasoff,[166] the Ober Prokuror or High Procurator of the Russian Synod,[167] and M. de Barante,[168] the French Ambassador. '"You will be surprised' said Clanricarde "to see a General of Hussars in his uniform, an Aide de Camp of the Emperor, holding such a position, presiding in the Synod, and directing the Bishops, and governing the Church"'.[169] Pratasoff must have been equally surprised to read, in Clanricarde's uncertain diplomatic French, of the 'désir [...] bizarre' of this 'jeune homme très instruit [...] etre reçu dans l'Eglise Greco- Russe, communier, et faire les etudes necessaires, dans une seminaire à Moscow [sic], pour devenu d' etre Pretre de cette Religion'.[170] Palmer certainly wished to be granted communion and study in the Spiritual Academy, but Clanricarde had otherwise fundamentally misunderstood the basis of Palmer's journey to Russia, although his misconceptions were shared by Lambeth Palace.

On 1 August the Archbishop of Canterbury had told Palmer he was willing to provide his countersignature to Dr. Routh's letter, but the next day Benjamin Harrison, the Archbishop's domestic chaplain, wrote to say that the Archbishop could not sign the letter, because it would commit him to Palmer's interpretation of the 39 Articles. If Palmer's application 'to be received into Communion' were then rejected, that would involve 'the rejection of the English Church, and the denial of its orthodoxy by the Russian'. Palmer explained that he was not asking or expecting the Archbishop to endorse his *Introduction to the 39 Articles,* but simply required a certificate that both he and Dr. Routh were in communion with the Church of England. Hearing nothing, but hoping the certificate would follow, on 11 August 'at half past 10 p.m. [he] went on board the Hamburgh [sic] steamer, the John Bull [...] which weighed anchor at about 1 o'clock am. We were in Hamburgh at 6 am. On Friday the 14th I went on shore'.[171]

Writing from the ship, Palmer asked Harrison directly whether the Archbishop disapproved 'of a member of the English Church seeking or accepting the Communion of any foreign Church or Bishop', providing he did not affirm or do anything 'contrary to the Doctrine of the Church of England'.[172] He reiterated that the English Church had never separated itself from the Eastern, and that he was not seeking to *leave* one Communion to *join* another.[173] Harrison replied that he thought 'it was rather *de trop* to have the Abp's signature [...] to testify that you & your College were in Communion with the Church of England [...] Dr. Routh's Letters were evidence enough'.[174] Less convincingly, he relied on the 'very grave consideration' of 'what is likely to promote or hinder, eventually, the cause of Christian unity at home & abroad, within our Church, and between it and other branches of the Church Catholic',[175] 'eventually' being a conveniently elastic term that left open the comfortable option of indefinite inaction. Zeal for unity with the East had not hitherto been a conspicuous feature of Howley's Archbishopric.

Palmer's father was known to the archbishop's wife. When she told him[176] that Palmer had a much better chance of success without the archbishop's signature, and that his son had 'created an interest and left a favourable impression behind [...] at Lambeth',[177] Palmer was even more confused. Writing to his father about the difficulties caused by his lack of proper episcopal accreditation, he confessed himself:

> considerably embarrassed by the contrary impressions which your report of some conversation with Mrs. Howley about me at Stowe and a note from Mr. Harrison (the Archb'p's Chaplain) had left upon my mind – for what you reported seemed to imply that the Abp had not refused to put his name to the President's Letters [. . .] but Harrison's note had already given me a contrary impression [. . .] I could not help feeling a suspicion that the Abp had not in fact [...] been much disposed to approve of that course which I intended [. . .] to pursue [...].[178]

The episode was a warning to Palmer that he could expect little, if any, support for his mission from the hierarchy of the Church of England.

4 Russia, 1840–1841

FIRST IMPRESSIONS

Palmer 'left by the Omnibus and reached the Stadt von Hamburg at Travemunde at 3pm. Went on board the Alexandra steamer, and dined. It was raining and blowing; but the wind was in our favour'.[1] The steamer arrived off Cronstadt at 11 am on 19 August, or 7 August in the Russian Old Calendar.[2] After a 'tedious inquest' from 'police and custom-house officers', they passed on between 'the pier and commercial port with its forest of masts, and then the naval port, with some thirty great men-of-war, many of them three-deckers'.[3] The city of St. Petersburg seemed, 'though still far off, to rise immediately out of the water'. The churches of St. Petersburg were

> unlike anything to be seen in the West; some of the domes, as those of the St. Catherine's Institute, were of a pale green, others of a bright copper colour. Those of the Trinity Church [...] were of a bright blue, studded with stars of gold. The tall, slender, gilt spires [. . .] of the Admiralty, and of St. Peter and St. Paul in the fortress, especially the latter, attracted my attention. As we came nearer, trees and lines of building were reflected upside down in the water along the shores.[4]

Making a turn to the left, they found themselves 'almost at once in the heart of the city, alongside of a magnificent granite quay, with rows of palace-like buildings, of light cheerful tints on either side of the greater Neva'. Palmer was struck by 'a bridge of boats' ahead of them, and the 'points of contrast' with London:

> the blue, cloudless sky; the clear, broad river; the quays, lined with palaces; the clean, lively tints of the buildings, without a trace of smoke or soot; the vast places comparatively empty, instead of crowded thoroughfares; while of the people visible few comparatively were women, and every third man seemed to be a soldier.[5]

Attempting to distinguish himself from the Protestant denominations of Europe, Palmer declared to the police that he was 'of the Orthodox or Catholic Religion, and a deacon'; but seeing 'le Révérend' in his passport, the police wrote him down 'as a *Prediger* or Pastor of the Anglican Reformed or Lutherano-Calvinistic confession of faith'. Leaving his books for a twelve-week scrutiny by the censor, Palmer established himself in an unlicensed lodging house 'in the Galernaia, a long street parallel to the English Quay' known as 'Miss Dees'', 'full of American Captains – with only one or two English', but 'very comfortable & I liked the people who keep it very well – & indeed they did all I wanted for me'. There were only two problems: its location – 'it was quite at one end of the City and a good way from every place almost I wanted to go to' – and its expense: 'living was dear there being at the rate of from fifteen to twenty pounds a month'.[6]

Woken the next morning between four and five am by the 'gong- like, booming sound' of the church bells, Palmer saw, under an arch at the end of the Galernaia, on the left the palace used by the Holy Governing Synod, and on the right a corresponding palace for the Governing Senate. Peter the Great had begun the transfer of the Senate to St. Petersburg from Moscow in 1712, and imposed the Synod upon the Church in place of the Patriarch in 1721. The Nefsky Prospekt, 'the chief street of all Petersburg', contained the churches of the Dutch Swiss, and French Calvinists, the German Lutherans, and the Roman Catholic church of the Poles, gave the street the nickname 'la rue de la tolérance'.[7] This tolerance was only for foreign visitors to Russia: any minister who received a proselyte from the Russian Church would be expelled from Russia, the penalty for the proselyte being 'civil death'. The Russian Church could receive proselytes from any of the foreign communions.[8]

That evening Palmer visited the 'Kazanski Sobor', then the main church of St. Petersburg, with its solid silver sanctuary doors, and silver icon lamps:

> The separation of the sanctuary, its richly ornamented screen, and the severe supernatural expression of the older icons, made on one an impression of mystery and awe. There was an abundance of pious gesticulations, bowing and crossing, kissing the icons, prostrating and touching the ground with the forehead (sometimes with an audible thump), and bowing and crossing again and again, and by men, young and old, as well as by women [...] there were a good many poor in and about the church, and beggars at the doors, to whom those passing in and out gave kopecks freely.[9]

His overall impression was of 'great splendour and magnificence, and of neatness too'. His first reaction to

> the outward devotion of the people [...] [was] one of wonder, curiosity, suspicion, and a certain repugnance (all being so contrary to English habits, and going far beyond those of Roman

> Catholics), mixed at the same time with respect for the simplicity and reverence, and for the almsgiving with which they were joined.[10]

The next day Palmer visited the Church of the Assumption, and recorded that:

> there was something so new and striking in the singing, which was sweet and distinct, and unaccompanied by instruments, and in the life and feeling with which the crowd joined in chanting frequent responses of *Hospodi pomilui* (i.e. Kyrie eleison) that I remained rivetted in attention for an hour or more, though I understood nothing. [...] I had never before heard anything so stirring and so congregational in divine worship.[11]

Later, he was 'surprized and edified at the sight of the numerous Congregations with which the Russian Churches are filled [...] even on common week days' there seemed to be 'a very fair congregation' for each of the three services, at 4 o'clock in the morning, the Liturgy at 10 am, or vespers at 6 pm. 'It is wonderful to see Merchants even leaving their business on a weekday to go to Church'.[12] 'The chanting and singing even in the smaller or common churches is most striking and sometimes makes one wonder if one is in Heaven or earth: I never heard anything at all like it'[13] he wrote, almost certainly quoting the emissaries of Prince Vladimir of Kiev who in 986 reported to their monarch that in Byzantium they had been led by the Greeks to 'the place where they worshipped their God; and we knew not whether we were in heaven, or on earth: for on earth there is no such vision nor beauty [...]'.[14]

Another striking difference from the Church of England was the social mix. 'It is pleasing to observe that all ranks and both sexes are equally believing: common soldiers – captains & generals with officers of the navy and peasants are all mingled together in one dense mass – and on the women's side the assembly is equally varied though I think the ladies manage to get more together'.[15] Again the almsgiving was noticeable: 'The crowd of beggars, who stood ranged in two rows both within the doors and without as we passed out, was great, and everybody seemed to give to them. I saw children giving'.[16] He could not resist remarking to his father that the deacon appeared 'with his scarf over his left shoulder'.[17]

THE STATE OF RELIGION IN RUSSIA

His English landlady's view of Russian religion was typical: the Russians had a great deal of religion 'in their way', but were 'very superstitious'. They were 'very ignorant, and it would be a good thing if they were taught to read and write'.[18] The Princess Dolgorouky[19] confirmed that although the peasants knew the Lord's Prayer, she doubted if they could repeat the Creed, and would certainly not know the Ten Commandments. They were generally not catechised, but if they were, the language was above them. If the Princess asked them what and how much they understood at church, they were surprised, replying 'How should we understand, as we cannot read?'; their illiteracy was seen by the priest as making instruction impossible.[20] When Palmer asked a serf to name the three members of the Trinity. The man replied 'God the Father, Jesus Christ, and the Most Holy Mother of God.'[21]

The Russians had in every room of their houses an icon of 'some Saint of the Church or of our Lord', which provided a point in the room to which to say prayers, and served to make 'a Chapel of every room.'[22] Mr. Blackmore once called up into his house 'a poor nun' whom he had seen passing. 'On entering the drawing-room she looked from one corner to another for the *Icon*, and seeing none, she crossed herself to an ornamented clock which stood just opposite.'[23] Princess Dolgorouky thought that the inability of the Church to fulfil the religious cravings of the people had led to a growth in the 'Raskolniki', or schismatics, and the inroads of Western sectaries. Tsar Alexander I of Russia, who saw himself as 'a universal Christian standing above dogmatic and confessional barriers',[24] had encouraged English evangelicals to proselytise among the Russian people. He himself became a member of the British Bible Society, which opened a branch in St. Petersburg in 1813. After initial success it met increasing opposition, and was defunct two years after the appointment of Metropolitan Serafim Glagolevsky as President in 1824. This may, as Zernov believes, have been because a non- hierarchical Christian democracy was seen as a threat to the fabric of the Empire, and presumably also to the Russian Church.[25]

The Jesuits had likewise for a time enjoyed considerable success in Russia, with 'houses in Petersburg, Moscow, Mohilef, Astrachan, Odessa, and other places', instilling in 'a considerable number of ladies of rank [...] sentiments unfavourable to the Greek Church.'[26] In March 1820, however, an '*oukaz*' was issued expelling them from the Empire, 'never to return under any name or character,' and confiscating their property.[27] Palmer had no patience with these 'foreign influences' as 'religious movements against the Orthodox Church'. About the Bible Society he was particularly harsh: 'a good deal of their mischief must have been corrected in passing through the Censura;[28] still no Russian seems to have any notion how subtle a poison is concealed and mixed with every portion of the enlightened zeal, or zeal for enlightenment, which they possess.'[29]

Palmer was told by one Russian[30] that his introduction to Count Pratasoff 'was the very best [he] could have'. Whether through this initial introduction or otherwise, the majority of Palmer's contacts were with the upper classes of St. Petersburg, and in particular with a number of society ladies who took an interest in religion and were both intelligent and honest enough to admit to Palmer the real state of religion in Russia. If the lower classes in Russia had a simple piety that, for lack of education, drifted into superstition, the case of the upper classes was arguably worse. There was an enormous social gap, and an unbridgeable cultural divide, between the gentry and the serfs. The language and culture of the upper classes was French, when it was not German.[31] There were some 70,000 Germans in Petersburg. The result was an impatience with Orthodoxy verging on scepticism, or a syncretistic liberalism and a 'religion of the heart'. Princess Sophia Galitsin[32] told Palmer on 9 November 1840 that

> Our upper classes are not very religious. The services of the Church are very fatiguing, and we understand but little of them, especially the Vespers and the Matins; and scarcely anybody (of the higher classes) goes to the Matins. They are very long and you must stand the whole time. We are more at home in the Liturgy, and can follow it better.[33]

The solution, suggested Palmer, would be to read through the services in the books beforehand, so as to become familiar with them. The Princess admitted that 'that is what some of the old people do; and so they are able to stand out all the services, without finding them tiresome, which we cannot'.[34] She gave no indication, however, that she intended to follow their example.

The priest with whom Palmer eventually lodged, Father Fortunatoff, was more blunt: 'The nobles are nearly all bad. In Petersburg scarcely any of the laity of the higher classes keep the Fasts, but in Moscow, very many do [...] the higher classes think it fine to be like the Germans and the French'. When the priests went round to the houses of their parishioners at Christmas, as was the custom, they scarcely ever went to the houses of the 'Kniazes and Grafs (Princes and Counts)'. The peasants loved to see 'the Frenchified or Germanized Russian nobles, who, they say, are *not* Russians' held up to ridicule in comedies. Fortunatoff told Palmer 'Truly, they are like *you*. They are quite against all ceremonies, as superstitious; they respect neither the Saints, nor their *Icons*. It would be a good thing for them to be a little more on their knees, and to bump their heads a little against the pavement like the *mujiks*'.[35] Fortunatoff believed all the professors and students in the University to be free-thinkers, and all the medical men unbelievers, who never communicated. This free-thinking influence came, according to Prince Meshchersky (himself once Ober-Prokuror) from the 'foreign Protestant preceptors and governesses' by whom 'all Russians' (presumably the higher classes) were bred up. Madame Potemkin[36] added that as a child she had been taught no catechism.[37]

When Palmer spent the first day of the Advent Fast, 15 November, with the Potemkins, they confirmed that children were often dispensed from fasting by their parents up to the age of seven, but few young people of the higher classes fasted thereafter until they were grown up. Then, however, they were 'so Protestantized, that very few of them observe the fasts at all', the influence of the Germans in Petersburg being blamed. Some kept the first and last weeks of Lent, although the poor kept the whole of each fast 'most religiously'.[38] The Princess Eudoxia Galitsin[39] also admitted the 'want of zeal' among the higher classes, suggesting that for some there was a 'social attraction' to the Latin Church that might induce them to convert, albeit out of weakness. 'The people are the real strength of our Churches'.[40]

The mischief among them, one lady told Palmer at a breakfast in January of 1841, was 'a foolish desire to imitate foreigners, which Peter the Great left as a legacy to his empire'. This was most likely the result of his upbringing among the foreigners of the Koukou or Nalivaiki suburb of Moscow, where his youthful playmates ('Germans and other foreigners, chiefly Protestants') grew up to form two regiments of guards, the Preobrajensky and Semenovsky, 'drilled after the German fashion, officered in part by foreigners', who had 'imbibed his anti-Russian ideas'.[41]

Of the religious liberals that Palmer met, M. Mallof,[42] a priest of the Isaac Church, was typical. He told Palmer: 'there are Christians everywhere and [...] the great thing is the religion of the heart'. Palmer would have none of it: 'It is not enough for men to have a good intention to practise virtue in the sect in which they happen to be; they must also seek to be Catholics in faith and to believe in the Catholic Church, as being the one only way of salvation'. And again, responding to M. Mallof's quotation of the example of Cornelius, 'Doubtless there are honest and good people in all the sects [...] but it is impossible for the Church to call their errors truth, or to regard truth as indifferent, or to call them disciples or brethren'.[43] He had indeed come a long way from his early sympathy for the Vaudois.

The Archpriest Koutnevich,[44] the High Almoner of the Army and Fleet, was unflinching in his conviction that the Eastern Church was right, and that the others had fallen away, going so far as to state that the Easterns 'could not give up even the non-essential perfections of the true Visible Church'. Nonetheless, he told Palmer that good Christians might exist wherever there was true baptism in the name of the Trinity, and that there was as it were a sliding scale of heresy. 'A fraternal charity' might be cultivated by the Eastern Church with those who had been regenerated in baptism, and had gone on to cultivate their inner life, not dwelling on their errors; there would be 'an invisible unity' between them and their Orthodox brethren, although an outward separation would remain. Palmer thought that this would encourage liberalism and indifference to religious truth within the Church under the name of Charity, and lead those in error outside it to underrate the importance of Orthodoxy and conformity to the whole will of God. Koutnevich's reply was close, though he may not have realised it, to being *ad hominem*: 'I would shrink from the very notion of a man in the Church, perhaps barely, coldly, intellectually orthodox, judging such Christians, whose regeneration and spiritual life is so evident'.[45] Palmer was not swayed: 'amabilis sane sententia, sed perniciosissima doctrina'.[46] Koutnevich continued to maintain that it was not 'formal Orthodoxy of dogmatic opinion or [...] rite' that constituted 'essential Christianity', but the 'principle of faith and love', which meant that 'some who are without the pale may be better Christians than many of those who are within', although the distinction of Baptism remained to define the limits of the principle.[47]

Nor would Palmer accept indifferentism as a virtue of the Orthodox Church. Mr. Skreepitsin,[48] an official of Count Pratasoff's Chancery, told him that:

> Our Church has, and we have, one good point; that is its *tolerance*. We are not like Rome, which anathematizes all others; we have our own rite, but can be at peace with others, for they are all essentially one. The same Christ is worshipped by us all, and all things else are matters of comparative indifference.[49]

Palmer thought that this was to admit 'two or more religions', and saw only a stark choice: 'either we are of the same religion, or one of us is a heretic. There is one faith, one Church, one baptism etc.'.[50]

With the various society ladies he met who held similar opinions he was equally direct. To the Princess Dolgorouky, the wife of the Governor of Vilna, who was inveighing against Catholic intolerance, he suggested that the difficulties of the Russian Orthodox arose because they did not really believe their own claims to be the true Church. Having abandoned their exclusivist position, they were at a loss as to where to draw the line, and degenerated into liberalism and indifference. The Princess, like the Archpriest or M. Mallof, thought the difference was between those who believed in Christ and wished to obey him, and those who did not. If a man took the former line 'with honesty of purpose', then even if he was 'out of the pale, one must feel and admit that he is a Christian, and in the way of salvation'.[51] As before, Palmer's objection was that such an open category was all but impossible of delimitation.

The condition of the Russian clergy would not easily remedy either ignorance or liberalism, for the Russians themselves admitted that the clergy were often as ignorant as their flocks. The Unter- Prokuror of the Synod, M. Mouravieff,[52] speaking to Palmer in September of 1840, conceded that 'the ignorance of the clergy is very great in Russia [...] there is little knowledge of theology'.[53] The chaplain at St. Petersburg, Mr. Law,[54] told Palmer that the Russian clergy were 'a caste apart', who received 'some kind of respect' while officiating, but very little otherwise. Few had received any education; they were 'mere peasants'. He thought that Palmer would find it 'utterly impossible' to live with them.[55] Princess Sophia Galitsin told Palmer that the clergy 'had by no means all left off their bad low habit of drinking'.[56] M. Mallof contrasted the education that he presumed an English priest would be given with the situation in Russia: 'we have scarcely any'. Some clergy 'seem sincerely to seek Christ'; others were 'mere bigots to outward forms, and think all religion to consist in them'.[57]

The monastic view of the secular clergy was as harsh. When Palmer visited the Sergievsky Hermitage, or Monastery, in the same September, he was told by a monk that 'the secular clergy are infected with liberalism' through the influence of 'Lutheran and other bad foreign books'. Father Tchihacheff went further, saying that the secular clergy were 'kept in a hypocritical orthodoxy only by fear of the people', in a Church that had 'preserved all the rites and ceremonies, and the creed of the early Church', but despite 'a fair outside' was 'a dead body', with little life. He feared a possible 'explosion of heretical liberalism'.[58] Count Pratasoff admitted to Palmer at their very first meeting that some Russian bishops were positively heretical. He asked if any of the English bishops held the same views and taught the same doctrine as Palmer: 'I will not ask if there are any among them who are heretics or heretically inclined. I know you must have such: *we* have such, even here'.[59]

As for Anglicanism, the view expressed by Count Nesselrode,[60] the Minister for Foreign Affairs, was typical: it was 'toujours le Protestantisme [...] toujours une hérésie'. He was in a position to know: 'Je suis Anglican moi-même'.[61] The French Ambassador, M. de Barante, identified the distinguishing feature of the Anglican Church as having 'preserved the hierarchy: in other respects they resemble the other Protestant sects'. Mde Potemkin's comment on this was 'Mais c'est une très grande difference, n'est-ce pas?', but she also categorised the English in St. Petersburg as 'ignorant and heterodox'. Count Pratasoff, comparing Palmer's views with those of the chaplains, would not accept that they were 'perfectly Orthodox'. 'Your English here are many of them quite Protestant, Puritan: and they make the Russians think that they are not only Protestants like the Lutherans, but even like the Reformed (i.e. Dutch or Swiss Calvinists), which is much worse'.[62]

This was not surprising given the attitudes and behaviour of the traders and sailors from England. Some had even taken exception to the cross on top of the English Chapel in Cronstadt, put there at the instance of the Tsar, until Mr. Blackmore had reminded them of a similar cross on top of St. Paul's Cathedral in London.

> Any internal ornament as a gilt cross in the middle of the Altar Cloth or a cross over the altar or candlesticks on it [...] or if the arrangements had been such as to make it look less to the eyes of the Russians like a "preaching-house" [...] especially if anything should have caused their [the Minister's] back to be turned to the people [...] would have caused great offence and scandal both to the English and more especially to the Scotch.[63]

When the Lutherans applied to share the English Chapel while their own church was being repaired, Mr. Blackmore refused them permission to set even unlighted candlesticks and a cross on the altar, 'for fear of offending the prejudices of his congregation'. Seamen arriving in or leaving St. Petersburg were required to take an oath, sworn by Russians 'on the Cross and the Holy Gospels'. Mention of the Cross had to be omitted when the English or Scottish seamen were sworn, 'as it would scandalize the men'.[64] To the magistrate's question 'When did you last receive the Sacrament?' the answer given by nine out of ten of them, according to Mr. Blackmore, was 'Never'. 'They even wanted Mr. Blackmore to certify for them that it was not their custom'.[65]

A story was told of a Russian merchantman trying to speak to an Englishman, who was in church during the sermon. The Russian doorkeeper, asked if the Englishman would be long, replied 'No, I think it will be over soon, as it is a long time since they all sat down to sleep'.[66] Anglican priests, like those in France who wore secular clothing, were not considered to be real priests, but Protestant 'Pastors', as Palmer's designation by the police officers on board ship had shown. Mr. Blackmore, invited to dine by a Russian colonel, was addressed by him by his correct civil title, i.e. 'as a *gentleman*, not as a priest'.[67] Prince Michael Galitsin, speaking of Mr. Law's 'unecclesiastical appearance', said that he should have taken him 'for a comfortable merchant, not certainly for a priest'.[68] Mde Potemkin said of Anglican bishops that they lived 'quite like gentlemen and men of the world [...] they have not that spiritual character which ours have, nor the veneration attaching to it'.[69] It was against this unpromising background that Palmer had to put his case for the Church of England's catholicity.

PALMER'S PROTAGONISTS

Four men were to be his interlocutors in discussing theological matters. The first, the 'General of Hussars in his uniform', was Count Pratasoff, the Ober-Prokuror or head of the Synod. Educated by the Jesuits, he was commissioned in the Guards Regiment of Hussars at fifteen,[70] and in 1834 transferred to the Ministry of Education. In 1836 he became Procurator of the Synod. Zernov describes him as 'thoroughly westernised in outlook', taking cues from the organization and discipline of the Roman Church, but locating authority firmly in the Tsar.[71] A monk of the Sergievsky Monastery told Palmer that 'if the Synod (through the influence of the Crown) were to do anything bad, why, we would have to submit [...] Pratasoff is our Patriarch, though a soldier, as he represents the Emperor'. The situation was anomalous; here was a *de facto* Patriarch who went 'to balls and theatres, dances well' and was '"un très galant homme – mais– [...] "'[72] His words were echoed by the Princess Eudoxia Galitsin, who declared it a 'scandal [...] when the Church is governed by a layman, Count Pratasoff, who (respectable as he may be) dances the Mazurka, "C'est un très galant homme, il danse très bien." That is the kind of remark made in the saloons about him'.[73]

The second was Pratasoff's second in command, Unter-Prokuror of the Synod Andrei Mouravieff. Described by Palmer as 'a tall, indeed gigantic man', he was 'a great traveller and prolific author',[74] more obviously devout than Pratasoff. The same monk who had spoken disapprovingly of Pratasoff said of Mouravieff that he lived 'a regular life, different from the rest, and is in a manner nearer to becoming a monk'.[75] Unlike Pratasoff, whose dealings with Palmer were friendly enough but cautious and non-committal, Mouravieff became far closer to Palmer and took a much greater personal interest in him. His letters to Palmer as Palmer prepared to abandon Orthodoxy and enter the Roman Church were full of passionate concern, not for the *amour propre* of Orthodoxy, but for the soul of his friend. In their discussions about Anglicanism he never minced his words but was brutally frank.

Palmer dealt mainly with two churchmen. One was the Archpriest Vasil Koutnevich, the High Almoner of the Army and Fleet. He was appointed to that post in 1852, joining the Synod a year later. He had taught languages (Latin, German and French) in the Theological Academy, and had held a chair in philosophy. He was 'an accomplished ecclesiastical bureaucrat', of particular use because of his grasp of the arcana of Synodical procedure. For this he had been decorated with the Order of Alexander Nevsky, 'a rare honour for a married priest'.[76] He took a conventional line with Palmer on the need to accept all that Orthodoxy held, without qualification, which led to bad-tempered exchanges over Palmer's insistence on the identification of a specific historical breach between Orthodoxy and Anglicanism.

The other was the Metropolitan Philaret of Moscow[77] – 'probably the greatest theologian of the Russian Church in modern times [...] his influence on the life and theological thinking in Russia was enormous'.[78] More broad-minded than Koutnevich, he would 'not presume to call false any church, believing that *Jesus is Christ*',[79] although he certainly believed that the Eastern Orthodox Church had preserved the pure doctrine of the original deposit of faith. So far as the divided Christian bodies were concerned 'You expect now that I should give judgement [...] but I just simply look upon them [...] in the end the power of God patently will triumph over human weakness, good over evil, unity over division, life over death'.[80] Florovsky describes him as 'invariably impressed by "warm piety" wherever he might find it',[81] which may explain why he struck up a warmer relationship with Palmer than Koutnevich.

THE DEBATE COMMENCES

Palmer's approach to the spokesmen for the Russian Church was by no means an apologetic one. He did not hesitate to confront the Russians with the weaknesses of their position. His most frequent complaint was of their inconsistency. The Russians received 'European sects' by

> anointing with the Holy Chrism which was the manner appointed by the Church in old time for the reconciling of Heretics & Schismatics to the true Church: This is now their practise [sic] by all alike: which involves the inference that their communion is the whole of the Catholic Church: but inconsistently enough, they still call themselves the *Eastern* Catholic Church, and speak of the Western or Latin Church.[82]

Palmer said to Mouravieff on 21 September that if the Greeks anathematised the Latins as heretics over the Procession (the *filioque*) then the Russians were entirely inconsistent. They continued to call themselves the Eastern Church, and to talk of the difficulties posed to a General Council by the current divisions, but if the Latins were heretics there was only one Church, and that Catholic, not Eastern; no General Council could be held with heretics.[83] He took a similar line with M. Mallof, suggesting that if the Russians really believed themselves to be the true Church, they should at once make efforts to convert the Latins as heretics. Mallof replied evasively that the Latins were 'presque hérétiques', although when Palmer mocked him for this, he added that some of their errors 'touched the foundation.' But Palmer insisted that 'presque' meant that they were still part of the Church, and the Eastern not the whole of it.[84] Similarly, Father Fortunatoff thought the Latins were 'in one sense' heretics, 'though in another they are not.' Palmer would not accept this; they were either out of the Church, or they were not. Fortunatoff simply stood firm on the historical claim of the Orthodox Church: 'Our Church has remained the same, and has preserved everything. We certainly answer to the definition of the visible Church; but we have no need to include others in that definition which is fulfilled in the Greco-Russian communion: she stands alone, and self-sufficing.' However, to define the boundaries of the Church with great precision would be, he felt, destructive of tolerance and the 'half recognition' that existed.[85]

Although the Orthodox made the *filioque* the great stumbling block to unity, Palmer pointed out that there had been intercommunion even after the West had adopted it. This was ascribed by M. Mouravieff to 'inattention' on the part of the East. The monks of the Sergievsky thought the heresy had developed over time, and the Latins had 'dissembled the question' whenever temporary reconciliation had taken place. They insisted that 'Eastern' did not denote 'any local circumscription *in space*', but 'historical origin.' Sounding almost Gnostic, they declared: 'Christianity was from the East: Ex Oriente lux; we pray towards the East: we expect Christ from the East; and Christ is Himself the Everlasting East. From the West the catechumen has to turn away when he is to be baptised, and has to renounce the powers of darkness.'[86] Palmer was not to meet this particular argument elsewhere in Russia.

Sometimes he was told that the Russians called themselves 'Capholics', as opposed to (Roman) 'Catholics',[87] but he would not allow any substance to this peculiar linguistic distinction. Speaking to the Archpriest Sidonsky[88] of the Kazan

Church or Cathedral on 13 October, he said that there was 'a real weight in popular language', which grew when there existed 'one Communion claiming distinctly to be the whole, and in point of extent and numbers having better claim than any other, which is named the Catholic Church by your own lips, and [...] by her enemies. You admit you are a part; she says that she is the whole.'[89] Even Mouravieff admitted that it 'told in favour of the Latins' that they had carried on the idea and the exercise of ecumenical authority by continuing with a succession of General Councils up to the Council of Trent.[90] Princess Eudoxia Galitsin,[91] too, admitted 'a discrepancy' between the Orthodox claims to be the one true church and 'the opinion practically held by all of them [...] that the life of the Latin Church cannot be denied without flagrant disregard of common sense'. The discrepancy caused 'a certain weakness'.[92] On this point, then, Palmer can be said to have forced unwilling agreement.

His second most frequently urged argument followed logically from the first. If the Russians believed that Orthodoxy was the true Church, where was their zeal for conversion of the 'heretic' West, especially when the West had come within their own boundaries? He reminded the priest Sidonsky that:

> there are some millions of Lutherans and Calvinists subjects of the Russian Empire, whom you ought to try to convert to the true faith and Church; then, there are the Latins, two-thirds of the Christian world; and not only have you shown no zeal or power to correct them, but you have actually been following and imitating them [...].

Take St. Petersburg alone: 'in this one city and diocese you have had a colony of English, 2000 or 3000, since the capital was transferred here. Now what have you done in 130 years for their souls more than if they were a herd of swine? *This* is the zeal and charity of the One, Holy, Catholic, Apostolic Church!' Sidonsky replied that the Orthodox Church had 'always shown great moderation and tolerance, and [. . .] been careful not to condemn others', which Palmer thought 'cruel to others, and suicidal towards herself.' Sidonsky conceded 'there has been a culpable negligence', but excused this on the basis that 'nothing has forced us hitherto to consider the question of the definition of the Visible Church: whenever circumstances require it, it will no doubt be examined'.[93]

The Archpriest Koutnevich, however, vigorously defended his Church's record. On 17 October Palmer suggested to him that the Orthodox Church did nothing by way of mission worthy of its claims. Would 'a colony of English heretics have remained one, two, three hundred years in France or in Italy, in Paris or in Rome, as they have here, without any one of them [. . .] having ever been so much as spoken to with a view to his conversion?'[94] Koutnevich responded that it was well enough known that Orthodox writers called upon other Churches and sects to come to her; that the zeal of the Romans was '*bad*; such zeal is always a sign of error', and that Russian history showed that they had converted many peoples. Some eight days after this conversation, Count Pratasoff produced to Palmer records for 1837, 8 and 9, showing the annual conversion of about 10,000 Raskolniks. In 1839 they had converted between one and two thousand proselytes to Roman Catholicism, 'some 100s of Mahometans, about 100 Jews [...] and 100 or 200 Protestants [...] in all, since 1827 above 180,000, and in the last four years above 85,000, without mentioning the two millions or nearly of Uniats who were reconciled all at once in 1839'.[95] Palmer later mentioned the Archimandrite of the Troitsa Lavra, Philaret, who after being made Bishop of Riga received into the Orthodox Church 70,000 or 80,000 Lettish Lutherans.[96]

On 23 November, Palmer encountered a living exemplar of Russian mission in the 'missionary to the Aleoutines', Father John Veniamineff,[97] later a Metropolitan and in 1977 canonised as Saint Innocent of Alaska, who had converted 10,000 of a population of 60,000 to Christianity.[98] Palmer spoke with him about his missionary work, and found him 'friendly, open and cheerful', with 'a rough, weather-beaten look [. . .] that bespoke a simple, practical, decided character'.[99] Fr. Veniamineff had been labouring among the Aleuts since 1822, composing a Cyrillic alphabet for the Aleut language, learning six local tribal dialects, writing an Aleutian course of Orthodox dogmatics and theology, and building a church with his own hands, as well as a hospital and an orphanage.[100] Remarkably, Palmer showed no embarrassment at reproaching the Russians with their lack of energy for mission even after meeting this future saint, who had laboured to win souls in conditions that would make most explorers quail.

Palmer more than once suggested that the Russians, if they believed the English to be in error, should send missionaries to convert them. Koutnevich was 'much surprised' at Palmer's suggestion,[101] and immediately countered with the political obstacles. Count Pratasoff, on the other hand, turned the tables on Palmer, saying 'our best hope is for *you*, that we may convert *you*, and make you a bishop, [. . .] and send you back'.[102] Predictably Palmer reacted to this unexpected and flattering proposal by reverting to the prior question of whether the Anglican Church was or was not in communion with the East. If it was, for him to change would be 'a bad conversion', becoming 'particular instead of universal', and starting fresh schism in England.[103]

Count Pratasoff may have been joking, as Palmer described him as 'laughing' when he made the remark, but less than a month before, on 10 December, M. Mouravieff had hinted strongly that the door to Orthodoxy was open, saying of the reconciliation of the Princess of Darmstadt that 'You saw on Thursday how an individual may be received'.104 Palmer had insisted on distinguishing her reconciliation as being from 'soul-destroying heresy', and persisted in his refusal to acknowledge the Eastern Church as the whole Catholic Church; nonetheless the Church authorities seem to have hoped that he might come to change his views and convert. On his second visit to Russia in 1843 Palmer was even told by the Archpriest Koutnevich that 'if I were to be reconciled, I might probably be received with my Order of Deacon'.105 The Russian Church, which after all had no reason to make concessions to the Church of England, must have seen in Palmer, with his extraordinary learning, and increasing knowledge and understanding of Orthodoxy, a unique opportunity for mission in England. However, it was an opportunity that was never taken.

Palmer identified the reason for the lack of effort towards restoring unity in the Church as lack of will: 'we English and you Greeks maintain the doctrine of the universal invisible unity, but in practice we both rest contented with our own *part*'.[106] It suited everybody, largely because of laziness, that the status quo should remain. Some, like Sidonsky, saw no 'great scandal or harm in the existing divisions'[107] in the Church, and thought that they might even be part of divine providence – that the liberties of the Church, and a pure testimony to antiquity, might be preserved for future unity'.[108] The most exhaustive discussion of the issue was between Palmer, Count Pratasoff, and the Metropolitan Philaret on 27 November 1840. Palmer set out the belief of the Church of England on unity, as contained in the Creed, that the Church is one. The Metropolitan replied in terms identical to Dr. Routh, 'It *ought* to be one, but it is not'. Palmer replied that the division that existed was 'impious and detestable'. The Metropolitan commented blandly that 'Unity, no doubt, is much to be desired'. Pressed on whether many other English people shared his ideas on intercommunion, Palmer asserted that the Roman Church was a schismatic intruder *when in England*, or Greece, or Russia.

This was incomprehensible to Philaret, for whom communion depended 'on unity of belief'. It was absurd to say that the Latins could be communicated with abroad, but not at home, or conversely excommunicated at home but not elsewhere. For him it was a simple matter of examining the various divisions of the Church and deciding which was 'right, or most right'. Palmer fell back on another idea crucial to his claims for the Church of England, that there was a 'necessary faith', with an accretion of secondary but non-essential opinions, in any given area of Christendom. This was flatly denied by the Metropolitan, who thought it 'contrary to all the sentiments of the Fathers'. Count Pratasoff remarked that this principle would make him a Universalist, changing his religion as he crossed national boundaries, and it begged the question of who decided what was or was not essential.[109]

The same point had become apparent to the French Ambassador, M. de Barante. The difference between essentials and non-essentials, he said to Palmer, would have to be drawn by private judgement. 'Not so', replied Palmer, 'but by the Church'. M. de

Barante persisted: 'Still, the principle of unity is necessary, and that principle existed in the first Councils; and it comes to the same thing (now, if you admit a perpetually existing authority) When you assert the Church to be divided, who is the judge?' 'You can only judge by probabilities if the Church is divided, God can only judge absolutely and circumstances, as time goes on, may make his judgement manifest'.[110] This pious but evasive response gave away the weakness of his position, and left a hostage to fortune in the hands of his opponents. What was the probability of the Anglican Church being 'the Church', or even united with it? And if circumstances may make God's judgement manifest, they equally well may not.

Palmer elaborated at their request on his concept of the Visible Church: that it was 'at this time divided by differences about secondary matters into three local parts, all agreeing in the necessary faith, viz. the Orthodox Eastern Churches and the Western; the latter being subdivided into the Continental and the British'. The Metropolitan expressed doubt that many in England could hold the theory: 'I think it can be anything but general'.[111] Both he and Count Pratasoff summed up the fundamental obstacle to Palmer's request, which echoed Dr. Routh's prediction to Palmer in July ('It will lead to nothing I fear, sir, for a separation there unhappily is'): 'These are matters for some future Council or Councils, but they cannot be treated of with individuals'. The Metropolitan pronounced that Palmer's language 'suits well enough for the fourth century, but is out of place in the present state of the world'. Perhaps one day his laudable quest for unity would come to be shared more widely, but until then 'individuals cannot be treated with or recognized in the first instance; now at any rate there is division'.[112]

It was at this point that Archbishop Howley's reluctance to approve Palmer's mission caused Palmer embarrassment; for if Palmer's language suited the fourth century, the letters he had brought did not, a fact that had not escaped the notice of Count Pratasoff. Palmer had to concede that a letter from his bishop or archbishop 'was the strict form', and his explanation that Archbishop Howley had thought Dr. Routh's letter enough was met by the Count with laughter: 'Ils ne voulaient pas se compromettre' he said to the Metropolitan, and dismissed Dr. Routh's authority as only that of a priest. 'His letter is nothing; you should have brought the same countersigned by the Bishop'.[113] However, the Count was probably teasing Palmer. His remark about the unwillingness of the Anglican authorities to compromise themselves showed that he knew very well why Palmer could only rely on letters from his College Principal. Despite the frank exchanges, the interview ended on an amicable note, with Philaret telling Palmer that they were glad to see him, and hoped 'that good might spring from this seed'.[114]

RUSSIAN SCEPTICISM

As this interview shows, the Russians gave Palmer as good as they got. When Palmer expressed to the Princess Meshchersky[115] his hope that the Church that had been one in visible and outward communion for 1200 years might be so again, she dismissed it as 'a beautiful dream'.[116] Some, especially Mouravieff, took an overtly sceptical approach to Palmer's depiction of the Church of England and its doctrine from the start. Palmer was frequently interrogated as to how representative his views were of the English Church. In their first interview, Count Pratasoff asked Palmer if the Anglican chaplains at St. Petersburg or Cronstadt would agree with him – and if he was right, why did the English Church not teach its people what Palmer had described? He asked, according to Palmer, 'over and over again: "If that be true, how can it be that it is so little known? [...] why do you not make Catechisms, and teach distinctly your doctrine?"' On 21 September M. Mouravieff made the same points:

> There may, no doubt, be individuals who think like you, perhaps even some of the bishops, – ([...] *are* there *any* of them who think like you?) – but *you* are not the Anglican Church [...] Do you mean to tell me that your friend the chaplain at Cronstadt, or the other, who is here, would agree with you?[117]

The Sergievsky monks too said 'you are only an individual; the thing necessary is to know what are the sentiments of your Church [...] what is the opinion of your *bishops* on these matters?'[118] When Palmer persisted, the response grew less diplomatic. M. Mouravieff spoke plainly to Palmer on 2 October: 'We know you only as heretics. You separated from the Latin Church 300 years ago [...] we think even the Latin Church heretical; but you are an apostasy from an apostasy; a progression from bad to worse'. His view was that the Pope had been the Patriarch of the English Church before the Reformation; therefore 'any communication must be through the Pope, and the Church of Rome [...] reconcile yourself to your Patriarch first, and then come and talk to us, if you think you have anything to say to us'.[119]

Mouravieff reiterated his view of the Reformation when he saw Palmer again in December, after he had been reading Palmer of Worcester's[120] *Treatise on the Church*.[121] 'You are obliged to apologize, and to cast about in order to defend yourselves, and your Reformation. But you cannot be defended'. Contrasting the Church of England with the Eastern Church ('calm and immovable'), he went on:

> It is plain how it [the Reformation] was [...] manifestly it was a violent irruption into the Church of laymen, who mangled and altered their religion to suit their own purposes. Union with such a church is impossible. Others may come into the Eastern Church and follow her; but she can yield nothing in any way, least of all to you [...] union with a national church, which leaves such latitude for denying or asserting all kinds of opinion, is impossible. With you

> everything needs explanations and apologies. One of you sees a thing in one light, another in another; no two of you agree.

Becoming more personal, he continued, 'There are your XXXIX Articles, which any one may subscribe, and be a thorough-going Protestant. You, in your Dissertation, allow some things to us, and do not allow others; you amalgamate and reconcile and eclecticise, that Protestants you may not be'.[122]

This was a more than fair point against Palmer, who had been forced, time and again, to field in his support Bishop Lancelot Andrewes' *Preces Privatae,* and the Canon of 1571. The former contained 'Prayers for the departed, the Intercession of Saints, the Eulogy of the Blessed Virgin, and faith in the Real Presence',[123] and the latter bound the clergy (according to Palmer) 'to preach nothing as of faith but only what is contained in Holy Scripture, and what the Catholic Fathers and ancient Bishops have collected from the same'.[124] But Lord Selborne remarks of the canon that 'it never had legal force';[125] and although Palmer assured the Archimandrite of the Sergievsky, when asked if Bishop Andrewes was acknowledged in England, that 'all agree to call him one of the best and greatest divines of their Church',[126] it is doubtful that the majority of contemporary Anglicans would have agreed with either the doctrines or practices listed above: they were private devotions, after all, not a public form of service. To show that the Church of England held the doctrine of the Real Presence, he was forced to rely on 'the *Scotch* Liturgy'.[127]

Mouravieff was not, therefore, attracted by Palmer's idea of using the Russian chaplains in London 'to acquire a better knowledge of the state of Church matters in England'. He remarked contemptuously that they had 'no particular reason for cultivating such studies – English is not a classical language'. When Palmer suggested that nonetheless, English theology might be a fair exchange for the German that they currently read, Mouravieff was curt: 'If we read here German books, we do not adopt the errors of the Germans, but can distinguish between good and bad without help from you'.[128] He used Palmer's own weapons against him when taxed with the 'superiority in various points' of the Latins to the Easterns. He allowed that 'Rome had the credit of activity'; but 'by that rule, the Dissenters beat you out and out, for they are in India, America, the Levant, Syria, and Abyssinia, everywhere, and they convert numbers'. Palmer's reply that they had not done so yet missed the point; it was the zeal of Rome for conversion, not the numbers that resulted, he had prayed in aid against the Orthodox. Mouravieff ended the interview by reverting to what he saw as the simple truth about the Anglican Church: 'You manifestly fell away from them [Rome], and it is of no avail now to try to explain things away, and to change all our convictions as to your past history'.[129]

Princess Eudoxia Galitsin echoed Mouravieff: 'How can you pretend that your religion is the same as ours when you have not the same sacraments or altars in our churches? You came out of the Church at the Reformation'. When Palmer objected to this she replied 'The English themselves speak as I was speaking'. His response – 'That is nothing to me' – was indicative of his wilful blindness to reality. He might treat the opinions of other Englishmen with disdain, but they contradicted and undermined his arguments. Prince Michael Galitsin[130] had asked his banker ('a Scotchman, an excellent fellow') about Palmer. He replied 'Oh! He is not of *our* religion; he is a member of some new sect'.[131]

Mouravieff returned to the theme of Anglican inconsistency in a subsequent interview on 25 February O. S./9 March N. S. 1841.[132] He again based his objections on the 39 Articles which he declared were 'quite contrary to your principles and opinions which you cannot defend by clear words of your Church herself in any systematic or full confession of faith, but part is only your own opinion, part a passage taken from one book, part a passage taken from another'.[133] Palmer retorted indignantly that Mouravieff could not have read the Synodal correspondence with the Non-Jurors, whose opinions reflected his own. Mouravieff was unmoved.

> Yes I have read it; it is true the British bishops in it speak your language, and seem to hold your principles; but then the 39 Articles are quite different; and while some of you may reject or interpret them away (for you may by interpreting make of any form what you please) there may be others, and a far greater number perhaps, who stick to them in their plain and literal sense.[134]

Palmer insisted that there was 'a constant and unbroken tradition for the correct interpretation of the Articles', but Mouravieff returned to his first criticism: 'You have had plenty of writers no doubt; but do they agree together? Does not every one of them hold a different doctrine from every other?' Besides, the Non-Jurors' correspondence clearly undermined Palmer's fundamental assertion that communion between East and West had never been interrupted, for it 'shows that there is a separation – for it was a correspondence to restore unity, and it proceeded on the assumption that there was a separation'.[135] As the separation did exist, they could not take

> the word of a Deacon with letters only from a priest or head of a College like an Archimandrite [...] and besides that your Rite was so totally unlike ours, if we were to believe your statement which you cannot prove, with all appearances against you, and admitted an individual to Communion it might cause enormous scandal on both sides.

Palmer himself would be regarded as 'a renegade or apostate' by half the Church of England. But, added both Mouravieff and the Metropolitan, putting pressure on

Palmer to reconsider his position, 'It is impossible to belong to two Churches at once; and to be suspended between two is not a sure road to heaven'.[136]

Palmer was prepared to concede the truth of some of the Russian charges against the Church of England. He admitted to Koutnevich with regard to confession in the Church of England that 'practically there is no discipline';[137] to the monks of the Sergievsky that 'the Anglican Church has by successive violences and other influences been stripped perfectly bare';[138] and to Pratasoff that the popular liberty that they had in England, far from being favourable to ecclesiastical humility and discipline, was 'the devil's liberty'.[139] He conceded that 'all the outward surface of things among us is Protestant',[140] and that his countrymen and popular opinion had both been 'thoroughly Protestantised'.[141] He admitted that 'others speak contrary to me',[142] and that few interpreted the 39 Articles as he did;[143] those who did, who thought the Church of England '*de*formed rather than *re*formed',[144] were attempting to rebuild 'a Catholic theology out of the ruins of a decomposed Protestantism'.[145] He quoted with approval Lord Clanricarde's comments at dinner at the French Ambassador's, that the Church of England 'a été toujours pour le fond Catholique, mais elle a été terriblement defigurée et mutilée'; and that the churches of England were 'bare and slovenly', and the services and ceremonies so 'lifeless and naked' as to be 'contemptible'.[146]

Some, rather than being sceptical, simply could not understand what Palmer meant by seeking communion. The Archpriest Koutnevich told him that 'You have your own chaplain here; you need not come to us'. Palmer explained again that in Russia he was no member of the Church of England, but of the Church of Russia.[147] The Archimandrite of the Sergievsky could not see why the English should not send out a bishop of their own to St. Petersburg.[148] The Metropolitan Philaret, having agreed that Palmer's application might have been considered had his case been one of necessity, ruled out that possibility for the very reason that 'there is an English church here to which you can go'.[149]

There were any number of reasons why Palmer's application could not be granted. It was a matter of far too great importance to be dealt with between an individual (and a mere deacon at that) and representatives of the Russian Church: 'union should be attempted only by Synods'.[150] It would cause scandal with a number of parties, such as the Greeks, whom Mouravieff described as 'unlearned, both laity and clergy, and they are blindly attached to all that they have received, even to the minutest details of their rites'. He illustrated this ignorance by recounting how he had asked the Patriarch of Constantinople to explain the heresy of the Armenians, which seemed to him to be 'very subtle'. The Patriarch had replied 'Oh, do not ask me, my son! Only know that all the heresies in the world which are most pernicious and wicked are united in the heresy of the Armenians'.[151] But however comical they might think the Greeks, the Russians would not run the risk of losing the communion of the Eastern Patriarchs.

The reaction of ordinary Russians had also to be considered. Koutnevich told Palmer that to give communion to the English despite the existing differences 'would be extremely dangerous, and it would scandalize the people beyond anything'. In fact he thought that 'your people too would be scandalized'. Mouravieff agreed; they had to 'keep in view the Raskolniks, not to scandalize our own people', adding as a more worldly consideration, 'What would the English and the French Ambassadors here say to it?'[152] A 'Russian lady' agreed: 'if you obtained what you are seeking [...] it would be to upset (bouleverser) all Russia. There are here different ambassadors [...] what would they say?'[153] Count Pratasoff's private secretary felt that 'unity of good will and sympathy' was all that could be practically had for the time being. He too was concerned that if the Russian Church granted Palmer's request, it might cause more Raskolniks, be taken as disrespectful by the Greeks, and inevitably set a precedent. Count Pratasoff himself was concerned about the implications of doing so: it would be 'the same thing as to offer union to all the West'.[154] Palmer's report of his progress to Dr. Routh,[155] was bleak:

> from what I have seen of the Orthodox clergy & of 2 members of the Synod I should suppose that there was no sort of probability of their either admitting me to Communion or even examining my belief with the intention of either admitting or rejecting me according to its correctness or heterodoxy.

This was partly because, as he had found, the Russians were far more aware of Roman Catholicism than they were of 'the claims & character of our Church', which to the Russians was 'one of the many sects of heretical Protestantism', and 'the external appearance of English manners & worship is not such as to undeceive them [...] we never keep fasts, never make the sign of the Cross – and reject Invocations of Saints & the external reverencing of Pictures wh. they consider to be two essential points of the true Religion'. He thought the Russians incapable of distinguishing between 'the essential & immutable Faith & Secondary matters of opinion, language or practise [sic]': Metropolitan Philaret had rejected Palmer's definitions of what was essential and secondary. The Russian definition of the Visible Church did not include the separated and therefore heretical West, still less the Sects that had left the Pope's jurisdiction. He enumerated the elements that they feared would be scandalised by any new step, viz. the Uniats and the Greeks.[156] Palmer recorded drily that after he had finished writing his letter, his host Father Fortunatoff 'criticized it freely, and ended by going to his piano and singing the *Trisagion* (Ἅγιος ὁ Θεός), the Cherubicon (Therefore with Angels, etc.), the Tersanctus (Holy, holy, holy); the Hymn (Φῶς ἱλαρόν) the *Nunc dimittis*, and the *Te Deum*.'[157]

APPLICATION FOR COMMUNION

On 21 March 1841 Palmer delivered to Metropolitan Philaret a formal application for communion in the form of a letter. In it he described himself as 'a Deacon of the Church which is in the Western dioceses of the English [...] unworthy for my sins of the communion of any Church', who 'ought rather to pass all my life in tears and penitence outside the doors of the Church'. He offered ecclesiastical obedience to 'particular local churches', and unconditional obedience to 'the oecumenical authority of the whole'.[158]

He had been warned more than once of the likely response. Mr. Blackmore had told him in mid-August that 'if you would be admitted to communion you will have to be confirmed with Chrism: you will have to accept all the traditions of the Orthodox Eastern Church, and not only those which you may call ecumenical [correctly anticipating the Metropolitan's rejection of Palmer's would-be distinction between essential and secondary matters of the faith]; you will have to confess before communicating [...]'.[159] This the Archpriest Koutnevich had confirmed on 28 August, telling him 'If any one would be admitted to Communion in the Sacraments, he must believe all that the Orthodox *Eastern* Church [Palmer's stress] believes'.[160] M. Mouravieff on 22 September told him equally plainly, 'Any one who would communicate with the Oriental church must take her exactly as she is, for she can do nothing to meet him',[161] and on 20 January 1841 he repeated, speaking specifically about Palmer's letter to the Metropolitan, 'To an individual the Church can concede nothing; and no one can communicate except with an unconditional acceptance of all that she teaches and practises'.[162]

Philaret's reply began by speaking of the pleasure that Palmer's request had given him, but as what *charity* seeks must be approved by *truth*, the *truth* of diocesan right was 'to admit to Communion of the Sacraments those who confessing the dogmas of the Orthodox Church, promise and render to her absolute obedience, without any conditions restrictions or reservations':

> You, Sir, propose certain conditions, and make certain restrictions and reservations, and propose to yourself to *await*, as you say, *in silence the result of conferences between the Bishops*. This if we are to speak plainly, is not to render obedience to the Eastern Catholic Church, but to make a kind of treaty with her; a thing certainly which it is not for the diocesan authority to admit, but for the synodal authority to decide upon.

Communion between their two Churches was 'not a matter to be attempted by a Deacon or Head of a College on one side nor one Bishop on the other'. Philaret concluded by expressing his own full satisfaction with the Communion of the Orthodox Catholic Church, and wishing Palmer 'like satisfaction and bliss'. He returned with the answer 'Welshman's Latin Edition of the 39 Articles, with the corners of the leaves turned down at Articles XIX, XXI, and XXII'.[163]

LOCAL DIFFICULTIES AND CUSTOMS

Although Palmer was to remain in Russia for just over a month longer, this politely expressed refusal had effectively brought his self- imposed mission to an end. The confident tone of the narrative of *Notes of a Visit to the Russian Church* might give the impression that Palmer's time in Russia was entirely happy and easy; this was not so. He faced a number of hardships and difficulties, of which the language was the most obvious. He had never learned Russian, and although he was helped by the fact that the Westernised middle and upper classes spoke French, and the clergy and monks Latin, to his mortification he found Russian much more difficult to learn than he had expected:

> I have however made very little progress in picking up those innumerable (but most necessary) phrases, which are required in common life and for want of which I still feel very helpless and wish myself well settled in the Academy or rather home again in England most heartily; but this will no doubt get better in a little time [...].[164]

He confided to his mother 'I can assure you that I am heartily homesick & shall return as soon as ever I have made sufficient progress in the language'.[165] Things were little better by the next January, at least as regards his spoken Russian:

> In speaking I have made no progress at all or *very* little – which vexes me a good deal and I am at a loss to account for my having so totally failed. I have it is true been very unfortunately situated for this – for I have little or no opportunity for practising: the Priest's family consisting only of his wife and two infant children – and he having been used to talk Latin to me for nearly three months and I to him – we cannot do anything else – and in other society I never hear anything but French spoken – add to this that my Priest speaks very rapidly and indistinctly.

As to reading,

> my state of proficiency is pretty much as follows: I can read the Church Service books (which are in Sclavonic [sic]) without difficulty, and have read three or four volumes through in Russ (Russian) – and with the priest's assistance can read from fifty to seventy pages a day – by myself I get on but very slowly having still many words to look out.[166]

After his intial forays into the cathedrals and churches of St. Petersburg he admired the piety of the Russians, but still wrote to his Aunt Eleanor that 'the people upon the whole are not well looking, neither men nor women [...] I cannot say that I very much like what I have seen of the country at present, or of the Capital'.[167] He seems to have been more willing to voice his doubts to his aunts than to his parents.

Although he was well looked after, his lodgings were as expensive as 'the most expensive Hotel in Paris or London'. [168] This, together with his desire to learn Russian, led Palmer to persuade Count Pratasoff to find him a room with a Father Fortunatoff, who lived at 'no. 10 in the suburbs in the Offitserskaia, on the Viborg side, across the Neva'.[169] The move left him 'In point of situation [...] no gainer but the contrary – for I am now at the other extremity of the City in the suburbs almost in the country – and not in any very desirable part of the town either'. He was separated from the southern bank of the Neva by two bridges of boats that had to be removed swiftly when the ice came down in 'huge masses' from the Ladoga lake, freezing over a couple of days so as to enable people to cross. Eventually sledges could be driven down the river to Cronstadt: 'the track is marked out with small trees all the way and station houses fixed with men to look out and give notice by ringing a bell in hazy weather or snowstorms'.[170] The house itself was one storey and wooden, with furniture that was 'scanty and poor in the extreme'.[171] Palmer found that he had

> considerable personal discomforts – e.g. – I have a trunk which is not long enough for a bedstead and for bedding a mattrass [sic] one sheet & a counterpane he insisting that I will let him stove the room up to such a degree of heat as the Russians live in I shall not want any more bedding which may be true enough – I cannot say I like the heated atmosphere in which they live at all.

This was caused by the 'great earthen stoves' or 'peeches' which were to be found in every room, heated up every day or two, on top of which whole families of peasants would sleep, lying there 'when it is so hot that their shirts or cloths [sic] are all but catching fire'.[172] Fortunately he had bought a wadded cloak which he could use as bedclothes. In fact he was lucky to have a separate bedroom at all:

> In the domestic arrangements of a Russian house of the middle & lower classes – and to a very considerable degree also of the higher – an Englishman is struck by the apparent absence of bedrooms – The fact is they use the same rooms very generally to sleep in at night which they live in during the day – sometimes a bed is concealed by a light moveable screen six feet high – often there is no bed at all but sofas are used instead – a Russian requiring nothing but his cloak and a light coverlet [...].

The servants, like the droshky drivers, often slept at their master's door in their sheepskin 'just like a dog'.[173] These arrangements meant that there was 'little taking off of clothes'. The Russians kept themselves clean by 'vapour baths', taken 'at least once a week', the custom being 'extremely ancient in Russia', and 'described by the chronicler Nestor as exciting the wonder of St. Andrew the Apostle'; 'if you like you may have the advantage of being flogged with light twigs [...] and after this you have cold water – the coldest water indeed thrown over you – are rubbed dry by the attendants' or if in the country 'the peasants commonly run out of the bath & take a roll on the snow [...] the Russians recommend their baths as a preventative or a remedy for many ails & diseases'.[174]

Fr. Fortunatoff was married with 'two little children who cry a good part of the day', and was 'Chaplain to a Government Hospital of Marines situated in the quarter – and the duties of this place are not onerous – he having to celebrate the Liturgy only on Sundays & Festivals – He also teaches an hour or two Sacred History & Catechism & Latin Grammar in a School in another Government Establishment'.[175] Fortunately the priest turned out to be 'good- natured – and very well disposed to work with me to teach me Russian'. The drawbacks were that he had 'one trick you would not like & that is of pawing every thing about which comes in his way', and the fact that 'as we sit & read together his long beard is forever coming into my face'. Palmer noted that 'the Priests wear their hair long behind like women flowing down their backs – (a custom said to be taken from the Jewish Nazarists) and at the same time they wear their beards especially long before – I admire the beards – but cannot say as much of the hair'.[176]

Although he wrote to his mother that he was 'agreeably disappointed [...] that I have not yet been seriously molested either by fleas or any other similar animals', he may have been sparing her feelings; for in *Notes of a Visit* he describes how after a sleepless first night the priest 'examined the crevices and corners of the room, and found long clusters of [...] vermin hanging like bees in a hive. They frizzled and fell into the candle, and almost put it out. This clearance was no doubt much, but still my nights are bad enough'.[177] He was to be similarly afflicted at the Sergievsky Monastery:

> I cannot give you any idea of how much I have suffered from fleas, bugs and mosquitos since I have been here – though I am much interested in all I see and hear, yet I assure you I pay for it *with my blood* both day and night – a monk said to me I am afraid you are troubled by the fleas – I answered that they might serve at all events to teach me patience – at which they said 'You speak like a monk'.[178]

The Russians had an extraordinary tendency to go to sleep regardless of time or place, the droshky Drivers in the street in their Kaftans or sheepskins, or the Mujiks flat out on top of tree trunks on timber waggons. A 20 year old servant girl at Miss Dees' disappeared at 10 o' clock in the morning, only to be found stretched out fast asleep on a shelf in a cupboard. 'She would fall asleep over her work not at the end of the day but as soon as she came down in the morning'. The Mujiks had 'little value for their lives & little sense of danger'. One, reproached by his Mistress for risking his neck while working on an outside window, replied calmly, 'Never mind, I am only a Mujik'.[179]

A Russian Mujik formed the subject matter of the first of Palmer's many 'significant dreams'. When in Cronstadt on the night of 31 August O. S./12 September N. S., he dreamed that he had killed the son or very near relation of 'an ancient, weatherbeaten, hard-featured hardworking Russian countryman of the lowest rank (i.e. of Mujiks)' who was taking it especially hard 'because he had suffered & been wronged in the same way once before either in his own person or by the loss of his own son'. In the dream he offered the old man four squirrel skins, and then sheepskins as 'blood price' for the loss, but the Mujik was implacable, instilling in Palmer 'a deep fear & awe of his vengeance'. The sheepskin was given an overtly religious significance as he heard himself say in the dream 'one of them is the fleece of his own dearly beloved Son'.[180] Palmer analysed the dream at length as a metaphor for how we each of us displease God and kill Christ anew by disobedience, although it might indicate that he saw God as vengeful and implacable.

Palmer was much struck by the way that piety pervaded everyday life in Russia. 'The Russians will not live in a house until it has been blessed [...] by the Priest',

> nor sail in a ship in like manner [...] every Russian ship has also Pictures of the Saints on board – & a monk for a Chaplain who says prayers for & with the ship's crew also on land every Government establishment & office without any distinction has a Chapel & Chaplain attached to it – & very many of the private houses of the richer people.

He enumerated the endless occasions on which the Russians made the sign of the Cross: 'on rising and going to bed – on entering a room or passing a Church – before & after meals – and above all during the performance of divine service – they also think that this custom is salutary and that people who have it not can scarce be Christian [...]'.[181] He was charmed by the custom of children seeking their parents' blessing night and morning, as monks did of their abbots and lay people on meeting priests they knew in the street. However, when he told M. de Barante that he had 'never been in so religious a country', the Ambassador responded that this was so 'as far as external observances go, but it is to regretted that they do not influence sufficiently the morals of the people – there is not only much drunkenness, but other vices besides'.[182] Palmer had discovered as much from personal experience:

> The bad qualities which generally strike foreigners & of which I have seen enough myself to make me fear that the accusation is well-founded are a disposition to cringing – lying & duplicity – stealing & drunkenness – I have had one or two small things stolen out of the pocket of my cloak by servants in houses where I was visiting: & the servants in the Church of the Hospital here were so drunk on Easter Monday that they could not stand – but I should add that they were punished & lost their places for it.[183]

On the other hand:

> The good qualities which strike you here as very general whereas in England Society seems to be full of a contrary spirit – are as much humility obedience – a kind of brotherly oneness & goodhumoured familiarity between all classes a reasonable & reverent disposition in all that relates to religion – The entire absence of that aversion to do or say anything in ordinary life which shall mark you to be a Christian which is so common in English Society – and a great development of good & amiable & tender feeling as distinguished from intellect.[184]

The last remark may refer to himself, for as his French diaries show, he felt himself overly intellectual and lacking in feeling.

Drunk or sober, the 'lower orders' presented a picturesque sight to Western eyes. They usually wore

> a very coarse shirt – a wrapper round their legs – a sort of drawers rather trowsers which go down into their boots – and a Caftan or long gown with large round sleeves, of thick dark blue Cloth – which is bound round the waist with [...] a sash of cotton – generally red – sometimes yellow – they never wear shoes but always boots & long beards – if the weather is cold in spring & autumn the middle classes often wear a very long & close great coat of the same dark blue coat [sic] [. . .] in winter the lower people all were [sic] sheepskins generally made as frockcoats with a leather band round the waist & the base skin outside.[185]

Although Palmer describes the unbound 'Caftan' as looking like an Oxford gown, he must have made an impression himself by wearing his cap and gown in Russia, as he did on 23 April to see Metropolitan Philaret, who was apparently 'much pleased', saying that it was 'the Eastern dress in its origin – and certainly much fitter for Ecclesiastics and more becoming than the modern tight European dresses which are not only unbecoming but scarcely decent'. The Metropolitan asked

> whether the clergy always wore it – I said the rule is that they should – but they do not except in Colleges, and there only the Gown. He said 'Besides that the thing is so proper itself – if it is the rule of your Church why do they not obey it – that is what I do not understand' – nor indeed could I explain either that or a hundred other discrepancies between the paper-theoretical Catholicism and the living practical Protestantism of our Church.[186]

His sartorial observations extended to Orthodox vestments; his remarks in August to his father about scarves being worn by the Deacons over the left shoulder produced no response, but in October, after a visit to the Sergievsky Lavra, he was trailing his coat – or scarf – again. 'The Deacons [...] put on [...] on the left shoulder their scarves or stoles [...] with crosses upon them: just as I wear mine – which pleased me much to see'.[187] This time his father rose to the bait: 'I do not see why you should have exulted so much when you saw the deacon wear his stole on the left shoulder like yourself – for I must own as you very well know, I should have thought it much more becoming in them than I do in you'. He astutely asked: 'Would they admit an Anglican to communion without rebaptising? And what possibility is there of an English Deacon being recognised as such and ordained priest?' [188] The answer to the second question was given by Koutnevich in 1843; but it was the different Russian and Greek responses to the first question that was primarily responsible for keeping Palmer out of the Orthodox Church.

The 'common vehicles of the country' made a great impression. They were

> called Teleggas and have no springs – & the sight of which has really something barbarous & surprizing in it. These are cradles on four wheels or rather frames, on which is mounted a sort of wooden boat or skeleton of open wooden ribs, the driver sitting outside of it in front it is commonly half full of straw or rubbish to break the jolts and, in it, sits like a great bird in a nest the traveller or passenger.[189]

Rather than pay 70 to 80 roubles for a coach and four, Palmer unwisely chose to travel in a telegga to visit the Troitsa Lavra on 17/29 May 1841. He set off from Howard's Hotel in Moscow at 4 o'clock in the morning, unaware that with: 'this sort of vehicle, having no springs, no one ought to use it, as I then did ignorantly, without providing himself with a mattress or feather-bed, and tying a sash or shawl tightly round his body, else he will run a risk of being jarred and shaken almost to pieces'.[190] The result was that 'though the distance is not more than fifty miles we were more than ten hours in accomplishing it, and I must say I never had so good a shaking in my life [...] though I had taken the precaution to tie a pocket handkerchief round my waist (or rather stomach)[191] I could hardly endure the jolting and for some versts there was no road'.[192] This last stretch he described as 'a mere cart-rut over a common'.[193] He had not learned his lesson when the time came for him to return to Moscow on 3 June (N. S.), for he 'started about half-past nine, and arrived at Moscow about seven p.m., nearly shaken to pieces, having neglected to provide myself with a mattress'.[194]

He wrote to his sister Emma that 'there are always I am told more than 100,000 regular troops in the Capital or in its immediate vicinity'. He found them

> to be "excellent conservatives" and to think with me that it would be more reasonable for the Christian Powers of Europe to take the first legitimate opportunity in concert to putting an end to the Turkish Power & the slavery of the Eastern Christians to unbelievers than to league together as now by a miserable jealousy of one another to "maintain the Integrity of the Ottoman Empire".[195]

He had had a similar conversation with one of the Sergievsky monks on the way back from the monastery to Petersburg. The monk regretted that 'nothing is worshipped but what is military', a 'mania [...] necessarily unfavourable to the strict morality and simplicity of early times'. Palmer responded that 'perhaps Russia is preparing for her great mission – the deliverance of the Eastern Churches and the overthrow of the Turkish Empire'.[196] Although he had at Dr. Routh's suggestion omitted the passage about delivering 'the East from the yoke of the infidels' from his address to the Tsar, he still cherished the same romantic sentiment.

ON SHIFTING SANDS

By January of 1841, Palmer was coming to feel that his defence of the Church of England was gallantry on behalf of a lady of doubtful ecclesiastical virtue. This feeling was the more uncomfortable because it reflected on his own integrity in making claims on her behalf. M. Mouravieff, although kind to him on a number of occasions,

> on matters of Divinity talks to me as if I were a kind of well-intentioned impostor, trying to whitewash and explain into an Orthodox and Catholic Church an heretical Protestant Act of Parliament "Establishment" which, by the way, he seemed to understand by the confident way in which he talks much better than I do myself [...].[197]

He was handicapped by the fact that apart from the merchants and traders who came to St. Petersburg from England and Scotland, such as Prince Michael's banker, 'every Russian family has had an English governess to teach their daughters [...] or has known English people or travelled – or read English books'. Count Pratasoff's immediate reaction on hearing Palmer's exposition of his Church's beliefs, after asking if the Anglican chaplains would agree with him, was to say that he would speak to his wife's 'English *bonne* or companion, a good woman enough'[198] about the matter.

The invariable 'final & conclusive objection' to his claims for the Church of England was:

> what is there Catholic about your people – if you are Catholics, for what earthly reason do you in all things that we can see follow the heretical novelties of the Protestants and differ from the whole Christian Church in all ages and in all places [...] Why they say your people will not even so much as make the sign of the Cross – your Pastor never says the Liturgy but only preaches – You have abolished the sacrifice and retained only as a separate thing the Communion – and to that your people go with full stomachs contrary to the practise [sic] of the whole Church – and communicate whenever they think themselves fit, without any shadow of ecclesiastical discipline, whatever sins a man may have been guilty of – then again you keep no fasts – you pay no honour to the Mother of Our Lord, or to the Saints and you call us Idolaters for kissing and bowing to their Icons [...].[199]

He was hard pressed to counter these accusations – 'which I confess I feel to contain only too much truth'. If he tried 'then they retort but your clergy even your Bishops are just the same – & this makes it necessary to enter into an Historical explanation of the Revolution of 1688 & its mixed religious & political consequences – and this they can seldom well understand'. No amount of Scottish liturgies or private prayers of Caroline divines could make the Russians see the Catholic silk purse that Palmer described to them, rather than the Protestant sow's ear that they and their English governesses already knew. Roundell had written to him on New Year's Day 1841, conveying the interest and accurate predictions of the eminent Dr. Moberly,[200] who had said 'that from what he knew of Russia [...] they never could be brought to think of you as an orthodox Christian; and considered, as the fact has turned out, that you would have great difficulty about the language'.[201]

Trying to debate ecclesiastical and theological issues with the Russians had its own peculiar difficulties:

> the character and appearance of Russian Divinity and of Russian ideas and conventions is very complex and puzzling [...] generally they are far less learned than the Latin clergy of the Continent – and less capable of entering into theological questions with any logical accuracy; they do not reason like the people of the West – but go all by feelings and analogies – twisting about like eels and flying from and about the point in question with the utmost provoking and baffling irregularity [...].[202]

Nonetheless he had by now formed a profound admiration for the essence of Orthodox spirituality:

> at the same time the spirit of their Divinity and their Clergy is far more wholesome than that of the Papists – and is in fact that of the Fathers and of the Early Church – being very pious and practical – negligent of all that is intellectual and formal or ecclesiastical compared with that morality and spirituality for the sake of which alone the others are valuable.[203]

This had been the proud boast of the Archimandrite of the Sergievsky Monastery to Palmer, who 'talked to me much about the Asketic [sic] Divines – with whom I was obliged to confess myself to be little acquainted. They are however all that he thinks about or values – they said they had conserved in their convents the asceticism of the Early Church'.[204] This led Palmer to conclude that 'if there is any Church which has preserved antiquity it is the Eastern, & we must look to it if there is to be peace – for it is plain that in the West we had been carried away into many novel abuses & errors by an exaggerated opinion of the Roman authority & infallibility'.[205]

Palmer could still write in all seriousness of 'the English Communion which alone holds the true definition', but his exposure to a Church that had preserved the 'pious and practical' spirit 'of the Fathers and the Early Church' had opened his eyes to what the Church of England lacked, thrown away or destroyed at the Reformation:

> it is only too evident that there has been a great and general departure in England and in the members of the English Church from Orthodox belief, opinion and sentiment and from Catholic practise [sic] and that the Church herself instead of being in her 'true and natural position' has been buried for 300 years under a cloud of Heretical Protestantism.[206]

This made the provincial self-satisfaction and ignorance of the English in Russia hard to bear:

> I assure you I have learned a lesson by seeing my countrymen (and in a manner through them our Church and Communion) in contact with the Oriental Church – to talk of Popery as people do in England is a farce – a most wretched farce, and to take a high line about our Church as if all was right in it as people are too apt to do in controversy is equally so and is really dishonest if we were not blinded by self-complacency.[207]

Writing of *Tract 90*, he thought that although the authors of the *Tracts for the Times* 'seem to have a knack of doing everything in such a way as to startle most and have the greatest possible appearance of novelty', it might 'be all the better in the long run, as it will effectively break up that wretched double compromising system which has so long prevailed: when truth was theoretically recognised as 'Orthodoxy' and practically denied with few exceptions even by the *High Church* men'. He concluded fiercely: 'My stay in Russia has I suppose greatly increased my sense of the utter rottenness of our 'Establishment' and of the necessity of a *thorough Reformation*'.[208] He returned to and dilated upon this theme in a letter written within a fortnight of his return to England, concerning a mission to the Syrian churches of 'Kurdistan' and the Chaldeans of Mosul in early 1842.[209]

> I do not expect to see any thing like efficiency in any Mission undertaken by her members till there has been a complete Reformation of the existing Theology and sentiment among us. No Church and still less a Missionary Church can exist without authoritative teaching not of the dead letter of meagre & ambiguous formularies, but of a living spirit of Orthodoxy, and discipline.[210]

Having for so long carefully distanced himself from the Tractarians, he here quoted Newman's introduction to *Tract 90* almost verbatim – 'the stammering lips of ambiguous formularies'[211] – but in his wording ('dead letter') arguably went even further.

He had to face, though reluctantly and with horror, the meaning and implication of the wilful dereliction of discipline in the Church of England, particularly in the context of passive communion:

> The Church ought not either for the sake of the Penitent or of others to give hastily and upon the mere expression of the feeling of repentance her absolution to persons who have incurred excommunication [...] by great or habitual sins.

To do so, at least ostensibly, was to attempt the impossible:

> That Church which should say that thieves, drunkards, whoremongers &c are not by her intention ipso facto excommunicated would merely commit an act of apostacy [sic]: [. . .] yet in practise this is, I tremble to write it, very nearly [...] the condition of our own communion.[212]

The laxity of the Church's discipline meant that

> People [. . .] do not feel that any sins however great, are sins against the Church or that she has any thing to do with them [...] the Clergy in the mean time administer the Sacrament to all indifferently [. . .] as for heresy or Schism few of the Clergy seem to consider them to be causes of refusal at all even if they know what they are [. . .] the neglect of discipline is the great sin & weakness of our Church, one which must be corrected if we are to preserve our existence.[213]

To enforce discipline an organisation must know what it believes; but in Palmer's view as in Newman's, the Church of England did not. The compromises of the Reformation had left it with 'ambiguous formularies' incapable of enforcement, even had the will been there to do so. His French and Russian experiences drove him to the inescapable conclusion that the Roman & Greek Communions were 'in this matter incomparably less corrupt than our own.'[214]

Palmer was an interested spectator of the ceremonies of the Russian Church's year, such as the Blessing of the Waters on the Vigil of Theophany, in January. This began with the celebration of St. Basil's Liturgy in the Chapel of the Imperial Winter Palace, followed by a procession of 'the singers – the eight members of the Synod, the Emperor and his suite all bare-headed' with flags and the Cross from the Palace to the Quay between three lines of clergy. The Metropolitan then descended the steps to the river and blessed the water, as the choir sang 'anthems concerning the Manifestation of the Blessed Trinity in our Saviour's Baptism.' The ceremony ended with guns firing from the fortress opposite, and the crowd rushing to the river to drink and carry away some of the water. Palmer had to stand 'full two hours with the thermometer some degrees below zero and a wind into the bargain and something like half an hour without hats.'[215] When the river broke up on 4 April (New Style), it was formally opened, as was the custom, by the Commandant of the Fortress. He went into the middle of the river with his fleet of boats, guns were fired from the Fortress and some of the river water was taken by him into the Palace to the Emperor – 'when the custom was, I know not whether it is still, that he should be rewarded by a plate full of Ducats'.[216] Palmer describes the scene as the ice broke up and floated away:

> The ice looked very black, spongy porous & rotten as it went away from the river – but some of that from the lake had white snow still remaining upon it – and the river presented a very mottled appearance of black, yellowish, and white with occasional streaks of water between; the ships & boats in great numbers appeared – suddenly in every direction after the river was clear and opened – one could not tell from whence – and gulls & other sea birds which we had not seen for some time began to skim & flap over the water.[217]

VISIT TO MOSCOW

The formal rejection of Palmer's application for communion at least meant that he was free to travel to Moscow, which he did in May. The journey, some 525 miles, took him three days by coach, past the wooden houses of the peasants, with their ornamented balconies, to the city.

> after the first view there is nothing particular to be seen in the City itself except the Kremlin – the rest is only remarkable for the quantity of open courts, gardens, & dead walls which fill up the length of the streets on each side [...] the roofs of the houses are either green or red – chiefly the former – those of the churches which are exceedingly numerous, almost always green – with bulbous domes either green or blue or gilded – sometimes they are painted with streaks of red or green & sometimes are mottled with brown: every bulb & pinnacle is surmounted by a Cross ornamented at the corners, and attached to the roof by wires from them: and standing upon or surmounting a Crescent.[218]

In Moscow he visited the Kremlin, and within it the Cathedral of the Assumption, which contained the tombs of the Metropolitans and Patriarchs. He was shown the Patriarchal, or Synodal, Hall and vestry. In the former the holy chrism was boiled in Passion Week, Synods were formerly held, and the Patriarch Nicon stood trial. Nicon came to embody for Palmer the principle of the Church's fearless independence of the secular power, and his last twenty-five years in Rome were largely devoted to writing a seven-volume history of him. In the vestry Palmer was shown the Saccos of St. Peter, the first Metropolitan to die at Moscow, dating from 680, and a vestment from Constantinople embroidered with 70,000 'grains of seed pearl', with the 'likenesses of the Emperor John Paleologus, and his Empress Anna [...] the Metropolitan Photius, and the Patriarch Nicon'. The whole Creed, in Greek, was embroidered round the garment in letters of gold.[219]

Palmer also visited the Choudoff Monastery, and endured hours of shaking-up in a 'triska' to visit the Monastery or Trinity Lavra of St. Sergius. On the road he saw thousands of pilgrims, male and female, in a 'peculiar dress of a whitish-brown colour, the head, chin, and face bound and muffled up in a handkerchief, a jacket or smock covering the body and reaching barely to the knees, while the legs were clad in wrappers, with either bare feet, or else shoes of bark, or sandals'. Some had walked 'from very distant provinces [...] even from Siberia'. [220]

On arriving, Palmer went into the Church at three o'clock for the Lesser Vespers, after which the Archimandrite gave him a cup of tea. From six to eleven he attended the Vigil Service, after which the Archimandrite gave him 'a good-sized piece of bread' to eat. With British understatement he wrote:

> It was now nearly midnight, and to one who had been standing above five hours, and before that had been jolting in a vehicle without springs under a hot sun over hard ground, part of the way a mere rough track, since four o' clock in the morning, it was no unpleasant thing to be able to lie down.[221]

The next morning 'amid a perfect thunder of bells, so that one could not hear a word said out of doors, and scarcely in',[222] Palmer went to the Liturgy, followed by a substantial dinner in the *trapeza*.[223] After dinner they visited 'a court where 1500 poor strangers had just dined [...] The monastery is bound to give refreshment to the number of 500 daily, if so many present themselves'.[224]

At 'the dependent convent or seminary of Bethany', founded by the Metropolitan Platon, Palmer saw the original coffin of St. Sergius 'in which his body lay for thirty-five years before it was discovered that it was incorrupt'. This meant that 'whereas the bodies all around in the cemetery have fallen to dust & utter decay so that nothing but bones remains – the body which is called incorrupt on the contrary *though dried*, and brown in colour – has preserved its whole frame, skin and flesh'. This was

> the only rule apparent in the Oriental Church for canonizing a Saint; and sometimes this discovery takes place in consequence of disturbance of ground for rebuilding or repairing or transferring a Church – sometimes of dreams and healings and testimony of individuals. I have heard some remarkable instances in which the remains of persons who were quite forgotten and the place of whose burial was not known were thus pointed out and found.

The Orthodox compared unfavourably this infallible sign of sanctity, revealed as God pleases, with the Roman Catholic procedure of canonisation.[225] In the vestry of the main Lavra Palmer saw too the Saint's robes and altar-service: 'a remarkable and instructive contrast to all the surrounding wealth and magnificence,' his *phenolion* [sic] ('not a cope, but the older round cloke') of 'very coarse plain dark cloth, not woollen but more like undressed hemp, darned and patched, and the sacred vessels were of maple wood, made, it is said, by his own hands'.[226]

FAREWELL TO RUSSIA

By early July, Palmer began to say goodbye to the several representatives of the Russian Synod. The Archpriest Koutnevich hoped that Palmer would 'retain a friendly recollection of the Russian Church' after his return to England, but that although they desired unity 'most heartily' they could not, to obtain it, 'make little of those doctrines or rules of conduct which we have received from antiquity'.[227] Palmer suggested the Russian Church should help the Western Churches by giving communion on the basis of essentials held in common, so as to keep the healthy portion of the Church in contact with the rest, and so that its influence might 'expel the disease'. Koutnevich replied that 'your bishops' should write to the Synod, who would be happy to correspond with them, and 'treat of whatever they propose'. Palmer was pessimistic as to anything of the sort happening: 'We have too much to do at home first'. Nor would the Establishment of the Church of England be likely to adopt the Archpriest's allied suggestion, to resume 'the correspondence of the last century', i.e. of the Non-Jurors. It would never admit to having been represented by the Non-Juring bishops, although, Palmer said significantly, the Scottish Church might do so. He himself deprecated the Non-Jurors' assumption of loss of communion. He still preferred that the Eastern Church should state when communion was lost, and the Church of England respond with explanations on essential doctrine, and possible concessions on secondary matters. As his parting gift Palmer gave the Archpriest a copy of Andrewes' *Private Devotions* 'which he seemed much to value'.[228]

The same day Palmer saw Mr. Skreepitsin, and had to disabuse him of the idea that he might return in an official capacity. His demand for communion had been 'a merely personal act', and even 'supposing our Church to be disposed to open communications', Palmer was not 'at all a likely person to be employed'. Skreepitsin cheerfully replied that 'Surely, having been already here, and knowing the language and our Church, you would be the man', and also suggested that the English bishops should write to the Synod. 'Our Government would like nothing better, if it could be'. The popular antipathy to Rome would, he felt, be a factor in favour of fruitful negotiation. The Metropolitan was 'just the man of all of us who most desires that your Bishops should write to the Synod'; if he had replied to Palmer as if Palmer had come to open negotiations after an admitted separation, that was because he, as a diocesan bishop, 'would no doubt be afraid of committing himself'. He assured Palmer that the answer was not intended to be cold, as the Metropolitan, like all of them, 'had been much pleased' with his visit to Russia.[229]

Even Fr. Fortunatoff was optimistic about the prospects for unity if the English bishops were to write to the Synod, although he thought that explanations would have to be made beforehand. He paid a handsome tribute to Palmer's achievement:

'We knew, here, in Russia, very little of your Church; you have done a great thing in opening the way to a better acquaintance; your bishops should write; our Synod would be very glad to answer and confer with them; and I think it would succeed'.[230] Perhaps Palmer had begun to feel a victim of his own propaganda on behalf of the Church of England, or more pessimistic about it; certainly his reply was uncharacteristically gloomy: 'I explained that, in our present state and circumstances, we can do nothing'. Like Skreepitsin, Fortunatoff was not to be discouraged. He suggested that Anglican 'symbolical books', and 'books of canons and laws of the Church', could be sent to Russia. 'Now that you have made a beginning others will follow your example, and come from England to study our Church'. He thought that the Russians should have 'a good church in London' and the Anglicans one in St. Petersburg.[231]

The next day Count Pratasoff stated the intention of the Synod to send to London as chaplain a young man who could learn English, study Anglican divinity, and report back on the state of the English Church. He asked Palmer to make himself known to him when he came, and introduce him to some of the clergy. This intention was acted upon, and Fr. Eugene Ivanovich Popov[232] 'a graduate of the St. Petersburg Theological Academy'[233], was transferred to London from Copenhagen.[234] Popov came to be seen as 'the soul of the Russian colony' in England, and developed close ties with Newman and Pusey.[235] This was 'the first practical, official step taken by the Russians in the nineteenth century to establish closer ecclesiastical ties with England',[236] and it is to Palmer's credit that his visit led directly to it.

Pratasoff's parting with Palmer was very cordial – 'he then expressed abundance of good wishes and interest about myself personally' – and even embarrassing – 'and on bidding me good-bye, embraced me after the foreign way'. Mouravieff paid Palmer an even more fulsome tribute than Fortunatoff: '[...] the impression you have made upon the Metropolitan and upon all of us is most favourable to your Church. We have all had the greatest pleasure in conversing with you, and I must say, though you are only a deacon, yet the cause of your Church could not have been better represented'.[237] In this he echoed the sentiments of the Metropolitan, who told Palmer that he was 'the excellent defender of a bad cause'.[238] This was praise indeed, since Mouravieff had all but accused him of lying about the Church of England. However, Palmer seems to have responded rather coldly, interrupting to say that he did not represent his Church, but had come purely to pursue his private studies. When Mouravieff asked, 'You will of course let your superiors and bishops know the result of your journey?' Palmer replied shortly that he 'had nothing to do in this matter with any bishop', nor did he see any good end in making any report except to Dr. Routh. The authorities of the English Church disagreed among themselves; public feeling in the Church would have to change. He did agree that he would publish translations of some of their books, as that had been his original intention in coming out and learning the language. Mouravieff reassured him that the Metropolitan had not thought him to be presumptuously attempting to open communications between separated churches, and hoped the time would soon come when they could grant Palmer's request to be given communion. In the meantime both sides had to be content with the consciousness of a unity of spirit between them and a desire of a visible union. And with that, 'he took a most friendly leave of me, and made me promise to write to him'.[239]

Dr. Routh had observed to Palmer's father 'I think, sir, after all, the time will not have been misspent and that your son's visit will have done some good'.[240] Palmer himself wrote rather less confidently to his father from London after 'a very rough and disagreeable passage all the way from both St. Petersburg to Lubeck and from Hamburgh [sic] to London', 'I trust it may be as they assured me – that my visit may have done some good to others besides myself'.[241] More than forty years later, Newman wrote that 'Mr. Palmer made many friends in Russia, and had no reason to regret his going there'[242] but at the time: 'Palmer of Magdalen is returning ἄπρακτος [unsuccessful]. The Russians will not believe him against the evidence of all the English they ever saw before. They think him a theorist or worse'.[243]

As Newman said, Palmer 'failed from first to last in the direct object which started him on these expeditions', but Palmer must have anticipated that his request was unlikely to be granted. It was perhaps more frustrating to him that the Russians refused to discuss relations between the Churches in his terms, and specify when and why they believed the separation to have occurred. But even had they wanted to, the gradual process by which East and West had become alienated from each another was not easily explained. Some reasons, such as the *filioque*, did not bear close examination; others, such as cultural differences and the legacy of the Crusades, could not easily be overcome by bishops writing to Synods.

Nonetheless for a young academic it was a great achievement to have succeeded in making such a favourable impression on behalf of at least part of the Church of England. Palmer could truthfully say to Mouravieff that he had not come to Russia to represent his Church, but in effect that was exactly what he had come to do; not the Church as she actually was, but as he would have liked her to have been. The Metropolitan had identified this in telling Palmer his language was suited to the fourth century; Palmer was in many ways harking back to a pre-Reformation, or, as he called it, *de*formation, Church of England. Even if, as Mouravieff pointed out, his witness was highly selective, there was truth in what he said. There was a Catholic element in the Church of England that had been made known to the

Russians, and they could now distinguish to some degree between her and the Lutherans and Calvinists.

HOLDING UP A MIRROR

On his return Palmer wrote, on 6 August 1841, what appears to be an essay[244] entitled *On the Popular View Taken by English Protestants of the Russian Church and Religion and vice versa: Also on the Indefinite Use of the Word Popery.*[245] In it he set out the prevalent criticisms in Russia of the English Church, and how despite its claims it conformed to their worst expectations of a Protestant sect. He mentioned English criticisms of the Russian Church, but in giving the incredulous and contemptuous Russian reaction to them, conveyed his own impatience at English stupidity and narrow-mindedness. The English, he wrote, while taxing the Russians with 'Idolatry' [of Icons] and 'the Introduction of many mediators', 'are charitable enough to speak generally of them as Christians & in the way of Salvation', although they would of course 'think a Protestant Missionary perfectly justified in converting them if he could & in inducing them to renounce their corrupt Church & religion [...] .' He described the common view of the Russian Church as a national institution 'for the natives only', and of the wider Orthodox Church as having 'a still greater degree of ignorance, barbarism, formality & superstition so that no civilized & educated European would ever think to learn any spiritual wisdom from them'.

> Rather he would feel confident that both there & in Russia his cheap Bibles, Tracts, schools, printing-presses, Missionaries & Societies must be looked to as the only means under Providence of eventually bringing about a change & introducing pure spiritual Religion & clear views of the scheme or system of the Gospel [...].[246]

Turning to the Russian view of the English Church, Palmer set the scene more widely than hitherto: first describing the initial Russian (and Greek) indulgence towards the West for its desire to reform Papal abuses, which disappeared when the Protestants introduced their own novelties and went from bad to worse. This, however, they still blamed ultimately on the Pope, in that

> the lawlessness of the Pope in setting himself above the Councils & Canons gave his subjects that frame of mind which afterwards for their own fancied expediencies or necessities trampled all authority & all Canons under foot: His one Great Schism produced innumerable petty schisms: his innovations & additions produced the equally novel denials & mutilations of the Reformers, and lastly his building Christianity & the Church upon his own power & responsibility – led to the endangering of the Church & of Christianity itself wherever his power & supremacy should come to be called in question.

The papal concentration of power and responsibility in 'one absolute Head' led to 'a contrary reaction of democratical rebellion'; thus the seeds of Protestantism were contained in Popery. However the Orthodox condemned 'strongly and unequivocally' the Protestant principle of substituting 'a written revelation addressed immediately to the Private Judgement of mankind at large for the traditional faith of a sacramental Church'.[247]

Palmer set out the 'notes of Heresy' in the Protestant sects, that they were named after their founders, as with Lutheranism or Calvinism, and had abandoned the old Orders of 'Bishops, Priests and Deacons' for spurious new titles such as 'Pastors or Preachers'. Although Palmer attributed these remarks to the Russians, they are suspiciously like his observations in France and elsewhere before he travelled to Russia. All the attributes of these new Sects, 'this new Religion & Clergy the one of which can never have faith nor the other authority – the form & furnishing of their temples or Preaching Houses, their worship, their customs & opinions all apiece', flowed from the 'one & the same negative principle & aiming after one & the same development of negation'.[248] The Russians thought all Englishmen Protestants, although they were aware of 'some Catholic peculiarities' of the Anglican Church, 'which are accounted for by the nature of the Reformation which was almost entirely Political'.[249] They thought that the Anglican Church would be constituted by its preservation, if such was the case, of the Orders of priesthood, and the Apostolic Succession. English accusations of idolatry, or introducing more mediators than one, the Russians regarded 'as signs of a perverse misapprehension & pitiable fanaticism'.[250]

The Russians were bemused by the 'great Rooms, in dwelling houses' that served the Anglicans for Churches at St. Petersburg or Moscow, with three wooden boxes out of which the Pastor and his Clerk read alternately to the congregation 'without any thing whatever in the outward appearance to give the notion of their leading the congregation or uttering in their name prayers & praises to God'. They were struck by the nakedness of the altar, without 'Cross, Ciborium, or Lights'; the 'silent Congregation hidden in wooden pews neither standing according to the Oecumenical Canon nor kneeling according to the rule of the Latin & indeed of their own Church for prayer – but sitting or squatting with books before them',[251] the lack of distinction of the different orders of clergy by dress, the absence of chanting 'and that when there is "singing" the words are indistinguishable & the one or two voices are drowned in the sound of the organ'.[252] The tendency of the English abroad to go to Lutheran or Calvinist worship for preference, rather than to a Roman Catholic service like the Russians, reinforced their suspicions. Palmer added that the Russians 'are much inclined to think that no religious life or zeal is to be found in the Dominant Church [...] they suppose that the rest are cold, dead, and worldly with the habitual prejudices of Protestants without their original fanaticism'. In fact the Russians Palmer spoke to were seldom this blunt; they were a device to voice his own criticisms of the Church of England.

He rose to almost Swiftian heights in describing the reaction of 'many of the Russian nobility' in London last summer to 'the nudity & meagreness of our Church & services':

> the entire absence not only of a splendid but even of a decent ceremonial [...] they were constantly expressing their surprize that the English should in any way pretend to the character of a religious nation – when though the richest, the most luxurious & self indulgent people in the world; the proudest & most jealous in keeping up all form & etiquette connected with their own social or personal consideration – they should yet by a most disgusting & transparent hypocrisy make it a point of their religion to banish every thing like ornament, splendour, costliness or ceremony from the Houses & Worship of God: We could listen perhaps with more patience they would say to their Puritanical maxims if they were only consistent with the Quakers in their private life, in the Houses of their Gentry Merchants & Nobles, nay of the Clergy themselves few of whom would think the Altar of their Church with its furniture other than contemptible and mean for a sideboard in their own House. Above all the decency, & respectful ceremony of their Queen's Court, & the splendid magnificence & Luxury of the Royal Residences contrasted strangely with the interior of St. Paul's & Westminster Abbey & the fashion of Divine service which is seen in them.[253]

The accusation of 'Popery' levelled at the Orthodox by the English was also stupid and unfair; unfair because the Orthodox were 'fierce accusers of the innovations of the Latins or Papists', and 'unconscious of having followed the Pope in any thing: boasting a superior antiquity for the Mother Churches of their Communion, and an inviolable attachment to the doctrine & discipline of the Oecumenical Councils'. Quoting Mouravieff on English prejudice, he said that the Russians would

> sometimes laugh most heartily and say Well Well it is perfectly inconceivable how so many people should be so stupid or fanatical – What progress the Latins must make among you if such is the state of your Church – and this among the English of all others – who think themselves the first for civilisation & intelligence and whose commerce & roving disposition brings them into contact with all the world – Surely our Churches – 80 millions of Christians are not so invisible! Who have been witnessing against Latinism & Popery some six hundred years before Protestantism was ever thought of – Really they have said to me your people seem to be so besotted with Puritanism, so completely beside themselves with their hatred of Popery that it is a wonder they do not hesitate to retain any remnant of Christianity itself.[254]

This ignorance was such that 'One would think they could not read – or had no books – but on the contrary they have abundance of books can all read & write, & have many learned men'. The Russian clergy often wondered why those in the

West had been so 'engrossed by their own party feelings' as to ignore the East; there was the primitive model to which they could have appealed for reforming abuses. Either they simply did not know about the East, 'which shews great inattention & carelessness', or were 'so self-confident as not to think it worth their while to consult her which argues an heretical disposition.'[255] The result was 'a number of new and spurious Religions', and the indiscriminate branding as 'Popery' 'whatever they have taken upon themselves in the course of their quarrel to condemn or abolish.'

5 The Cursing Deacon

Although his closer acquaintanceship with the Russian Church made him more jaundiced with the Church of England, Palmer did not yet think of leaving it. Roundell, who described his brother's influence upon him at this time as 'greater [...] than at any other time, before or afterwards' said of their correspondence about *Tract 90* that whilst he 'showed great dissatisfaction with the actual state of things in the Church of England' he had made 'no change from his former point of view, and no nearer approach to Rome'.[1] In his *Letter to a Waverer*,[2] Palmer allowed that if a wavering member of the Church of England had paid her 'a constant and dutiful obedience, and by the very practice and cultivation of her precepts and doctrines come to the painful sense that she herself is not that which she has represented herself [...] then I can say nothing against a change';[3] he must leave the 'false and erroneous sect, whatever it may be [...] and must join the true Church'. This would be his own case, if he 'felt such a temptation of intellect or feeling to condemn my own Church'. For now, to renounce the Church of England, even after rigorous self- examination and tearful prayer, would seem 'to be committing Matricide and what [...] I would rather die a thousand times than do'. But he was keenly aware of the difficulties presented by the discrepancy between Anglican theory as he held it and the reality:

> I have hitherto found my conviction ever increasing, at once of the real existence of the English Church, and yet of the unparalleled defects of its members – of the weakness and rottenness of the existing outward system, and the Divine strength of that Spirit which has been kept alive within; of the difficulties which the habits and opinions of her members, and her external circumstances, present beyond those of the Roman or even of the Greek Communion.

Nonetheless, he could still write with apparent sincerity of 'the much greater satisfaction which really, and in her *theory*, she offers, both as to the definition of the Church, and as to particular doctrines, than the Roman'.[4] He had staked his credit on the Church of England's living up to her best, Catholic side, and showing herself in what he had represented to the Russians and the French as her true colours. Almost immediately, however, a controversy arose which seemed as if it were designed to prove incontrovertibly her truly Protestant nature, and Palmer much worse than a 'theorist' in the eyes of his Russian friends.

THE JERUSALEM BISHOPRIC

In June of 1841 the Emperor Frederick William IV of Prussia had sent the 'experienced diplomatist and versatile scholar'[5] M. Bunsen[6] to England to discuss with Archbishop Howley and Bishop Blomfield[7] of London the possibility of establishing a bishopric at Jerusalem which would, while retaining the independence of the 'Evangelical Church of Germany', unite it with the Anglican Church in Jerusalem. The clergy and missionaries of the Prussian Church would work under a bishop alternately nominated by the Prussian and British monarchs, and ordinations by the bishop would be valid in Prussia. The aim was largely political, to secure for Protestants in the Holy Land the same influence as the French had as protectors of the Latins, and the Russians as protectors of the Orthodox.[8]

Both Archbishop and Bishop eagerly adopted the suggestion. The approval of a meeting of bishops was obtained in August 1841, and the means to implement the scheme, 'The Foreigners Consecration Act Amendment Bill', introduced into the Lords at the end of the same month, receiving the royal assent in October. A letter commendatory was sent by Howley to the Patriarchs in November, reassuring them that the intention was not to proselytise from the Eastern Churches:

> we have sent this Bishop our brother [...] we have charged him in no wise and in no matter to invade the jurisdiction of you, the Bishops, or others having rule in the Churches of the East, but rather to show you due honour and reverence, and to be ready, on all occasions and by all means, to cultivate diligently whatever promotes brotherly love, intercourse, and unanimity.[9]

Howley added his expression of 'longing desire to renew that ancient love towards the ancient churches of the East which has been suspended for ages'.[10] That the scheme had precisely the opposite effect is testified to by the Rev. George Williams,[11] who went to Jerusalem as Bishop Alexander's[12] chaplain. 'Deeply interested' himself in the Oriental Churches, he wrote that

> instead of contributing to heal the divisions of Eastern Christendom, it has aggravated them rather [...] instead of conciliating the Prelates of the Oriental Church, it has incurred their suspicion and contempt, if not their enmity, by petty aggressions on their lawful jurisdiction – feebly emulating the Latin Propaganda, without the same excuse [...] besides exhibiting the public scandal of faith broken before the infidels, it has rudely shaken the confidence of learned and pious members of our own Communion, and alienated their attachment from the Church of their baptism [...].[13]

Inexplicably, he went on to exempt from blame Howley, Blomfield, and the King of Prussia.

Some Evangelicals saw the plan as ushering in the restoration of Israel; churchmen like Samuel Wilberforce anticipated the restoration of episcopacy in Prussia.[14] Gladstone,[15] on the other hand, deplored the scheme as 'approximating to a union with foreign Protestantism', arrived at without any theological examination.[16] Lord Selborne thought it 'extraordinary enough' that such an innovation could be brought in

> without any synodical act of the Church of England, without open consultation with or any concurrence of the English Episcopate generally, – in fact, by no ecclesiastical authority, except that of the Archbishop of Canterbury and the Bishop of London for the time being, fortified by a permissive Act of Parliament, obtained with the assistance of the ministry of the day [...].[17]

'Acquiescence in it seemed impossible' he said 'to those who thought with Newman or my brother' – particularly the latter, as the scheme 'appeared to violate at every point' the principles that he had been recently asserting to the leading authorities of the Russian Church.[18]

November 1841, arrived in the Holy Land on the steamship 'Devastation' in January 1842, and died in 1845 while travelling back to England. DNB.

Palmer had to act, which as ever for him meant furious composition, initially of a 'Memorial'. The original draft had several characteristic touches of hyperbole: 'I therefore, a sinner and the meanest and vilest of all sinners, who am not worthy to communicate in the Church of God, but ought rather to pass my whole life in public Penance [...]', he began, before describing how he had heard that Lutherans were to be received into communion with the new bishop without renouncing the 'principle of Protestantism' or being confirmed. He therefore presented his

> most humble petition to Your Grace and beg to ask if this thing is really so – And if it is, as I fear, then I roll myself (in thought at least) at your feet, I clasp your knees, I intreat you with tears, I implore you by the Blood of Our Saviour Jesus Christ to interfere and preserve the Church from this great & ruinous Sin [...] what is here written with ink I sign with my blood [...].[19]

Surprisingly, Dr. Routh approved this draft, although Palmer's father and brother 'who also saw it, noticing the strength of certain expressions of feeling, said that the Archbishop would not understand it, but only think the writer out of his senses. So they re-wrote it'.[20] It was largely re-written by Roundell. Palmer wrote of the new draft: 'I think myself it is so much better than my own, in method of expression, and in avoiding dogmatising (as he calls it) [...] I am glad to get rid of the dogmatical tone, but rather regret the loss of the "insanity" which however is incompatible with the decency and reasonableness of conventional form.'[21]

The new Memorial also objected to the unqualified admission of Lutherans to the communion of the Bishop. It added that the *right* of private judgement as opposed to the *duty* of ecclesiastical submission was destructive of the substance of all Apostolical Churches, and elaborated on the authority for Confirmation, which the Lutherans had dispensed with for three hundred years. Should the rumours of the scope of the plan be true, Palmer ended, then 'the integrity of our religion is in danger' and he was duty bound to try to prevent the danger of his brethren being driven into separation from their Mother Church.[22]

However, neither reasoned pleas nor bloodstained petitions had any effect on the consecration of Michael Solomon Alexander as the first bishop of 'the United Church of England and Ireland in Jerusalem' on 7 November, the same day that Palmer delivered the rewritten Memorial into the Archbishop's hands. Alexander's Jewish origin made him attractive to those of a Millenarian or Evangelical persuasion, who according to Newman 'boasted' that 'we are sending out a Bishop [...] who is of the "the pure blood of Judah", and his wife of "the pure blood of Levi" –as if this was not the very error of the Galatians, as if the Jewish Law had not been abolished once for all.'[23] Although Palmer wrote deploring the appointment of 'a Bishop of Jewish blood upon Mount Sion', his real objection was to 'the principle of his mission', which was to offer 'to unite all sects and sectarianized Churches in one communion, upon a footing of the most perfect equality'. Palmer even saw a 'fearful danger' of Alexander 'becoming the Precursor of some great Antichrist'.[24]

No answer to the Memorial came from Lambeth Palace. Palmer drew up a Protest. This too was vetted and redrafted by his family and Dr. Routh, with 'much anxious consultation [...] we all agreed with him in substance, but by no means with everything that he wished to say'. Palmer was persuaded, with some difficulty, to omit 'certain statements on doctrinal points [. . .] unnecessary for his purpose, and sure to be misunderstood',[25] namely 'the prayers of the blessed virgin [sic] and all the saints'.[26] Dr. Routh, having seen the rewritten Protest, 'praised it much; though he seemed to have some good-natured apprehensions on my account; but said nothing against my doing it. He suggested several prudential amendments; and ended by giving me his blessing'.[27] In favour of amendment he argued that 'what I said would be all very well if I were at a Council board negotiating with the Russian Bishops – but that with respect to my immediate object it would be causing an unnecessary diversion [...].'[28] A proposal by Palmer that Roundell and even the younger members of the family should sign the Protest was dropped, after 'strong objections' from their father, but on 12 November he was still hoping to 'get something or other which all who like can sign', to express their 'concurrence in the adjuration of Heretical Protestantism and profession of Catholicism and desire of communion with all other branches of the Catholic Church.'[29]

Palmer showed the Protest to Newman on 8 November. Newman felt the 'protest had given him a very clear view of the case and made him quite resolved to make one himself also'. Newman told John Keble that in making his own protest 'Palmer's intended protest is what determined me', and that he had sent copies to the Bishop of Oxford – who 'knew nothing whatever of the Jerusalem matter – had never been consulted'[30] and to Harrison. Palmer wrote of Newman's protest that it 'is at present only a disclaimer of Lutheranism and Calvinism', whereas he wanted 'to get something also, if possible, indicating desire of unity with the Eastern Church. He also said that he addressed himself 'to private judgement upon which others as well as I are virtually thrown back',[31] something necessitated by the 'delinquency [...] of the authorities who abdicate their own functions and throw them back upon private conscience'.[32]

The Protest made its several points in a series of paragraphs beginning 'And whereas [...]' in the manner of a royal proclamation. Palmer differentiated between the sense in which the English Church called itself Protestant, which was 'against certain accidents, blemishes, and errors, in the Latin Churches of the time', from the 'mixed multitudes' of the Lutherans and Calvinists who made their protest into a 'principle of anarchy and individualism, destructive of all real and Apostolical Churches'.[33] This principle he identified as the 'principle of Dissent' that martyred Charles I, and which the secular authorities had attempted to foist onto the Church. It was a 'pernicious heresy', abhorred by all true Churches; the Lutheran and Calvinists who held it were excommunicated by name by the Latins and the Orthodox Churches, unlike the English Church. Again he objected to letting 'foreign sects' into communion with the English Church without conversion, reconciliation or Confirmation, and recognising them as 'professing the Public Worship of Almighty God according to the principles of the Church of England'. This he said 'commits our Church in the eyes of all the world, and especially of the Eastern Churches, to their principle of Protestantism'.[34]

Palmer contrasted Howley's words in his letters commendatory to the Eastern Patriarchs with his reluctance or refusal to provide Palmer with a certificate to take to Russia, and repeated Count Pratasoff's statement that a 'distinct disclaimer' of the 'principle of Protestantism' was necessary before negotiations with the Eastern Churches (something they were willing and even desirous to enter upon) could hope to begin. He later referred with understandable feeling to 'those dignitaries of the Russian Church and Empire, who honoured me with their confidence, and believed on my representations that our Church had some better thing in her than mere sectarian Protestantism', which bound him to them as much as to his own countrymen. The complete subversion of those representations, and the clear-eyed betrayal of every catholic principle of the Church of England, were the 'circumstances' that 'conspired to make me feel that I am called upon to do this act, which yet, if I know myself, I would rather die than do'.[35]

Palmer anathematized the principle of Protestantism or Dissent, refusing to recognise any union with Lutherans or Calvinists, or Dissenters, except on their conversion 'to the obedience of the Apostolic Episcopate both in faith and discipline'. He declared his recognition of the Orthodox Eastern and Catholic Churches, and vowed never to proselytise them or allow them to be taught that it was lawful to renounce their own Church. Nor, he said, unable to resist being provocative, would he allow them to be taught that 'the blessed Eucharist is a mere sign, or that there is no sacrifice in it'; that intercessory prayer to the departed 'interferes with the unity of Christ's mediation'; or that veneration of relics, the Cross, the doors of the Church, the priest's vestments, hands etc., 'are either wickedness or idolatry in themselves, or in the Church'.[36] He concluded by pleading that vital questions be settled 'by Authority in lawful Synods, as in old time',[37] and appealed to any that might be lawfully called and held, before formally protesting against what had been done without Synodal Authority.

A proof of the Protest was sent by Palmer, apparently unprompted, to the Archbishop of Canterbury with a letter explaining that he wished the archbishop to have the opportunity to see it 'while as yet it is [...] within my power to omit or alter any thing, or to suppress it altogether; which last I should desire above all things to do, if I could only be enabled to do so without damage to that cause, which I have felt myself called upon to undertake'.[38] In this as in most of his other controversies, Palmer acted very much upon the principle of private judgement, or at least feeling: 'circumstances conspire to *make me feel*', 'I have *felt myself* called upon to undertake'. Ironically, he was using the freedom granted by the Protestant principle he so despised to champion the Catholicity of the Church of England.

Howley wrote immediately to Dr. Routh, describing Palmer as 'a member of your College, for whom on account of his family, as well as his personal qualities, I have much regard', but deploring the 'pamphlet which he calls a *Protest*, the most extraordinary perhaps which was ever put forth by a Deacon of our Church'. He specified 'the tone of disrespect, to our Church, and its Bishops, which pervades the *Protest*', anticipated that publication 'would certainly subject him to much censure', and therefore asked Routh, 'as a friend to Mr. Palmer',[39] to use his influence to suppress it.

Dr. Routh duly sent for Palmer and dissuaded him from publishing the Protest, on the grounds of 'deference to the Archbishop's station and wishes, and considering that the full details of the convention with the King of Prussia were not yet known'.[40] Palmer agreed with reluctance, as he 'could not understand upon what principle, agreeing with me as he did, he could advise me to defer to the very Authorities whose acts I was protesting', and showed him *The Times's* extract from *The Prussian State Gazette*, which clearly stated the principles of the scheme.[41] He did ultimately agree, however, on the basis that he knew 'they were really of one belief', and as Routh was his Superior. The pill was sweetened by Routh's suggestion that Palmer could still, in order to make the Protest and assuage his conscience, send a copy (what he had already sent was only a proof) to the Archbishop, and afterwards publish his objections to the scheme 'in some other form'. Routh himself was later to write to the Archbishop expressing his own objections to the scheme in terms that he felt Palmer would have approved.

Palmer received what he described as 'a short note in very kind words' from Howley. His description is odd, as the tone of the letter is terse, and Howley's aim is clearly to avoid defending or justifying his actions. He urged Palmer 'from motives of personal regard, as well as considerations of a higher nature'[42] to 'reflect again and again, before you give publicity in any way to the *Protest*, which you have sent me'. He declined to enter on 'the several points which I deem objectionable' partly because of lack of time, and partly because he knew that Palmer intended 'to ask the advice of the venerable President of your College, and to act under his direction'.[43] Howley had suggested to Dr. Routh that the Protest would impede 'the prospects of unity, both with the other Protestant Churches, and also with the Greek Church'.[44] Palmer might reasonably have responded that the whole aim of his Protest was to impede union with the Protestant Churches, and that, even supposing Howley to have any genuine interest in union with the 'Greek Churches', renunciation of Protestantism was the necessary first step in any negotiations for unity with the Greek Churches, a renunciation made by the Protest in forceful terms. Howley did not seem to understand or acknowledge the fact that union with both Protestant and Orthodox Churches was inherently contradictory. Howley attempted to refuse to accept the Protest, 'on the ground that he who made it could have no voice in the matter,' but when informed that the alternative to acceptance was publication, he gave way and received it.[45] The Archbishop was later said to have shown the Protest to Bunsen, 'with these words, "See what a letter I have received from a Deacon"'.[46]

Palmer had also received a communication on 25 November from Harrison, the Archbishop's chaplain. Although Palmer charitably described this letter too as 'very kindly worded as regards myself', it combined pomposity with a disingenuous refusal to face the implications of the Jerusalem Bishopric, and ended with a thinly-veiled threat. Harrison began with a mild reproach to Palmer for disrespect to the Archbishop, making the fair observation that such disrespect was inconsistent with Palmer's ostensible views of church authority: 'I was glad to find that you did not *mean* to be disrespectful in your use of the pronouns in your letter; – it certainly *sounded* less respectful than, on your principles, you would wish it to be, towards those in high places of spiritual authority'. 'I do not find,' he continued, 'the principle of the right of private judgement [. . .] put forth in the Confession of Augsburg' [WP[47] – 'assumed'] '[...] we ought in fairness to deal with them as we do with Romanists [...] looking to the principles laid down in their symbolical books [WP – 'But if they notoriously maintain any heresy whether it is in their book, or no?'][48] Harrison disputed that Palmer had the right to assume that 'our Bishops are unavoidably going to commit '"[...] the great wickedness" of allowing [the Lutherans] [. . .] to join our Communion and receive our Sacraments' [WP – 'It *is* commonly committed: the King professes that the integrity of their Confession and rite is acknowledged, and so unless a stipulation be made it is clear'.] '[. . .] why should we not suppose that individuals joining our Communion might be willing and offer of their own accord [...] to receive Confirmation?' [WP – 'Perhaps they might, perhaps not, what then?'] And if the "Congregations" which desire "to place themselves under the authority" of our Bishop should be allowed to use a Liturgy of their own [...] there would strictly speaking be no joining our Communion or receiving *our* Sacraments. [WP – 'save as being under our Bishop and Clergy ordained by him!! Ordination no sacrament nor involving communion!'][49]

So far as unity with the East was concerned, Harrison would not concede that the Church of England should disclaim heretical principles which the Prayer Book showed were wrongly attributed to her [WP – 'Yes but a book is not a Church'.[50]] Harrison then used 'the Archbishop's kind and gentle feeling towards you personally' to try and dissuade Palmer from publishing the Protest; and if that would not sway him, he 'might feel myself called upon [...] to protest, and that strongly.' [WP — 'and make no *rejection*'.] He again attempted to make Palmer feel guilty: 'I do feel that the exceeding kindness and condescension of the Archbishop ought not to be abused' [WP – 'so indeed do I'[51]] 'I cannot but hope that [...] you will not allow a document to go abroad [...] unjustly exhibiting our Church and its chief rulers in so very unfavourable a light – will represent you as so *undutifully* [WP – 'painfully rather, that it may not be also the shame and ruin of the Church'] proclaiming what you regard as their shame and reproach'.

It is hard to see the logic of Harrison's criticism. If the Jerusalem Bishopric was justified, and in accordance with the principles of the Church of England, then there was nothing for Church or Archbishop to fear from the Protest, which after all was only the opinion of one deacon. Only if the Bishopric were in some way dishonest or wrong would that have been the case. The letter ended with an apparently friendly warning about the implications for Palmer's future prospects in the Church of England: 'I cannot feel as much regard as I do for you [...] the deep sorrow with which I should see you take so unhappy a step, and one so injurious to your own character and usefulness'.[52]

Palmer may have genuinely believed these letters to be 'very kind', or he may have been trying to allay his father's fears that he was alienating the Church hierarchy and damaging his career. Had his father known the true state of affairs and the increasingly steely tone of the communications from Lambeth, he might well have insisted, or tried to insist, that the whole Protest be dropped. His letters reveal ambiguous feelings about his son's actions. He was happy that Palmer intended to consult both himself and Dr. Routh. 'So far', he wrote, 'I entirely approve'. However, he still felt it necessary to say, referring to Sibthorp's conversion to Rome, that he was 'in no fear that you will quit your vessel in the midst of danger, not even if she were to appear to sink'.[53] Clearly then this possibility had entered his mind. He later wrote that although he well realised that his son had 'profited more' by learning and knowledge, yet 'wisdom and discretion' were 'more immediate gifts', and that he 'had the advantage' of his son in experience 'by a few years', and Dr. Routh by a few more.[54]

He was apprehensive that his son's initiative in the affair might have repercussions on the whole family: 'These are very weighty matters, and important and serious subjects to us individually, from the part which William feels himself called to take in them'.[55] These remarks may have coincided with his objections to other family members signing the Protest. It is clear that he by no means felt that William was necessarily called to take the action he was taking. He went on to refer to '"a sort of excitement", unfavourable to a sound judgement and due caution, in so great an affair'.[56] He voiced 'serious misgiving'[57] to Roundell: it was 'the strangest way in the world [...] to vindicate the Catholicity of the English Church' by doing anything 'which might drive a weak brother out of it, and send him over to Rome [...] it is, as appears to me, a pertinacious adherence to indiscretion of this sort, that gives me any uneasiness'.[58] The acts of 'one or more of the bishops of the day', could not possibly affect the catholicity of the Church of England, therefore 'to leave it for Rome on account of the offence of others, would be nothing short of spiritual self-destruction'.[59] Dr. Routh had made the same point: 'It is very bad, sir, certainly: but two Prelates cannot overturn our Church'.[60]

Given all these reservations, it was as Lord Selborne said 'all the more generous' of him to defend Palmer as vigorously – and justifiably – as he did in December, after receiving a letter from the archbishop via Palmer's Uncle Horsley. This congratulated Palmer's father on Edwin's election to Balliol, but added the hope that Edwin would not 'be perverted by the indiscreet zeal of his elder brother'. The response of Palmer's father was at first icily polite; he thanked 'the friend who offered his congratulations' for his kind wishes, and as to the remark about 'indiscreet zeal', 'I am not offended at it, but thank him for that too'. He continued:

> I should like to ask him whether he considers the willingness with which the intention to publish has been laid aside as a mark of intemperate zeal; whether the communication of the intended publication in the first instance to those who might have the power to stop it was indiscreet; whether it was indiscreet to advise, before anything was done, with a person of so much learning as the head of his College, whose suggestions and alterations were in every instance adopted? In a word, whether (in point of fact) in this affair he has been guilty of any indiscretion whatever [...].[61]

Palmer could surely not have asked for more; but this was the last time on which he could rely on such unqualified support from his father.

A bizarre twist to the affair was that Bishop Alexander's chaplain, George Williams, with whom Palmer was 'not acquainted', wrote to ask if Palmer could 'give him some hints' about his new post, 'saying that "of course he sees immense difficulties; and if I can guard him against any mistakes into which he is likely to fall, I shall do him a great kindness, and may benefit the Church"'.[62] Palmer told Roundell he was 'thinking of writing to him to offer to go out with him, if he or his Bishop think my knowledge may be of any service to them; only stipulating that I am not to be considered as recognising "the essential unity of Protestant Christendom"'. Lord Selborne speculates drily as to whether 'this singular offer [...] was actually made; probably not; at all events, if it was made, nothing came of it'.[63] Palmer, who had written in the same letter 'I really cannot endure without doing something or other', fired off a series of semi-serious queries to be put by Williams to the Bishop, in order that Williams 'come to a distinct understanding, if possible, before he sailed'.[64] They were designed to point up the inconsistencies of the scheme, and began from basics. Were they 'to profess consistently the *principle* of Catholicism *or* the *principle* of Protestantism in the name of the Church of England, or [...] to try to mix the two together, and if so, by what rule?' Were the Lutherans, and later the Calvinists, to be admitted to communion at once, or to be required to renounce the 'principle of Protestantism', embrace the whole Apostolic Faith, and be confirmed? Was the Greek Orthodox Church to be regarded as truly Orthodox and Catholic, and therefore offered communion, or were they as Protestants 'to regard it as heretical, and corrupt, and idolatrous', to be converted 'by all means to Evangelical Protestantism' – or were they 'to attempt to trim between these two opinions?' If other Protestant 'Ministers' converted Orthodox as heretics, would they 'accept and allow' that? If members of the Orthodox spontaneously came asking to abjure their own Church, would they reject them? Were the Nestorians and Jacobites 'to be viewed as heretics or orthodox brethren'? Would they be admitted to communion at once, or only upon renouncing their heresy?[65] Williams' reply, if he made one, is not recorded; it is doubtful that he felt the 'immense difficulties' he mentioned had been lessened.

CONTROVERSIAL CORRESPONDENCE

The Archbishop had succeeded in stifling Palmer's 'Protest'; but Palmer's next controversial encounters were very much in the public arena. The first was with the Revd C. P. Golightly[66] of Oriel, Protestant arch-foe of the Oxford Movement. He had written in *The Standard* newspaper[67] that 'a member of the University' was surprised and concerned to find 'that the *via media* was deserted; that Rome was no longer regarded as a schismatical community; and that there was a strong desire for union with her'.[68] Worse, Golightly alleged that the members of the Oxford Movement

> instead of fighting under their proper banner, [...] have hoisted the flag of Anglicanism, and under those false colours, are taking advantage of their respective positions as [...] Clergymen of the Established Church, to propagate Romanism [...].[69]

Whilst denying that he was offended, Palmer felt compelled to reply. He reiterated his view of the Church of England as Catholic, and went on to deny any expression of regret that any friend of his should desert the *via media*, saying that

> truth is sometimes in a mean, I admit, but it seems to me to be a very bad rule to teach it by. It is of its own nature positive, not like Protestantism, negative; it is a beacon set on a hill, not a mixed puddle in a valley.

This contemptuous description of what the Church of England chose to regard as its cardinal virtue, the middle way, might in itself have aroused sufficient hostility; but what followed gave the greatest offence:

> Certainly, I am for no middle ways [...] for myself, I utterly reject and anathematize the principle of Protestantism as a heresy, with all its forms, sects, or denominations. And if the Church of England should ever unhappily profess herself to be a form of Protestantism [...] I would reject and anathematize the Church of England, and would separate myself from her immediately as from a human sect [...].[70]

Distinguishing the sense in which he could justifiably be accused of Popery from simple, but presumably covert, allegiance to Rome, he wrote:

> if to desire the restoration of unity with those Churches ['the foreign Churches of the Latins'] [...] and above all with the Church of Rome itself, be Popery, then I for one am a Papist from the bottom of my soul; but [...] my Popery is of a kind which takes in not only the Churches now in actual communion with Rome, but also the Eastern Catholic Churches, and the British, if their Protestant members will allow me still to call them Catholic.

Speaking from his accustomed viewpoint of nostalgia for the pre- Reformation unity of the Middle Ages, this would also have been unremarkable, but it is unlikely that in the theologically overheated atmosphere of the time the sense in which he saw himself as 'a Papist from the bottom of my soul' was understood. He returned to his solemn rejection of Protestantism, turning his fire on the hierarchy that had apparently embraced it:

> anathema to the principle of Protestantism, [. . .] and to all its forms, sects, and denominations, especially to those of the Lutherans and Calvinists, [. . .] Likewise to all persons, who *knowingly and willingly, and understanding what they do,* shall assert either for themselves or for the Church of England *the principle of Protestantism,* or maintain the Church of England to have one and the same common religion with any or all of the various forms of and sects of Protestantism, or [...] go about to establish any intercommunion between our Church and them, otherwise than by bringing them [...] to renounce their errors [...] – to all such I say anathema.[71]

This bombastic[72] outburst earned Palmer the derisive nickname of 'The Cursing Deacon',[73] and 'drew upon his name no small obloquy'.[74] Both Roundell Palmer and his father 'had advised against the publication of those rash passages in his letter to Mr. Golightly which raised the storm; but we were too late'.[75]

Among the responses to the exchange were a letter to Palmer from his cousin William, and a letter in the *Oxford Herald* from 'A Protestant Catholic'. Writing to his cousin, Palmer asserted that Protestantism was not merely 'a protest against certain errors'; it had no limits. 'You cannot mention to me any single article of the Christian Faith, however necessary to salvation, which it is absolutely necessary to believe in order to be a Protestant [...] any heresy or error, which a man may not believe, and yet be a "Protestant" and of "the Protestant religion"'.[76] 'He who *protests* is *inferior*'; if the Church of England was '*at variance*' with Rome and was right, then she was Catholic and the guardian of truth.[77]

Palmer enlarged on this point in his response to the 'Protestant- Catholic'. Many churches might protest against the doctrine of Papal Supremacy; that did not make them Protestant. They held a common 'Catholic principle of dogmatic and traditional authority in the Hierarchy [. . .] opposed to the spirit and principle of Protestantism'. English 'Protestantism' was a protest against the Latin Church on certain secondary and accidental points, and was not to be confused with the 'Dissenting or Heretical Protestantism' found abroad.

Palmer was happy enough to fight against Rome, but not 'with a host of evil spirits and infidels for our allies'. He would not be joined 'under a unity of ambiguous words [. . .] with opinions and sects which I abhor',[78] no doubt a reference to the Jerusalem Bishopric. The writer of the letter had stated that he was confident that Palmer did not believe in the Supremacy of the Pope, Transubstantiation, or the

Council of Trent. Palmer's response was an Orthodox one. The jurisdiction taken away from the Pope was not

> of Divine right, nor even according to the spirit of the Oecumenical Canons, nor safe for the Church at large; nor do I believe that the definition of the visible Church is necessarily limited by practical obedience to Rome; nor that the Bishop or Church of Rome, or any given Council of Bishops, are to be viewed in themselves and strictly speaking infallible antecedently to the reception of their decrees by the Church at large.[79]

Transubstantiation was a 'Mystery [...] far too great for words to express [...] it were dangerous and irreverent to attempt it, being as it is an object for faith only to apprehend'.[80] As to the Council of Trent, 'I have nothing at all to do with it'. Let it be examined 'in a Synod of our own and foreign Bishops' to see if it should be received or rejected. The Church of England *should* rightly be called Catholic and not Protestant, for talk of Protestantism 'stops short at the Church- porch, as if paralyzed by some ancient exorcism'. Inside Church we hear only of 'the Catholic faith to be kept whole and undefiled', 'the Catholic Religion', 'Holy Catholic and Apostolic Church', 'good Catholic Fathers',[81] etc. This was 'more than a mere chance'. Our 'Orthodox Divines' must have been 'very far indeed from intending to recognise any such principle' as the right of every man to follow his own private interpretation of the Bible, which was a 'pernicious heresy'.[82] Although the whole tone of this letter was more moderate than either his letter to Golightly or the Protest, he still ended by 'most sadly and seriously' repeating his anathema of those who knowingly professed or recognised 'the principle of Continental Protestantism'.[83]

Despite the furore his anathemas had caused, Palmer published the materials relating to the Protest, as Dr. Routh had suggested, under the title *Aids to Reflection on the Seemingly Double Character of the Established Church*. The Introduction argued that if the Church of England concurred with *The Prussian State Gazette* about the existence of one 'Evangelical' or 'Reformed' Protestant Church, 'upheld by a superior unity, the Head of the Church Himself', she would 'unchurch herself, and render it impossible for any one [...] to justify his allegiance to her on Catholic principles'.[84] If the authorities of the Church of England agreed with *The Prussian State Gazette*, union with the Eastern Church would become impossible, and the Catholic character of the English Church destroyed. Palmer hoped to show, before it was too late, that there was still a desire for unity with the Eastern Church, which could be acted upon if it were finally realised that simultaneous recognition of both 'Catholic Churches and Protestant Persuasions' was impossible. Lutheranism and Calvinism, Palmer said, were not founded on any particular heresy, 'though they have several', but on 'Heresy itself made into a principle'. The German Lutherans, dissecting the Bible in reliance on their individual understanding

> descended deeper and deeper into enquiries concerning the history, composition nature, and object, of the Bible, and its component parts [...] The only limit to their attempts to find a resting-place – to find bottom [...] in the waters of "subjectivity," was when they had come either to positive insanity, or to a state of doubt of the existence of God and of their own souls. [...] once assert the principle of rebellion, and you must follow your own reason and feeling, one or both, [...] and oscillate alternately into worse and worse depths of heresy, fanaticism, and heresy again – and so on, even till all ultimately subsides, if uncorrected, into atheism and suicide [...].[85]

He quoted from his Russian journals to show how the Russians had come to perceive the Church of England as Protestant – for example, M. Mouravieff in October 1840:

> There can be no unity between us as long as it is possible to mistake your Church for a sect or confession of Protestantism [...] but [...] she looks at present so much like Protestantism, and suffers herself so patiently to be confounded with it by all the world, that she must excuse us if we do not take the word of an individual that it is otherwise; she must speak to us herself, and tell us that she is Catholic, and we shall be ready enough to believe her.[86]

Again in January 1841, when Palmer was reading to Count Pratasoff the Archbishop of Canterbury's last Charge, which spoke of a reconciliation of the Churches of the East and West, the Count took it from him and read '[...] I am not without hope that *more cordial union* may, in time, be effected *among all Protestant Churches.* At this he exclaimed – "Ah! so your Primate admits the other Protestants to be Churches, and speaks not of correcting their heresy, but of more cordial union with them. He admits then that you are all one community already"'.[87] Pratasoff found it 'inconceivable that any should be so blind and infatuated as to seek to express the substance of their religion, (if they have any), by a word which really expresses nothing but negation. And yet this is the constant and recognized language of all your English people [...].'[88] In ending Palmer again cast his gaze back to the days of King Charles I and Archbishop Laud:

> We had Bishops once, and Clergy, and a King, who would have taught, and led, and ruled us in the faith and fear of God; who desired the unity of the whole Church, East and West, on Catholic principles [...] and we cut off their heads. We made to ourselves such Bishops and Priests, and such a Civil Government, as was after our own hearts, and now we have no business to complain. The same people which sinned must repent, if they would regain the opportunity they once lost, and have their rulers such as they were before. We who demanded license formerly, must demand authority now [...] with the definite teaching of the whole Orthodox religion [...].[89]

Able as these last two publications were, they 'did not counteract the impressions to his disadvantage, which the "anathemas" of the letter to Mr.

Golightly had produced'. 'William, as you will have seen, has brought everybody upon his back, and I fear will have prejudiced the public against anything he can say [...] But I will not be the person to blame him now. He has enough to meet [...] '.[90] Undaunted, in 1842 Palmer attacked the Jerusalem Bishopric in The *Examination of an Announcement made in the Prussian State Gazette*, published anonymously, which analysed and satirised the proposals for the Bishopric. Prefixed to the pamphlet was an extract from the Sixth Canon of the Second Ecumenical Council of Constantinople: ' [...] We define those also to be heretics who, while they claim to be sound in the Faith, have been rent, or have rent *themselves* off, and gather congregations apart from *Our* Canonical Bishops, etc.'.

Palmer began with a plea that King Frederick William ascertain that he and his subjects were in communion with the Church of England 'really, canonically, and of right', and quoted Frederick's letter to his Minister of State, Eichhorn,[91] about the 'German congregations of the Evangelical religion in Palestine, which are inclined to place themselves under the jurisdiction' of the new Bishop; likewise the 'young divines of the German Protestant Church [...] [who] will certainly think it desirable to avail themselves of the offers contained in the letter of the Archbishop of Canterbury'. These young divines were to be 'thoroughly grounded in the doctrines of the Protestant faith, according to the Augsburg Confession'.[92] Feigning innocence, Palmer pondered the meaning of the King's orders to his Minister:

> The orders [...] are "in respect of the relations of the Bishop [...] " to certain other parties; it matters not for the present to whom; whoever *they* may be, we have already something here which concerns *ourselves*. [...] Here is something to set us thinking, – and in which we are deeply interested.[93]

The relations of 'an Orthodox Christian Bishop' with those in or out of his flock were surely dictated by necessity; but 'perhaps further light will be thrown upon it as we go along'. As for 'the German Congregation':

> Why only of Germans? [...] seeing that many Germans are not subjects of the King of Prussia [...] the words which follow look as if they would in some degree limit this congregation, about which we are enquiring: it is "the German [...] congregation *of the Evangelical religion* in Palestine". "The Evangelical religion": what is that? The religion of the Good Message: but message implies [...] a sender.

Was this then part of 'the one true Orthodox Catholic and Apostolic Church [...] or of some other falsely-called Evangelical religion and Evangelical Church which is not identical with ours?'[94] The 'young Divines' must be of the same religion, because otherwise they would have to 'become so, and obtain his [the bishop's] *Communion*, and [...] be ordained and sent by him, before they can be under his pastoral care [...].'[95] They will, in accordance with the Canons of the Church, bring with them a certificate signed by their Bishop showing that they are in communion with him; and if on examination they are found to be orthodox, they will be admitted to communion. But 'the language used by the King of Prussia [...] seems to make their relations with the new Bishop dependent upon private choice'. Nothing is said 'about *communion*, or the terms of obtaining it'; the 'young Divines' accept the Bishop's 'protection and pastoral care [...] as a matter of choice and expediency, to obtain "a greater freedom of action, and a more successful result of their labours"!' Palmer commented sarcastically

> The announcement of such an extent of liberty to Christians in the Evangelical Church will be astonishing, no doubt, to many [...] the knowledge of our rights, if rights they be, may have been reserved to be revealed to us by the King of Prussia and those with whom he has negotiated just at the moment that it is most likely to be most wanted.[96]

Presumably, Palmer speculated, in Germany some chose to follow, others not to follow, 'the Evangelical Bishop of the district; while yet both parties are equally of the Evangelical religion, equally Divines, and equally qualified to be ordained, whether for submission or rebellion, by the accommodating charity of the Evangelical Synod'.[97] Having listed five possible categories of members of the Evangelical religion in Palestine, Palmer concluded that this theory of the Evangelical Church 'presents to our view a truly wonderful combination of the most opposite principles'.[98]

Why also did the Archbishop choose to communicate through the King - 'a layman, and not in any sense representative of her Apostolic authority?' Surely he should write to the Evangelical Bishops of that country, or their Synod?

> Perhaps he would have preferred to do so; but the King of that country, it may be, is jealous of the spiritual power, and allows no missives to come from foreign Churches without passing through his own hands [...].'[99]

However, there was no request to pass on the communication to 'the Spirituality and to the Church'. The letter mentioned 'relations in which the German congregations will stand' to the Bishop, which would be a matter of necessity, unless they were 'capable of being made the subject of negotiation, on matters of local detail and arrangement'. But in virtue of what necessity '*will*' the relations be 'of such or such a kind?' And again, '"The Bishop," we learn, "will consider it as his duty". Will he so consider it indeed? Why will he? In virtue of what law or necessity?'[100]

The congregations of the German Evangelical Church could obtain ordination for their clergy from the English bishop, without pledging themselves to follow the English rite. There was mention of "the German Liturgy" to be used by these clergy; but this must mean that 'the Canons have either been altered by competent authority, or else are now arbitrarily relaxed in favour of this class; – unless the same Canons can bind one set of Clergy to use, and another not to use, the same forms'.[101] And how, he asked, can the Archbishop canonically enforce his assertion that the new Liturgy *will* be used by these Clergy? What was 'the Orthodoxy or validity of the new Ritual'? Why had the Archbishop thought it necessary to add that he had 'carefully examined' the Liturgy in question? With blistering scorn he observed that

> It raises one's thoughts of the dignity of our Primate's Chair to see him re- examining with the eye of a Judge a Ritual and Liturgy transmitted to him in the name of the Evangelical or Apostolical Churches of the whole Prussian kingdom, if not of all Germany, and compiled from those Liturgies previously received from those Churches, – Liturgies derived perhaps from the times of St. Boniface, at any rate of such antiquity that their authors and the dates of their introduction seem to be unknown; and their authority is rested only upon prescription, on the fact that they "are received".[102]

The truth was that it was 'notorious' that 'neither the Prussian Establishment nor its Clergy has any fixed definition or existence,

which is capable of being recognised by the Canons of the Apostolic Church'. There was 'no such thing in existence as [...] the "German Protestant or Evangelical Church"'.[103] He trusted that the Archbishop of Canterbury and the Bishop of London would 'suffer us [...] to Protest against their acts and doctrines' lest 'by a blind submission to their views and policy, however conscientious, we bring the distinct and formal anathemas of the Eastern as well as the rest of the Latin Church upon our heads and the heads of our children'. Equally he trusted, not altogether convincingly, that they would not find 'anything in the tone of our reflections to imply either a spirit of insubordination towards their Office [...] or any personal disrespect or discourtesy towards themselves'.[104] The submission of Catholics to their bishops was, however, 'due only so far as the Bishops themselves profess and uphold the spirit, the principle, and the tradition of the Catholic Faith. Every one is bound to expose and accuse heterodoxy [...].'[105]

Palmer accused the Primate and the Bishop of London of being 'ready on the first suggestion of a foreign King to change the basis and nature of our religion, and to precipitate us into a union with all the sects and heresies of that Babylon which is called the Reformed Church'.[106] Nonetheless, what they purported to do 'in the name of the Church, and with a high hand [...] cannot *proprio vigore* bind the Church; because they are of themselves illegal and uncanonical, and subject their authors to deprivation, and even to excommunication: for the Bishop, and still more, the Archbishop, is set to keep and enforce the laws of the Church, and not to break them [...].'[107] It was the duty of those who disagreed to appeal to a Synod or Convocation, or, if that was impossible, to decline to accept the communion of Bishop Alexander or of 'his Senders-and-Consecrators' until they again upheld the Canons of the Church of England. To do otherwise was to become a link in a chain running from the German Lutherans and Calvinists via all the Nonconformists and the Scotch Presbyterians to all the Dissenters of Scotland and America, and from them to the Dissenters of England and Ireland, who were excommunicated by those same Canons. Acquiescence would mean that 'we, by our own act, should have ceased to be even theoretically Catholics'.[108]

6 The Galitsin Affair

Palmer was now at the height of his powers and influence. The highest in the Church of England flinched at his thunderbolts; the highest in the Synod of Russia paid him compliments. True, he was a maverick; but had he moderated the violence of his rhetoric and gathered to himself the followers that Spencer described, he might have rallied the Oxford Movement and been a mighty force for change within the Church of England. Had he knelt before the great Metropolitan Philaret in humility and asked to be received into the Orthodox Church he would have been received with joy, perhaps to be a beacon of Orthodoxy in the West. Instead, he stubbornly followed his own path, which led, so far at least as the world was concerned, into the wilderness, to alienation from his closest family and friends, to humiliation and ridicule. He was ultimately to blame for this, but the cause of his fall was a woman, Maria Arkadievna, the Princess Galitsin.[1]

Her husband, Prince Michael Galitsin, had been introduced to Palmer by Madame Potemkin at a dinner party in St. Petersburg in October 1840. The Prince spoke dismissively of the Church of England, but then revealed that his wife and eldest daughter, who had been living in Geneva and France, had purportedly 'been converted from the superstition of the Russian Church to the Anglican religion'.[2] A conversion to Rome he could have borne; but for his family to turn to Protestantism made him very unhappy. Palmer was unperturbed. The affair was nonsense; the conversion was to 'Calvinistic Methodism',[3] if it was anything. Rashly, he pledged himself 'to prove that the ladies have not in any way been admitted as members of the Anglican Church, and, if I fail, am ready to be converted myself to that Russian Church which they have renounced and left'. The grateful Prince told him he had given him a ray of hope, and, fatally, that Palmer's credit 'was quite as much implicated in the matter as his [the Prince's] interest and feelings'.[4]

Palmer saw this as a chance, surely God-given, to vindicate his view of the Church of England as quite distinct from Protestantism. His chivalrous character responded to the appeal to rescue the Princess and her daughters from soul-destroying error, and his credit and honour as an English gentleman had been staked on the successful outcome. Sadly, events were to show that the Prince was merely using Palmer to procure the return of his wife, and avoid the severe civil penalties for apostasy from Orthodoxy. The Prince had reminded his wife that if her conversion became known, 'the Synod [...] would anathematize them; and the Government might confiscate their estates';[5] but neither this possibility nor reasoned argument had changed her mind. The Prince was 'au bout de mon Latin'. He begged Palmer to write to him a letter to be forwarded to his wife, which Palmer willingly did. It expressed his willingness to help, and his hope that if only the Princess and her daughters would give his arguments 'serious and reasonable attention', he could convince them that they 'ought to continue dutiful members of that Church in which they were baptised'.[6] The Anglican chaplain at Geneva had no more standing than 'a Chaplain in a ship at sea', with no authority to convert Russians. 'I make no doubt that it would be easy to procure an authoritative declaration to this effect from the spiritual heads of the English Churches, if it were required'.[7] He remarked prophetically to the Prince that 'Intellectual argument with this class of religionists is generally thrown away; indeed it does harm rather than good'.[8] The Prince was pleased with the letter, even considering publishing it in Russian, though that would be 'publishing at the same time the disgrace of his family'.[9]

A few days later Palmer wrote again with a copy of Bishop Jolly's[10] *Treatise on the Church*[11] to be passed on to Galitsin's wife and daughters. The following February, the Prince called again, begging Palmer to answer a letter from the Princess. Palmer took up the pen 'with a heavy heart', as the Princess had not even acknowledged his previous letter. He wrote nonetheless of the dangers of judging 'great Bishops and whole Churches', of the necessity of prayer for the right notions of the Church and her authority and parental duty towards one's children, prayer that might be accompanied by the shedding of tears. To trust 'to one's own understanding' in religious matters was dangerous enough with only one's own soul at stake, but 'doubly so' when children were involved. He expressed alarm at the judgemental and combative tone of the Princess's letter to her husband ('Je *defie* un Papiste d'y repondre') which he saw as stemming directly from the prejudices of the sects, and urged instead prayers for the Pope and action for peace and unity.[12]

In March a letter arrived from the eldest daughter, Princess Zinaida,[13] indicating that her mother was too ill to read Palmer's letter of November, and asking about the respects in which the Church of England seemed to conform to the Bible, and 'the Greek Church' to be contrary to it. She begged Palmer to answer each article of her letter 'by the authority of the Bible, and not by that of "Councils" and "Bishops"', and to remember that she was 'no theologian, but a poor girl, who often fails in her efforts for her salvation, and who hopes to be saved through her faith in Christ'.[14] Palmer's response was almost a dissertation, being 'some sixty pages in length'.[15] Its tone was affectionate and concerned, although reproved her for being unwilling to listen to the wisdom of saintly bishops and the Councils of the Church, particularly as she gave such weight to the opinion of the Anglican clergyman who had 'converted' herself and her mother. He expounded his theory of the one Catholic Church, which meant that she had the right to intercommunion in an Anglican Church without any necessity for 'conversion'. Again he unwisely anticipated that 'the Spiritual Heads of the Anglican Church' would provide a formal declaration that they 'do not, and cannot [...] recognize any conversion of the members of the Greek or Russian Churches to theirs'.[16] Even if she frequented the Chapel of the English Embassy at St. Petersburg for the rest of her life, she would never be a member of the Church of England. '[...] by right a Catholic Christian is a member of the diocese of London when in London, of Rome when at Rome, and of Moscow when at Moscow'.[17] If she were to go to England, she 'would desire to Communicate in the English Churches, and even ought to do so'. As to his own position in Russia, he had to concede that reality had failed to conform to his theory. 'If I go to any separate English Chapel, I do so only because the Bishop here will not or cannot give me the Communion upon Catholic principles'.[18]

On 11/23 March, the Prince came to see Palmer with a letter to the Archbishop of Canterbury, ostensibly written by himself, seeking clarification of the exact relation of the English Church to the Russian. If the Prince did write it, it is remarkable how closely the style resembled Palmer's, as in the legal precision of the opening questions:

> My Lord, I am a Russian, and as such Orthodox. I would ask then:
>
> I. If the Church of England does or does not excommunicate the Catholic and Apostolic Church of the East?
>
> II. If an English Bishop, in his own diocese, pretended to make one of my country and faith renounce the Russian Church, and reconcile him, as a heretic or idolater, to the Church of England, could such a Bishop ground himself upon any canon or law of his Church [...]?[19]

The letter asked if, in the absence of any canon, the chaplain at Geneva had not acted *ultra vires* in purporting to convert the Princess and her daughter; if any law or canon of the English Church excluded an Orthodox Russian from her Communion; and whether an Orthodox, by taking Communion in an Anglican Church impliedly renounced the Orthodox Church.[20]

On 2 May (N. S.) the Prince dined with the English Ambassador, Lord Clanricarde.[21] He told the Ambassador that he had written to the Archbishop, and what he had said. Clanricarde was amused. He said, smiling: 'I can tell you, you will embarrass him extremely: you cannot conceive how such a letter will embarrass him to answer. He is one of the most timid and apprehensive men in existence. But he will probably give the letter to one of his Chaplains, to answer for him'. Clanricarde also indicated that he was glad the Prince had written the letter; and that should no answer have arrived by the time the Prince returned from Geneva, where he was going to speak to his wife and children, then he would 'do his best to induce his Grace to send an answer with as little delay as possible'.[22] Palmer had declined to accompany the Prince, as the Princess continued to ignore his letters, and the eldest daughter had yet to receive his reply. The Princess had, however, written to the Emperor – a strange act for one who later constantly enjoined Palmer not to publicise her conversion in any way, for fear of condign punishment – describing her conversion as being 'to the Evangelical Religion,' and declaring 'We are Protestants'.

When Palmer visited the Prince on 5/17 June there was still no reply from the Archbishop. Palmer thought that 'both his personal rank and the very sufficient excuse he had for troubling the Archbishop were such as to make the civility of an answer due to him'.[23] The Prince took the Archbishop's silence to indicate that he 'was a mere Protestant like the multitude, and was unwilling to send him an answer', something he repeated when Palmer saw him on 17/29 June, the night the Prince was leaving for Geneva.

Palmer's resolution was bolstered by his parting conversation with Count Pratasoff on 2 July (N. S.). The Count, who knew all about the affair, told Palmer he 'should do a very good deed [...] who should bring those ladies out of their errors'. The Russian chaplain at Berne had tried and failed to persuade them to return to Orthodoxy; they had softened their stance on Icons, being used to them, but still would not admit the Real Presence, 'so it will be all the more to your credit, and to the credit of your views [n. b. not your Church] if you should be able to do anything with them'. All possibility of union was out of the question while the English Church assented to, or failed to dissociate itself from, 'proselytism of our people'.[24]

On his return to London, Palmer asked the Archbishop of Canterbury if he had received the Prince's letter. He had: 'he well remembered it "from the strange ignorance which it shewed of the present state of the Church of England; attributing to her the exercise of a much greater degree of authority than she in fact possesses"'. This may well have been a hint that Howley suspected Palmer had 'directed the pen of the Russian Prince'.[25] Howley added 'The Church of England anathematizes nobody'. Palmer commented sarcastically 'forgetting, perhaps, one of the XXXIX Articles, which begins with these words, "*Sunt et illi praeterea anathematizandi,*" &c.'.[26] The Archbishop claimed that he thought he *had* answered the letter; but his private secretary, 'sitting at his elbow', said that His Grace "*had thought of answering it*, but had never done so"'.[27] Embarrassed, Palmer wrote to the Prince that 'our

Bishops in England & especially the Archbishop who is now quite an old man are altogether overwhelmed with letterwriting [...] so that an involuntary neglect or omission will sometimes occur – at the same time I am greatly surprized & vexed that it should have happened in your case [...].'[28] It seems hardly credible that Palmer was genuinely surprised at this turn of events, but as with his later rebuff by the Scottish bishops, he appears to have convinced himself that events and people would conform to his expectations.

On 7 September Palmer received an excited letter from the Prince, regretting 'exceedingly' that Palmer had not gone with him to Geneva, where he 'would have been of the greatest use', and asking him for a copy of his 'long letter', which had not been received. The Princess would only say that she was 'of *the unity of the Gospel*', and would be no more specific about her religion; his daughter was communicating in the English Chapel, whose 'Programmes' were pasted about the walls of Geneva, 'just like the play-bills of a theatre'.[29] The Prince was satisfied that the chaplain, Mr. Hare,[30] was 'a complete heretic', who denied the Real Presence. The Prince begged Palmer to come to St. Petersburg, and wanted to know when he could hope to hear from the Archbishop; in the meantime, did the Bishop of London acknowledge Mr. Hare? Palmer replied that Mr. Hare was obviously '*a regular Protestant,* and just like the "Calvinistes" or "Evangéliques" of Geneva', probably nominally licensed by the Bishop of London, but more likely just hired by the English expatriates at Geneva, and so 'really responsible only to them'.[31] Nonetheless, he would write to the Bishop as requested.

This he did on 8 September 1841. Bishop Blomfield replied that he had 'no real jurisdiction' over clergy not within his diocese, but that it was customary for him to license those chosen by Congregations abroad. He had done so in the case of Mr. Hare, who had not made any attempt to convert either of the ladies concerned, but had admitted the daughter to communion on the recommendation of Lord Edward Chichester,[32] and the mother a month later, when she came demanding 'admission to the Communion of the Church of England'. The Bishop was happy to condone his action, but ambivalent as to whether it was by way of conversion from the 'Greek' to the Anglican Church, or simply by way of intercommunion.[33] Palmer wrote back by return, asking whether the female Galitisins had been admitted to communion as converts, or on the principle of intercommunion. If the former, then Palmer's representations to the Russians would be shown to be 'mistaken', and the Russian Church to be heretical and idolatrous in the eyes of the English Church. The Bishop replied that

> If a person of good life and conversation presents himself to a clergyman of the Church of England, declaring his assent to the doctrines of that Church, and desiring to be admitted as a Communicant, I conceive that it is the duty of that Clergyman to admit him.[34]

Whether this person was a convert or not was 'a question which concerns the conscience of the party himself, but which the Clergyman [...] [was] not called upon to determine'. The Bishop did not 'feel it necessary to decide in the present instance' whether the Greek Church taught doctrines 'which disqualify those who hold them from communicating in our Church'.[35] Mr. Hare, he felt, had not exceeded his authority in admitting the ladies to Communion; he did not see that he, the Bishop, could 'be required to interfere any further in the matter'.

Palmer promptly tried this principle on the nearest Dissenting Minister ('of the Independent Denomination'). Could a Dissenting Minister give communion to someone without finding out their status, whether proselyte, or brother? Further, was this solely a matter for the conscience of the party communicating, and of indifference to the Minister admitting him to Communion? The Minister 'smiled at what seemed to him to be the absurdity of the question', and said that

> in every religious community [...] it must be for the Authority to determine what persons are admissible, and upon what conditions each person is admitted to its privileges: that if these were left to be taken at the discretion of private conscience, the community would no longer be any real community at all.[36]

Palmer made a copy of his long letter, and sent it to St. Petersburg to await the return of the Galitsins; but 'of all this correspondence, and its result', he 'made no report at that time [...] being ashamed to write any'.[37]

A fortnight later, however, shame was turned to rejoicing when the Prince's eldest daughter, having at last received Palmer's long letter, returned to the Orthodox Church. 'My daughter has been brought back, under God's grace, by your letters', but his wife was still lost in the darkness of heresy.

> Who shall restore a mother to her children, a wife to her husband, unless it be yourself? I implore you then, in the name of Jesus Christ, to cross the Channel, and go to Paris to see my wife. She will make no difficulty of receiving you [...] No one can be more capable [...] of convincing her.[38]

Palmer agreed to travel to Paris as soon as he could. Only if the Princess sent him away, or if 'I see that the case is absolutely hopeless', would he abandon his attempt to reunite her to the Communion of the Russian Church. However, he was not so carried away by the good news as to forget to ask:

> I hope that in reconciling herself to the Russian Church your daughter did not renounce or accuse the *Church of England*, but only that heretical Protestantism, Lutheranism, or Calvinism, and those particular heresies or errors which she had been taught [...] Pray let me know exactly how this was.[39]

Palmer was well aware that it was 'the settled usage of the Eastern Church [...] to reconcile Anglicans, as Lutherans, or Calvinists'; the only response to his question was a guilty silence. This however made 'no change in his resolution to go to Paris'.

Palmer's success in reconverting the eldest daughter bewildered his fellow Anglicans. The British Ambassador, Lord Stuart de Rothesay,[40] mishearing a conversation between Mr. Blackmore and his fellow chaplain Mr. Law, asked: 'What, are you speaking of that man, Mr. P[almer], who turns people away from his own Church?'.[41]

M. Mouravieff, on the other hand, praised Palmer's efforts to Metropolitan Philaret, who answered 'rather drily, "Truly our Church is greatly indebted to that English Deacon!"'.[42] The affair had become the talk of society in St. Petersburg, 'among the higher circles'.

In early January, Palmer left for Paris and his old friend Bishop Luscombe. Luscombe had been consecrated by the Bishops of the Scottish Episcopal Church on 20 March, 1825, with the full consent of both the English Hierarchy and the Government, to look after the 'members of the United Church of England and Ireland and the Episcopal Church in Scotland'[43] on the continent. When they met in Paris Luscombe spontaneously mentioned a Russian lady who had a seat in the English Chapel, who usually left before the sermon. He did not know her by sight, and had not spoken to her.

There then followed a game of hide and seek. Palmer called on the Princess; she was unwell. Palmer would not succeed in bringing her back to the Greek Church: 'I am not *seeking*; I have *found*'. Palmer's religion was 'an *association of souls*, a *religious discipline*'; hers, the '*cry of one shipwrecked* towards the Saviour'. She made another appointment, but cancelled it, pleading her 'continued indisposition'. Palmer wrote that 'the character of the Anglican Church' was implicated in the matter', and, 'knowing that she was not altogether confined to the house', to ask her 'not to trifle' with him, and grant him quarter or half an hour's conversation. The Princess replied with maddening disingenuousness that whilst she 'had been well enough for some days past to go out', she had been forbidden 'to attend to any business that requires thought'! What followed set the tone for their future exchanges, with herself the victim, and Palmer the villain. 'It is impossible for me to conceive how a poor obscure woman like myself', she wrote, 'who seeks to keep herself under the Gospel of Salvation, and live the *life which is hidden in God,* can be any thing so important to the existence of the Church of England'. She was puzzled that 'a disciple of Dr. Pusey, i.e. a Dissenter', should tell her so; besides, Palmer thought 'too much of the *form,* to be *spiritually religious.* All these *formal* dissertations are the things which destroy *peace*'.[44]

Palmer calmly replied that he would eagerly hear the proof of his being a Dissenter, and that no doubt he did think too much of forms. Her prejudices against Dr. Pusey, 'a good and learned man', were mistaken, and he had a right to request her assistance when 'the *character* (*not* the *existence*) of the Anglican Church [...] was seriously and publicly compromised'[45] by her alleged conversion to it. By now something of the Princess Galitsin's character was becoming apparent. She was a descendant of the famous Fieldmarshal Suvorov, and Zernov suggests had inherited both his 'energy and eccentricity'. She

> was intensely egocentric and her sudden conversion to Anglicanism provided her with the means of keeping everybody occupied with her fortunes. She was a restless woman, full of misdirected energy, constantly changing her residence, resolute and ready to use any weapons for defence or attack. Palmer's appearance on the scene provided her with a an inexhaustible supply of dramatic situations [...].[46]

Although she was constantly complaining of her poor health, she 'could hit back hard and this Palmer soon discovered to his discomfort'.[47] It could, however, be said in the Princess's defence that she had the right to use any available means to keep Palmer, who was extraordinarily persistent, at bay. After all, she had done nothing to deserve to be made a test case for Palmer's ecclesiastical theory, and was entitled to become an Anglican if she wished without interference from him; ultimately, it was none of his business.

Palmer enlisted the help of Bishop Luscombe, who suggested that he and Palmer exchange letters, in which he could express agreement with Palmer's views. When the letters were shown to the Princess, 'if she were a person [...] of good sense and feeling, this ought to weigh with her'. The Bishop duly wrote that he 'did *not* allow that a member of the Russian Orthodox Church or of the Oriental Orthodox Churches *can* be received into the Church of England as a convert, because those Churches certainly form part of the Catholic Church'. A member of those Churches would be admitted to communion on the basis of intercommunion, if they had been rightly Baptized and Confirmed.[48]

The day after receiving the Bishop's reply, Sunday 23 January, Palmer had a lengthy interview with the Princess. She spoke of 'the persecutions and martyrdom she had suffered, and was still suffering', and of the futility of trying to make her change her mind, accusing Palmer of pride and formalism in trying to do so. She 'roundly declared that she belonged to the Anglican Church [...] as a convert from the Russian, which she had left'. Palmer responded that she had never done so, except in intention. She taxed Palmer with arguing from an entirely unreal position:

> It is a pure theory of yours, and utterly vain and absurd, to suppose that the Russian and Anglican Churches can ever be reconciled, or a mutual Communion exist [...] it is very strange indeed, that after seeing Anglican Bishops and Clergymen, and so many English people, and none of them ever questioning my being a member of the Anglican Church [...] you should now be the first to tell me I am not![49]

Palmer then played his trump card by producing the letters between himself and Bishop Luscombe. The Princess 'seemed at first to take this as a sort of persecution of her', before demanding to know what the Bishop would do.

When they met again on Tuesday 25 January, the Princess correctly identified

> two Anglican Churches, the one 'Catholic,' the other 'Biblical' or 'Protestant': [...] she saw perfectly well the two had nothing in common: that I belonged to the 'Papistic' or 'Catholic' Anglican Church, she only to the Biblical or Protestant: that she belonged to that which was popularly and really the religion of the English people; and of the Parliament [...] You are the first who has attempted to call in question or deny my membership.[50]

Palmer agreed that one or other of them must be right, but it was 'the laws and constitutions of the Society' that decided the issue, not 'popular opinion'. Pressed on her understanding of the Church, the Princess 'flew off to the invisible Church, and the New Jerusalem'.[51] Palmer was to have some difficulty in dealing with the Princess's approach to theological debate, which mixed logical argument with flights of evangelical rhetoric and emotional conviction impervious to rationality. At other times she would patronise Palmer:

> I see clearly that you are a long way off from being truly religious: but you are still young; and by the grace of God that may come; but indeed, indeed, you lack much of that state of the soul: you have not got your passport signed: I am sure of that.[52]

This sort of attack must have been unsettling, for Palmer did indeed go very much by theories and 'the laws and constitutions of the Society', making him vulnerable to charges of spiritual deadness and formalism.

The Princess, on the other hand, was determined to claim the title of Anglican, but prepared to ignore Anglican authority (such as there was) when it suited her, perhaps the most convincing proof of her Anglican credentials. She dismissed the idea of seeking a decisive ruling from the Archbishop of Canterbury with the words: 'What need is there, when I have all that I desire already?', and noted the Archbishop's tact in not answering her husband's letter. Although she had read the two letters between Palmer and Bishop Luscombe, she 'still attached no importance to Bp. Luscombe's judgement'.[53]

Despite this, Palmer determined to bring the Bishop into play again. Having heard of the Princess's response to his letter, the Bishop decided to write to her himself. He listed the 'necessary qualifications' for the Princess to be admitted to communion: that she believed all the Articles of the Apostles' Creed in the same sense in which they were held in the Church of England, that she should have been validly baptised and confirmed, and not excommunicated by the Russian Church. The Bishop was happy to take the Princess's 'presentation of herself at the Communion' as assurance that she had them.

On 28 January the Princess proposed a final meeting at which Palmer could 'say all that you still have to say about religion'; she could no longer receive him thereafter. However, she rejoiced 'to think of the spirit of peace, charity and good will which has presided at our two conversations'. Palmer replied that 'the tone of your note, though very kind and civil to me, seems to whisper in my ear "Now I hope I shall get rid of you at last"'. He enclosed for her a draft of a letter that she might write to the Archbishop of Canterbury, did she wish to question Bishop Luscombe's judgement. Palmer seems to have taken peculiar pleasure in putting himself in the shoes of his opponents, and pleading their case for them in hypothesis, a manifestation perhaps of the legal career that he never had. His imaginary letter on the Princess's behalf was so able that the Princess, when they met on 30 January, told him that he had given her 'an arm against him', although in the same breath she complained that Palmer had added 'to her persecutions and difficulties [...] she could not tell what she should do'.[54] Stung by the Bishop's note into being more combative, she told Palmer that 'in our Church [the Anglican] there is life; and there has been *progress* [...] while the Greek Church is a dead skeleton'. Again she accused Palmer of being 'a most infatuated and zealous formalist; of not being Christian; nor having hope in me'. Palmer retaliated by telling her that unlike her eldest daughter, she 'did not appear to be at all reasonable', which she 'seemed surprised' to be told.[55]

Palmer returned to England and to Oxford on 17 February. Unknown to him, he had been under attack in his own College days before. The Bursar, Richard Clarke Sewell,[56] had written to Dr. Routh to protest against the association of Magdalen with Palmer. This appears from a sort of deposition that Dr. Routh wrote on the letter, to the effect that the letter he sent with Palmer to Russia:

> expressed his private wish, that Mr. Palmer might be admitted to Church Communion in Russia with the provision, that he affirmed [...] nothing contrary to the Faith and Doctrine of the C of E ... the recommendation I gave Mr. Palmer [...] was given in my own name & merely points out who I was, by the mention of my being the head of a College in Oxford.[57]

Bishop Bagot of Oxford, to whom Sewell also appealed, reassured Dr. Routh on 3 February 1842 that he was 'resolved not to take any steps, or make myself a party to anything wh. may tend to renew agitation from whatever side or quarter it may come'.[58] Three days later he politely squashed Sewell:

> I trust you will not think me wanting in courtesy if I decline answering the several questions contained in your letter, to an individual member [of yr. College] with whom I have not had the honour of any acquaintance, and when the questions do not appear to come officially under the general authority of the College.[59]

The Vice-President, Francis Faber, took a similar line when Sewell requested that his letter, and Dr. Routh's reply, be sent to the Archbishop of Canterbury, the Bishop of Winchester, and the Bishop of Oxford: 'I declined having anything to do, in my official capacity, with his intended communication to the Bishops, reminding him that he had acted throughout as an individual, disjoined from his College, and that he must proceed & terminate in the same character'.[60]

Sewell was not pacified by Dr. Routh's reply. He, and allegedly 'many others', still thought that

> the *form* in which Mr. Palmer published your letter, was such as to induce a belief [...] that the letter [...] was the act of the President representing the Body in his own person - and not of yourself as an individual – And if the College [...] had given any such letters, it would [...] have been exposed to the charge of Impertinence and Arrogance in meddling with matters Ecclesiastical, & of disrespect to the Episcopal authority rather of our Diocesan, or the Primate, in treading upon the privilege belonging canonically & ex officio to them or one of them only. I wish indeed the College could be altogether relieved from the effect of Mr. Palmer's late publications. I cannot but fear the notoriety he has achieved for himself will be anything but beneficial to the interests of the Society. And there are but two ways in which this [...] can be accomplished, either by his retiring from the tutorship, or by some public disavowal on the part of the Body of a participation in the sentiments & opinions he has lately given to the world.[61]

However, neither took place. Once more Palmer had reason to be grateful to Dr. Routh.

In mid-March Palmer received a note from Bishop Luscombe, to the effect that the Princess had been among the previous Sunday's communicants, thereby ostensibly conforming to his wish that she came as a member of the Russian Church, and not a convert. Palmer's fears that the Princess might 'put off a few civil words upon Bishop Luscombe, without ever really accepting his terms', were confirmed when just over a week later, a letter arrived from Paris, from a Mr. Bosanquet.[62] He and his wife were friends of the Princess. Palmer had made their acquaintance and asked them to speak to her, in the hope that as friends they might make more headway. Mr. Bosanquet was 'something of a Puseyite', but as the Princess depended upon his wife for advice and help, the couple were careful to be impartial, and had told the Princess of their acquaintance with Palmer. The letter disclosed that the Princess was unconcerned about unity, but wanted 'to glide calmly into a community *whose tenets coincide with her own,* without enquiring how far they may differ from those she quits [...] to quit the Greek, and *to take the Anglican* [Church] *only on her own terms and conditions*'.[63] Alarmed, Palmer sought clarification, and wrote to the Princess, asking her to confirm the basis on which she had taken communion. This letter he enclosed in a letter to Bishop Luscombe, indicating that the Princess's opinions were apparently unchanged. He requested the Bishop to send it to the Princess with a covering note written by Luscombe, as that was more likely to evoke an answer. If the Bishop thought that inappropriate, Palmer's letter alone could be sent on.

Palmer had gone too far. Luscombe sent the letter on without any note from himself, and reminded Palmer that he had told the Princess that her attendance at communion would be taken by him as assurance of her possession of the necessary qualifications: she had gone further in giving written notice of her intention to take communion.

> Mde. A [the Princess] *did* present herself on that day. It is not for me to question her sincerity: therefore *I wish to avoid any discussion of your last communication. I have done all that I think it becomes me to do* [...].

The postscript drew the sting a little: 'I duly appreciate *your* motives, and I beg you to do justice to mine, and to my regard for you'.[64] However the Princess' notice was highly ambiguous, stating that in coming to take communion 'she was perfectly at peace with her conscience before God'.[65] She was indicating, for those who had eyes to read, that she was both a Russian Princess and a true Protestant, and it would be she, and not the Bishop, who would decide whether she should take communion or not.

Palmer wrote back that he certainly would not have understood the Princess's notice as the Bishop appeared to have done; the situation was now 'far worse', as she had 'obtained the Communion *of a Bishop* by apparently professing to believe the faith of the Anglican Church', whereas he knew that she disbelieved a number of fundamental doctrines. It would be almost impossible in the circumstances to defend the Anglican Church in Russia, to which the Princess was set to return, as Palmer had tried to do; he 'must be content to be regarded there at present as a sort of impostor'.[66] He thanked Luscombe gloomily for his personal kindness 'in this distressing affair'.

The letter passed on by the Bishop produced an hysterical and angry response from the Princess, which, although intended for Palmer's eyes, was written to Mr. Bosanquet, who warned Palmer that 'any chance of further communication' had been lost. Palmer was eventually given a copy by the Princess in 1848. In it the Princess denied, with reason, that Palmer had any right to question her, or that she had any obligation to answer him. She would not answer him, nor ever speak with him again. She accused him of falsely interpreting their three conversations, held only to please her husband, suggesting that Palmer had 'laid aside that tone of false gentleness and charity' by which he hoped to change her mind; but God's grace had armed her against his 'egotistical and cruel agitation'. Palmer manifestly had not 'the Spirit of God', indeed 'is for the present abandoned of God. The end of his letter is an open declaration of hatred and of war. I accept his defiance with boldness [...].' The Princess 'a woman, without strength and without support [...] and suffering from an aneurism of the heart, which alone may kill her at any time', whilst claiming to be 'not at all the person to relish the strife of war', was plainly enjoying the rôle of Protestant martyr.

Mr. Bosanquet added that 'further interference for the present would be productive of no good', and that if the Princess's welfare was Palmer's motive, that would be 'only endangered by any immediate interference or persecution on the subject'. It was natural for a woman to shrink from being the battlefield for a controversy over the reunion of the Churches, and 'hardly fair to make use of her as an instrument, or a test: more especially, as no one can have any right to interfere with her'. The Princess was shortly to start for Russia: 'When there, kindness and good management may do much with her; harshness and persecution nothing'. It should have been abundantly clear by now to Palmer that the Princess had entirely brought the Bosanquets round to her point of view, as indicated by the frequent use of the word 'persecution'; he had lost two more allies in his cause.

In replying to Bosanquet to explain his motives, Palmer significantly shifted his ground. He was no longer simply responding to the Prince's appeals to bring his wife back to Orthodoxy. The Princess was 'most cruelly and publicly wronging that spiritual family of which I am a member', and Palmer found 'her representation of the Anglican Church opposed and confronted with my own'.[67] Palmer 'had a right to take legal and public measures to vindicate the character of our Church and Religion'. His tone was markedly more combative. If the Princess refused

> to study the questions between us [...] such conduct on her part leaves me no choice. If we were both reasonably-minded, we should be willing to examine the matter together. But if that cannot be, the only thing that remains is, to seek out the competent tribunal, and to go to law together, either amicably or otherwise, and to work out the question by legal and public methods.[68]

A more 'reasonably-minded' man might indeed have stopped to consider why it was that so far he had 'totally failed' in his self- appointed rôle as champion of the Church of England, and taken stock before expending himself further in a lost cause; Palmer was not that man.

A month later Mr. Bosanquet wrote from Paris that the Princess's 'opinions [...] were not to be shaken'. To pursue her further would only 'drive her to Calvinism'.[69] Palmer wrote to the Prince in April, suggesting canvassing the Church authorities to see if they objected to the Princess's opinions. If not, then, said Palmer: 'I for one will lose no time in looking out for some other religion, wherever it may be found'. However, this proposal was not adopted. Palmer himself was told by 'a barrister who had given much attention to the Ecclesiastical branch of his profession', almost certainly Roundell Palmer, that 'nothing could be done to any purpose';[70] and the Prince, when he eventually replied, made no reference to Palmer's suggestions. He quoted his wife as saying that Palmer had had

> no success either in pleasing her, or in persuading her. She represents that in her discussions with you she had always the best of it, and you always the worst: that you knew not what to say against her arguments; but were ready to cry: and that even on one occasion you were taken unwell [...] she regards me as her persecutor, and you as her accomplice [...] she says that 'you have written to her from England a letter which is perfectly frightful' ['une lettre affreuse']; and that 'even a mutual acquaintance' of you both [namely Mr. O] 'could not refrain from expressing his indignation at it.'[71]

She had received communion from Bishop Luscombe despite Palmer's best efforts, which meant 'the triumph of Protestantism over Catholicism'. It was Palmer who 'ran some risk of being turned out of the Anglican Church'. It appeared, then, that Palmer would have to accept defeat; but as with the reconversion of the eldest Galitsin daughter, events were to ensure that Palmer's destiny continued to be linked with that of the Princess.

The Princess proposed to return to St. Petersburg, 'to bear her testimony to the truth', and asked Bishop Luscombe for a written certificate of Communion. This she might have had, if she had not specifically asked him, when he called on her, 'to say nothing in his certificate about intercommunion'.[72] The Bishop realised that he had been fooled, and refused the certificate until she could satisfy him that she believed the doctrines of the Church of England, and came to communion not as a convert, but as a member of the Russian Church. This clarification was requested in a letter, which, in Palmer's dry phrase, 'the lady did not think it necessary to answer'.

Unaware of this development, Palmer had decided to arm himself for a visit to the Episcopal Lutherans of Sweden with Canonical Letters from the Bishop of Oxford. A formal letter to his father, in whose parish of Mixbury he served as deacon, led to the obtaining of the necessary certificate;[73] although the bemused Bishop observed that 'although he had no objection to give the certificate asked for, he could not help asking, "Cui bono?"',[74] 'which question my Father [...] could not answer'.[75] The day that Palmer received the certificate, Prince Galitsin wrote to say that the Princess was no longer admitted to communion by Bishop Luscombe, and to ask Palmer to come to St. Petersburg to 'work upon the heart and understanding' of his wife.[76] Palmer immediately travelled to Paris, to be briefed by Bishop Luscombe on what had occurred. The Bishop felt that as the Princess was now 'setting him [...] at defiance, it was his [...] duty to disavow her', and was now prepared to give Palmer his full support. Palmer proposed that he become the Bishop's clerk,[77] which the Bishop accepted.[78]

Determined to pursue his theory of the Catholic Church with rigid consistency, Palmer then called upon the Roman Catholic Archbishop of Paris and presented his Bishop's certificate with a request to be admitted to communion. The Grand-Vicaire brought back a predictable refusal, on the grounds that despite the absence of any formal synodical judgement, or excommunication of the Anglican Church by the Gallican, nonetheless 'the Anglican Church had separated herself *in fact* [...] it was self-evident that there must be a Head; and [...] Henry VIII was not that Head which God had appointed, nor Queen Victoria'.[79]

Palmer then drafted an emollient letter to the Princess, asking her 'most sincerely and humbly [...] to forgive' him, if he had 'in any way hurt, or wronged, or offended' her personally, and assuring her of his 'regard and respect'.[80] He tried to present it at her Paris address, but found that she had left, he presumed for St. Petersburg. Privately, he continued to think the Princess 'terribly prejudiced against everybody whom she thinks desirous of changing her opinions', with 'no idea of viewing the Ecclesiastical question in a practical light [...] [she] told me I was lost in formalities [...] inconsistent with spiritual religion'.[81]

Palmer next obtained Letters Commendatory from Bishop Luscombe, agreeing with the Bishop that to disarm the criticism that they came from one bishop alone, and were unsupported by a Synod, Palmer should seek the approval of the Scottish bishops. Palmer saw his attachment to Bishop Luscombe as separating himself entirely from the diocese of Oxford for the time being,[82] which was to be a contentious issue between himself and his father.

Having cautioned the Prince to treat his wife kindly, avoid religious discussion, and distance himself from Palmer's zeal in defending his 'theory about the English Church', Palmer travelled to Aberdeen, where he met the Primus, the Bishop of Aberdeen, and the Bishops of Brechin and Edinburgh. The three bishops were not enthusiastic:

> Bishop Luscombe might be doing very right; it would be time enough to seek for further support to his declarations, when their sufficiency should have been actually called in question in Russia; and that then it would be rather matter for a Synod; whereas they [...] answered me only as individual and Diocesan Bishops.[83]

Palmer's relative Dean Horsley,[84] the Dean of Brechin, told him that the Bishop of Edinburgh had been anxious to impress on him that

> the reluctance of the Scotch Bishops to take any decisive steps in the matter [...] did not arise from any improper fear of, or deference to the English Hierarchy, but from want of sufficient time to deliberate on the momentous points submitted to their consideration.

The Bishops feared the reaction of the laity to any declaration of intercommunion with the Greek Church, 'the more likely from the evil communications with which the Church in this quarter of the island is beset, and the horrible low Genevan atmosphere by which she is oppressed, and in which she can scarcely do more than vegetate'.[85] A Synod of both Chambers should assemble to investigate the question.

Palmer responded that he was 'the last person to be impatient', if 'time and full information' were all that were required to 'lead to a good result'. With a breahtaking disregard of his own stubbornness in pursuit of principle, he told Dean Horsley: 'The whole matter has come to me, and upon me, of itself; without my anticipating or seeking it'. He was nearer the truth when he continued: '[...] and it is, properly speaking, none of mine: my only desire is to do what seems right for me to do in it myself according to my own views'.[86] He disagreed that synodical acceptance of Bishop Luscombe's letters would entail declaring intercommunion with the East, although disavowing heretical propositions and acknowledging 'the seven points of Faith to be orthodox' would pave the way for the restoration of intercommunion, if lost.

Although he had 'an ordinary and canonical right to address the diocesan bishop, wherever I may be, in order to obtain from him the Communion', he had no such right so far as a Synod was concerned, which he rightly anticipated would leave him in a dilemma on his return to Russia. If he presented Luscombe's Letters to the Synod, they would direct him, as an individual, to the diocesan bishop. The bishop would then object to Letters signed by only 'a Chaplain-Bishop at Paris' as not sufficiently representing 'the real doctrine and religion' of Palmer's Church, and say that they should have been signed by a Synod. The lack of support from the Scottish bishops was the more regrettable, because 'the Scottish Church is the only Church in our Islands which *could* treat with the Russian or any other Synodically'.[87] J. M. Neale felt that when Palmer's application was 'passed over in silence', the three bishops 'missed one of the noblest opportunities of promoting union [...] since Archbishop Wake's negotiation with the Gallican Church'.[88] As for the laity, Palmer felt that if intercommunion were publicly declared forthwith, only 'the most fanatical Evangelicals' would be shocked.

In mid-August Dean Horsley told Palmer that whatever the Bishop of Edinburgh had said, his own diocesan had confirmed that the Scottish bishops would never 'act synodically or authoritatively [...] unless they first ascertain that their doing so will be *perfectly agreeable* to the English Hierarchy'. Moreover, 'from the present anything-arian character of that Hierarchy' assent to a declaration of intercommunion by 'the Scotch Bishops' was most improbable. Nonetheless, he thought that Palmer should submit the matter to a Synod of the Church, not merely an Episcopal Synod, in order to take the opinion 'of the Presbyters as well as of the Bishops'.[89] Events were to show that Palmer would have done better to have learned the lessons of this first rebuff in Scotland, and abandon any attempt to find support there as hopeless from the start.

7 Return to Russia

On 1 September Palmer sailed for St. Petersburg on the 'Jupiter' steamer, arriving on 9 September, his departure giving his family at home 'two or three years of comparative rest'.[1] Calling immediately on Prince Galitsin, he found an extraordinary change. Far from being penalised, the Princess had been received at Court; she received Palmer 'so graciously and good-humouredly, that I was [...] astonished'. The Prince cheerfully remarked 'Now I hope you will be good friends'. Palmer, the wiser for his previous encounters with the Princess, replied steadily 'It is impossible we should be otherwise, so long as [the Princess] does not pretend any right to the communion of Bishop Luscombe, from whom I come; and I trust and suppose that she no longer does [...].' Grace and good humour vanished at once, as did the Princess, not to reappear until Palmer had left. He was informed that when the Princess had left Paris she had gone to London, to seek a ruling from the Archbishop of Canterbury, the Bishop of London, and

M. Bunsen, returning 'quite triumphant', vindicated in her conviction that Palmer was 'a maintainer of paradoxes', and the Church of England Protestant. Letters had been given her, allegedly instructing the English chaplain to give her communion, which she had already taken in the chapel of the British factory.[2] '"So that," continued [the Prince], "things seem settled in a worse state for you than ever"'. The Prince had recovered his wife; any remaining problem was Palmer's alone. His eldest daughter asked innocently how Palmer could still be a member of the Anglican Church. She

> urged strongly, that it was of no use for me to try to oppose her mother in her proceedings here [...] for she had "obtained all requisite authorizations from the Archbishop: that he was the first Prelate of our Communion; and that Mr. L[aw] the Chaplain, was bound to obey him: that it was evident the question was settled: that there was nothing left for me to do but open my eyes to the real nature of the Anglican Church, and to submit: that the best thing I could do

would be to quit it, and turn either *Catolic* or *Capholic,* (Roman or Russian); and they hoped I would do so".[3]

This might be thought to be both right and sensible; but Palmer maintained that since the power of the Archbishop and the Bishop of London was not absolute, the more their acts involved the Church in heresy, 'the more every one of its members was bound to protest against and resist them'. Palmer himself 'would never rest' until he had done 'all he could'. This was not what the Prince wanted to hear:

It was a very serious matter for his wife, and for them all, to cause no open scandal; nor give occasion for the matter to be noticed by the civil or ecclesiastical authorities: that at present she acted with the greatest circumspection; went to the English Chapel only in a hackney coach [...] that she was unobserved; acted privately, without any publicity; scandalized nobody: and that in short, there was no reason to interfere with her; and I had no business or occasion to do so.[4]

So much for passionate appeals to Palmer to bring his wife back to the true religion. Now Palmer's obduracy threatened to destroy an accommodation with the Russian authorities at the highest level, for the Emperor himself had given permission for the Princess to return to Russia, letting it be known that 'no notice would be taken of her illegal acts, so long as she was 'quiet, and caused no public scandal'.[5]

When Palmer retorted that the Anglican Church was 'outraged and scandalized' by the Princess' behaviour, the Prince and his daughter smiled, saying 'There is no scandal; nobody is scandalized but you'. The daughter fairly pointed out that as 'any one might communicate, even a heathen' in Anglican Chapels, Palmer could 'prosecute everybody who communicated at all', as much as her mother. He was of 'the sect of the Puseyites', not the Anglican Church. Palmer replied that the Princess, by communicating when she held the beliefs she did, imputed heresy to the Church. The Prince countered that not only the Archbishop's Letters, but the whole affair of the Jerusalem Bishopric, gave the lie to that. Palmer's quarrel lay with the Archbishop of Canterbury and M. Bunsen. Palmer 'was the party beaten, and [...] ought to acquiesce: [...] it was not for a deacon to contend against the Archbishop'. If Palmer wanted to be a Catholic, let him quit the Anglican Church, and 'join the Church of Dr. Wiseman'. If the Princess was let alone to act discreetly, 'she might at any time, if she came round, be reconciled [...] without any publicity'.[6] Palmer objected that if she were, she would renounce the Anglican Church as heretical. The Prince 'did not seem to care a straw about this, plainly, because he had made up his mind that such is indeed the case'.[7] Palmer must not come to their house any more, although the Prince would come to Palmer's lodgings 'as often as might be desirable or necessary'.

Now, if ever, was the time for Palmer to quit the field with whatever dignity he could muster. Lord Selborne, balancing fraternal loyalty with judicial objectivity, describes him as proceeding:

> with a bravery, patience, and perseverance which would have been admirable if the cause had been more adequate; constructing out of the materials which that case furnished an ecclesiastical problem, on the solution of which he staked his future life; blending with great tenderness and consideration for the persons concerned an inflexible determination to work out that problem to some practical result, and an absolute insensibility to all reasons against the claim of one like himself to force such public issues, arising out of private matters, upon his Church; sustained, however, in that attempt by the sense of a vocation, which he collected from signs intelligible to himself alone.[8]

Palmer's resolution to continue was fortified, first by the chaplain, Mr. Law, who stated that if he discovered that a person such as the Princess had actually taken communion from him, he would 'do what he could to prevent it, from fear of the civil penalties, which might cause the most serious embarrassments to all the English residents'.[9] Moreover, the Prince's daughter had, as Palmer feared, been reconciled to the Russian Church as from Lutheranism and Calvinism. 'Having contributed materially [...] to bring back his daughter to orthodoxy', Palmer had 'every right to expect that some regard should be shewn' to the honour of the Anglican Church. He could not 'remain silent or careless' when he had been characterised as someone 'who turns people away from his own Church'. The Prince dismissively retorted that: 'Your Church is only known as a heresy to ours: all the circumstances of this particular case fully bore out our views of it [...] do you mean to pretend that your opinion is that of the Anglican Church?' When Palmer replied that he did, the Prince said that 'with your Bishops and Archbishop and all your own people against you', Palmer must 'have very different ideas of submission from what I have'. This was a shrewd point, identifying Palmer's reliance on Catholic principles when it suited him, but readiness to ignore authority when it did not; ironically, in much the same way as the Princess. The Prince quoted William Hare, the chaplain at Geneva, who, taxed with Palmer's interpretation of Anglican doctrine, 'asked contemptuously What authority there was *in your opinion*?' Palmer said that if the Prince was so convinced of the Protestantism of the English Church, let him or his wife 'carry out our controversy', and no doubt the Galitsins would be right. The Prince replied loftily 'Oh that is your affair; we have nothing to do with that'.[10]

Despite his fighting talk, Palmer's feelings were anything but confident. He wrote to his father:

> My prospect is anything but satisfactory – and I do not as yet see my way at all clearly before me [...] I wish myself back in England many many times every day – this indeed I am much in the habit of doing whenever I find myself at a distance – and especially at first – but I have never felt it more than I do now – which I take to proceed from the fact that I am occupied with a disagreeable business which has to do with, and depends in some measure upon other people.[11]

His father's response was worried: 'I really think the way you propose to act is like taking upon yourself more than is well becoming in a private person, and that is not likely to lead to any good result'.[12]

A week later Palmer wrote in similar terms to Dr. Routh:

> I am sorry to say that I have hitherto met with nothing agreeable but only with what is mortifying & painful with respect to my own business here & I shall either return now completely failed in my attempt to make good my own representations of the Character & principles of our Church – or else I shall have to defer my return for some time & pursue the controversy between myself & the Lady under very painful & difficult circumstances [...] I [...] propose that you should accept my resignation of the Tutorship & appoint some other Tutor [...]. [13]

On this occasion his resignation was not accepted.

Palmer now told the Prince that since he had 'such dispositions and views, as he had evinced, I feared we must thenceforth consider ourselves in some measure as antagonists'.[14] Assuring him that 'he could not desire my speedy departure from St. Petersburg more ardently than I desired it myself', Palmer laid down three conditions for his departure 'by the next steamer'. First, the Princess should 'give up her pretensions to be a member of the British or Anglican Communion'. She should acknowledge that she 'had no right or claim to the Communion of Bishop Luscombe, and was sorry for having unintentionally deceived him'. She must promise Palmer not to take communion again in the English Chapel at St. Petersburg without giving notice to the chaplain, and showing him whatever certificate she had obtained in England, or at least obtaining the chaplain's permission. This amounted to an abandonment of taking communion in the English Chapel; Palmer knew Mr. Law would prevent any such attempt. As for the certificate, Palmer may have been calling the Princess's bluff, suspecting that it was not the blanket permission to take communion she described.

The Galitsins declined to comply. Palmer told the Prince that he would consequently 'be obliged' to present Luscombe's Letters to the Metropolitan of St. Petersburg, or the Synod, and seek communion on the basis of 'a profession of faith drawn up against his wife's profession of heresy'. This might 'lead to results [...] disagreeable to them'. To the Prince it was tantamount to a denunciation of his wife; he 'tried to work upon my feelings of honour, charity, &c.: speaking of her weak state of health; and saying, that I ought not to persecute a woman'.[15] Palmer was unmoved. The Prince refused to exchange letters explaining and qualifying the acts of his wife and daughter: 'he could not know, or appear to know, any thing about his wife's illegal acts [...] of his daughter's reconciliation, that the business was none of his: that he was a soldier, not a divine'. Palmer pointed out that the reconciliation was public, and a matter of record. The Prince asked Palmer to alter Luscombe's Letters so as to be general, rather than particular. Luscombe had, by coincidence, recently given Palmer permission to make such alterations to the Letters as he saw fit.

Palmer duly left a copy of Luscombe's Letters Commendatory at the house of the Archpriest Koutnevich, asking whether their presentation to the Synod would involve any public scandal to the individuals involved. On 4 October Palmer received a reply which clearly showed that the Prince had been putting across his side of the story, and trying to spike Palmer's guns. The Synod 'knew very well what the Anglican Church was', and the Latin pamphlet Palmer had presented 'could do nothing whatever to make its character either better or worse'. Moral pressure was exerted, and this time it was Palmer who was threatened:

> after the confidence which the Prince had placed in me, it would neither be honourable nor Christian to divulge, or draw into public notoriety his family matters & private correspondence; that he had a regard for me, & gave mecredit for good intentions; & therefore should be sorry that by showing about that Latin Document, I should give people a bad opinion of me, and get myself perhaps shut out altogether from St. Petersburg, if not from Russia.[16]

Palmer wrote angrily to the Prince:

> I do not understand exactly what you have been about; and fear that you have been seeking to do harm rather than good both to your own interest and to mine. [...] it is exceedingly bad policy to pre-occupy the mind of [a] third person with your own view of the case [...] pray do not diplomatize with me, for that will do no sort of good; unless, indeed [...] you could manage to procure an order from the High Police to make me leave the country. This [...] would indeed be something positive: and it would be equally agreeable, so far as personal wishes and convenience are concerned, to both of us.[17]

He genuinely wished to be able to leave. Complaining of having 'had the Jerusalem Bishopric thrown in my teeth from all sides', he wrote to his Aunt Mary:

> How I wish I was back again, sitting and talking with you in your drawing room at Finmere! – but I have two tendencies in my mind one of which drives me away from home in spite of myself and the other makes me most earnestly long to be at home again, as soon as I find that I am actually separated by any considerable distance from it.[18]

When he met the Prince on 11 October, they 'parted apparently very good friends', the Prince even thanking him for the omissions and alterations he had made to the Letters.

A further message from the Archpriest confirmed what he had predicted to Dean Horsley: the Synod 'could not engage in communications with an individual Clerk, nor even with one Bishop: nothing short of a Synodal communication could be attended to'. Palmer should address himself to a particular bishop. He replied that the Synod effectively *was* a particular bishop, since it was in place of the Patriarch. Angered by the Archpriest's argument that the reconciliation service made no mention of the Anglican Church, he suggested that the Archpriest put in writing his opinion that the Prince's daughter had not been reconciled from the Anglican Church; no mention then need be made of it in his petition to the Synod. When Palmer met the Archpriest on 7/19 October, the question was largely resolved by the Prince's apparent happiness with Palmer's alterations, so that after discussion of the 'theological bearing' of Bishop Luscombe's Letters, they 'parted very amicably'.[19] The Archpriest told Palmer he had no doubt of his sincere acceptance of all the dogmas of the Greek Church, and rejection of all heresies; understood that he could not be reconciled from Lutheranism, etc., but 'they had no form to suit my case'. However the problem caused by the caution of the Scottish bishops remained:

> He said to me that it would not be safe to accept the Letters of one Bishop, however orthodox their contents, or the profession of one individual: other individuals & Bishops might write different Letters from the same Church, or claim Communion in virtue of their being of the same, by mere formal letters, while they held all manner of heresies.[20]

Count Pratasoff told him that if he made application to the Synod, 'it was a weighty matter, and they moved very slowly in Russia in such things: that they might very likely keep me a year at St. Petersburgh: I must make up my mind to that; and consider how I liked that prospect'.[21] Pratasoff could not receive anything from Palmer himself; the papers would have to be transmitted via the Ambassador, to the Foreign Office, and thence 'to the proper Department'. He would then pass them to the Synod, but 'all that cannot be done in a hurry'. The implication was obvious; Palmer should drop the matter, and go home. Rumours had begun to circulate among both the Russians and the expatriate community of St. Petersburg, that Palmer 'had come out to insult and persecute, on account of her religion, a Russian lady of rank; whose husband had turned me out of doors, and forbidden me the house'.[22] As Palmer had gone out of his way to be discreet, the rumours could only have come from the Galitsins themselves. Palmer later heard that the High Procurator had been forced to take Prince Galitsin aside and caution him, 'saying, "Your wife must be careful and hold her tongue: you know we may be forced to put her into a convent"'.[23] Whilst this could mean that Pratasoff merely suspected the Princess of spreading the rumours, something she vehemently denied in 1847, they certainly reflected the Princess's viewpoint: Palmer almost certainly thought her responsible.

After some debate, Mr. Law indicated his willingness to receive Palmer on the basis of Bishop Luscombe's Letters. This gave Palmer the lever he needed. He immediately required the Princess, as was consistent with his duty as deacon, to leave the English Chapel immediately after the sermon, and not to present herself for communion, 'inasmuch as you are a stranger; and have never been validly admitted to be a member of our Church'.[24] Although the Princess complied with the request, and did not come to the English Chapel again while Palmer was at St. Petersburg, she had by no means admitted defeat.

On 12/24 October, Palmer presented his petition to the Synod by way of the British Ambassador. He asked that the Russian Church cease to require that Anglicans seeking communion abjure Lutheranism and Calvinism *qua* heresies held by the Church of England. That anathema might be said, but as precursor to the acceptance of 'all the articles of faith, as held in the Eastern Church', and a promise of conformity in matters of discipline to the Russian or Eastern Church, while living in its dioceses. Alternatively, Palmer asked that the specific Lutheran or Calvinistic heresy that he was supposed to hold as an Anglican be objected to him; or finally, what prevented 'your giving credit to those Letters Commendatory, which I now present [...] from a Scottish Bishop'.[25] Palmer realised that

> the answer which I shall probably receive, if I receive any will be that the testimony of the Bishop is insufficient to prove the nature or *principles* of his Church – his Church being the Scottish and not the English Church.[26]

M. Mouravieff, no longer Unter-Prokuror,[27] agreed:

> he expected the Synod would not give me any answer or else one still more evasive than what I had received before that I came referring to Canons &c., but that things here and in Greece too are not really administered by the Canons, but Policy & Intrigue & custom & ignorance influence everything [...] that the Greek Patriarchs would be only puzzled – still more than the Synod &c.

Palmer's 'exertions were not likely to have any success', because

> they had here only a Political or National idea of religion, & connected their notions of the Protestant Bpric at Jerusalem & English Policy with the English Religion: that so they would suspect me in spite of all I could do or say of being in league with the same system.[28]

The strains upon him may account for a dream he had recorded in his diary, that:

> Roundell was amusing himself with fighting a lion in a room like the Dining Room – and I was both angry and horribly afraid for him, seeing that the sport was a serious battle and wondering that it had lasted at all – and feeling quite sure how it must end; – I went away at length out of fear for my own safety [...] & soon feeling ashamed for having left him.[29]

As with the dream about the Mujik, anxiety and guilt are the dominant themes; perhaps Roundell symbolised himself, engaged in 'a serious battle', and all too aware of 'how it must end'. He wrote again to Dr. Routh to resign his Tutorship, acknowledging the pressure on him to go:

> there are as you know a considerable number of members of the Society who wish that that place should be filled by some other than myself [. . .] the circumstances of my present absence together with the length of time that has elapsed since the expression of their wish – offer a good opportunity for the individual who has outraged their feelings to withdraw himself, without giving any triumph to those opinions upon which their feelings are based.[30]

The answer from the Synod came on 11/23 January 1843,[31] and was much as Palmer had anticipated. Palmer could not be admitted to Communion 'otherwise than by the Rite prescribed for converts from heterodoxy', since

> the British Church has never yet [. . .] expressed her purpose of restoring that union with our orthodox Catholic Church which she has lost, by disavowing all dogmas contrary to our orthodox Confession

and secondly,

> the present Letters of a single Bishop with the Petition of a single Deacon, as expressing no more than the opinions of individuals, are in nowise matter for Synodical deliberation.[32]

Pratasoff hastened to tell Palmer that 'the Bishops and Prelates' had spoken in the Synod 'with tears of emotion in their eyes [. . .] if there were only a few in Britain, nay if there were only twenty, who thought with the Bishop from whom I came, unity must sooner or later be restored'. The Synod would have gone further in the form of its Answer, but they were 'obliged to be very cautious'. Bishop Luscombe had not addressed the Synod directly, but even if he had, was 'unsupported by his brethren', and only implicitly agreed in Palmer's acknowledgement of the Russian Church as orthodox. They should persevere in their efforts for unity; 'God is manifestly drawing us all together'.[33]

To Pratasoff's dismay, Palmer responded that he would present another petition requesting a Confessor who could specify the heresy held by himself or his Church, enabling him, if appropriate, to abjure it and be reconciled. Pratasoff warned him that he: 'should have to begin all over again [...] and that would keep me another six months'. However, he agreed that the request was reasonable. Palmer reported to his father that while 'they seem [...] to be very full of good will, and hope for ultimate reunion',[34] he did not think that Pratasoff 'understands much' about his further petition, 'nor desires that anything more should be done in the matter'.[35] This was confirmed to him by way of 'friendly advice from one individual', which included a warning:

> [...] Count [Pratasoff] did not see his way very much in the matter [...] they were afraid or rather desirous of evading than forwarding it, that at the same time they thought well of me personally – and would by no means deal unhandsomely with me – but that I must be cautious how I left off having once began, as there was no telling but that their own fear or caution or backwardness might be put off upon me, if I gave them the opportunity.[36]

Palmer therefore faced the added difficulty that if he threw up the matter and returned home, as both those in St. Petersburg and his family at home wished him to do, any failure to resolve it would be blamed on him.

The Rector of the Academy felt it would be an important and desirable step to clarify the true character of the British Church, as the Synod wanted above all to provoke 'some Synodal act in Britain'. The Synod already recognised the British Church itself, and its orders of bishop and deacon, as the precedent had been set by the Eastern Patriarchs' correspondence in the time of Peter the Great. The Archpriest told Palmer that they would be 'most happy' to admit him to their Communion 'with affection, for my good feeling towards them; but only on condition I renounced the errors of my Church'.[37] These were contained in the XXXIX Articles, which were 'plainly Luthero-Calvinistic, and must necessarily be rejected [...] we cannot but understand the [...] Articles in their plain and natural sense'.[38] Mouravieff's response to Palmer's draft petition was forthright:

> He dissuaded me from presenting it saying it would detain me an indefinite time & it was of no use attempting to force a question which on the other side it was desired to evade: that I talked as if I was in the Fourth Century: [...] it was not at all a satisfactory answer [...] if the application was renewed or repeated they might easily set it aside and return to the old accusation of Lutheranism & Calvinism.[39]

The Archbishop of Volhynia,[40] who had presided in the Synod when Palmer's first petition came before it, was more positive. He 'had read what had been sent in to the Synod with the most lively joy [...] there was nothing in what I and the Bishop from whom I came had written, that offered any difficulty'. He hoped that the Scottish bishops in particular would 'Synodically express their desire of union; so that the Russian Synod may be able to treat with them directly'.[41]

Palmer presented his second petition to the English Ambassador on 10/22 February, and then wrote to Bishop Luscombe seeking his approval of guidelines drafted by Palmer for his appearance before any Confessor appointed by the Synod. Luscombe returned the guidelines in Latin, transformed into formal Instructions; he thought Palmer had 'a just cause to ascertain why' he had been refused communion, but feared that his claim would 'not be regarded'. He had also begun to feel the futility of one bishop and one deacon attempting to force reunion between churches: 'I fear that I and you are not of sufficient weight and importance for this object [...] I hope that you will not again call on me individually; but, if occasion shall require, I hope you will apply to the Episcopal College in Scotland'.[42] Palmer reassured Luscombe that no further act or declaration could be called for from him individually, and that they had both done their duty by the Church. Remarkably, Palmer was quite confident that both he and the bishop had 'been acting strictly, and clearly, within the sphere of our personal duty':

> for me, [...] who was neither Priest nor Bishop, any attempt to busy myself with the general interests of the Church would have been as presumptuous, as it would have been impracticable and absurd.[43]

His father and brother were not the only ones to think that this was precisely the case.

Palmer then turned to 'a circumstance [...] which has given me considerable annoyance'. A month earlier, Palmer had met 'an acquaintance Mr. R.,'[44] who had accosted Palmer 'open-mouthed', asking him if he knew 'what an ill turn' Bishop Luscombe had done him, by publishing a volume of sermons 'attacking everything that is Orthodox. And have you seen the refutation? It is so triumphant! I suppose it is still to be had in the shops here'.[45] The shops, however, had sold out, and the results could not have been worse for Palmer.

His Russian friends later told him that this was

> the only thing against him: up to this point all had been going on very well: that nothing could be more favourable than the impression which the Letters and Petition had made upon their Synod; and that a very friendly expectation had been excited as to the possible result of the second Petition: but now people were perplexed, and knew not what to think of me or of the Bishop.[46]

The Galitsins were to blame. The Bishop had given the Princess a volume of his sermons to study; the Prince had found 'a Popish refutation' of the sermons in a French bookshop, and had taken both volumes to their confessor, none other than the Archpriest Koutnevich, 'upon whose mind they produced the most unfavourable impression'.[47] This effectively put them before the Synod. Friends of the Galitsins had bought up the only copies available. Palmer dismissed the misunderstandings caused by the book as 'merely technical and verbal differences', but without a copy he had no idea of precisely what it said, and was powerless to defend himself or Bishop Luscombe. He was now paying the price for his success in excluding the Princess from communion at the English Chapel.

Days before, Palmer's father, unaware of Palmer's self-created status as Bishop Luscombe's clerk, had:

> ventured to put your name down as a candidate for Priest's Orders on Trinity Sunday. I could see no reason for putting it off longer and could have no doubt you contemplated priest's orders at some time or other [...].

Although he knew 'so little of the nature of your communications with the Russian Synod as to be unable to form a judgement of the results', he was neither approving nor optimistic: 'I know you are a private unaccredited person – and that whatever you do will be scanned with no favourable eye by many. I trust you will be discreet at all times [...].'[48] Dr. Routh, who regarded Palmer 'with something of the same feeling that I do myself', also regretted 'the sacrifice you appear to be making of your own fortunes, and of some place or station for which he thinks you may be fitted, and which might enable you to act with more effect'.[49] Palmer replied that his father had been 'too precipitate'.[50] He 'neither did contemplate, nor do contemplate, seeking Priest's Orders without some sufficient reason',[51] and 'wished he had explained more fully [...] my present connection with Bishop Luscombe'. To attempt any act involving formal communion with an English bishop now would involve 'the necessity of throwing up the whole affair', which depended on his letters from Luscombe. He affected not to understand what his father meant by 'sacrificing my "fortunes"', etc., adding that he felt it was essential to have found the truth before attempting to teach it to anyone else, as for example a deacon to a layman and so on.

> If a man feels that the Faith and Church, of which a layman ought to have full assurance, is a matter of great doubt and strife and contention, he certainly will not seek [...] to influence others, till he is quite sure himself, of his own standing and action being right and legitimate.[52]

Nor would he take on additional responsibility 'without a very clear call to do so'. Far from feeling such a call,

> my thoughts [...] make me wish to be a layman in the Church of England rather than a deacon, a woman rather than a man, a child rather than a woman: and, in like manner, not only not to

> seek other fortunes or places or stations in order to act with more effect, but rather to be poorer and lower in worldly rank and station [...].[53]

He remarked to his Aunt Mary on the same day that the expressions his father used such as 'more effect' and 'private fortunes' seemed to him to 'have reference to that sort of life which is according to the spirit of society as it exists', adding 'If I had been told when I left England last Autumn how long I should be detained in Russia I should have gone with a very heavy heart indeed [...].'[54]

His father's reply began resignedly: 'I was by no means confident that you would view it in the light I wished', before becoming heavily ironical:

> I am sorry that you do not understand my meaning, when I say you seem to make a sacrifice of your private fortunes [...] however, I must not complain of your not understanding me, because it is owing perhaps to the fact that I do not understand you. [...] what your relations may be to Bishop Luscombe, and through him to the Scottish Church, superseding those which may lie for the present dormant with our own, I cannot divine. Being where you are, your relations with the Bishop of Oxford may be for a time suspended; but the moment you return, especially as my deacon to Mixbury, no one can doubt that you will be subject to him [...].[55]

He also expressed alarm at the mention of 'Faith' and 'Church' being matters of 'doubt', and 'strife', and 'contention'.

Palmer thanked his father politely for 'taking care, so far as you could, that it should be in my power, if I returned, to do that which seemed to you fit for me to do'. As to Orders, Palmer 'was ready to seek them as soon as I should receive an official and authoritative notice to do so'. As for sacrificing his private fortunes, unless it was by his daily faults, he could not see how he was doing so, 'nor do I know any other private fortune which is to be desired, than the opportunity of doing the work of one's present station and circumstances, and grace to enable one to do it'. This made the large assumption that what he was about in Russia was rightly the work of his present station and circumstances, as against the normal duties of an Anglican deacon, or an academic. 'What may appear to me [...] to be properly and naturally my duty under circumstances, may not appear to be so to others or even to you. All I can say with respect to this is, I am sorry for it' – scarcely an adequate justification. He expressed his readiness to give up his own judgement in favour of his father's, or Dr. Routh's, 'in anything in which you or he can rightly claim the power [...] but, so long as you and he only give counsel, or express wishes, I must necessarily judge as well as I can of the justness of my own principles and views, and the degree in which I can or cannot, rightly conform to yours'.[56]

> You regard perhaps what I am about as useless or improper or at least think that I have gone out of my way to seek it for myself and that I ought to throw it up at once [...] I am not at all disposed, to defend my own judgement against yours –[57]

He knew that his relatives thought of him 'as a member of the Established Church of England, going from that Church, as 'an unauthorised individual', to busy myself about you do not clearly see what in other countries or Churches', who ought to come home to carry on as his father's deacon; but

> I suppose myself on the other hand, not to come from the Church of England at all; but yet to come from a Bishop, with whom I had a strictly canonical relation, and having also all the authorization which the canons of the Church require, and that I myself could in the first instance even wish to have.[58]

– not to be wondered at, when the relations had been brought about and arranged entirely by himself.

Roundell Palmer, who entirely concurred in his father's views, gave vent to the misgiving he had had all along

> as to the propriety of an individual, so situated as he is, acting as he has done in a matter which [...] is of public, not private, concernment. I fear, both in this matter and in that of the 'anathema,' he has taken upon himself without warrant to speak for his Church; and, when led to doubt how far his Church would adopt his statements, began to distrust his Church instead of himself.

He put his finger on the fallacy at the heart of his brother's arguments:

> That he should talk about relations established between himself and Bishop Luscombe as if they were not a mere creation of his own, – much more, as if they could supersede or modify his previous relations to the whole English Church, – does certainly look like a very painful delusion.[59]

He was at least as frank with Palmer himself, as Palmer's self- consciously humble reply to his letter shows:

> I thank you for the earnestness of your remonstrances. The things which you blame, and the appearances of which in me give you uneasiness, are all very bad; namely, "inventing new and fictitious relations[60] for ourselves, and then claiming a right to supersede and throw aside, for their sake, those under which God's Providence has placed us"; and, "running into the very excesses of private judgement," [...] "placing scandals in the way of others", etc. etc.[61]

Palmer claimed that 'nothing could please me better' than to live with their father 'and serve him in his parish, so far as he could or would order me, whether as deacon or priest', although his careful qualification effectively left him free to ignore any such 'order'. 'As a member of Magdalen College', he desired 'nothing better than to have my work and duty pointed out to me by my superior; and I am ready to do it, whatever it may be'. This was a difficult assertion to sustain, when he had only recently resigned those duties to which the College *had* appointed him, because they conflicted with his self-imposed mission. He was after all a member of an Oxford college, not a private soldier, and his performance of his college duties depended at least as much on his willingness to do them, as on direct orders from Dr. Routh. After an involved exposition of the difficulties created by his becoming Bishop Luscombe's clerk, he ended: 'I fear I shall have only puzzled you still more, by entering into a subject on which we do not understand one another's views'.[62]

On 12/24 May, Palmer heard from Pratasoff that the priest appointed to examine him was the Archpriest Koutnevich, confessor to the Galitsins. Pratasoff had also seen Bishop Luscombe's sermons, which had made such a bad impression on Koutnevich. Although some pages seemed to him to be heretical, he charitably remarked that 'the Bishop might have changed his mind since'. Palmer bluntly contradicted this, but said that it was mere language, which left room for agreement 'in the basis of the true faith underneath it'. To Pratasoff's question, 'How many of the Bishops are orthodox?' he was equally frank: 'Probably not one single Bishop of our Church would seem to be exactly orthodox'. The Count was shocked: 'that surely must be going too far'. Palmer agreed that perhaps they were not deliberately heretical, but orthodox 'in intention and submission to the Church'; but 'from the body at large [...] nothing can be looked for for a long time, say for fifty or sixty years to come, or even more'.[63]

Palmer had an informal interview with the Archpriest on 14/26 May. It was clear that his credit had been badly damaged by the sermons and the refutation. The Archpriest began by telling Palmer that when officially appointed, he would object to him 'the heresies of which the Eastern Church accuses the British; than which (taking up from his table the volume of Bishop Luscombe's Sermons, and the Romish Refutation of Them) "nothing can be easier"'. The Archpriest later told the chaplain at Cronstadt that the books had 'fallen [...] out of the clouds into his hands, just at the right moment, before he wanted them'; otherwise, going only on the papers Palmer had put before the Synod, 'he should have been rather at a loss how to accuse me as a heretic'.[64] Beginning in the manner of a cross-examining barrister, Koutnevich opened the *Sermons*, and asked Palmer if he knew his own bishop's signature and handwriting. When after some attempted explanation Palmer asked the Archpriest what he thought the motives had been for the books being given to him, 'and so virtually to the Synod', Koutnevich first laughed, but then said more seriously, "I do not wish to say anything harsh, or painful to you, nor to think of you as if you had been trying to impose upon us; but really when I consider the divergence, not to say contrareity, which there is between those documents which you have sent in to the Synod and these 'Sermons' of your own Bishop, and the XXXIX Articles of his Church, I do not know what to think of you, or of that Bishop".[65]

All he would have to do was to copy out passages from the 39 Articles and the *Sermons*, and ask Palmer to reject and anathematise them. Palmer pointed out that the Bishop's later *Letters* had as much force as the earlier sermons, and might even be taken as a explanation or retraction of them; the Articles Palmer took in a very different sense. Koutnevich however had lost patience with Palmer's attempts to make black equal white:

it is not, as you say, a question of *interpretation*. We must not trifle or quibble dishonestly in matters of faith: and after that fashion, by interpreting and explaining away, the most blasphemous book might be made into a book of devotion.[66]

Palmer nonetheless handed over to the Archpriest some Dissertations written by himself for Mouravieff and translated into Latin, which set out Palmer's view of the true sense of the 39 Articles, in which they might be received by the Easterns. These Koutnevich very reluctantly promised to read. Palmer now stated that if the Synod of the Scottish Episcopal Church disallowed the interpretation which he put on the 39 Articles, then he was 'ready to renounce the Articles, and them, and their Church' at the Archpriest's bidding.

A series of interviews followed, summarised by Palmer in a Report to Bishop Luscombe of 9 June. It was made clear from the start that the discussions would be on the terms laid down by the Synod, and not by Palmer. Koutnevich's instructions were solely 'to declare [...] all that is necessary to [...] being admitted to the Communion of our Church'. This relegated Palmer to the standing of a catechumen or enquirer like any other. The Archpriest confirmed that

he had received no order either to answer, as in the name of the Synod, any questions from me respecting our loss of union, or to examine my conscience, after the manner of a Confessor, on the Faith which I might hold [...] only to declare to me, all that was necessary, if I pleased to go over to the Communion of the Russian Church on the usual terms.[67]

Palmer 'observed, that while I had asked for one thing, the Synod had [...] answered by granting me another', and objected that he had to be convinced of the reality of a separation before he could seek reconciliation. Koutnevich replied 'of his own common sense, and speaking of a matter generally notorious', that the British Church had lost communion at the same time as the Roman and other Western

Churches, at the time of the Patriarch Photius. 'My attempting to reopen a doubt of the legitimacy of the separation when both sides Latin Roman & Greek agreed in assuming it was captious & argued some insincerity'.[68] The original Photian anathema had been reiterated in subsequent Synods, and was finally confirmed by Michael Cerularius. The union was lost 'most deservedly, on account of real and damnable heresies', chief of which was the *filioque*.[69] Palmer relied as before on those 'Orthodox Latin Fathers' who had used this expression without condemnation from the East, and, after giving his interpretation of the *filioque* clause, expressed his willingness to listen to whatever the Synod wished to state.

The Declaration that followed clearly drew on previous experience of dealing with Palmer. He must

> honestly and simply admit this principle, that the Eastern is the Oecumenical Church; and then not question curiously or captiously, or rather deceitfully, at what point of time, or by what Synodal act, or by the Synodical admission of what heresy, the British Church has lost her original union with the Eastern [...] for that this is not the way to begin: nor do such cunning questionings merit attention or favour, but rather anger or indignation [...] Nor, again, was I to make too careful or curious distinctions as to the importance of particular differences; nor to question whether some things may not be secondary [...].[70]

Koutnevich was equally determined to have no endless qualification of the meaning of the 39 Articles. 'He had read my Treatises & knew that I interpreted them differently – but [...] they needed no interpretation [...] my statements did not come out naturally from the Articles themselves'.[71] He warned Palmer that to be admitted to the Communion of the Russian Church, he must

> acknowledge those Articles to be a full and perfect Confession of the Faith both of the Scottish and of the Anglican Churches, a Confession not to be interpreted, filled up, or corrected by any other Documents, Homilies, Liturgies, or writings of Divines, but to understood and taken in the plain literal sense and spirit.[72]

He then enumerated a series of 'false and heretical propositions, [...] expressly contained in the XXXIX Articles', that Palmer must confess to be so contained, and renounce and anathematise them, together with the Articles themselves, and the British Church. Palmer countered by distinguishing 44 'real heresies [...] which destroyed the integrity of the Catholic Faith', but which could not in his view be imputed to the British Church. He said anathema to these propositions in his own name and that of Bishop Luscombe, but declined to say anathema also to the 39 Articles and the Church which maintained them as her Confession of Faith, on the basis that they were not a full Confession of Faith, having been framed 'not as a general exposition of truth, but only with a view to certain specific controversies'.[73]

He must appeal to the Bishop from whom he had come, and the Synod of Scottish bishops who had consecrated him, to see if they agreed with the sense in which he understood the 39 Articles, or allowed the heresies to which he had said anathema. If they did the latter, or 'attempted by an evasive silence to yoke faith and heresy together', he 'would return to Russia, and seek to be reconciled by the prescribed Form from the Scottish Church, as from heresy'.[74] He was later to regret this, his second rash pledge in Russia.

The flummoxed Archpriest asked Palmer what report he should make to the Synod. Palmer reverted to the need to know 'some reasonable proof' that the British and Roman Churches had lost their original union with the Eastern 'by some real and apostatical heresy'. The Archpriest, 'somewhat provoked,' told Palmer 'with some air of asperity' that he had already identified the *filioque* clause as the reason for the loss of union. The Archpriest was 'quite angry that I insisted at beginning from the beginning [...] the Synod he said will [...] only be angry as I am at such captious and subtle questions which only show insincerity: the Roman Church and all the world admit the separation – why should you doubt it?'[75] Fortunately their parting on 5 June was amicable. Palmer assured the Archpriest that he 'had no intention of dealing deceitfully, nor of trifling with the Synod in the matter' and Koutnevich in turn apologised 'for any asperity of manner he might have used in taxing me or Bishop Luscombe with dishonesty'.[76] However, the impression caused by the sermons was clearly ineradicable: 'he would *try* to think well of me; though he did not see, in the face of such clear evidence of heresy, how any good could result from my appealing to Bishop Luscombe, and to the Synod of his brethren in Scotland'.[77]

There was nothing more that Palmer could do in Russia, particularly as he was suddenly afflicted by 'a weakness of the eyes', perhaps psychosomatic, which left him 'unable to write or read more than a few lines together'.[78] He therefore left St. Petersburg on 4/16 June, returning home by way of Sweden.

Six years later, in June of 1849, the young James Barmby[79] travelled to St. Petersburg armed with introductions from Palmer to 'several Russian families, & really their kindness & hospitality is amazing'. He wrote to a friend about the impression Palmer had made there. Those to whom Barmby had introductions 'speak of [him] in the most affectionate terms'; but 'Among the English with only two exceptions, one of whom is of course Dr. L[aw], he is mentioned as "a fool", "a Madman", "an extraordinary fellow" "a strange enthusiast", "an ass" "a Papist" etc. etc.'. Not that the expatriate English knew much about church matters: they were

> generally in Church notions where England was 50 years ago; besides they are all commercial parties, and cognizant of few ideas beyond their counting houses; – also singularly ignorant

of the Russians, & of their religion, which they generally regard as a cross between Popery & heathenism. Well: fancy the effect likely to be produced by turning old P – *in his cassock* – loose among those gentry; his head crammed full of the Greek Church; & without the least tact or discretion spouting [?] his startling notions right & left [...] going to Russian Churches, bowing & crossing himself, & kissing pictures as well as Priests: you may conceive that the effect of all this would be what it was: that they neither understood what he meant, nor sympathised with him in any thing; were set against him ab initio, and in fact never came to know the least of his character at all. I stick up for him everywhere, to the surprize of people, who begin to suspect me of insanity in consequence.[80]

Nonetheless Barmby thought that Palmer had 'done good work among them [...] in making the position of the Anglican Church known to them, as different from that of mere Lutherans'.[81] His first impressions of Russian services were as mixed as Palmer's had been:

The music in the Churches is *delicious*; but the solemnity of the Service not half what I expected: the *reader* [...] generally a snob[82] in his own dirty plain clothes [...] does nearly all the psalms, Lessons & Prayers in a most abominably irreverent way, as fast as he can go, & strangely troubled with fits of spitting.[83]

8 Struggle for a Soul

Back in England, Palmer managed to overcome his illness sufficiently to edit *The Doctrine of the Russian Church* with his friend Mr. Blackmore, who had come over to England from Russia. 'This volume was [...] published at Xmas 1844'.[1] Palmer also occupied himself 'in preparing an Appendix to the same under the title of *A Harmony of Anglican & Eastern Doctrine*', which was not published until June 1846. He was, however, scrupulous in avoiding any clerical duties in the diocese of Oxford that would have been inconsistent with his association with Bishop Luscombe.[2]

In early 1844 he noted from newspaper stories in French and German newspapers that the Princess had left Russia, and was living, now in Berlin, now in Switzerland, and now in Paris; describing herself as having 'suffered much for having embraced Protestantism, but [...] *firm in her faith*'.[3] Her gypsy life was explained when Palmer 'learned from Private Letters that she had had a purse of 8000 ? Roubles a year made up by her relatives to enable her to travel again, as she & her husband were tired of each other'.[4] Perhaps the bond created by a common opposition to Palmer had broken down in his absence.

Palmer's eye problems meant that it was not until March 1844 that he travelled to Paris and delivered his Report to Bishop Luscombe, and was authorised to appeal to the Synod of the Scottish bishops on the 44 propositions he had anathematised, as well as 48 additional disciplinary propositions added by the Bishop. His preparation for this, which included re-writing his Latin Disssertations, was again delayed by his bad eyesight, so that by the spring of 1846 'certain of the Authorities at St. Petersburg were enquiring "whether anything had yet been done in Scotland?"'[5]

By 1846 he had 'come to give up the Latin language & theology on the point of the Procession in consequence of reading carefully Zoernikav's Treatise',[6] and was therefore in full doctrinal agreement with the Eastern Church. Despite this, and his pledge to Koutnevich, his correspondence at this time showed an increasing drift towards Roman Catholicism. Newman had been received as a Roman Catholic in October 1845; Lord Selborne thought that his brother was 'profoundly affected by the secession [...] of Mr. Newman, and the friends who accompanied or followed him'. [7] Previously, Palmer had been ready to discuss with his father the claims of Roman authority in hypothesis, and without heat; he now became more belligerent in advocating the claims of Rome, and dismissing the pretensions of Anglicanism: 'I can safely follow the interpretation of the Church of the 4th Century [...] but I cannot safely follow the rebellion of the 16th Century'.[8] His refusal to listen to the arguments or the emotional appeals of his father put their relationship under an increasing strain.

For it was not, for Palmer, ultimately a matter of 'setting up one private opinion against another', but 'what seems to me[9] a paramount and anterior authority', against which

> not even a whole National Church, nor a particular synod nor bishops, – much less any individual king or reformer, or individual thinker, whether older in age, or father by relation, – can rightfully maintain their particular view of religious truth [...].[10]

Palmer had had 'the knowledge and recognition of an outward authority [...] forced upon my own unwilling, reluctant, and prejudiced mind'.[11] Although his father 'in things really belonging to private opinion stands to me, I may say it, in the place of God [...] he cannot be right, in any matter [...] to think contrary to the Catholic Church'. William Palmer senior wrote on the letter that the question was 'the true and correct notion of that authority, its nature and extent; [...] It is not enough to say, I have gradually arrived at such and such conclusions, and that very unwillingly, and contrary to the notions in which I was brought up'.[12]

When in January 1846 Palmer mentioned in conversation 'a consciousness of uncertainty as to the issue in his own case', his father relied on 'the first and last clauses of the famous Bull of Pius V against Elizabeth I'[13] as exemplifying the errors of the Roman Church – 'No one can desire to be united to her *as she is* without great danger and imputation of blame'. He entreated Palmer to 'be on his guard', and

> abstain from recommending, by any overt act, a kind of devotion unknown to the Primitive Church, in particular [...] in respect of them for whom I shall one day have to answer. I allude to Mary's asking me, whether she might accept a crucifix, and Dorothea and Emily your book of poems. The "overt acts" I had in mind were of this kind.[14]

He decried the ways 'simple-hearted souls' were led off to Rome: 'either commending her practice, and thence deducing her authority, or insisting on her authority, and thereby silencing all objection to her practice'. He might be 'poor and weak and blind and prejudiced', but believed 'from my soul that God has given me the means of Grace in the Church of my baptism; and that, if I use them faithfully, I shall be saved, and you with me'. He prayed God to 'protect and defend you from the evil'.[15] He pleaded with Palmer not to commit himself in any way before 'hearing and considering everything I may have to say on every point relating to it '[...] endeavouring to divest yourself of all prejudice; for [...] you are no more free from it than others'.[16]

Palmer's reply, 'the only occasion in which he gave way to irritation',[17] pointed out that it was his father who had

> desired my sisters to speak to you whenever I put anything into their hands, which they might suppose you would dislike [...] and therefore I told them when they asked me for copies of my printed verses, that there were things in them that you would probably dislike, so they had better speak to you of it – the same of the Cross or Crucifix which I gave Emma.[18]

He could no longer hide his feeling that

> Our heads are turned then two directly contrary ways: I am very sorry for it, but I cannot help it. I respect your conscientious conviction that you ought to do all you can to keep all your children steadfast in that tradition or opinion in which you find yourself; – but my own conviction being against this, and in favour of the older traditions and superior authority, I shall necessarily be bound to do all I can to recommend obedience and conformity to authority and truth (as I now view it) rather than to rebellion and error.[19]

This expression of a reluctant necessity to act on his convictions hardened into something like a declaration of war in what followed:

> [...] whenever and wherever I have the unhappiness to find that you are firmly bent on following yourself and recommending others to follow either your own sense or that of a particular and inferior authority against the general and superior authority of the Church in matters of religion [...] your opinion or feeling is to me simply as though it were not [...].[20]

He was not to be dissuaded that St. Basil was wrong to address the Saints, nor St. John Damascene to defend Icons; nor would he conceal his belief that 'the doctrine of the Church is the truth, and the contrary doctrine, though you maintain it, is an error and a rebellion to be avoided by piety'.[21]

His father declined to defend himself 'from the imputation of setting up my own opinion against the great saints and Fathers of the Church', relying instead on the 'best authorities', SS. Peter, Paul, James, John and Jude. He professed his ignorance that 'the invocation of Saints and the use of pictures and images [...] were ever [...] accounted necessary and essential parts of Christian faith and practice', or that 'they are so accounted either in the Greek or Latin Churches to this day. If I ought to know this, shew me where I am to learn it'.

> the object of my fear and dread in the movement towards Rome [...] in which the conduct of persons eminent for their learning and piety, who have already gone over, suggests the idea that it is possible for the *best Christians* and *most learned men*, in any period, (not gifted as were the Apostles), not always to have seen to what their studies, will and opinions really tended, and of what *development* they were capable.[22]

He '*required*' an opinion from his son on his 'critical test of the Papal pretensions',[23]

> the Pope's assertion that he hath been constituted by our Lord "super omnes gentes et omnia regia Principem" etc.; and of his assuming on *our Lord's authority* to depose a reigning sovereign from her throne, to absolve her People from their oaths and allegiance and excite them to rebel against her power.[24]

As to what Palmer had said of their relations, 'upon reflection you might want to qualify it a little, and not speak so confidently on those points on which you think we differ'. If their heads were really turned two different ways, 'are our hearts also?' Were they

> so opposed [...] that all common attentions must be thrown aside as useless? I cannot believe that we are so opposed, that you are justified in separating yourself from me. I request further of you to consider and answer the question, *how far* sons and daughters are '*sui juris*', in matters of religion, in their father's house?[25]

Palmer's response on the necessity of Icons and addresses to saints was magisterially evasive:

> those Churches (Greek and Latin) expressly teach, that these things are not essential in themselves. But the duty of obedience to the Church is not bounded by that which is in itself necessary for the Individual to believe or do, but extends to all lesser things which have more or less direct relation to the same.

How direct or otherwise this relation might be Palmer did not say. Of their heads being turned two different ways he remarked: 'Your kindness and affection for me makes [sic] you feel pain at the expression. But I think nothing is to be gained by blinking what is true'. He elaborated on his meaning:

> [...] you have made me feel, on the whole, that the whole energy of my life and the employment of all my faculties has been deliberately directed for the last thirteen years (and

> is still so directed) upon an end which, the more I advance towards it, the more it shows itself reprehensible to your feelings and opinions. I feel that there must be some cause for this [...].[26]

Everybody – 'the worst and most Protestant [...] the very best [...] in my own Church [...] the Roman Catholics themselves' – joined in telling him that he deceived himself in thinking that 'a certain kind of pursuit after truth was consistent with my position, or that the Church of England could consist with those principles which I assumed as true'. This testimony, together with that of others,

> hitherto [...] in the same path as myself, and who have come to allow that their ground was untenable; – and feeling, moreover, that I have actually myself in many things come nearer to Rome, and got rid of feelings and opinions against her; – I cannot help contemplating, intellectually at least, the possibility of a further change [...] Either I ought to find some means to conform myself to the sense and wishes and opinions of the Anglican Church and its heads [...] or I ought to see that my place, whatever it is, is not by rights in their Church [...] such a person as I ought to be naturally and sensibly in and under the Church, whatever the Church is, not over it.[27]
>
> Even if I might once think that there were signs of a revival or improvement such as agreed with my own opinions, yet even then the very leaders of that movement [...] were equally in my own illegitimate position, and have now felt that they were so, and yielded to circumstances.[28]

Conforming himself to the Anglican Church seemed to him '*impossible*'; he left open only the slimmest of possibilities that he might 'in due time find the way' to give up the conviction that he was doing his duty as a member of the Church of England in 'following out those indiscreet, prejudiced, imaginative, unpractical, questionable, or Romanising studies', as they seemed to all who did not follow them. But to do so seemed to Palmer 'extremely disagreeable and shocking, and what I am as yet by no means prepared for'.[29] Determined to show how far apart he and his father now were, he cast back in his father's teeth epithets that had perhaps been angrily flung at him:

> I would take any trouble to progress, even in the least degree, in the knowledge of the sense and doctrine and law of the Church. I would willingly walk over Europe to get the smallest particle of that knowledge, which would only move your mistrust or aversion – would make you think me, more and more, a 'self- willed and wrong-headed young man', or (at best) 'a good lawyer spoiled' [...] Is this to be united in heart?[30]

The response to his father's 'interrogatory about the Pope', was an ominously qualified one:

> my present opinion is sufficiently strong, not only against his temporal pretensions, as represented by the Jesuits and the Ultramontane party. At the same time [...] I feel my opinion

has become more favourable to the Papal Supremacy, and less favourable to the pretended rights of the so-called National Churches [...] than it was in 1834.[31]

A heartfelt cry followed:

I most heartily wish, that I could reasonably and with a good conscience submit to Rome, or to any other authority which should relieve me from the pain and difficulty which I now experience in having to ask for truth by my own study, and that with an increasing sense that the results of my studies make it more and more hopeless to look for any such authority to govern me where I am.[32] [...] the cases in which you talk of your opinion and mine, are really cases of Church Authority – and in such wherever I am convinced that the Church has spoken [...] I have no intention to pay your opinion, no, nor the opinion of a whole English Convocation or Parliament, the slightest respect whatever.[33]

It was a declaration of which any Elizabethan martyr would have been proud, but Palmer's father ignored the rhetoric, and fixed on the fundamental question, the 'end' towards which Palmer's life had been directed for so long:

Can you at length tell me, at the end of those thirteen years, what that end hath been, what it now is? Have you yourself known? Did Mr. Faber know? Did Mr. Newman? Have they not both been taken in the meshes of their own net? Are you not yourself now like a poor bird, ever and anon fluttering about the jaws of a hydra till she drop into them?[34]

He recalled how his loyalty to his son had turned to dismay:

I always took a most earnest and affectionate interest in your pursuits and objects. I lent myself to them, when I did not always clearly apprehend them. I defended you, I took your part, I assisted you by all the means in my power [...] On one occasion, when I asked the Bishop for a document [...] the Bishop, in granting it, somewhat prophetically asked, "*cui bono*?" And, somehow or other, from that day to this, you have been separated from us. Could that be the fulfilment?

I went on confidently till I began to feel you had taken on more than you had authority to do, and till I heard from your own lips that the pusuit, whatever it might be, in which you were engaged, was leading you to desire a reconciliation with the Church of Rome on her terms, or on any terms, without being aware of what (as it appeared to me) made any such desire very sinful and dangerous.[35]

He was resigned to the fact that his son would not step into his shoes at Mixbury and Finmere; but what he had never expected was to find himself

contending, as it were, for life and death, on a point the success of which involves our separation before the time, and whether you are to look upon me as a heathen man and a publican, or whether we are to walk in the house of God as friends.[36]

Before these questions were answered, he wrote again in more sympathetic and persuasive vein:

> I see the difficulty, not to say distress of your present circumstances and situation; and I see nothing satisfactory before you – no profession – no calling [...] visit Egypt – Syria – Arabia – Mesopotamia – Asia. Learn the state of the Christians in all these – their civil, moral and religious state; and let us profit by what you learn. This is a branch of theology you have not yet studied, to which I look with intense interest.[37]

This was sound psychology, but ahead of its time; only in the last twenty-four years of his life would Palmer travel regularly to Egypt, albeit as an amateur archaeologist. For now Palmer had

> something to do here, which has come to me of itself in which I am actually engaged [. . .] you may be assured that I shall be delighted [...] to travel in the East, whenever, and as soon as ever, I can find or make any opportunity of doing so, without deserting work, which I like much less, but which is already in hand.[38]

Besides, he was physically unable to work: 'I cannot make my own eyes to be strong or weak'. Writing the previous day to answer his father's query about the end toward which he had been advancing, he maintained that he could:

> very easily tell you what *end* I have always proposed to myself ; viz. to learn accurately the truth of that religion which the Church of England had professed to deliver to me, and [. . .] whatever errors or imperfections might attach either to my own personal or generally to the Anglican, belief or practice.[39]

This seems a disingenuously broad aim, in that its achievement hardly required two forays into Russia, still less the pursuit of Princess Galitsin. So far as his possible conversion to Roman Catholicism was concerned:

> Far from having your horror of the hydra, I feel that it would be the happiest day of my life that should enable me, with a full conviction and a clear conscience, to cast myself at the feet of so great an authority as the Roman Church, against which I now find myself at war [. . .] most gladly would I, if I could, submit to the Roman obedience, even if it cost me all that is most dear to me on earth.[40]

To his father, Roman authority was 'indeed vast, *immense*, awful; awful, if it be well founded, awful, if it have no just foundation at all'. He worried to Roundell that Palmer's 'state of mind and feelings' were much the same as Newman's and Ward's had been, and although neither of them was satisfied with everything the Roman Church holds, nor is William, yet they are gone; and when I hear him say he wishes he could be reconciled, and that he is sensible of progressing in opinion in the same direction, that, surely, is enough to alarm one who does not wish it.[41]

Equally disturbing was his professional position:

I see him in the maturity of strength and age without a profession and without the opportunity of adopting one. I see him also without means, excepting only an enhancement of his fellowship, which if he goes on he will soon be incapable of retaining. I see no way of extricating him from the atmosphere in which he lives,[42] and introducing him to something, if not new, yet different, which may possibly break the spell by which he seems to be surrounded.[43]

He recounted how Palmer had, with massive but unconscious irony, accused him of 'tilting at windmills' in opposing

Romish views, rites, and doctrines. [...] he rather quickly withdrew the allusion, when he saw that I was ready to retort it upon himself. But, seriously speaking, I do really apprehend that, like the knight of La Mancha, he has been absorbed too much with one idea, and that almost detached [...] from the realities of life, and (in a manner) not quite consistent with his age and station.[44]

Both parties still strove to be conciliatory. Palmer described the differences between them 'as only straws on the surface', not regarding 'first principles *in themselves*, but [...] the channels through which we are to seek and receive truth.'[45] Nonetheless, for him that channel was increasingly

an Ecclesiastical Unity and Authority, above and beyond that of the Anglican Established Church [...] I totally and confidently refuse to obey her, so soon and so far as I perceive her to commend or counsel anything contrary to the law of the *whole*. I was not baptised into "Anglicanism," nor did I promise to believe in "The Anglican Church", but in "The Church", of which the Anglican must be a homogeneous member, if she would be a member at all.[46]

Palmer wrote to a M. de Mestral[47] in July of 'the impossibility of explaining the phenomenon of the Anglican Church, unless you allow that her Reformation (or Deformation) was only superficial and that she has preserved underneath it the contrary principle of Catholicism'. To him it had become a matter of simple logic:

notwithstanding the peculiarities of the Anglican Church, the prima facie presumption is decidedly against her, if we allow that the Reformation generally was essentially heretical and the first impulse of a generous mind would naturally be to return to that authority and to that state of things against which we [...] unjustifiably rebelled.[48]

The choice on the Continent was starker: 'the Roman Communion on the one hand and simple sectarianism on the other'. Into the scales had to be put the example of 'the most eminent and religious men among the so-called Puseyites in England', who had come to find 'that their position was untenable'. Logically, 'to be a member of the Church of England is a self-committed absurdity'.[49] His misgivings about the intellectual convictions that forestalled his submission to Catholicism were amply borne out by the qualified nature of his eventual conversion:

> [...] I should shrink very much from following a mere feeling or impulse which might leave me afterwards, or from getting up an unreal conviction, by impatiently smothering or setting aside intellectual convictions which might return upon me afterwards. I would be very careful to make sure that I could not only accept the base letter of the Roman formularies, but also the practical spirit of the zealous and religious among her clergy and people [...] my own convictions are by no means altogether Roman.[50]

Some of his friends were impatient with this cerebral approach to spiritual matters. Frederick William Faber wrote

> you seem to regard conversion as merely a subjective process of intellectual adjustment of difficulties: this seems very odd to us who seem to have heard God's call so plainly [...] I hope by God's mercy that the time is not far distant when your long search will come to an end, and both your "reason" and your "feelings" be satisfied, where alone they will be, in doctrines and practises of which no amount of erudition can give an extern the true idea.[51]

Perhaps Palmer was trying to convince himself when he wrote to another correspondent that same July that the reception of Newman and his followers might 'damp and discourage', yet could not

> destroy either the essential character of the Anglican Church or that spirit and effort after improvement which has been gaining ground during some years past among her members [...] the less we think about it as individuals and the more heartily we do our own particular duties the better it will be.[52]

He was dismissive too of Newman's *Essay on the Development of Christian Doctrine*. The 'easy way' in which Newman 'disposed of the Eastern Church "in two or three lines", noted by 'a Russian of high rank' Palmer had spoken to at Paris, showed 'a very great prejudice'.[53]

9 Pearls before Swine

On Tuesday, 2 April 1844, Palmer finally delivered his report to Bishop Luscombe in Paris. The night before, he dreamed that he 'was going in a carriage or chaise under some trees in the West of Scotland to see the Bishops', before stopping at a house where he was met by

> a very wrinkled bustling fidgety peevish old woman who asked me sharply What do ye want? I said I wanted to see the Bishops – What do ye want with the Bishops? You can't see the Bishops" she replied. I said, I must see the Bishops, for I have important business with them. You can't see the Bishops she repeated, We have a great deal to do; we have a great deal of company in the house: you can't see the Bishops.[1]

Nonetheless, in the dream Palmer managed to enter the house and see three bishops. He kissed the hand of one, whom he recognised from engravings as Bishop Jolly. Leaving the room, he was accosted again by the old woman, 'more fidgety & peevish than ever', who asked him if he had done with the bishops:

> 'No', I said, 'I have not even begun with them; for my business is long & difficult, & it is not easy to enter upon such a business all at once on a first interview.' 'But ye must have done with them' she replied, 'You can't see any more of them.'

In the dream Palmer pressed her:

> And at last as if to get rid of me, and being tired at my obstinacy in keeping her so long she said very peevishly – Well, perhaps if ye come on Friday, I can't say. And so I went out.[2]

Palmer saw this dream as foreshowing the reception of his Appeal in Scotland, and even recounted it to the Scottish bishops that he spoke with; events were to show that it was indeed prophetic.

His journey to Scotland began on 10 August 1846, 'by the Steamer City of London', which took 39 ½ hours to carry its cargo of 'men dogs sportsmen, horses & carriages & 140 passengers' to Aberdeen, arriving at '3 ½ pm'.[3] The next day he saw the Primus, Bishop Skinner of Aberdeen,[4] in order to be 'put into the right course of proceeding'. The Bishop was far from encouraging:

> He seemed much alarmed at the magnitude of the questions raised: said he saw no end to the difficulties [...] wished my papers were all on the back of the fire, as the best thing: asked whether I was not casting pearls before swine in taking so much trouble though with the best intentions about that Lady: and whether it would not be much better for me to 'take a charge'.[5]

Palmer responded that 'was doing the work of a Deacon in this very thing', and told him about his dream. The Bishop confirmed its tenor by clearly implying 'that he thought they would all agree to get rid of the business if they could', but advised Palmer to see each of the bishops in person. Palmer left with him a printed copy of the Letters to be presented to the Synod, as the Bishop 'declined to take charge' of the originals.

Palmer first visited Bishop Torry, the Bishop of St. Andrews, Dunkeld and Dunblane.[6] Bishop Torry was to be Palmer's only real ally and sympathiser among the Scottish bishops, but his support was apt to wax and wane, perhaps because of his great age, eighty-three. Palmer instantly liked him: 'The Bp on my entering gave us both his blessing most solemnly, & let me kiss his hand. His manner was most simple, open, & free from all tinge of worldly fear or policy'. Palmer

felt 'from the moment I saw him to the time that I took my leave, that it was impossible to have any fear of differing from such a man'.[7] Torry 'entered heartily into my affair – on my observing on the difficulties, & that they would get rid of it if they could, he said with energy "I do not see how they *can* avoid entering into it"'. However, he later remarked that the Bishop of Edinburgh[8] 'might perhaps be unfavourable', and that 'though he wished with all his heart [the other bishops] would enter upon it & thought they might, he doubted or feared they would not'.[9] Although he himself would not attend the Synod, he told Palmer he would write to him and to the Primus. Palmer 'put into his hands' an authenticated copy of Bishop Luscombe's Letters, leaving with him, as with the other bishops, an unauthenticated printed copy.

Torry saw Palmer's Appeal as an historic chance for the episcopal church to try to finish what the Nonjurors had started:

> [...] a Negotiation which was deem'd worthy to be entered upon by such distinguished men as Bishop Campbell, Bp Gaddener, Bp Rattray, Bp Hickes is still worthy of renewal, if it can be

entered upon with any prospect of ultimate success [...] What they deemed desirable & worth of attainment then, has lost none of its value to our Church since [...].[10]

Not only was it a worthy aim, but, as Bishop Torry told the Primus, Bishop Skinner

the Disavowal of this Church in its Synodal capacity, of its having adopted the 39 Articles of the Church of England in a Calvinistical sense, is a Duty, which the Synod owes to itself [...].

This was exactly what Palmer wanted to hear, as in Torry's words 'it will strengthen your Testimony given to the same effect in Russia [...] which it would appear the Holy Synod of Muscovy received with incredulity'. Torry had also told the Primus that in his judgement, Palmer's 'desire of intercommunion with us ought to be freely conceded'.[11]

Palmer had been warned by Dean Horsley that Torry's brother bishops did not share his sympathy for Palmer's enterprise: 'The Bishops will not meddle with the matter if they can help it: they will find some way or other to get rid of it, if they can; you may be quite sure of that'. However, he thought they could scarcely avoid sanctioning the XLVIII Propositions on Discipline; to do otherwise would be 'completely cutting away the ground from under their own feet'. Bishop Moir[12] of Brechin was simply bemused:

[...] he had much to think of relating to his own diocese – wondered, as did the Primus, what should make me so desirous of Communion with the Russian Church – seemed to understand nothing of my business when I had gone over the whole, but treated it as some undertaking of my own caprice or zeal [...].[13]

Bishop Russell of Glasgow[14] 'shewed the same disposition as the rest', but gave a strong hint that the bishops would all follow the lead of Bishop Terrot of Edinburgh, who was 'their great man [...] all would depend on him'.

When Palmer saw Bishop Skinner on 1 September to enquire about the 'time and manner' of his appearing before the Synod, to be held two days hence, the Primus was unhelpfully vague. He told Palmer that the Synod was opened with 'one or two short Collects [...] & the Lord's Prayer'; but when Palmer evinced his intention to be present at the constitution of the Synod, as representing Bishop Luscombe, the Primus agreed only 'hesitatingly, & with an attempt to evade it, on the ground of the shortness of the prayers, & the trouble I should be putting myself to, if I came on purpose'.[15]

A friendly clergyman, 'Mr. Jones', had shown Palmer the room in Edinburgh where the Synod was to be held, which was Bishop Jolly's Library, on the first floor of a house in Hill Street belonging to the Pantonian Trust.[16] There, at 10 am on 3 September, Palmer faced the Bishops of Aberdeen, Glasgow, Brechin, and Edinburgh. They began by addressing the preliminary question, 'how far they should allow me to sit & represent Bp Luscombe & subscribe eventually to the Acts'. The tone was set by Bishop Terrot of Edinburgh, who 'spoke in such a manner as to make one feel (the others being silent) that my whole business was with him, and him alone', saying 'sharply, that I could pretend to nothing more than to deliver a Letter: that I could not be received as Bp Luscombe's representative, nor indeed had any right to be present at their deliberations on the Letter I should present'. Palmer retorted 'that whatever directions on those points I was to receive, it was for the Synod to give them after being constituted but what passed at present was only private conversation: that probably it might judge as he said'.[17] Palmer remarked to his journal that he was aware that Bishop Luscombe himself could have had no right to sit with the Synod on Scottish business, but 'had no notion of being turned out while they deliberated'. But turned out he was, and told to return at 1 pm. Seeing the way the wind was blowing, he separated from 'the longer document' his credentials from Bishop Luscombe, which he handed to the Primus, before retiring to the room below. On returning, he was informed by the Primus

> with great blandness, & a certain air of self-complacency, that the Synod had taken into its consideration & had settled the whole of my business: & that as Bp Luscombe had sent them a Letter by me, they had determined, as the more becoming course, to deal with him directly, & send him another Letter in return. So that you will not have, he concluded, to put yourself to any further trouble in the matter.[18]

Although his initial account appears dispassionate enough, later in the same journal Palmer gave full rein to his bitter anger and contempt:

> [...] as we see no necessity for the employment of special messengers, we shall send our letter by the ordinary Post, which now costs only a penny. ' [...] Answ. The Synod, it seems, is pleased to be merry; but it might remember the fable of the boys & the frogs. Your Missionary Bishop would no doubt have appreciated such courteous & becoming behaviour [...][19]

Anticipating the response of the bishops, Palmer had determined to wrong-foot them, hoping perhaps to postpone the final dismissal of his application. He therefore

> begged to be informed, as if surprised, what business the Synod could have considered or settled: saying that I certainly had business to communicate in Bp Luscombe's name, but at present I had actually communicated nothing whatever, beyond my own Credentials.

The puzzled bishops produced the copy papers Palmer had given each of them, asking if this was not his business. Palmer replied blandly

> that it might or it might not be; but that at any rate I had never presented it to the Synod: that it was wholly unauthenticated by any seal or signature: that if I had in fact as they said given those papers away to the Bishops, yet I had done so for their individual information, to prepare them for my mission to the Synod, not to supersede it or to assist them to set it aside.[20]

Having confirmed that he wished for a decision 'on this preliminary question only', Palmer again retired. No doubt unimpressed by this legal quibbling, the bishops recalled Palmer and told him that

> [...] they could not receive me as Bp Luscombe's representative [. . .] that their Synod meets by Canon; & none but Bishops of dioceses in Scotland can sit in it: nor any of them by their representatives: that Bp Luscombe even if he were present himself, could not sit or be present still less by proxy.

Bishop Torry later confirmed that this was correct, saying that Bishop Luscombe 'could not as our Missionary claim a right to a seat in our Synod, having no *portio gregis*[21] committed to him in Scotland; and far less could appear there by a representative, a privilege not accorded to any of ourselves'.[22]

Palmer attempted to persuade the bishops that, while this 'might be so', there must be other ways in which they might meet to consider the Appeal; but the bishops, as Palmer must have anticipated, were not interested in taking the bait. 'Perceiving that they were quite as fidgety as the old woman in my dream, & quite as desirous to get rid of me', Palmer tried to read out what he had been frantically writing while waiting downstairs, a Report to the Russian Synod of the response, or lack of it, of its Scottish equivalent. He would have read that the Scottish Synod

> [. . .] declined to receive me, meets only for national affairs, & that they, the Bishops, are incapable or unwilling to act in concert with any other bishops or Bishops out of Scotland in any cause whether of faith or of discipline, or to constitute any other Synod in which other Bishops may be admitted to act in concert with them either personally or through their representatives [. . .][23]

but at the words 'only for national affairs', was brusquely interrupted by Bishop Terrot: 'No we say nothing of the kind. I do not say what we could & could not [do]: [he] utterly disallowed any comment or explanation to be sent to Russia [...].' He and the other bishops were equally quick to quash the idea of an alternative Synod or enabling Canon, and to leave no possible loophole for Palmer's ingenuity to exploit:

> There is no other way. This is the only Synod: at least this is the only way that we know of [Bp of Edinburgh] No I won't say that either. I won't say what we could do, or what we could do in some other way; what might or might not be: only, you have your answer: Here it is from the Minutes. Take it word for word as it stands: put no interpretations upon it: draw no inferences of our own from it: [but (aside) be gone]. [...] Bps. "You have your answer. Cannot you see that any attempt to enter further into conversation is considered by the Synod impertinent & intrusive?[24]

Palmer's remonstrations to the bishops now became more urgent, as he was faced with the prospect of being left 'in the hands of the Easterns Synodically cut off or abandoned', with 'the acts & pretensions of the Lady my antagonist [...] thus synodically countenanced or tolerated'.[25] The only alternative would be to withdraw his 'disclaimer of heresy & share together with "swine" that passive communion which it seems you wish to continue to all comers'. The possible consequences were appalling: 'the next case perhaps may be that of a Universalist or an enlightened Jew, of a liberalizing Hindoo, Turk, or Pantheist'.[26] The bishops, however, 'did not seem to attach the slightest importance to the tendency of their refusal and further silence and animus to leave me without any ground to refuse to be reconciled', except that Bishop Terrot said he would be concerned on Palmer's own account, and another 'that it would be wrong & a great sin'.[27] Despite the sharp exchanges that had taken place, as Palmer was shown out the Bishop of Glasgow reiterated an invitation to dinner at his house that night. Palmer was in no mood to accept: '"To be left cut off from your Communion is too serious a matter to be dined upon". Bp. "Indeed we did not mean any thing of the kind; but you see we are incompetent"'.[28]

The next day Palmer called upon each of the bishops in turn. Bishop Terrot was unrepentant: 'they could do nothing else than they did, & I must take their answer as it stood'. When Palmer said that he had wanted to say more about the consequences of the bishops' refusal, but thought they were becoming impatient, the bishop agreed: 'He confessed that he had been himself very desirous that nothing more should pass, & thought it very inconvenient to have more conversation (in the Synod)'.[29] Bishop Skinner, upbraided by Palmer for causing him to 'run my head against a point of form', likewise said that

> there was no other way of proceeding that he knew of: and besides he confessed that they desired to avoid entering into the matter; & thought that they were quite powerless to deal with such questions as it involved; & that it would be inexpedient in the highest degree to raise them.[30]

Palmer sympathised, but 'the first question is what is duty; the next what will be the results of doing our duty, & *how* it may be best done'. The bishop was unable to say how Palmer might counter any Eastern demand that he should take the bishops' silence 'for an allowance of or indifference to the charge', and attempted to laugh the matter off, saying Palmer 'was too conscientious [...] if all others were like me perhaps I might do something. [...] he saw I was in a difficulty now & felt for me; & respected me [...] "My good friend [...] you take it too much to heart & make too much of it"'. They argued for a while about how Palmer might have done things differently, until the bishop, perhaps out of exhaustion, 'at last gave up his objection'. Palmer remarked that 'for the inaction of the Anglican Church there is the excuse of a civil bond; for the silence of the Scottish there is no excuse, at least none that can be pleaded or sound reasonable to the Easterns'; the bishop that he saw Palmer's difficulty, but should be sorry to see him reconciled to the Eastern Church. Palmer 'reminded him of my dream & made him remark how it was coming true & that I had some grounds for hope in it – He said "perhaps others may some day stand in our places, & you may succeed with them"'.[31]

The dream was also 'talked over' with Bishop Russell of Glasgow, who

> said I must have recognized something of the old woman's sharpness in Bp Terrot. He said he confessed the result of the day's business so far as I was concerned was painful to his feelings (without implying that he would have done otherwise) [...] that I did not owe the Bps many thanks.

Returning to Palmer a glove he had dropped in his house, and 'asking if I had thrown that down as a gauntlet?', the Bishop said that though they had been sorry not to see him, Palmer had after all done the right thing in refusing the invitation to dinner. Like the others 'He could not suggest any excuse for my not reconciling myself to the Easterns,' saying with ponderous Victorian humour, 'We shall be very happy to see you even if you *do* come back [in quality of an Eastern Priest or Deacon] with a beard, though then you'll be a *barb*-arian'.[32]

A further blow was struck to Palmer's hopes by the announcement in the London papers of the sudden death of Bishop Luscombe.[33] It was not a complete surprise, as Luscombe had told him two months before, in Paris, that he thought his death was 'probably very near';[34] but it removed at once a pillar of a support, a sympathiser with his views and aims, and his connection to the Scottish Church. Bishop Russell remarked tactlessly, but no doubt with feeling, that he was 'sorry to see Bishop Luscombe's death in the papers [...] but not at all sorry that that *link* should be broken'.[35] Palmer consoled himself with the knowledge that the Appeal 'had been brought into Scotland before Bishop Luscombe's death, and [...] accepted and sustained by the Senior of the Scottish Bishops', and that legally speaking it had not been formally presented to the bishops either singly, or collectively in Synod.[36]

However, even Palmer recognised the realities of the situation: 'It seemed that the Controversy was pretty well decided: [...] nothing remained but to return to the Russian Arch-Priest, and to confess that there was no longer any thing to be pleaded against his imputations'.[37] Or, as he put it more bluntly in his journal, 'Having been thus summarily rejected or rather jested with by the Scottish Bishops & their Synod, [...] I ought to redeem my pledge by coming back to Russia, & renouncing the Scottish Church & Communion, in whatever words may be put into my mouth, as being really, as the Easterns object, heretical'.[38] Unwilling to take this course, he cast around frantically for reasons not to. Since 'the Apostle' had decreed that a heretic should not be rejected

> till after the first & second admonition [...] surely must it be allowed to be reasonable & proper that an individual under authority should shew at least a like patience towards that which he has hitherto regarded as the authority of a true & orthodox though particular Church, before he submits to the voice of another similar particular authority [...] I trust therefore I shall not be thought to be merely trifling, or shrinking from the performance of my pledge, when I say that before I definitively submit to the sentence of the Eastern Church, I will once & again [...] renew that application, which has now been so summarily dismissed.[39]

This was specious nonsense. No 'sentence' had been passed by the Eastern Church; he had given an undertaking which he had not expected to have to fulfil. The answer of the Scottish Church through its bishops had revealed its true character, on his own principles; there was no longer any possible equation between it and the Eastern Church.

The immediate consequence was that Palmer refused to worship in the dioceses of the Scottish bishops. This was inconsistent if he genuinely thought the matter was still undecided, and 'noticed with [...] expressions of surprise and annoyance; and was attributed to some sort of pettishness or irritation'.[40] Bishop Skinner wrote in exasperation to Dr. Routh about 'the nature & circumstances of your talented friend Mr. Wm Palmer's recent visit, and interview with the Bishops of our Scotch Episcopal Church'. He related the progress of Palmer's application, and how his 'singular request' to be admitted to the Synod as Bishop Luscombe's representative had been denied. He concluded

> we have all been grieved to find that Mr. Palmer feels, I fear, most indignant at his uncurteous [sic] reception, and hesitates not to talk of it and characterise it, as in fact an act of excommunication thrusting him out of our communion - insomuch that he would not even go to Church with us last Sunday, and talks very foolishly of becoming a Convert at once to the Greek Church. I have troubled you so much at length with this absurd affair, with the view of your having it in your power to mollify the wrath of your poor friend, who possesses

> many estimable qualities, altho' upon this unfortunate subject he really acts the part of a crazy person.[41]

Crazy or not, Palmer needed some connection with the Scottish Church in order to take matters further. He therefore wrote to Bishop Torry, expressing himself 'most desirous of finding any good ground for keeping the matter still open', and suggesting that Torry judge the case 'as an individual Bishop, and afterwards with your Diocesan Synod'. Palmer offered to reside for this purpose in Peterhead, and become Torry's 'Deacon and servant'. Bishop Torry, however, failed to understand why Palmer should be obliged to reconcile himself to the East, or withdraw from public worship in other Scottish dioceses. If Palmer were in communion with Torry's diocese alone, it would make him (Torry) 'leader of a Sect'.[42] Palmer on the other hand thought that to continue in Communion with the other Scottish dioceses would be to condone the bishops' indifference to passive communion. After a discussion with 'two or three Presbyters of friendly disposition towards the Appeal' from another diocese, Palmer cut the Gordian knot by casting the matter in terms of obedience to his bishop. Bishop Torry had surely made it a condition of sustaining the Appeal that he resume communion with the other dioceses; it was therefore his duty to submit to his Bishop.[43]

Torry could now give Palmer official accreditation, which he did in the form of a Certificate that Palmer was now his clerk. He also provided a document declaring that Palmer had not, in the Bishop's judgement, cut himself off from the communion of the Scottish Church, and that his Appeal had a just claim to be 'examined into', and if found legitimate, to be heard and judged by the bishops of the Scottish Church. It also officially received him into Communion, and authorised him to assist the clergy, and in particular to preach, while resident in the diocese. This would be so while the bishop considered the Appeal to be still pending, and Palmer did not withdraw from the Communion of any other Scottish bishop or diocese. Palmer visited all the clergy of the St. Andrews diocese, who agreed with Bishop Torry that the Appeal deserved examination, and a fair hearing. Palmer now prepared to return into England to write up the Appeal, preparatory to its being put before the various diocesan synods, in the hope that a majority would demand a hearing by the bishops.

10 The Struggle Continues

In November 1846 Palmer wrote to his father from Edinburgh to take stock of his position:

> I am received by one Bishop in Scotland, and do not yet despair of being ultimately received by the rest. I have no intention of returning to reside in England, still less of returning to any formal and regular ecclesiastical duty in England, so long as my *Appeal* may be pending in Scotland.[1]

In the event of a final decision against him, Palmer supposed he would give up his Oxford fellowship, and be reconciled to the Eastern Church, after 'as long a delay as possible', spent perhaps travelling in the East as his father had suggested. Significantly, his first stop would be Rome, to make himself acquainted with 'all that they can say against the Greeks, on the great point of the Procession especially'. He was quite frank as to why: 'if my convictions could be altered on that point so as to bring them into agreement with the Roman doctrine [. . .] I should greatly prefer submitting myself to the Roman Communion here in the West, to submitting myself to the Eastern Church'.[2] In the meantime, the work he had to do would be as well done at Mixbury as anywhere, and that being so, 'though I certainly do not mean to do any act to bring myself into ecclesiastical connection with the Bishop of Oxford, nor even with any parochial clergyman in his diocese', he put himself at his father's service, 'because I suppose that I might, very likely, be occasionally of use to you [. . .] provided only that there be no reference to the Bishop of the diocese'.

His father declined this 'offer of assistance affectionately though singularly made':[3]

> Much as I stand in need of assistance [...] I think you will honour me for saying that I must decline it, as it would clearly be inconsistent with his duty for any priest [. . .] to use the services of a clergyman [. . .] who is unwilling to be found in ecclesiastical connection with the Bishop.

Lord Selborne does not quote that part of the reply that betrayed his father's hurt at Palmer's breach of Communion with his family:

> However in appearance it might remove the offence of your not communicating in the Church, where I officiate, and your Mother and Brethren are partakers, and though you might be willing to take passive communion at the hands of any other servant of the Church of England and of America, who would be strange in a manner to you and you to him [...] yet I feel it a thing quite impossible for *me* to receive *my own son* and *my deacon*, upon that footing.[4]

Nonetheless, and to his credit, he welcomed his son home, and was content to let the future take care of itself:

> You may be assured that we shall ever rejoice to have you here, comfort you, nurse you, work with you, and share with you in every good thing wherewith God has blessed us. What is still in the womb of Time may never come to its birth.[5]

He could not approve, however, of the prospect either of reconciliation to the Greek Church, which, 'while she persists in anathematising the Roman, would be to make oneself a partaker in her sins', nor of travelling to Rome to go into the question of the *filioque*: 'it would be to no purpose, so long as the Bull *Regnans in Excelsis* remains upon the record'.[6]

Palmer must have made substantial progress with *An Appeal to the Scottish Church* by the following February, as his father was able to write to Roundell that:

> I consider the introductory narrative which runs through 3 or 4 books extremely interesting and creditable, and productive of so strong a case with respect to the true character of the English Church [...] and the unworthy inconsistent conduct of its professed members, that I think nothing but indiscretion and want of judgement in the management of it can prevent its having a considerable effect and being much read and considered.[7]

He was 'less satisfied' as the book went on:

> my impression is that it would be better to go far less into the detail of what past [sic] in his last visit to St. Petersburgh than he has done – it is in this part that I fear he will both tire and be thought to have taken more upon him than he need have done, and not known when he might have retired without discredit from the field.

He rightly commented that 'the results of [...] his last journey to St. Petersburgh must have been personally mortifying', because of the behaviour of the parties 'for whose sake he appears to have done so much, or rather whose private affairs and feelings he somewhat incautiously makes the occasion of a great and important public controversy'. He accurately forecast the results of his son's stubbornness and inconsistency:

> A fear is awakened in my breast that he will *by persisting drive himself from* our communion, from which assuredly he cannot be driven (where if he stays, and knows how to use his weapons, he is so strong that he may by God's helping be an instrument of much good), and that quite at variance with principles he himself lays down.[8]

THE PRINCESS REAPPEARS

At this same time an unexpected letter arrived at Mixbury from Paris, where a female cousin, Mrs. George Palmer, had met Princess Galitsin. The Princess seemed 'very much excited on matters of religion, but [...] an interesting and cultivated woman'. The Princess had heard a report from Russia that Palmer 'was going into the Greek Church', and feared that the Russian clergy would urge him to attack her. 'She thinks he has great power to harm her, and knowing the intensity of his religious beliefs, she fears he may consider himself obliged to do so'.[9] She therefore sought an assurance that he would 'promise not to interfere further in her affairs, nor attack her in Russia'.[10] Palmer replied at length, enclosing copies of all the documents relevant to his appearance before the Scottish Synod. Whilst being unwilling to do anything unnecessarily to 'annoy or disoblige' the Princess, he would still do his duty towards the Church, regardless of personal considerations. He could not see any grounds for apprehension on the Princess' part, and denied any personal ill- feeling towards her. He undertook to keep her informed, and in a postscript agreed not to attack her in Russia, on the bizarre understanding that she would 'interfere in his affairs' by writing to the Scottish Synod to put her point of view. Typically, he enclosed a draft of the sort of letter she might send.

Mrs. George Palmer wrote again in August, hoping that Palmer 'would [...] embrace any opportunity [...] of ceasing further proceedings', as any further denunciation or publicity would lose the Princess the protection of the Emperor, and leave her liable to the legal penalties of '*death*, or [...] perpetual imprisonment with flagellations, or banishment to Siberia [...]'.[11] Enclosed was a note from the Princess, which said that if Palmer thought she might take his salutations

> as an impertinence [...] he knows me very little. My rule is *charity, peace, concord*. Nothing of what he has done [...] will ever prevent my holding out the hand of brotherhood; and I forgive him, as I desire to be myself forgiven by God.

She accepted the idea of an interview, 'on condition that he sets aside all irritation and ill-will'.[12]

Palmer replied to his cousin that there were certainly many motives that might persuade him to give up further proceedings, but not if the alternative were

> renouncing [...] and despairing of the Anglican Church and Communion, separating from all my family, and becoming to my own kindred and people nearly as unintelligible a fanatic, as if I were to turn Chinaman, and wear a Mandarin's dress and tail[13]

illustrating how culturally alien Palmer feared he would become if he embraced Orthodoxy. To the Princess herself he wrote that appearances 'are certainly much in favour of your pretensions, and much against mine', and assured her that he would not be putting himself to the heavy expense of publishing the *Appeal* 'from a desire to persecute a Lady, whom I had no expectation of ever coming across again'.

In the meantime, Mrs. George Palmer was anxious to persuade Palmer 'of the reality of her [the Princess'] sufferings':

> her letters are really opened; her servants are really bought and converted into spies, by the Russians, she has twice been poisoned – (acetate of Morphia) & now she is fed from the public Table of Tivoli, not daring to have food dressed in her own house.[14]

Palmer's reply spoke of the Princess in surprisingly warm and generous terms

> It is quite unnecessary [...] to seek to engage sympathy & pity on her side. I well know that she is a lady of very agreeable manners & of cultivated mind & good talents; & that she has many amiable qualities; & further, I believe her to be quite sincere in her religious opinions, [which] are much freer in her from the mixture of mere sectarian prejudices than is commonly the case with native Anglicans [...].[15]

Knowing that she must be unhappy, he said, he pitied her, describing his feelings towards her in intriguing terms:

> The collision into which I have been accidentally brought with her [...] has inspired me with a sort of interest in her which I cannot easily explain, & which is certainly the very contrary of anything like personal enmity.[16]

September found Palmer back in Edinburgh for the Episcopal Synod, for no other reason, since he was not yet ready to make application to the Diocesan Synods, than his dream of the old lady. His reliance on the dream appeared to be vindicated when the Bishop of Glasgow invited him to dine with the Bishops 'on *Friday next*'; and Palmer was struck by the significance of Bishop Skinner's parting words of the year before when he discovered only three out of the five bishops of the previous year present. It is entirely characteristic of Palmer that in the *Appeal* he went on from these observations, which were eccentric enough, to a digression about 'a vision caused by ether', and popular belief in supernatural punishment for blasphemy.[17] Other, practical, reasons for returning to Scotland were to show his face in the diocese of St. Andrews, and to ensure the communication to the Synod of a letter he had written to Bishop Torry. This year he accepted the invitation to dinner with the bishops, and found that the letter had not been read to the Synod. When Palmer suggested to a Mr. Ranken the next day that 'the Bishops could not see anything but a whim or extravagance of my own in the affair', he agreed, saying that 'the Bishops had used the expression "a sort of well-intentioned monomania"'.[18] Palmer noted that they thought 'the whole business at an end [...] I had probably made it up, and am now good friends with the lady, and so it would no doubt drop'.[19]

While in Edinburgh, Palmer was visited by Count Alexander Tolstoy.[20] He, together with the Russian chaplain M. Popov and 'a Scottish clergyman', Mr. Gordon,[21] visited churches, or, in Palmer's phrase, 'lionized'.[22] At St. Columba's the visitors were gratified to see a Rood-screen being erected, as well as by the 'images' in the stained glass, and the 'Scottish Communion-Office', with its variations from, and corrections to, the English Office. One of the visitors remarked to Palmer that here was something to justify his pretensions: 'One might well suppose that people who hold this belief, and who so furnish their Churches, would easily unite with us. But we saw nothing of this yesterday in York Minster. All there was thoroughly Protestant, and made one shudder'.[23] Palmer dissuaded them from going into other, larger churches nearby:

> You will find in them nothing but an area covered with boxes, and perhaps surrounded with galleries. There are, as [Princess Galitsin] rightly says, "two contrary Anglicanisms", joined together within one external organisation. "It is inconceivable," the Count said, "perfectly inconceivable, how you can go on thus holding two different religions at once, which are directly contrary one to the other."[24]

Having 'attended personally upon the Bishop [of St. Andrews] "as his Deacon"', Palmer went to London to meet Princess Galitsin. If the account in the *Appeal* is taken at face value, the encounters between Palmer and the Princess were, if frank, entirely harmonious. The Princess, having confirmed that Palmer had anathematised the 44 Propositions at the bidding of the Russian Synod, told him, 'Then there is not a shadow of Anglicanism remaining in you: no, not a shadow! And I am quite astonished, that you should have found a Bishop in Scotland, though it *is* only one, to give you any countenance'.[25] Although at a friend's insistence she listened as Palmer read over to her the letter he had drafted for her to send to the Scottish bishops, she declined to adopt it or petition them. She was happy enough that Palmer had 'failed in his efforts against her', but despised the bishops for avoiding the issue. She maintained the truth of the Gospel by professing and acting upon it as an individual, not by addressing 'Authorities or Synods'. Besides, 'the Scottish Bishops would no more attend to the Appeal as coming from her, than they had attended to it as coming from their own Missionary Bishop. [...] it would be all the more ill-judged in her to make the experiment, as she could gain nothing by it'. Even Palmer 'could not but recognise that there was force in some at least of these reasons'.[26] The *Appeal* suggests that she added that 'it would be displeasing to her husband'; Palmer's journal, however, records that it was he who 'suggested adding to the other reasons [...] that it would annoy her husband, who before called me and her by the name of two characters from *Notre Dame de Paris*'.[27]

The parties agreed to disagree amicably, the Princess reflecting that 'all had been brought about by higher powers, for evil on my side, and for good on hers'. She confessed to having sent Bishop Luscombe's *Sermons*, and their refutation, to the Archpriest, and when Palmer told her that far from being displeased by this, he had 'admired her tact and boldness', she said if so he must be 'very generous; as her sending those documents had certainly done me much harm; and had made a very unfavourable impression against me, and against Bishop Luscombe'.[28] These remarks were made in the course of Palmer's reading over to the Princess, at her request, the entire manuscript of *An Appeal to the Scottish Church*. The harmony described in the book[29] is not reflected in Palmer's journal, which on 25 October recorded that:

> After dinner at Lowndes St. I read to her all that related to my first visit to Paris [...] She said that I had placed her in a bad & ridiculous light - as a vain, dissipated, egotistical, talkative vapourish woman, when illness at the time was problematical – that now I knew her in her true character, I ought to rewrite all that part, which I had written before from my own pride & pique calumniously for her: that her husband & friends would be excessively annoyed to read such misrepresentation: that some of her friends at Paris had been afraid for her lest I should print calumnies – but they had never dreamed of my setting her in a ridiculous light [...] she warned me – I should suffer for it, as God punished all those who illtreated her & most severely too [...] I must remember that she also had written her memoirs in full: that now we were good friends, she had resolved to retouch & alter all that she had written of our relations from a false point of view with any illfeeling or dislike & I ought to do the same [...] I should open my eyes & give up my pride & spite [...].[30]

Peace seems to have been restored by 1 November, when Palmer wrote to his Aunt Mary that: 'she seems satisfied that I have no personal pique or animosity against her; and we have parted very good friends, though still essentially antagonists as before'. He had learned 'that her flightiness and excitement in religious matters is even greater than I had supposed – and, if it went only a little further than it does, would lead me to the idea that she was not altogether a sane person'. He reflected, apparently without irony, that 'I know how very difficult it is to say, at what point sanity becomes insanity. Most people, perhaps, are more or less insane, or have the seeds of insanity or a tendency towards it, on some point or other'.[31]

The Princess continued to correspond with Palmer and those of his family with whom she had become acquainted. In December the same year Palmer even sent her a 'Chatelaine'[32] as a present. Mrs. George Palmer was 'much amused with a story she heard from a dear friend of hers the other day, viz. that you had converted the Princess who consequently driven from her own country had come to find shelter & live with you in England'.[33]

In the Autumn of 1848 Mrs. George Palmer[34] died suddenly 'of a premature confinement'. The Princess wrote to Palmer to ask 'in what belief she died'. In the course of his reply, Palmer set out with extraordinary frankness his 'religious convictions & occupations':

> I become more & more a fool or a monomaniac to the apprehension of all around me, even of those I love best & most respect: Certainly this is not *pleasant*: also as I find myself more & more disowned by the Anglican Communion to which I naturally belonged, & more & more obliged by my convictions to fight against all around me; I cannot help sighing to be free from so odious & egotistical a position.[35]

He could not submit to Rome, because he was not yet convinced of the 'nullity' of Anglicanism, nor could he believe Roman doctrines; but the prospect of being reconciled to the Eastern Church was 'not inviting' to his feelings:

> To say nothing of the utter isolation among my own people which such a change would involve, the Eastern Church itself, in practise, has its faults, & faults for which I have no sort of liking. I see the narrow bigotry of its members the ritual formalities, the gross ignorance of the people, the unquestionable superstition which is popularly mixed up with their Icon & Saint Worship, & which is practically shared & defended or winked at, from a feeling of necessity by the Clergy.[36]

Although he added that he disapproved of 'Civil Rulers' assuming the position of Heads of the Church, this confession shows that Palmer was, despite his wide knowledge of Orthodoxy and his many Russian friends, still very much an Anglican in his approach to the Eastern Church. There was also the cultural divide to consider:

> if I [...] joined the Eastern Church, without dissembling my utter aversion for such abuses, should I do you think, be "received with open arms by the Orthodox"? And if not, can you conceive a less enviable position [...] than that of causing distress & astonishment & misconception to all those with whom I naturally had most sympathy, & being utterly separated from them, without even being acceptable to these new brethren by whom you were received![37]

His previous confidence was deserting him: 'I feel more & more that the person who is maintaining what I believe to be the truth is [in] every way unworthy to maintain, & incapable of maintaining it'. This was symbolised by a dream involving the Princess, in which he saw 'a very beautiful falcon with bright blue & partycoloured feathers: And you were the falcon: And you said in a tone of annoyance & aversion "What does the Man mean? He has been twice offering me baked pork"'. He interpreted this to mean that the 'food' he had been offering, in the form of his belief or opinions, was 'the flesh of an unclean animal, filthy and forbidden food', and therefore the Princess refused to listen to him

> not because her opinions or desertion of the Russian Church are good, (for she is represented as a Falcon) but because he who offers her better opinions, is sinful & unworthy & turns that which ought then appear [sic] as the flesh of a lamb into unclean food.[38]

The Princess' reaction to this unusual letter must remain a mystery, as from this point on she disappears from Palmer's journals and correspondence. When the failure of the Scottish Episcopal Church to support him became clear, Palmer had to concede that she had been right in her view of the Church of England, and he had been wrong. There were no grounds on which to oppose her any longer: the field was hers.

11 Passing into Oblivion

In February of 1848 Palmer had received what in other circumstances might been a heartening tribute to his achievement in Russia, in the form of a book published by Mouravieff, dealing in part with English ecclesiastical history. Palmer's influence is apparent in Mouravieff's description of the Oxford colleges, 'which are rather Ecclesiastical than secular bodies, semi-monastic Foundations'. Mouravieff went on to say that

> Though the Orthodox Church could not take a single Deacon who came as an individual into Russia, to represent a whole Church, or accept his explanations as sufficient, still the visit of Mr. Palmer has done much good for his Church, in making it known to the Orthodox Church. He has established a distinction in our ideas for the Anglican Church from the Protestant, with which we frequently before confounded it.[1]

This was Dead Sea fruit. Palmer could take little pleasure in having recommended to the Russians a Church that regarded him as a maverick and a nuisance, that refused to conform to his interpretation of its character and doctrines, and that he feared he would inevitably have to leave. He regretted taking the course that had brought him to this point:

> The conclusion often forced upon my mind is, that those are not only happiest, but *best*, who are mercifully left in comparative ignorance, or even positive error, while they have upon the whole dispositions and grace to act up to the light that they have [...] if it is good and right in one sense to pursue truth yet in another sense it is a painful and terrible responsibility [...] Certainly for myself, when I began the study of Divinity I very little dreamed what it would lead to.[2]

By November 1848 Palmer was back in Edinburgh, 'lodging with a Landlady of a singular name'.[3] Although he had the benefit of 'the most charming look out from my windows possible upon Princes St Gardens and the Castle and Old Town opposite', it was a dangerously unhealthy place to be:

> We too have the Cholera now in London, Hull, Newcastle and Edinburgh from whence I now write – here in Edinburgh it has shown itself about a week, and has killed about 35 persons, nearly all the cases that have occurred. Certainly, if filth and stench have any thing to do with it, the Scotch ought to have it in its worst form.[4]

When he sought the approval of Bishop Torry for the publication of his *Appeal* – since 'a cause involving important public questions of Discipline and Doctrine' could not be 'conducted by an individual Deacon' – the bishop seemed anxious to distance himself from Palmer. He granted Palmer's request – 'although I do not see how it can be useful to you' – to have his name inserted 'in Oliver & Boyd's Almanack, after the *instituted* Clergy [Palmer's stress] of the Diocese', but begged 'that there may be no reference to my Name, in regard to any – whether Clergy, or Laity who are not within the precincts of my Diocesan Authority', adding that he felt 'quite incompetent to take any concern in the circulation of your book, or the destination of the Money that may arise from the sale of it. All must be solely determined by yourself, without the smallest allusion to my name or authority'. Palmer commented laconically that 'the Bishop [...] did not seem to feel that he had undertaken to exert himself personally in the matter'. His reluctance was understandable. As he wrote to Palmer:

> Twelve days (if granted me) will carry me into my eighty-sixth year. It is therefore, time for you to get another Scottish Bishop to take you by the hand – a comparatively young & active person.[5]

Palmer's immediate response carefully prefaced his concern with an expression of 'gratitude & affectionate reverence [...] for that support & sympathy which you have given me hitherto', but wondered whether Torry 'had either forgotten much of what passed before; or else wished to have nothing more to do with the matter [...] at any rate there must be some misunderstanding somewhere'.[6] Torry reassured Palmer that he still supported the Appeal, and gave Palmer an 'Advertisement' to be prefixed to it, indicating his permission for its publication and consideration of 'its intrinsic importance', which entitled it to 'an attentive consideration by the Synod', although he dissociated himself from its contents.[7]

Palmer himself had written to an aunt that the issue of the Appeal seemed 'hopeless', and questioned his ability to continue in the Church of England. This prompted his father to ask 'how far the Bishop, to whom you have attached yourself, is or is not acquainted with the state of his Deacon's mind?'[8] Palmer replied that 'his Deacon's state of mind' had 'nothing to do with it'. It would have to follow 'the issue of the affair, which seems hopeless'. He had told Bishop Torry 'two years and a half ago [...] that I would turn Papist, if I could'. Nonetheless 'I should inevitably, upon the issue of this Appeal in Scotland proving unfavourably, be reconciled, as from heresy, to the Eastern Church'. This was 'perfectly well known, or ought to be [...] to Bishop Torry; because it is involved and very distinctly avowed in all those documents which he has seen, relating to the Appeal'.[9]

His father pounced on the crossing-out of the word 'might,' and the substitution of 'ought', which he took as 'equivalent to an acknowledgement, that you do not certainly know that he is aware of it: and this I think that *you ought* to know certainly'. Seeing that his son's mind was made up, he urged him to be sure when he came to say anathema 'to the [...] Churches of this Realm, and *therein to all their members*, [...] that the Lord hath bid thee say it'. He recalled an occasion after a service when Palmer had asked him 'where I got the orthodox doctrine you heard me preach'.

> If I know or have learned anything that is true, I must have learned it in and through the Church; the Church to which I belong; the only Church of which I ever had the benefit; *that Church*, which you have now come to *think so rotten* and *heretical*.[10]

Palmer was unsympathetic when he complained of the treatment of the Church of England by the Roman and Eastern Churches:

> [...] your expressions, of our "unhappy Church", the East and the West concurring to anathematise "an unfortunate, that lies between them at their feet", – are good, and touching to any one who views the Church of England through *your feelings*. But to me, I confess, they have no truth or reality in themselves.

The Reformation Churches had

> found out that, mighty as their movement had been, it had failed to subvert or reform the older Churches: and so they began to come down from their original tone, and to talk of mutual recognition; and now they think it sometimes very hard upon them to be still anathematised. The waters of the Reformation reached their height; and then came the ebb; and the ebb has left us stranded [...].[11]

As 1849 drew on, Palmer's tone 'became more gentle'.[12] In May he wrote that 'a prudent man should be very slow and cautious in making any change for himself, and [...] distrust himself if he feels any disposition to be carried away by the example or influence of other men [...] beyond his depth', even if he 'seemed [...] to turn away from plain and glaring truth, which might lead him [...] to see the error of his sect'.[13] His birthday, 12 July, brought gloomy reflections:

> This day I am 38 years old; and wish that I had spent them better: but I feel painfully that I am like (in more than age) the paralytic in the Gospel. My faults have grown up with me; and, as

> I grow older, I am less and less able to do anything energetically against them, and all my good intentions or resolutions seem to have been abortive, and to have died in the bud.[14]

To his father, however, he was more cheerful, expressing his gratitude to God for the example of his relatives, whilst distinguishing between their virtues and 'their inherited ecclesiastical state or opinions' as 'I have long felt the ground on which I stand in the Anglican Communion narrowing under me year by year, and promising to the merely intellectual eye to become, before many more years pass [...] untenable'. If that happened 'I should be inclined not to take any step immediately, but simply to announce to you the fact; and then do whatever you advised and wished [...] on the ground of the junior members of the family being one with the head'.[15] This was indeed a change from the angry exchanges over Palmer's gifts to his sisters.

His father was 'well pleased' that his son was likely to 'keep his position for a year or two,' and hoped that 'the standing place will not give way [...] even so soon'. He paid generous tribute to his son's qualities:

> When a grave question has been raised, it ought to be settled [...]You have raised the question; and, if you do not desert it, you may live to see it settled, pursuing it with the judgement, temper, and ability you have shown, – qualities all of which will improve as you advance in the exercise of them.[16]

Palmer had acknowledged that 'the Clergy of a Scotch diocese are very little likely to read with much attention a book of 700 pages',[17] but his hopes must have been raised by the decision of the St. Andrew's diocese to apply to the Bishop to hold a special Synod in March before the annual Synod in June, to enable the other Diocesan Synods to consider the matter that year. The special Synod met on 27 March, presided over by the Dean, Bishop Torry's son John,[18] and recommended the Appeal to the consideration of the other Synods. The idea of passive communion was solemnly disavowed and repudiated, and Palmer formally thanked 'for the stand he has made in defence of our Communion'.[19]

Palmer wrote to W. E. Gladstone to inform him of the result, urging a clear distinction between the objects of the Appeal, and the subsequent approach to be taken (if appropriate) to the Eastern Church. He responded to Gladstone's earlier criticism of an 'exclusive principle [...] naturally connected with somewhat of an exacting & domineering spirit'[20] by observing that

> the "exclusive principle" is, I suppose, inseparable from Truth - and so long as there is a division must produce [...] very much of an exacting and domineering spirit [...] but in the Russian *religion*, as such, there is nothing like an exacting or domineering spirit, otherwise than as to

> insist upon law may seem domineering to those who are resolved to claim the right of breaking law.[21]

It is highly likely that Gladstone was the 'layman of eminence connected with the Scottish Church' quoted in the *Appeal* as saying that he 'should feel sorely grieved and wounded for the honour of our Communion in Scotland, were [Palmer's] Appeal to be passed by'.[22] Gladstone would have been able to confirm Palmer's fears about the attitude of the Scottish bishops towards the *Appeal,* as Bishop Skinner had written to him on 4 April to say that as he suspected

> that we Scottish bishops are not in good odour with Deacon Palmer, if we do not lie under his anathema, I have never seen nor do much care for seeing, his strange book. The poor man I fear labours sadly under a Monomania on the subject of the Church.[23]

Although Bishop Torry's diocese had responded favourably to the Appeal, when Palmer called on the bishop on 12 June he found him 'fidgeting ever since he heard of my coming for fear of trouble', namely the opposition of his colleagues: 'the Bishop of Edinburgh and the Primus were sure to be against him, and he had no reason to expect that Bp. Forbes[24] & Bp. Trower[25] would differ from them; and he thought Bp. Low[26] would also be against'. He felt that he himself 'had done enough, having already done [...] all that was asked for, in the document which he had given me before [...] he felt sure his Colleagues would wish to get rid of the matter'.[27]

The St. Andrews Synod met on 20 June, and voted to reject the motions before it, and await the views of the other Synods. The diocese of Ross and Moray decided that the Appeal had legitimately arisen, and recommended its submission to a General Synod. The diocese of Glasgow and Galloway postponed the formal presentation of the Appeal to the following year, as did the Synod of the diocese of Brechin. The Bishop had refused to discuss the matter with Palmer 'except in the Synod itself, saying that he so highly disapproved of my having printed papers of private conversation etc.'.[28] On 10 July Palmer called on him again, to make his application to the Episcopal Synod, of which the Bishop was Clerk.

> He asked respecting the Latin on the loose paper "What object can you have?" & [...] again with the air of a man in severe pain – "Where can you find in the primitive Church a precedent for a Deacon doing such things?" I professed myself quite ready to make any explanations but reminded him that he had shortly before absolutely declined holding any communications on the subject except officially in his Synod. So we parted.[29]

Palmer called on the Primus, Bishop Skinner of Aberdeen, on 2 August. Knowing that the Bishop had 'always from the first thought it not legitimate', Palmer 'suggested that if he would say that he would not allow his Synod to take the matter up it might save trouble. He seemed to feel this would be going too far but added that certainly he should wish it to be put off & got rid of, when received'. Asked how he would like Palmer to present it, the Bishop replied 'that certainly he should not wish me to appear in person [I should talk them all dumb]'.[30] The Aberdeen Synod approved all legitimate endeavours 'to defend our Communion from the intrusion of strangers and the imputation of heresy', but declined to go into the Doctrinal or Disciplinary Propositions before it in detail. Palmer's application to the Bishop for a copy of these resolutions was refused, and he was forced to obtain a copy from the Synod Clerk of the Synod of St. Andrews.

The same gentleman was able to assist Palmer again, when they met by chance as Palmer travelled west, as he thought to the Synod of the diocese of Argyll and the Isles. The Clerk told him that the Synod had already been held on 8 August, despite promises from both the Bishop and the Dean[31] in person to Palmer that he would be informed of the date as soon as it was fixed. The Synodal Resolutions were blunt; the Appeal did not legitimately lie to the Synod, no General Synod was required, and the existing laws of the Church with regard to Holy Communion were sufficient. A copy was sent to Palmer, accompanied by 'an expression of regret from the Dean, (dated on the Sunday, two days before the Synod) that his promised notice had not been given earlier, owing to some mistake, as he expressed it, between himself and the Bishop'.[32] Palmer wrote to the Synod Clerk remarking on how much more 'to the point, more decided, and more consistent' the Resolutions were than those of the other Synods, but pointing out 'a slight informality about them', namely that they had been passed before the Appeal had in fact been communicated to the Synod. 'When people have made up their minds what to do', he remarked suavely, 'they will often anticipate the due course of proceedings, and will leap to results'. He asked for the Appeal to be communicated 'to the Bishop and Clergy at their *next* Annual Synod'.[33]

A furious letter, which does not appear in the *Appeal*, came in reply from the Dean of Argyll and the Isles:

> You must permit me to recall to *your recollection* the fourth resolution passed at the 'Special Synod of the United Diocese of St. Andrews Dunkeld and Dunblane on Tuesday March 27 1849' in which it was resolved that the present Synod recommends this Appeal to the consideration of the other Synods of the Church [...] the official communication was consequently made by the Dean of St. Andrews to me, and to the Bishop of Argyll & the Isles [...] and you will allow me to add will not require to be repeated next year under any circumstances.[34]

Palmer in reply distinguished between the Address relating to the Appeal, and the official communication of the Appeal itself, and ended dismissively

> Whether there will be any need for them [the Bp. & the majority of the Synod of Argyll & the Isles] [...] to make any excuse to the Synod of St. Andrews for the precipitancy with which they forwarded this year the result of their "consideration of the Appeal" (not of the Warden's Address) before the Appeal had been officially communicated to them to be considered, it will of course be for the Bishops & the Synod to determine for themselves, when the time comes.[35]

This may have been satisfying, but it did not affect the eventual outcome. Palmer had already failed to obtain from each of the Bishops, with the exception of Torry, signatures concurring in the resolutions of the special Synod of St. Andrews in March, to be shown to the Eastern Patriarchs[36]; on 7 September the Episcopal Synod decreed that 'the Appeal has not legitimately arisen'. The idea of a General Synod was dismissed, and it was announced that 'the existing documents of the Church sufficiently shew the care of the Church to guard the sanctity of Holy Communion from the intrusion of unworthy applicants'. The Bishops' third Resolution, which appears to cast Palmer as a dangerous disturber of the ecclesiastical peace, defended their inaction in sanctimonious terms:

> [...] the Bishops, remembering their solemn commission to '*watch as those who must give an account*' over the peace and prosperity of the Church, entreat the Clergy to discourage all attempts to disturb the confidence which the members of the Church so generally repose in her authorized Declarations and Liturgical Offices; and to remember that any measures affecting that full Communion which exists between this Church and the Churches in England, Ireland and America, and which is of the most unspeakable importance to the cause of true religion at home and abroad, must issue in results most fatal to the great object for which our prayers are offered, namely, that all who confess God's holy Name may agree in the truth of his holy Word, and live in unity and godly love.[37]

In the summer Palmer had written to Dr. Routh reminding him of an intention expressed 'some time back' to seek admission to Priest's Orders in Scotland. Bishop Torry was willing to ordain Palmer on provision of Testimonials and written proof that a Fellowship at Oxford was held in England to be a sufficient title. This last Dr. Routh was to provide.[38] Palmer also asked Bishop Torry if his name could be added to the list of Clergy attached

> to the Episcopal Church or Cathedral at Perth [...] at any rate it cannot be improper, I would hope for a Bishop to have at least one *Deacon* attached as such to his own person & to the central Church & Cathedral of his Diocese.[39]

Palmer had approached John Torry, the Dean of St. Andrew's, and the Warden of Trinity College,[40] to sign the Testimonials for Orders,

& they both said they would. But the next day the Dean having called the Warden's attention to the words in the form "Nor has he at any time (so far as we know or have heard) maintained or written any thing contrary to the Doctrine or discipline of the Episcopal Church in Scotland", the Warden withdrew his promise, the Dean still continuing his. So I requested the Dean to send the Testimonials to the Clergy of the Diocese in order of seniority, and he sent them to the two seniors who both declined, upon which he himself also declined.[41]

The Dean also handed to Palmer a letter from his father, which summarily delivered the *coup de grâce* to Palmer's connection with the Scottish Church:

it would appear, if I understand it rightly, that all your efforts hitherto, in regard to "passive Communion etc." have been completely palsied, & that you are even refused a hearing; as in their [the Episcopal Synod's] judgement your Appeal has not "legitimately arisen".

I infer, therefore, that I am entirely precluded from taking any further concern in the matter; and I think your wisest course will be to let the whole pass into Oblivion, – as if your Appeal had never been raised.

As to the "list of the Clergy" to be in future connected with the Cathedral, or central Church of the Diocese, no such list has yet been formed; and therefore, I can give no direct answer to your application; but I always remain your affectionate Brother & Friend.

Pat'k Torry.[42]

Palmer's last resort was now the Episcopal Church of America; he asked if he rightly understood that he was not to use Bishop Torry's name in sending the Appeal there. The Bishop's reply was affectionate but firm. The decision of the Episcopal Synod

completely ties up my hands respecting the said Appeal, if I wish to remain in Communion with my Colleagues; – any departure from which, you may believe, has always been, & still is, quite foreign to the feelings of my heart, and the convictions of my understanding [...] so far as personal regard & friendly wishes towards you are concerned, I continue unchanged; but I conceive myself inhibited from any further connection with you, in relation to your Appeal, which by the decision of a great majority of the Episcopal College, seems finally dismissed.[43]

The Appeal was sent to America in the Autumn of 1849, initially to Palmer's correspondent Mr. Forbes[44] of St. Luke's Church, New York. Ironically he had become a Roman Catholic just before the letter arrived, and it was therefore passed on to a Mr. Parks. He in turn submitted it to the Reverend Dr. Samuel Seabury,[45] the grandson of the first Anglican bishop in America consecrated by the bishops of the Scottish Church at Dr. Routh's suggestion. Mr. Parks felt that the 'Reply & Opinion' given by Dr. Seabury was 'so full and [...] so satisfactory' that he sent it on as he had received it. In it Dr. Seabury displayed more courtesy than the Scottish bishops in his assessment of Palmer and the Appeal, beginning with a glowing tribute:

> If there are any persons who can read Mr. Palmer's book without loving & admiring the man, I am not of the number. His ardent love of the Church, & his noble devotion of his powers & faculties to the achievement of the great design which he had conceived are worthy of all commendation [...] Acuteness, learning, & a liberal sense of mind are impressed on the volume.[46]

He felt that Palmer had erred in undertaking to leave the Communion of the Scottish and Anglican Churches, if the Appeal failed. Such a promise was 'null & void, because it is a violation of prior & higher obligations.' He fairly suggested that Palmer

> could not in reason hope to do more than call attention to the subject and make men feel its importance; and he ought, I think, to have been content to have wrought in with & under his own Church, during his natural life & let his Church, after he had gone to his reward, avail herself of his labours.

As he wisely put it, 'The problem of the Reformation will not, I think, have been wrought out [...] by the case of Mde A', and until it was wrought out, 'every clergyman in the Anglican Church or Churches derived from her, is bound to remain at his post. So it seems to me.'[47] As for the American Church, it could not consider the Appeal because it was of a judicial nature, and the American Synods had only legislative powers.

Mr. Parks thought the most beneficial effect of the Appeal would be its effect on the minds of its readers:

> the good to be effected by your book depends not upon the Appeal being sustained, but upon its being *read*, by the most influential minds in the Church, its clear & discriminating statements of doctrine & its enuntiations of the principles of Catholic unity, intercommunion & discipline being *pondered* [...]

He added a prescient warning:

> The only thing that can prevent the most wholesome & lasting effects following upon the dissemination of your book will be the fact [...] of your separation from the Anglican Communion.[48]

12 The Correspondence with Khomiakoff

So ended, with the 'various Resolutions more or less favourable, evasive or dilatory'[1] of the Scottish Synods, and the compliments of Dr. Seabury, Palmer's active connection with the Church of England. Palmer had, in the meantime, been engaged in correspondence with Alexis Khomiakoff[2], polymath, writer, inventor, and leader of the Slavophile movement. The Slavophiles looked back to the Fathers, and strove to free the Russian Orthodox Church from its captivity to Western scholasticism and modes of thought. Khomiakoff refused to debate with Roman Catholic and Protestant opponents in their terms, looking instead 'upon Latinism and Protestantism from *the Church's* point of view, and therefore from *a higher* standpoint'.[3] The result perplexed foreign theologians, for 'they had at last heard the voice of a theologian, not of the anti-Latin, nor the anti-Protestant, but of the Orthodox School'.[4] The correspondence began when in 1844 Khomiakoff thanked Palmer for translating a poem he had written on the death of his children. Khomiakoff privately grumbled that he was

> dragged into this correspondence with Palmer. The subject [...] is doubtless so important that I cannot grumble about the necessity of continuing it, but I do not expect any great usefulness, and I am especially annoyed that my name is mixed up in this. I should have preferred to remain anonymous [...] however, I feel and am deeply persuaded, that it must be continued and that the religiou argument contains in it all the essence and meaning of those religious questions confronting us.[5]

For him this was simply why Orthodoxy was right, and why Anglicanism, defined by its opposition to Roman Catholicism, was wrong. His theory that all Protestants were 'Crypto-Papists' was expressed in an algebraic formula:

> All the West knows but one datum, *a*; whether it be preceded by the positive sign +, as with the Romanists, or with the negative, - as with the Protestants, the *a* remains the same.

Therefore 'A Frenchman, a German, an Englishman, will go over to Presbyterianism, to Lutheranism, to the Independents [...] indeed to almost every form of belief or misbelief [sic]; he will not go over to Orthodoxy'. To do so would be like 'rushing into a new and unknown world, a bold step to take'; it would deprive the convert 'of his rights of citizenship in the civilised world of the West'. [6] The Western communities had 'a deep enmity and an incurable disdain' for the East, which could only be changed by a fundamental reassessment of their past, and the recognition that they had 'been schismatical for ages and ages, ever since the dawn of [their] intellectual life'. This required 'in a man an almost superhuman courage', and 'in a nation an almost incredible humility'.[7] Only Orthodoxy could give the assurance of truth: 'Romanism, though seemingly active, has received the deadly blow from its own lawful child, Protestantism [...] the ark of Orthodoxy alone rides safe and unhurt through storms and billows. The world shall flock to it'.

Palmer in response reverted to the criticisms he had made when in Russia. If the East sincerely believed itself to be the true Church, it should work 'with unwearied energy' to evangelise 'the unbelieving world'.

> Do not go on for ever folding your hands in a shocking self-complacency, outwardly showing not tolerance only, but something like fraternal recognition to worse heretics than either Romanists or Anglicans, while you inwardly say in your heart, 'We alone are the true Church, and *they* are all heretics in the way of darkness and destruction,' – *they*, whom you do not lift so much as a finger to bring into your exclusive Ark of salvation![8]

Although Khomiakoff conceded that Russia lacked 'the burning zeal of the Apostles', he dismissed Palmer's peculiar idea of sending a missionary to Oxford, since the Christian message was well enough known in the West. A 'spirit of proselytism' was not, per se, the criterion of religious truth; and the proselytism of the Latins, far from being admirable, was merely 'the necessary result of a particular national ecclesiastical organisation [...] in many respects too un- Christian to be admired, as having produced and being always ready to produce more persecutors than martyrs'.[9]

Khomiakoff did not hold back in criticising Anglicanism. There could only be union with Orthodoxy 'as the consequence of a complete harmony [...] *a perfect Unity of doctrine*'.[10] It was a 'strange and dangerous delusion' of Anglicanism that every particular Church could run into partial errors without ceasing to belong to Catholicity, and that Truth could somehow be 'distilled out of the corrupt mass'. The consequences were either that the Church became 'a mere word without a meaning in it', or, in a description that perfectly fits contemporary Anglicanism, 'a society of good men differing in all their opinions, but earnestly seeking for Truth with a total certainty that it has not yet been found, and with no hope at all ever to find it'.[11] The simple question was whether the West had 'maintained the ecclesiastical tradition unimpaired'. If not, there was no possibility of unity, for 'the Church cannot be a harmony of discords; it cannot be a numerical sum of Orthodox, Latins, and Protestants' – what might be termed the 'ecumenical fallacy'. Some Anglican 'Bishops and divines' might be 'quite orthodox',

> but what of that? Their opinion is only *an individual opinion*, it is not *the Faith of the Community*. [...] we may and do sympathise with the individuals; we cannot and dare not sympathise with a Church which interpolates the Symbol [Creed] and doubts her right to that interpolation, or which gives Communion to those *who declare* the Bread and Wine of the High Sacrifice to be mere bread and wine, as well as those who declare it to be the Body and Blood of Christ.[12]

Besides which there was a more fundamental problem. Suppose Anglicanism to be wholly orthodox, and

> [...] their Creed and Faith quite consistent with ours, the mode and process by which that creed is or has been attained is a Protestant one; a simple logical act of the understanding [...] If we admit this, all is lost, and Rationalism is the supreme judge of every question. Protestantism [...] is the admission of an unknown [quantity] to be sought by reason [...] do not, I pray, nourish the hope of finding Christian truth without stepping out of the Protestant circle [...].[13]

He saw the strong reaction to the 'Papal Aggression' of Pius IX in re- establishing a Roman Catholic hierarchy in England with territorial titles as attributable to the loss of lingering Anglican claims to Catholicity:

> Now Rome has decidedly rejected them, and has shown that she denies, or, rather, willingly ignores their existence as a Church. They are forced into Protestantism, which they feel to be the death of Religion, or reduced to confess that Anglicanism is no Church, but simply an Establishment.[14]

The 'numerous defections to Rome' by 'those who long for Catholicity', came because 'tatters of Tradition, arbitrarily chosen, without continuity and authority, and constantly exposed to doubt, cannot constitute a Catholic Church. [...] the position of Anglicanism is completely defined. It is a narrow ledge of *terra firma*, beaten by the waves of Romanism and Protestantism, and crumbling on both sides into the mighty waters.[15] The position cannot be maintained, but where is the egress?' There was only one answer to the questions: 'Where is unity without tyranny? Where is freedom without revolt to be found?'

> They are both to be found in the ancient, continuous, unadulterated Tradition of the Church. There a unity is to be found more authoritative than the despotism of the Vatican, *for it is based on the strength of mutual love*. There a liberty is to be found more free than the licence of Protestantism, for it is *regulated by the humility of mutual love*. There is the Rock and the Refuge.[16]

Khomiakoff was, despite his trenchant criticism of Anglicanism, careful to stress to Palmer the goodwill of the Russian hierarchy towards England. Count Pratasoff had listened to Khomiakoff's account of religion in England 'with serious, and, I hope, sincere interest'; the Metropolitan Philaret of Moscow had displayed a sympathy 'unexpectedly warm and strong', and although nothing had been positively promised, 'everything that can be done without offending the Christian conscience will be done'.[17] 'Let a few men' he wrote in 1851 'speak and act boldly, and though as few as the first Apostles, they may begin a course of spiritual conquest, as did the ancient teachers of Christianity'.[18]

Palmer mentioned in 1849 individuals 'of considerable reputation among our clergy', who had been consulted by one of the Scottish bishops, and had recommended making the Appeal the occasion of an approach to the Eastern Church to open negotiations for unity.[19] He himself was not in favour of this, believing 'a great practical reformation on our side' to be necessary first. Despite this disclaimer, he was thought to be behind the subsequent approaches to the Russian Synod, which led to some confusion.

Gregory, the Archbishop of Kazan,[20] had informed Khomiakoff of the proposed Memorial to the Synod. Khomiakoff, like others, mistakenly assumed that it was from some of Palmer's friends. Palmer had complained to him of the inconsistency of the Russians and the Greeks on the method of his reception, the Russians being happy to receive him by chrismation, but the Greeks insisting on rebaptism. This, to Palmer, contradicted Orthodox claims to be the True Church. He either had to profess himself 'to be as yet unbaptised, contrary to my own belief and the declarations of the Russian Church, or being received by a part only of the whole of the Eastern Church, the Russians, while another part, the Greek, tell me that I am as yet unbaptised, and have been received as improperly baptised by the Russians'.[21] Khomiakoff cheerfully predicted that once the petition was forwarded, 'every difficulty shall disappear', but the truth was that the Archbishop was unsympathetic to Palmer's complaints about the Greek insistence on rebaptism. Palmer had come to Russia 'full of his private opinions'. Let him now submit humbly to the Russian Church, and any obstacle presented by Greek demands would be irrelevant. It was no wonder that the Greek Patriarchs could not 'trust the zeal of an English deacon, which with the present diplomatic intrigues would seem strange to anyone'.[22] The Archbishop had heard, (as it transpired, incorrectly) that the Memorial 'existed only as a project and the Synod had been informed that in Palmer's absence people had stopped signing it'.[23]

Khomiakoff, refuting Palmer's criticisms of Orthodox indifference to his spiritual welfare, urged him to become Orthodox at once:

> Do not be tardy, dearest sir, in the service of God's Kingdom! Hasten your return! Hasten to take the last and decisive step. The door of the Church is open. Brothers are ready to meet you with brotherly love.[24]

The 'brothers' were, on the contrary, becoming anxious about the working-out of Palmer's questions. Archbishop Gregory wrote on 16 April:

> To grant him what he asks is out of place. This is especially difficult now that he has raised incautiously the question of Baptism in the East. This is a question which, of course, can be solved favourably in it own good time; but our easy rapprochement with heretics at the present moment could easily bring about doubts about us in the East. I am not talking about the need for a new Baptism for Palmer and his adherents, but about the difficulty in which Palmer has placed us with regard to the East. Until this question is cleared up, which can, of course, not take too long, we must take care lest in concluding a new union we break the old.[25]

Palmer's determined adherence to 'his private opinions', and his refusal to let sleeping dogs lie, meant that he was now regarded as an eccentric nuisance by both the Anglican and the Orthodox Churches.

Oblivious to the stir he was causing, Palmer had had his request for conditional baptism refused by Patriarch Anthimos II of Constantinople. He had published *Dissertations on Subjects relating to the 'Orthodox' or 'Eastern Catholic' Communion* and had had it distributed in 'different parts of the Levant'. No more could be done in relation to the Greek Orthodox. As for the Russians, he would be 'a fool or a madman' to try to ignore the insurmountable difficulty of the 'relations of the Spiritual and Civil Powers', which were 'such as to be inconsistent with the due exercise of the Apostolical Office'. He could not defend this state of things to 'reasonable men [...] in the West'. As a test, he would send copies of the *Dissertations* to the Russian State Censor; if they were passed, he '*might then* seek admission to the Communion of the Russian Church'.[26]

This left him in an obvious dilemma: he was in complete doctrinal agreement with the Orthodox Church, but with no way into it. He could not be received into the Roman Church as he 'could not profess to believe what I do not believe'; the only solution was to wait until time produced a change in either Greece or Russia. That time might be spent 'in the Levant, perhaps at Mount Athos'.[27] Even allowing for Palmer's tendency to represent himself to others as a monastic, this was a strange proposal, particularly given his next remark, that 'the *Greek* character (though they have some admirable natural gifts) is by no means attractive in a religious point of view'.

He began to pave the way for an eventual move to Roman Catholicism, declaring that the points on which he differed from Rome were points of detail only, whereas the points of difficulty in the Russian Church were 'such as affect the definition of the Catholic Church itself'. He proposed that, 'having done all that I could do towards the Greek and Russian branches of the Eastern Church', he would 'probably go and study at Rome', as 'I ought to study more closely the Roman Communion, which [...] seems [...] to be left, by a kind of exhaustive process, the only claimant on my allegiance'. The 'only necessary question' was

> What is that Church now on earth which is identical in essence (*e.g.* in the spirit and idea of universality, in zeal and charity for particular souls, and in its attitude of independence and, if need be, opposition to the powers of this world in spiritual things) with the Church of the first ages?

Khomiakoff at once foresaw the result of Palmer's journey to Rome. He wrote to a friend:

> Palmer, on returning from Greece annoyed and vexed, fell into a real ambush. The Romans very skilfully planned their attack and ask only one thing: Come to Rome! You have been to St. Petersburg, Athens and Constantinople; justice demands you visit Rome. If he but goes there, he will, of course, never get out alive except as a Roman Catholic.[28]

This was true enough, but blind to Palmer's increasing willingness to be persuaded into becoming a Roman Catholic.

Khomiakoff pointed out that 'the discipline of a whole Church' could not be expected to be altered for an individual; conversely, if Palmer was acting on behalf of others, then 'the greatest and even the most unexpected difficulties' would inevitably arise. Khomiakoff accurately predicted in what state of mind Palmer would be received:

> To get rid of the difficulties of your present position you may lull your convictions to sleep, you may silence them, even conquer them; you will not uproot them. You will enter the Roman Communion, as it were, double-minded [...] does any Symbol begin by with the words: 'I *will* believe,' or 'I *will not doubt*'? Do not all of them begin by the words, 'I *do* believe'?
> Now let us return to Greece and Russia.
> Here you have no need to say: 'I *will* believe', but you say with all your heart I *do* believe' that the tenets of their doctrine are in every respect concordant with the ancient and traditionary Faith of the Church Universal.[29]

He ascribed the 'obstinacy of the Patriarchs' to ignorance, brought about by belonging to 'a poor enslaved community'. It amounted to nothing more than the error of a local church, that would soon be dispelled. He confessed that he too was 'suspicious of the Greeks', who could not

> get rid of a dangerous inheritance from Antiquity. [...] they are perhaps unconsciously too proud of their having been useful to the Church; Christianity belongs too much to their national history, and their hearts are not completely free from a certain aristocratical feeling which makes them look down upon other Christian nations, though Orthodox, as their inferiors.[30]

True, the Russian Church was 'not quite independent' of the State, but this was due to the weakness of the higher representatives of the Church, and their desire for State protection. Had Palmer in fact played fair by the Orthodox Church? He could, after all, have been received as an individual by any Russian priest, once he found himself in doctrinal agreement with Orthodoxy. Thereafter a congregation could have formed, first on a parochial, then on an episcopal scale. Alternatively, he and his friends could have approached the Synod as a 'society'; but there had been merely 'a project of address', vague and not sent as it could have been to 'a member of the Synod zealous enough to have undertaken the whole business by himself, and so to have been your advocate and guide. [...] all has been going in a secret and stealthy manner, quite unworthy not only of the Church, but of those earnest and pious men who wanted to join her Communion'.[31]

Khomiakoff set out with military precision what should now be done instead: deputies should be chosen, a short Profession of Faith drawn up indicating belief in the faithfulness of the Orthodox Church 'to the ancient Tradition and to the seven Oecumenical Councils', Western innovations repudiated. Unconditional admission should be sought; priests, a short Liturgy, and a bishop requested when numbers required. To head off any hostile intervention, the deputation and its instructions should be 'made known and public by way of print as much as possible'.

These requests should be sent direct to the Russian Synod, making it clear that the Russian Church was being addressed because of her more indulgent discipline, but not questioning the right of the Greeks to maintain their own. It should be made clear that the bishop was requested to be sent to England not only to obtain information, 'but with a commission to admit converts, ordain priests, and introduce a Liturgy'. Khomiakoff added intriguingly that he was 'partly commissioned to make these communications'.[32] The alternative was to be received as individuals, and leave the rest to God, 'who can develop an atom to the size of the world'. Whichever course he took, Palmer had 'called into life a question between Russia and Greece which, though productive of a temporary disturbance', would certainly in time produce 'favourable results'.[33] Khomiakoff put Palmer's choice in stark terms: 'Romanism is nothing but Separatism, and [...] humanity has only one choice: – Catholic Orthodoxy or Infidelity. All middle terms are but preparatory steps towards the latter'.

In April 1853 Palmer told Khomiakoff of his intention to resign his Magdalen fellowship and sever his connection with Oxford, something he had been unwilling to do during his father's lifetime. He returned to his plan to study in Rome, and again mentioned the *Dissertations*, which as he had anticipated had been suppressed by the Russian Censors. He finally disabused Khomiakoff of his 'indistinct and inaccurate idea' that he was part of 'an organised party or school, with distinct views of union with the Eastern Church. This is not the case'. Anglicans who thought and spoke favourably of the Eastern Church only did so while they were still 'tenacious adherents' of the Church of England. When they came to the point at which they contemplated the necessity of abandoning Anglicanism, their enthusiasm for the East invariably diminished and disappeared; 'the thought of submitting to Easternism [sic] as being the true Catholicism or Universality never so much as crosses their mind'.[34]

He could not accept that the differences between the Russians and the Greeks on the reception of converts were simply a question of local use, not essentially affecting the continuing existence of one Eastern Church. The two parts were to be regarded 'as separate and divided, until they speak to me with a single, and not with a double voice'.[35] The Greeks were not 'over-warm', but hypocritical. The 'very Patriarchs and Bishops' who had refused Palmer the chance of conditional baptism 'by a hypocritical dissimulation or economy' cheerfully received all those chrismated by the Russians; worse, they made occasional exceptions for V.I.P.s such as the wife of the Russian Consul at Athens, a French Roman Catholic, who was received by chrismation after her husband obtained a special licence from a previous Patriarch of Constantinople. To 'mock and perplex individuals with a double voice' in this way might seem of no great consequence to the Churches concerned, but Palmer refused to become 'a party to such trifling'.[36]

The relation of the Russian Church to the Civil Power drew from him the blunt conclusion that '[...] if I were inclined to repeat the attempt to obtain admission to the Eastern Church, or to any part of it, the Russian is the very last part which I should think of'. Such a step would appear merely 'as an innocent, though unintelligible, extravagance or monomania, so long as the proselyte was not mixed up with the politico-ecclesiastical system of Russia'. Imagine a Greek or Russian submitting themselves on religious grounds to the supremacy of Queen Victoria, and the Acts of the English Parliament – the idea was absurd. The Russian State had assumed that power of the Church which rightly belonged to the Apostles, for example administering the property of bishops and appointing, paying and dismissing their servants, something to which the bishops submitted. 'The admission of such machinery into the permanent institutions of the Church is the indirect admission of a principle subversive of the Apostolic mission and authority'.[37]

Palmer acted 'for the sake of my own conscience and personal responsibility only', not expecting to move 'ecclesiastical or secular mountains'. He saw it as his 'duty' to act as he did, although what exactly imposed this duty on him, whether in his capacity of Oxford fellow or Anglican deacon, he did not divulge. He declared that he felt no pain in discovering difficulties in the way of his joining the Eastern Church, having 'no sort of reason to wish to find the lesser section of Christendom right rather than the greater'. Conceding again that he could not, 'to please Rome, or to join her communion, say that I believe, or will believe' what he did not believe, still he 'would wish to agree with Rome rather than Constantinople'. Palmer provided no rationale for this wish other than personal inclination; his subsequent remarks, that he proposed to 'listen attentively to all that the superior authority can say to me, and do my best to find out that it is right, and that my individual mind, and the inferior authority [...] is mistaken', simply prejudged the question, and signalled an uncharacteristic intention to sacrifice his intellect to the dictates of Rome.

He had never been acting 'upon some general plan, and for some public object, or in concert with others' in his dealings with the Eastern Church; he was merely 'an individual blockhead or monomaniac, who was led on from one thing to another'. He had had nothing to do with the project of an address to the Russian Synod, and the two individuals most concerned in it had since become Roman Catholics. Two years later Palmer followed them, and although he exchanged further friendly letters with Khomiakoff, the Crimean War and Palmer's conversion in 1855 ended the correspondence.

13 In the Levant

1. ATHENS, DAMASCUS AND JERUSALEM.

Palmer had written to Khomiakoff in 1849 that he might well find himself accompanying his brother, Edwin, whose chest was delicate, to a warmer climate next winter; and so it transpired. Edwin had been forbidden by his doctor to spend the winter in Oxford, although 'if he went abroad of his own choice he gave him the whole run of the Levant'. Egypt was 'objected to because of '"RC or Romanising" friends' and the lack of Anglican chaplains. Palmer's father, in a manner reminiscent of the nervous warning of Palmer's Uncle George in 1839, forbade Edwin to remain in any Roman Catholic or Greek Church during divine service, or, if they went to Syria, to communicate or worship with Bishop Gobart, successor to Bishop Alexander in Jerusalem. 'Rhodes would have been preferred to Athens, but there was no Chaplain there, & no regular communication'.[1] Leaving London on 26 October, they reached Athens on 22 November, via Marseilles and Malta. In Athens they made the acquaintance of a missionary, Mr. Hill, who introduced them to Constantin Oeconomos,[2] 'a venerable Priest who lives at Athens, & who after being a schoolmaster at Smyrna was for many years a refugee in Russia'. Oeconomos alerted them to an obstacle to any approach by Palmer to the Greek Synod, that 'the Synod & Hierarchy of the Kingdom of Greece were then not in Communion with the Patriarch of Constantinople in consequence of their anarchical declaration of independence'. Shortly afterwards they met 'Pharmakides the great rival of Economos – he is a monk & Sec'y to the H. Synod of the Kingdom of Greece'.[3] Mr. Hill had told them that it was 'the custom of the Graeco-Eastern Church to rebaptise all proselytes from the Westerns whether Roman Catholics, Lutherans, Calvinists & Anglicans', and Pharmakides provided a striking example. Two Latin priests had petitioned the Bishop of Patras to be received as priests, but were told that they had to be rebaptised. When Palmer protested that this was contrary to the Canons, the reply was simply 'this [...] is the custom of all the Easterns'. By contrast, the

> Archimandrite to Russian Legation in Athens while returning home received 2 RC Servian [sic] Priests w/o rebaptism or derogation to their Orders.
>
> The discovery of such a difference as this between the practice of the Russian & the Greek Churches seemed to interpose an insuperable obstacle for the present to my admission to the Communion of the Eastern Church.[4]

The Professor of Dogmatic Theology at Athens University, Archimandrite Michael, or Misael, Apostalides, confirmed the policy on rebaptism, saying that it would need consultation by the Patriarchs or a General Synod to change it. However, as Alexander Mavrocordato[5] told the Palmer brothers, 'it would be a most dangerous step for the Synod at Athens to introduce any innovation in such things. The Clergy at CP have still great jealousy towards us, and would seize any opportunity for giving them an ill character with the common people & so make a schism. Wherefore they have every reason to be cautious and to give no opportunity'.[6]

Although Palmer and his brother engaged a hierodeacon[7] to teach them Greek, they 'made *very little* progress', and '& consequently cannot use it much to make inquiries'. Palmer and Archimandrite Misael spoke in French instead.[8] Palmer's impressions of Athens, and the Greeks in general, were not favourable.

> the first thing that struck me here was, that the Greeks seem to be entirely occupied with secular ideas, and especially with politics [...] there is a great coldness and indifference to religion here[9], and that many of the rising generation, who wish to be civilised and enlightened, incline much to scepticism. Of Protestantism, the Priests say there is no sort of danger; but of infidelity, which is worse, there is considerable danger.

Nor was there any 'rallying point or nucleus of learned and religious people, around which a better school and spirit might rise up'. The clergy were poor and uneducated, forced to live on the offerings of the people; the only theological education was provided by a privately endowed seminary, 'only just coming into operation', with about 28 or

26 students, and the three courses of Theological Lectures at the University. The three bishops they had met had a pleasingly 'simple and religious manner of conversing', but two of the three 'were wholly uneducated': 'one of the two has recently shown at once his humility and his desire of learning, by attending as a Student (though a Bishop) the theological lectures at the University'.[10]

> I am told, too, that besides the general ignorance and poverty of their Clergy, there is a good deal of remissness and inaccuracy in their way of performing the voluminous services of their Church. They reduce them, practically, by omissions, to little more than half the length which they have in Russia, and this makes the neglect of the laity to attend them, even when thus reduced, so much the less excusable.
>
> [...] they have, I am told, the same rapid and irreverent way of reading the Psalms and Canons, and even many prayers [...] as I used to remark in Russia; so that it has become a by-word; and if any one speaks or gabbles foolishly and unintelligibly with great rapidity, they say to him, "that he speaks like one reading the Psalter".[11]

The 'ignorant vulgar' seemed 'to the most enlightened of their own clergy 'to worship their Pictures [Icons] in the grossest way.[12] They attach, too [...] a superstitious importance to the observation of the numerous fasts of their Church'. As in Russia, the upper classes sat light to the demands of Orthodoxy: they kept 'only two weeks, the first and the last, of Lent, and eat what they please (not only fish, but even meat), all the other five'.

Despite 'all the laxity, and disposition to free-thinking', there was also 'a vast profession of attachment to Orthodoxy'. Palmer's Protestant acquaintances in Athens explained that 'the Greeks worship, above all things, the idea of their nationality, and the hope of acquiring for it hereafter some increase of political importance: and their Church and Religion and Orthodoxy they regard as [...] the main bond of national unity for all who speak their language'. Palmer summed up the Greeks with Victorian disdain:

> If [...] one looks off to the general character of the Greeks, they seem to be very much the same people that they have ever been ; – equally clever, restless, volatile, vain, boastful, full of lying and cheating, petty intrigue, and party spirit. They are very much inclined to admire and imitate the French [...].

He later wrote that 'the people seem to be light, vain, changeable, and quite careless about religion here [...] they seem, however, to be good-humoured, and I have heard very little of violent passions, or great crimes'.[13] Nonetheless ' [...] it is surely possible that after a time a spirit of serious improvement may rise up; especially as the Greeks, with all their faults, have certainly some striking natural talents and excellencies'. He reflected on the enduring power of Christianity:

> It is also pleasant to the eye, materially, to see a City and a Capital, (nominally, at any rate, Christian) rising from its ruins, and extending itself on all sides: to see among the numerous ruined Byzantine Churches of the old town (which were all on a very small scale) some 10 or 15 repaired or repairing, so as to be fit for use, and 4 or 5 other churches in process of erection. The very sight of the solid and magnificent ruins of Pagan antiquity, of the Christian-Greek Empire, of the times of the Latin Frankish Dukes, and of the Venetians, and lastly of the Turks,

> mixed confusedly together – all shows how great that power was, which rose up from beneath and subverted the Heathen idolatrous Empire, and which has outlived since so many and great changes of fortune, and now, (having survived all the rest), remains in possession.[14]

In March 1850 Palmer and his brother went to Smyrna to meet Palmer's friend Admiral Count Poutiaine[15], who conveyed them in a Russian corvette to Beirut before joining them in Jerusalem. Edwin Palmer found the streets of Smyrna 'amazingly narrow & dirty with open drains etc. enough to drive a Sanitary Commission mad', and on Easter morning noted the 'Guns & bells [...] to herald the arrival of Easter. Innumerable *kites* flying in all directions, which seems quite the rage of Smyrna children'.[16] By April they were on the outskirts of Damascus:

> Damascus burst upon our view from the top of the last ascent, its long lines of walls and buildings rising beyond and amidst a dense elongated grove of verdure formed by its gardens – a green meadow & shining water in the midst of the trees & buildings – around on either side of all the above is a wide treeless plain of the richest verdure – Breaking this plain purple and orange- tinted hills, some of them clothed halfway up their sides with green or yellowish-green crops & then with wood: In the distance both to the right and to the left isolated mountains, and in front to the East in the far background like a wall with unequal tops the mountains of the Haourán.[17]

In Damascus the Russian Consul showed them the opulent house of 'a rich Turk[18] of his acquaintance. Outside it was ordinary & dirty enough, but inside perfectly gorgeous'. A fountained court gave on to a reception room with gilded and painted ceilings and walls; 'in the court there were orange trees in the corners and rose trees against the wall'. They were taken into a saloon, also with a fountain, and divans at the ends.

> The whole of the walls & ceiling both of the middle & the ends was covered with gilding, painting, arabesques, mirrors etc. The pavement was mosaic, of pieces of marble; & the sides of the fountain formed a beautiful specimen of the same solid mosaic. On the wall opposite the doors was a representation of the Golden Horn etc. [...] the general effect was really very tasteful & gorgeous, quite reminding me of the descriptions in the Arabian Nights.[19]

A week later they had almost reached Jerusalem. They were not alone on their journey:

> At 4.30 pm we pitched our tent West of Djenin, & close to this little stream, on the opposite side of which was a large camp of pilgrims, with asses, horses camels & tents going like us from Damascus to Jerusalem. Altogether it was a most picturesque and oriental scene, (& later a noisy one with singing, shouting & discharging of pistols.)
>
> The little town in front with five palm trees before it, three or four domes, and a tall minaret & cactuses on the left, hills on all sides: to our right half a dozen tents, more fires and many

more carpets, bags and occupied by owners in many-coloured dresses with the beasts of all kinds loose or tethered feeding behind them up the olive-sprinkled hill. And through all this confusion one saw apparently endless flocks of goats winding their way into the town for the night in a long narrow orderly train. Towards evening we had two respondent choruses of frogs & pilgrims. The songs of the former were ceaseless, but those of the pilgrims more mirthful to which were added occasional pistol-shots to inform any evil neighbours that there were arms in the camp.[20]

In Damascus, Palmer had presented Patriarch Methodius with a copy of his Petition; in Jerusalem they were 'visited [. . .] by 5 Bishops (Abp of Petra, Philadelphia, Neapolis, Sebaste & Gaza).[21] They brought with them besides Deacons [...] the Chief Secretary [. . .] talked to E. freely & in a style full of Classical allusions, amusing him by his flowery sentences e.g. by saying that we were "bees flying everywhere & sucking the flowers of orthodoxy"'. In answer to Palmer's questions, 'they unanimously affirmed that it was their constant & correct practice & that of the whole Eastern Church to Baptise all proselytes coming from the Latins [. . .] "just as Turks". If the Russians did otherwise, it must only be from some economy. The Patriarchal Vicar however remarked that the Latins had not been rejected μετ' ἀρᾶς (with a public anathema) like the Armenians'.[22]

Edwin Palmer, forbidden by his father to enter Orthodox churches, recorded the long hours spent by his brother and Admiral Poutiatine in the services. On Palm Sunday

> [...] The Admiral, the Doctor, & W[illiam] returned from the Church about 8.30pm having spent 13 hours in it & taken part in the second Liturgy at 5am (as well as the first at midnight).
>
> W. & the Admiral [...] went in soon after 7pm, lay down about 8, rose at 10 for the service which lasted till 2.30; then lay down again till 4.30, when the second service began – so they had four hours' rest.[23]

Palmer himself described the extraordinary scene in the Holy Sepulchre at the 'Miracle of the Holy Fire' on Easter morning:

> At 1.30pm I went with the Admiral & other Russians to the Church of the Holy Sepulchre & we were placed in the Gallery near the top of the Iconostasion so as to look down from the openings in the woodwork into the Greek Church; and beyond to the door of the Holy Sepulchre itself. We had each our bundle of 33 small tapers. The Church itself was full of Arabs who shouted incessantly in their own language "There is only one true Orthodox Faith." The Banners of the Church 8 or 10 in number were carried out from the holy doors of the Sanctuary below us by small troops of men *running* to the front of the Holy Sepulchre; the Turks keeping the middle way partially open, and the men running to escape the Crowd which pressed to touch & kiss the banners. Presently the Clergy came in Procession, the Bp. Samuel of Nablous, who officiated for the Patriarchal Vicar, last, with only a few boys behind him, in mitre etc. Without much delay after they had sung something & he had entered into the tomb (the

> Armenian Patriarch who receives the light from him, going as I was told only into the Ante-Chamber, the Clergy came running back to avoid the crowd, singly or by twos & threes, into the Sanctuary. Then the fire having been given out through the orifice window on the North side of the Holy Sepulchre (the Antechamber) appeared on the north side of the Sepulchre & before it had spread far from the Door of the Sepulchre it was already brought up to us in the Gallery. Presently the whole area of the Church, & the Galleries above were covered with fire & smoke, the people rushing & pressing in all directions to take it from one another, & having the appearance of fighting; & the shouting of the Arabs being incessant; By & by the tapers, which soon ran together & dropped scalding wax on their holders, began to be extinguished; which seemed only to increase the rushing about. The smoke remained last. The scene was really alarming lighted tapers swinging up to the wooden galleries by packthreads, huge torches with red flame and abundance of smoke in all directions close under the beams and carving of the wooden galleries, the area below a troubled sea of red lurid flame and smoke, besides the agitation of closely wedged crowds as if furiously fighting, & the shouting or roaring of the Arabs. All together there was more to suggest the idea of Pandemonium than of Heaven, and no greater contrast to the descent of the Heavenly & Spiritual fire upon Mount Sion could well be conceived. It is indeed an annual miracle that the Church is not burned down to the ground.[24]

Even when the ordeal of the services was over, there was more hardship to endure on their journey from Jerusalem: 'Our luggage having been sent to Jaffa the day before together with that of the Russian officers, we left Jerusalem at 6am but were nevertheless 11 hours on the road & nearly 10 in the saddle'.[25] They travelled on to Alexandria, where they noticed 'the unfinished Churches of the English and the Greeks, the building of both these being suspended for want of funds'. Only the French Roman Catholics of Alexandria, more numerous than the Orthodox, seemed 'to have plenty of money to spend & the will to spend it. '"They are united", said our guide; "whereas our rich people are so full of petty divisions & jealousies, each fearing that he will not obtain his due share of influence by his contributions – that they cannot agree to forward the work; & so almost the only subscribers to the new Church are of the middle and poorer sort, & so insufficient for the expenses"'.[26]

The journey had started predictable rumours in England about Palmer's intentions. Palmer's father wrote to Edwin that 'about three weeks ago his name was going the rounds of the Papers as having been reconciled to the Greek Church at Athens ('*united himself* that was the word)'. He fretted over the apparent aimlessness of Palmer's life:

> my earnest wish is, that he would be *a-doing*. He hinted to me, some months ago, that the time was short. I feel it to be so. And if I may not have the happiness of seeing him at work here, I should wish to hear of his being at work elsewhere. [...] it would be more to my mind still, if he would apply himself to preach the word of truth to any who might be ready to call out, "Come over to Macedonia & and help us", that he might at once turn his learning and his leisure to account, illustrating his teaching by the holy tenour [sic] of his life, and recommending it by his self-denial and his bounty – I pray God to bless him – if he blesses not me.'[27]

They left for Smyrna by 'the Austrian Steamer, Arciduca Giovanni', which had an exotic cargo:

> Half the Quarter deck was railed off into pens for Abyssinians, Nubians, & the other dark coloured or black people; one pen was full of women slaves going to Constantinople another was occupied by Turkish ladies, with their mattresses etc. an awning being always over them. The Nubian slave girls were the merriest part of the Company always joking, laughing, singing etc. & sometimes fighting.[28]

From Smyrna they went to Constantinople, where Edwin complained of the 'inconvenient hospitalities of oriental visiting' necessitated by their 'visits in the Fanar today [...] we had to eat sweetmeat (or once honey) three times, smoke two pipes, and drink four cups of coffee before 11 am in the interval between our own first and second breakfasts'.[29] Better entertainment was had when

> the Latins of Pera or some of them made a grand bonfire, which alarmed all this Quarter of the city, and gave us an excellent opportunity of witnessing the conduct of the Turks when there is an alarm of fire. Fires are indeed very frequent and very dangerous at Constantinople, so large a part of the city being built of wood. There is a lofty tower on this side of the Golden Horn (i.e. in Galata) and another on the other side (i.e. in Constantinople properly so called) on the top of which there are watchmen constantly on the look-out, and when they descry a fire they give notice by a flag, if it is by day, or by a light, if it is during the night. There follows a great hubbub of cries, and people rush wildly about shouting and yelling and dragging a very odd-looking kind of fire engine. How they obtain sufficient supplies of water I know not, for the ground on which the city is built is everywhere almost very hilly – and the hills are steep.[30]

They began to make arrangements for a visit to Mount Athos, but found that the depredations of Western manuscript collectors had aroused understandable suspicion about their motives:

> We then called upon the Hegumen of the Metóchi[31] of Mount Athos [...] I fancied that at first the announcement of our wish to visit the Holy Mountain was received with some coldness, till I fully explained that my object was simply ecclesiastical; I was going [explained one of the Ecclesiastics to another] "purely & simply, μόνον καὶ μόνον, to study the Services" etc. & not to search the Libraries.[32]

They called also on the ex-Patriarch of Constantinople, Constantius 'the Wise'[33], on the island of Antigone. He said of Palmer's proposed Petition to the Patriarch and the Synod of Constantinople that 'the Synod would not believe me alone, nor write anything for an individual'. He gave Palmer a paper which berated the Church of England for having 'destroyed together with her & no less than Rome herself the concord & union with the original Eastern Church' by retaining the *filioque*, and the Nonjurors for having 'passed over in profound silence these replies of the three

Patriarchs and the Synod, preferring their state of separation, and as holding tenets incompatible with those of the Eastern Church declining to become one body with her'.[34]

Dr. Millingen[35] confirmed the Greek view of the West: 'they affect to speak of all the Westerns as unbaptised; (a common term for Franks is "σκυλόφραγκοι" – "Frank-dogs"), without troubling themselves to make much distinction between Protestants & Roman Catholics'. He deplored the equivocal character of Anglicanism, which made reunion unnecessarily difficult. 'We should have had some basis at least & possible foundation of union, if our "Reformers" had got it laid down definitely to what ages or Councils we really acknowledged allegiance as incorrupt. As it is there is nothing to refer to but the documents of the Reformed Anglican Church, which seem to let in, whether they were meant to or not, not only minor varieties on points of detail, but two or more utterly opposed tendencies or systems'.[36]

At the end of June, Palmer met the Metropolitans of Crete and of Heraclea, and the 'blind lay-Professor Elias Tantalides'. He discovered that 'a monk or dragoman had been sent from the Patriarchate to the English Embassy to inquire whether Queen Victoria was favourable to my undertakings! The conversation was to this effect that if any man seeks to come to the Eastern Church, the door is always open; but that she would do nothing to proselytize even bodies, still less individuals'. They also ascribed the different Russian practice to economy[37]; 'that economy might be used by their Church with bodies but not with individuals, *they* would not follow their example'. Dr. Kara-Theodori[38] agreed that the practice of the Russians was either economy, 'or forced by the Civil Power: otherwise they ought to be corrected'.[39] Palmer summed up the results of his Levantine consultations:

> 1. The Eastern Church cannot write to the Scottish or British Bishops at the suggestion of an individual
> 2. Nor make any such indirect observations on my Appeal in writing as is desired [...] she seeks not to proselytize, but rather repels, and examines cautiously & even suspiciously the motives of such as would approach her. You must be re-Baptized, they say, or to speak more properly Baptised. (& make up own mind if we or [the] Russians are right or wrong) "As to the manner of coming over, we shall be happy to recognise you as a true member of our Church after you have actually decided upon your own responsibility."[40]
> The recent decision of the Privy Council on the subject of Baptismal regeneration being acquiesced in or ineffectually protested against, added to other considerations made me feel my position as an Anglican to be untenable.[41]

In Jerusalem he met two men who had felt as he did, but had already made their decision: 'We also saw at Jerusalem two of our English priests Wynne[42] and Patterson[43] who had become Roman Catholics there, and were lodging in the

Franciscan convent', adding pointedly 'they seemed very happy in their change, as I have before remarked to have been the case with other similar converts'.[44] At the same time they were joined by 'Edwin's friend Meyrick[45] [...] with his pupil Lord Lothian'.[46] Meyrick was so ill with 'one of the agues or low fevers so common in the East', that he had to be carried into the hotel in a chair.

2. ATHOS

Travelling to Mount Athos has never been easy; in 1850 'it was a decided adventure' for Palmer and his brother. Edwin wrote that 'The Agency attempted to get the steamers to touch regularly at the Mountain, but the directors absolutely refused. This struck me as something like Oxford asking for a railway'.[47] They therefore had to hire for their journey a schooner, 'really a Greek vessel but sailed under Russian colours, being the joint property of the Russian Consul at the Dardanelles (a man of Armenian extraction) [...] & of her captain a Greek of Tenedos, who in some unexplained manner was stated to be a British subject. His name was Demetri Andrea, that of his vessel "The Virginia". She... was navigated by three men and a boy (all Greek) besides the captain'. Thinking that four of them would be going,[48] they had reserved both the captain's cabin and the hold; but 'a glance at the cabin satisfied us that we might resign our claim to *that*. Fleas apart, suffocation was there a certainty'. The hold was full of wet sand for ballast, but they

> got some boarding laid on this, with sailcloth laid over it, and our own coverlets & pillows above all; and there during the nights & as much of the days as we were disposed we lay crosswise with our heads propped up against the windward side of the vessel and our legs either coiled up on the beds which were too short, or projected under the square opening by which people descended from the deck.[49]
>
> Here with our heads against the side of the vessel & sometimes with an umbrella over them when the spray oozed through from the deck we lay and practised patience tormented by hungry flies, & looking in the face a hen-coop of lean fowls which Gregoire had bought for our provisions.[50]

Their food had to be eaten 'resting on our elbows in a fashion far more classical than convenient', as they reclined in the hold. These 'exquisite repasts' consisted of

> boiled fowl morning & evening, with the liquor in which they were boiled made to represent vermicelli soup, and both fowls and liquor having a taste & smell strong & curious – though far from agreeable – which was derived from the red & yellow paint on our new CP earthenware plates. For drink we had bad wine [...] & water: for garnish mouldy bread & peas past all hope of digestion. The best part of our resources were lemonade & sea-biscuit, though the latter threatened instant destruction to our teeth. For sauce to these luxurious banquets we had instead of hunger qualmish sickly appetites grievously disordered by the heat of the hold (into which we could not prevent the sun coming down the hatches), by the slow pitching & rolling

> of the vessel from lack of wind to keep her well on her course, and – last but not least – by our internal dissatisfaction at the tediousness of the voyage.

Surrounded on the left by 'trunks, saddlebags, carpet-bags etc.,' and on the right by 'a most elegant assortment of chains, ropes, oars, spars', "all the conveniences of civilised life" were – wanting, simply & utterly wanting, on board our good ship [...] & we did not dream of taking off our clothes till we found ourselves once more on dry land. I must not omit some of the company below: – a band of *flies*, whose appetites seemed to have been wonderfully sharpened by sea-air and who really bit very hard (at our hands & faces when we would let them, but at all times) at our ankles [sic] where they found an undefended region between the trouser & the shoe. Of course we were a good deal on deck in the daytime; but there it was by no means easy to keep always in the shade, & the sun was very powerful. [...] It was a decided adventure.[51]

They finally landed at 'the Arsenal of the Lavra', whose 'only garrison' was 'a single old lay-brother, dressed in a sorry monastic habit, and of decidedly rustic mein, garb & language'. He offered to guide them, carry their smaller things, and fetch mules.

> On the road he chattered to us in the lowest description of Greek, but contrived to tell us a number of things about himself, viz. that he was by origin a Spartan ("Σπαρτιάτης" he said) had been a soldier: in the war against Buonaparte: in the English Service: under General Stuart: at Messina: and had now been 23 years on Mount Athos. He knew still a few English words, such as "beef" & "rum". We had been announced to him by our servant as pilgrims, προσκυνηταί, but on our telling him we wished to make a tour of the Monasteries, he observed σὰν Μιλόρδοι "as Milords"; and added that Englishmen, and therefore we also, were made of dollars, (ὁλλοτάλληρα [sic]).[52]

Their tour of Athos was to take them from the Great Lavra to Caracalla, to Philotheou, Koutloumousi, 'Karyes (& the Protaton); Stavronikita; Baitopaidi [Vatopedi]; Esphigmenou; Chilandari; Zographou; Castamonita; Dochiariou; "Xenophon"; Russicon; Xeropotamou; "Simopetra"; Gregoriou; Dionysiou; St. Paul; S. Anne'.[53] From the Lavra to Caracalla the 'Milordi' were provided with a colourful, indeed alarming, escort:

> W. led the van, his mule being led by a Bulgarian attired in the common sheepskin jacket & fustanellos[54] (exceedingly dirty) with an Albanian gun over his shoulder & powder & shot bags in his belt. I followed led by a monk from the convent in long black habit. Our servant came after us not only unled but leading the baggage-mules which were tied one behind the other. The Bulgarian (to the great annoyance of his mule) fired his piece as a leave-token at starting and again to announce the approach of guests when we drew near the monastery of Caracalla. (I must not leave out in our train a lively little ugly white cur seemingly owned by the same

> Bulgarian). Often we were in absolute shade, more often perhaps there was no shade *over our heads* (and the sun was powerful enough to make us glad of umbrellas as well as turbans).[55]

Conversations with the monks, 'who had resolved that William was a Russian, but I was not',[56] were wide ranging. One of their first discoveries was that a monk could if he wished 'keep a servant or two servants', although this would necessitate bringing more than the usual portion of money. Knowing that hens were not allowed on the Holy Mountain, Edwin asked where they procured eggs from. The answer was from their

> farm or μετόχια without the sacred precinct; à propos of which one of our hosts told us that the servant of a Frenchman, who had come here lately ignorant of their rules, had amused them by demanding for his master eggs laid & milk milked *that day*. They told him they could promise eggs of that *year*, more they could not undertake to say.[57]

As so often with enclosed communities, the monks were eager to discuss what was going on in the world. They 'conversed about modern inventions – of other countries – ships of war – Mehmet Ali – Balloons – Railroads – Population statistics – Electric Telegraphs – distances – canals – monster-trains – rapidity of locomotion – mines – California, etc.'. At Iviron, there were 'questions about England (where like all foreigners they had heard of the *Thames Tunnel*)',[58] and at St. Paul's the monks 'began by enquiring whether "we did not live in London", "whether London was not an island" etc. This by the way is a common view of the Athos monks – that "London is an island". In what relation they supposed it to stand to England I never made out'.[59]

The discussions naturally also addressed questions of theology.

At 'Xenophontos' the reaction was hostile:

> He (one of 'the superiors') received with unusual coldness and opposition what W. advanced in favour of the Anglican Church. He had a strong (and as it seemed to me not an unjust) impression of the aspect of the English Church in reference to the Eastern: viz. that on the essential point of difference between East & West, the English held with the Latin innovators: and that the so-called Reformation had not affected this point but had only still more embarrassed our position as regards the East by involving us in a medley of Lutheran & Calvinist heresies.[60]

At the Russicon, however,

> The monk [...] showed great pleasure at W's interest in matters ecclesiastical. They said it was not uncommon for them to have English travellers here in search of the picturesque, who went up Mount Athos etc.: but all these seemed to look down upon the monks as miserable

superstitious people, and showed no interest in them or in matters of religion. This was the first instance they had seen to the contrary.[61]

Palmer and his brother were for their part often dismissive of the capacity of the monks they met to engage in theological argument. 'Finding no monks of a superior caste we decided to go on to the next monastery' noted Edwin at the Lavra, while at St. Paul's Palmer found the monks 'quite unfitted to talk of theological controversies [...].'

On the reception of Western converts, the monks 'took strongly the line "Our Church receives those who like to come to her but forces nobody" alias does not proselytise, alias does not trouble her head about the matter'.[62] It does not seem to have occurred to either brother to look in the monks they met for any quality of holiness or spiritual attainment. Edwin Palmer portrayed Athos as a sort of asylum for inadequates: 'Athos has been a refuge for "the Nation", a resort of all who suffer from bodily or mental afflictions which unfit them for the storms of life'.[63]

Palmer exhausted himself trying to last through the long monastic services. At 'Chiliantari', he sat through the Lessons '(which is proper enough) & slept from fatigue', and at Zographou he 'was so sleepy that I might as well have not gone to the Church there at night [The handwriting of the Journal kept during this tour sufficiently shows that the writer was often only half awake, illegible words – breaks – and incoherent fragments like parts of short dreams, being of frequent occurrence in it, besides scratches where the pen has run away from the fingers]'.[64] At the Lavra 'W. & the monks were engaged with Nocturn, Mattins & First Hour from 1.45 to near 5am & with the Liturgy in a smaller church from 6 to 7 or thereabouts', and at St. Anne's Skete there was an '*18 hour* service [...] (less ½ hour between First Hour & the Liturgy)'.[65] The monks were sympathetic: 'In allusion to W's nodding several times in the church (which was not wonderful as he had not had a regular night's rest since we landed in Athos) they said that they themselves with all their habituation to it scarcely knew how to bear the long standings'.[66]

Even in 1850 secularisation was seen as a problem. A Father Paisios complained that while a few shops were needed in Karyes 'to supply them with the necessaries of life, imported food, iron tools etc.', there were too many, and they imported 'many superfluous things: yet he did not see how the community, which has no customs-house, could prevent them. No doubt his jealousy is well-grounded: the metropolis of Caryes is their point of contact with the world, and the readiest source of secularisation which threatens them'.[67]

14 Leaving the East

1. BACK TO GREECE

The brothers returned to England in August, 'Edwin's health being much improved'. Palmer wrote from Magdalen to Mouravieff, responding to his exhortation 'to bring my studies to an end and join the Eastern Church'. He was 'in some respects much nearer this conclusion than I was in 1843'; but 'the contradiction existing within the Eastern Church on the validity or nullity of Western Baptisms' now made joining the Eastern Church 'more impossible for me than ever'. Were he to do so, 'I might indeed be received by the Russian Church or by the Greek Church but I could not be received by the Orthodox or Eastern Church. For [...] one Church cannot commend and forbid, do and not do the same thing'.[1] The Russian Synod and the Greek patriarchs must be persuaded to come to some common agreement, 'if you would see me or any Western Christian join the Eastern Church'. The only answer he had been given to his petition to the four Greek patriarchs was

> an indirect and verbal one given through the Metropolitan of Crete, Nicomedia and Heraclea, to the effect that I must judge as well as I can for myself. And this is, I suppose, what I must print in England or Greece as the result of the whole to the great satisfaction as I anticipate of our RC controversialists.[2]

Towards the end of November, Palmer received a reply, via his friend Admiral Poutiatine, who disapproved of the spirit in which it was written and hoped that Palmer would not take offence, 'but rather attribute the harshness of many of its parts to the excessive zeal which Mouravieff always shows in defending Orthodoxy'.[3]

'Harsh' is a fair description of the letter's tone, which reviewed Palmer's activities in a sceptical and at times merciless light. Beginning with an 'expressive

Russian proverb [. . .] "To him that is wilful his will, to him that is saved Paradise"', Mouravieff asked Palmer to examine what he was doing:

> Is it really to seek out Truth, and with the desire for union, that you move heaven and earth, and cover oceans and distant lands? No, you only seem to, but really you are on the contrary only looking, in each Church, for a good reason for *not* reuniting, to excuse yourself in your own eyes. A lowly deacon, you make yourself Supreme Judge of the Churches, throwing down the gauntlet to Patriarchs and Synods, asking for encyclical responses to individual questions; questions which are refused an answer, even in your own communion, and when you are given no answer, for important reasons, you condemn a whole Church, arraigning it in your mind before your solitary tribunal.[4]

Instead of accepting with humility the teaching of the Church, he found it more suitable to harden himself against her, and find fault with her. Mouravieff urged him to calm himself and not lose precious time. It was certain that the Patriarchs of the East would not reply to Palmer, any more than his own bishops, because it was unreasonable for them to become involved, at the instigation of an individual, in polemic with another Church that was completely unknown to them, and whose members they only knew through the violence they exercised on their compatriots. 'The Church of the East is still in the catacombs, and you want to start a quarrel between two Churches, united between themselves, on a subject which they are not arguing over, because they see it as a matter of discipline and not of dogma!'[5]

Besides, was Rome itself always consistent? Was not Newman's rebaptism something extraordinary? The Pope shamelessly declared that his temporal power was indispensable for the good of the Church, and to protect it, he had summoned the help of armies of Catholics – was Palmer so blind he could not see how scandalous such behaviour was? If Palmer thought the Russian Church was subordinate to the State, the papacy was no freer, but at the mercy of the Catholic powers, the Pope's independence upheld by French bayonets. And why did he speak at such length of Rome?

> Because you are leaning towards Rome, and I can foresee that all the quarrels you are trying to pick with the Eastern Church are to justify, in your own eyes, the last step that you want to take in the wake of your colleagues, albeit with a few pangs of conscience, because you have looked into the Church of the East more deeply than they have. No doubt the new Cardinal Archbishop of Westminster will enjoy shaking the hand of his antagonist Allies, and then of the explorer of the East William Palmer.
>
> You do well to say, 'I accept the Orthodox teaching, even the Procession of the Holy Spirit'; then suddenly the time comes when you reject the East, and accept everything from the West - 'the tiara covers everything.'

> Saint Peter, common father of all the faithful ... that is truly a magic word, especially at a distance, and one falls at the feet of the sovereign of Rome, shutting one's eyes to everything he is responsible for.
>
> The one thing that seems very extraordinary to me, in people of such profound learning who are coming to reunite themselves with Rome, is that having laid down very difficult conditions to the East in demanding the recognition of a pretended orthodoxy in England, they suddenly fall, without the least condition, into the arms of Rome, and accept everything completely blindly.[6]

If people had turned to the East with the same humility as they did to the West, and a few enlightened people had reunited themselves with the Eastern Church without setting unacceptable conditions, then the speed of change might have accelerated, and an Orthodox Church in communion with the East, and with services in English, could have sprung up in England. Having asked Palmer's pardon for having been 'peut-être trop dur', Mouravieff ended wearily, 'I don't think there is any use in continuing the controversy on this subject, because it leads nowhere, except to endless discussions. You will go your own way without listening to me, I already know that. May the Angel of peace be with you, and direct your steps on the thorny path you are travelling'.[7]

In March 1851, Palmer returned to Greece, travelling first to Malta with his sister Eleanor and her husband, Cyril Wood, who were going to Ceylon. Palmer stopped at Patras[8], and from there travelled to the Megaspelion monastery, 'the largest in Greece'. His introduction to what appears to be retsina was not successful; he was offered 'two kinds of wine of the country one red & one white, but both in taste much alike, rather poor, & utterly disguised & poisoned with resin'. His guide Nicolai gave him an alarming warning: 'if any one drinks freely of this resined wine, it affects his head with a strange heat, and makes him break out into pustules, but without any ill effect whatever, and the cure for this is to go on drinking the same wine'.[9] One suspects that Nicolai was having a little fun at the serious Englishman's expense.

At Megaspelion he was earnestly proselytised by a Father Ignatius, 'one of the most voluble & original Greek monks I have yet seen'. The monk 'was most vehement against the English & their religion',[10] particularly for

> having made the Crown the head of the Church; which alone made it impossible for them to have Bishops Priests or Sacraments; & this wickedness the English Government is seeking to introduce everywhere, & is a party to a deep-laid and atrocious conspiracy to destroy Orthodoxy & the Orthodox Church. But all enemies which have attacked her have found to their cost that they were fighting against God.
>
> He exhorted me earnestly to come over to the Eastern Church observing that there had often been proselytes who had done so but always almost [sic] for some mixed or questionable

> motives, which afford no ground for satisfaction, whereas one ought to do this simply & sincerely.

Palmer responded to this heartfelt plea by 'silencing him by stating & dwelling upon the discrepancy now existing within the Eastern Church as to the validity or invalidity of my Baptism', although he 'had some difficulty' in talking him down.[11]

From Megaspelion Palmer returned to Athens, where he worked on translating into Greek *A Harmony of Anglican Doctrine with the Doctrine of the Eastern Church*, eventually published in Athens in 1851, and Διατριβαὶ περὶ τῆς Ἀγγλικῆς Ἐκκλησίας,[12] published the same year. He was as dyspeptic as before about the Greeks, writing of the congregation in the Church of Rhombé on Holy Thursday:

> The crowding & confusion both at the N. side door at first, and throughout the communion at the Holy Doors was most unedifying - & precluded any appearance of solemnity or devotion - several small children too, who might better one would think have been brought any other day, were squalling lustily, & many of the women were chattering, smiling & laughing both just before & just after having communicated.[13]

On Good Friday he noted that 'All day the streets have been full of people carrying lambs slung over their shoulders as in the picture of the Good Shepherd: & no end of shops have appeared for wax lights & various rather tawdry Crowns, Chandeliers, etc. for lights & fireworks'. On Easter Eve

> [...] the streets have been running with the blood of lambs – the Houses & Yards resounding with their bleatings, men & boys meeting you everywhere with live lambs over their necks & shoulders & the legs in their hands in front & with skins in their hands. But what is worst is that every street & almost every house has been splitting one's ears without a minute's interruption all day with the discharge of guns – & in the morning a salute of small cannon were [sic] fired.[14]

He was more impressed with 'the Greek Officers of the Court' who attended a service at St. Irene's, 'mostly in their national costumes embroidered with gold & silver, & transporting the imagination back to the Court of the Byzantine Emperors'. He was likewise pleased to see, a week or so later, that

> all the very dirty little children off the opposite dwellings who were much as usual yesterday were decent & many of them rather showily dressed; & the open balconies of the upper storey of the opposite cottages were full of gaily dressed girls & ladies instead of the dirty barelegged dingy-looking population of the week. The red caps, clean white Fustanelles, blue or red gaiters or leggings [...] blue cloak & coloured sashes of the men made a great shew; [...] sometimes there was added to all the rest a waistcoat of many colours.[15]

The news of 'the secession of Manning, Jas. Hope & the clergy of St. Saviours' to Rome reached Palmer in Athens in April 1851. His father hoped that Palmer would not, by acting on his own convictions, preclude 'father and mother from receiving the holy communion in common with you and you with them', effectively saying anathema to them, and exposing himself to the sentence 'Whoso curseth Father or Mother, let him die the death'. In reply, Palmer distinguished between those who deliberately and sinfully adhered to 'a false Church or sect', and those who, like his family, adhered to it 'from circumstances not of their own making'. He was not confusing the Anglican Church with its unworthy members, nor 'its relations to the State'. The problem was a wider one: 'the Anglican Church seems to hold one Article of the Creed, and by consequence all that relates to the Church and Sacraments, as open questions. For me, the judgement of the Privy Council submitted to as it has been by the Clergy and the Church generally, is alone quite enough'. Moreover, 'all those persons and parties and systems of opinion, which seemed to represent the contrary or good element within the Anglican Church, [were] insufficient to support either me or themselves. It is not on account of the power of the "unworthy", but [...] rather of the utter hopelessness and intrinsic helplessness of the better and more "worthy" side'. He had no 'lingering doubt as to the propriety of quitting' the Anglican Church, indeed he only delayed because of the difficulties that prevented his reception into Orthodoxy. There still remained a struggle between his emotion and his intellect:

> I confess that having come to think so differently of the Anglican Church from what I naturally did at first; and seeing the choice between Roman and Eastern by no means free from doubt; and most of those whom I respect in England already decided in favour of Rome; I have some idea, that I may possibly myself come to the same conclusion, – and, I confess, a considerable wish to do so; though my understanding has pretty consistently and uniformly carried me the other way.

As he was not yet 'perfectly confident of the durableness of my present opinions in favour of the Catholic Church', he would study the points in controversy 'longer and more attentively'.[16] He did not take this course out of personal inclination: 'if wishing could change my mind, I should wish with my whole heart to think well of the Anglican Church'. He spoke with reluctance about the question, 'because my opinions and my position are equivocal, and unsatisfactory to myself, and therefore still more so to any other person'. To his Aunt Mary he confessed that he was 'in such a state' that he could only trust that 'by God's help' he would get out of the difficulties he was in.[17]

2. BACK TO RUSSIA

In July 1851 Palmer sailed from Greece to Constantinople to leave with the Patriarch his 'Memorial or Question', asking 'to be admitted to the communion of the Orthodox Catholic Church [...] by a *conditional* baptism, if any doubt as to the essential validity of my present baptism could be discovered'. The Memorial reviewed the differences between the practices of the Russian and Greek Churches on rebaptism, before describing the response of Palmer's 'Latin (convert) friends [...] that such a discrepancy, and such inability or unwillingness or carelessness about reconciling it, are sufficient reasons for him to stifle his private opinions in favour of 'Orthodoxy', and look rather to Rome'.[18] Palmer indicated his intention to return in six weeks or thereabouts, to receive from the Patriarch 'such answer, written or verbal, as he might think proper to make'.

From Constantinople Palmer went on 26 July to Odessa, and from there to Kiev, Chernigov, and Sviatie-Gori, the latter 'a country house of Madame Potemkin, on the banks of the River Donetz, in the government of Kharkov'. In Odessa he met Innocent, Archbishop of Cherson and the Crimea,[19] who thought the Greeks 'clearly wrong' in rebaptising merely because of one immersion, or affusion, but that they 'might not consider the matter otherwise than from a Greek point of view'. He feared that Palmer would find the Greek Bishops 'too narrow, and too *Greek*'.[20] He also wondered at the movement of so many in England to Rome, and 'how they can bring themselves to believe the Papal Supremacy, which is so plainly contrary to the ideas of the Primitive Church'. This was a topic reverted to often on this visit to Russia: the Metropolitan of Kiev

> was yesterday much against the Pope: regrets that the English movement should take such a direction [...] Popery is a human growth of this world & the devil, and has not the truth: Why should they not rather have looked to the Eastern Church, which adheres to all those dogmas & rules of the Universal Church from which the Papists have departed?" I in vain restated the considerations which weigh with Anglicans in favour of Rome, & make them dismiss without so much as a thought the claims of the Eastern Church.[21]

When Palmer told the professors of the Kiev Spiritual Academy that he could more easily choose the Latin Communion, as Catholic and Universal, they dismissed the idea as 'a personal prejudice'. Palmer retorted that 'the Latin superiority lies not only nor chiefly in extent & numbers though these too have [...] great weight; but in the same & claim & spirit of universality, which the Easterns want & the Latins have. They said they are taught to have such a spirit & for no good end'.[22]

A 'young Swiss dressed in black with a white neckcloth who announced himself as the Pastor of Odessa', presumed that Palmer would agree with him in supposing the Russo-Greek Church far better than the Roman Catholics and nearer to the truth. Palmer replied that this was so, 'according to my private opinion as to some details [...] but [...] there is no absurdity in supposing a Universal Church to have a central point at Rome, while the very expression Universal or Catholic Eastern, Greeko-Russ or Greek Church is an absurdity'. He added testily,

> You may therefore think that I am an inconsistent & indefensible individual who am either a heretic or a schismatic for all Churches & parties, & therefore that my opinions are of no great moment nor worth inquiring after. [I was thinking also, though I did not of course say it, that just then I desired nothing so much as to be left alone and able to drink my tea before the teapot got cold].[23]

Palmer was equally impatient with the Archpriest Paulofsky,[24] who suggested to him that it would be 'Christian [...] to submit humbly to the Greek practice, the fault if any would then be theirs, and 'the merit of humility' with Palmer. Palmer responded that 'there was 'neither sense nor propriety nor humility in such absolute submission to a particular Church'; and when Paulofsky tried to argue that the Greek Church was universal as being one with the Universal Church, that the same argument could be made for the Anglican Church. The Archpriest hoped that the Liturgy of St. John Chrysostom might be imported into England:

> As well the customs of the Chinese, I replied; If there must be a total change restore the Latin Ritual, the Roman Mass & Breviary if you please. We are Occidentals, Latins if you like, not Greeks or Easterns. But you seek to join the Eastern Church? Not I. But you have studied & selected it as the true Church? By no means. If I selected a Church on general grounds it would certainly be rather the Roman.

Certainly Palmer would be a member of the Eastern Church, 'but not to be exclusively a member of her qua Eastern except when within her 'Eastern Dioceses'.[25] It was disingenuous of Palmer to maintain that he did not seek to join the Eastern Church, when he had pledged himself to do so to the Archpriest Koutnevich in 1843.

Swiss pastors were not the only nuisance in Kiev. After a walk around the town, Palmer returned to his room 'but was so beset by fleas there that after having twice undressed, & drowned more than I could count of them, (I suppose a hundred at least) I gave the matter up, and went out, & walked about, & reclined on the wooden steps of the Bp's house on the other side'.[26]

Palmer moved on to Donetz, and his friend Madame Potemkin, who was hoping to 'establish a convent in [the] Crimea'. She admitted to Palmer that the Russian Church suffered from 'want of zeal [and] life & spoke particularly of the difficulty of finding a Confessor capable of anything like direction. She has been recommended to many but has constantly had to change them, finding them so exceedingly cold

& formal, merely going through the routine'.[27] They were unexpectedly joined by Mouravieff, who had come 'to talk over the question of Rebaptism' with Palmer. On 2 September (N. S.)/23 August (O. S.) Palmer and Mouravieff called on the Archimandrite Arsenius[28] of Sviatie Gori to say goodbye. He 'exhorted' Palmer 'not to delay too long', saying of his objections to Baptism:

> the matter was plain, that I could not expect the Greek Patriarchs to tell me they were ignorant blunderers etc. that it was a trifling & captious objection: a snare of the enemy etc. & especially when I said that if I had held my present views about the Filioque & the Anglican Church 10 years ago I should have joined the Eastern Church through the Russian without suspecting any such difficulty or difference they both exclaimed see what are the snares of the enemy [. . .].

The Archimandrite gave Palmer 'an Icon of the BV & recommended me specially to her intercession, & Mde P[otemkin] after gave me another of St. Nicholas'.[29]

Throughout this excursion into Russia, Palmer had had a number of alarming accidents, none of which had yet caused him any serious harm. On 20 August (N. S.) a young unmanageable horse had caused his carriage to be 'run away with in the most dangerous manner, getting off the road, & the driver not knowing where we were being hurried down'. On 21 August 'we were overturned sharply in some deep sand: I bruised my leg, and skinned some part of it & got a bloody nose, & the driver hurt his leg, but we lifted the carriage up again & went on'. On 24 August Palmer had 'a very narrow escape', when 'a vicious horse which had shyed [sic] at first starting' got half loose and galloped off up a steep bank, 'so steep that the carriage seemed to be set on its hind end'. Palmer managed to jump out as the carriage came level with the top of the bank, as did the others on board; the carriage somehow managed to avoid overturning, and the horses were caught and held.[30] When he left Donetz on 27 August, however, Palmer's luck ran out. As they left a place called Bielo- ozersk, the horses were set

> off at full gallop before either Anatolias had mounted or the Driver had got the reins in his hand; they soon turned sharply round and upset the carriage, when I fell out on my head on my left eye, which was completely closed. [...] Adm. Korneloff[31] [...] took me into his own house and received me as if he had been Adm. P[outiatine] himself & having established me in a room or set of rooms, sent for a Doctor who ordered some goulard [?] lotion & six leeches behind the ears, saying no more were necessary. I had a confused headache, & slept a good deal after the leeches were taken off.[32]

After convalescing, Palmer visited Alupka,[33] where he was welcomed to the house of Prince Woronzoff,[34] who was celebrating the marriage of his son; and later Sebastopol and Balaclava in the Crimea. On 24 September he returned to Constantinople by steamer.

3. THE FINAL BLOW TO ORTHODOXY

On his return to Constantinople, Palmer resumed his round of visits. The ex-Patriarch Constantius remarked 'So you are still disquieting the Patriarch: you want more *proof* etc.'.[35] The 'Belgian Minister', M. de Blondil, told him that several people had asked him if Palmer was going to be baptised at Constantinople; 'one said "everybody says he is"'.[36] The Patriarch of Jerusalem, who resided at Constantinople, told him that the Russian practice was only

> κατὰ παραβλέψων, κάτ᾽ οἰκονομίαν[37] on account of secular influences, & great men [...] to say the truth, the Russians do wrong: you are not baptised nor regenerate, but I am not obliged to examine you, nor to cause scandal & difference: God is great, and if we only confess our faults, can make all good; but strictly & properly the Russians do wrong [...] if you would follow the clear sense of the Eastern Church you must be baptised rightly, and in being baptised you must not say you have what you seek, but must seek simply from God what you have not, & what the Church has to give, viz. regeneration.[38]

At last on 5 October Palmer 'was received by the Patriarch of Constantinople, in a lesser Synod'. 'The Patriarch had with him ten other ecclesiastics apparently Bishops (or some of them at least)'. Several other letters and papers were read aloud or in silence, the conversation being almost entirely in Turkish; then 'after the usual coffee and pipes' the Patriarch mentioned that 'there was a Question relating to Baptism to which I desired an answer'. Turning to Palmer, he gave his verdict:

> "There is no need of any long answer; we have, and know, but One Baptism. If the Russians do otherwise, we know it not, nor recognise it. We admit only One Baptism, and that without any addition, subtraction, or alteration" (alluding under this word, no doubt, to my question about conditionality) "whatever."

At this point, the Patriarch 'turned himself to the right and left, to the Bishops seated nearest to him on the divan, and said: "That is the answer, is it not?" And they assented, either verbally, or by bowing towards him in return'. Palmer 'observed that I understood, then, that it was unnecessary for me to wait any longer at Constantinople, or to expect any further written answer?' The Patriarch replied that he understood rightly, upon which Palmer 'thanked him for the answer given, and so took my leave. Thus, then, so far as I am concerned, I have fully stated the difficulty to the authorities of the Greek Church, and have received my answer'.[39]

This answer brought Palmer's 'relations and Efforts with regard to the Eastern Church pretty well to a close', as the 'Chief Authorities of that Communion' had 'completely or sufficiently defeated' his attempts to gain admission to it, The Anglican Church did not afford him 'a reasonable basis of authority for belief or teachings', but he could not 'practically join the Eastern Church without doing or saying something clearly wrong or false', although it taught 'all that faith which I believe and does not teach nor tolerate any heresy contrary to it'. He therefore proposed to wait, and devote himself to the closer study of the question of the Procession, the Church of Rome, and the Roman Supremacy. Despite an 'inherited duty and necessity' of hostility to Rome, he had come to feel that it was probable that the Roman Church, which was so much larger, was right in condemning both the Anglican and the Eastern Churches; 'and, since I must sacrifice my private judgement in favour of one of the three, I will sacrifice it in favour of the strongest and most consistent and most probable claimant'.[40] His doctrinal agreement with the East against Rome was a bar to this, still he *wished* to find in favour of Rome.

The failure of his approaches to the Orthodox Church came as a relief to Palmer's family. Roundell Palmer had anticipated not only a denominational but a physical separation: 'I should think it likely to lead also to a permanent residence in the country of his adopted Church'. This, though painful, was at least preferable to his returning to England 'to be an author or promoter of more divisions in our poor distracted Church here'.[41] William Palmer senior wrote in September describing the 'feelings of anxiety' with which he would open his son's next letters – 'seeing it will be, as it were, for life or death in one so near and dear to me as you are' – and after the news from Constantinople arrived, that 'we shall rejoice in as much of our company as you can give us here'. Towards the end of October, he wrote again reminding Palmer of his promise of 'a respite, which will save me [...] from witnessing your final rejection of a Communion in which, one way or the other, you seem to think we can be saved, though you cannot'. He hoped that as Palmer's studies, embarked upon to strengthen his position in the Anglican Church, had only served to weaken it, so his projected studies of Roman claims would issue 'in a direction contrary to the avowed wish and object'.[42] Edwin frankly expressed his

> satisfaction at [your] final renunciation of personal reconciliation to the Eastern Church [...] because I have a strong misgiving about the propriety of *joining* a communion so distinctly non-Oecumenical in its claims and feelings. Besides I am disposed to agree with your extract about the question of rebaptism [...] [though] you offered the Patriarchs a *compromise*, which from your formal and technical mind, I never would have expected
>
> [...] the extent of your concession (as the Patriarchs were, as I expected, peremptory) only widens and strengthens the barrier which now separates you from the Eastern Communion. I rejoice: for, be the Easterns ever so right, your pledge to the Russian Arch-Priest must always seem to me rash and inconsequent.[43]

At the urging of his Russian friends, Palmer had written to the Tsar from Sviatie Gori, but no reply was ever received.[44] He therefore replied that Edwin's conclusions were true 'so far as the *Greek* Church is concerned, but not absolutely so, so far as the Russian & the Eastern Church as a whole are concerned: though I think it most probable that it will be so for that also; and a very little time will now suffice for me to bring my efforts in that direction to an end'.[45] He did not see that he had offered the Patriarchs a compromise, as he was 'sufficiently convinced that their Rebaptisms *are* in point of fact *conditional*, & only wished to be distinctly allowed by individual Bishop or local Church in this opinion'; besides which it was a question of discipline or ritual, not of the 'confession or denial of Articles of faith', about which any compromise was 'inadmissible'. He believed what the Eastern Church believed and taught, and so could join it 'more easily even now. To join Rome I must obtain a change in my own belief [...] I too think my pledge given in Russia either is already or soon will be redeemed and at an end'.[46]

4. LAST LETTERS

Palmer and his father continued to correspond on 'ecclesiastical subjects' until early 1853, but 'the tone was happier than before'[47], both parties no doubt aware that the time left to William Palmer senior could not be long. In September 1851 Palmer's father thanked him for 'those kind and affectionate expressions, which testify in you a religion of the heart; showing that you are quite sensible of an Invisible Unity among the humble and honest members of various Churches in the outward world'. Palmer replied that he was inclined to view

> all religions and Churches and sects [...] as being [...] so many *permissive dispensations*, in which that portion of truth which has been retained retains its living and quickening power [...] so far as any people are well and religiously disposed [...] they belong to the Church

It might be wondered why, on this logic, Palmer did not simply remain within the 'permissive dispensation' of Anglicanism and seek his salvation there, particularly when 'it is not, absolutely speaking, necessary for the salvation of individuals belonging to it, that they should either understand the defects of their tradition, or be moved to change'. The case was different where a 'teacher or preacher is sent by competent authority',[48] but otherwise 'for the unsent and unauthorised individual, there cannot be a greater mistake than to suppose that mere knowledge of Divine or ecclesiastical truth is a good, to be sought for in the first instance for one's self, and obtruded upon others'.[49] Here there seems to be a new humility, and awareness on Palmer's part that he had all along been acting 'on signs intelligible to himself alone' in his quest for ecclesiastical purity. Also detectable are the first notes of regret that became a recurrent theme of his correspondence from now on.

In January 1852 Palmer wrote to his father that he no longer had a pledge to redeem in Russia, and recounted two dreams: in the first, Palmer stood by 'a House and a Church,' which he identified with those at Mixbury. The house was strong and solid, 'built of enormous stones of Cyclopian [sic] Masonry', but the church was 'built [...] in the most wretched way, with loose rubble; small stones, and dirt'. In the dream his father apologised that, solid though it was, he had not been able to spend more on the house, but said of the church, '"*That* was not *my* doing". In the second, he and his father were together; 'and you said, "Do you love me, Willy?": and I answered, "Dear Papa, I love you very much'.[50] His father recognised this affection in a letter to Palmer's sister Emily:

> Your brother William, it is true, has caused us all much very much pain, in his alienation from our own Church. But then it is a great comfort to us to know how much he wishes to do what is right [...] when we notice how he has given up all his prospects to carry out his own views, though I fear he is very much mistaken in them. He has no want of talent or learning [...]
>
> I say again, we cannot doubt, either of wish to do right, or of his great affection, in which he is by no means wanting. Though he has cut off from himself a path of usefulness, which might have been his here, yet there may be many where he is to whom he is doing good, and of which we know nothing.[51]

In February his father wrote that although we ought rather to endeavour to amend what is amiss at home, than 'in despair to relinquish our posts', nevertheless, every man has to seek his own salvation first; and I hope I shall not love you the less, if, *for the sake of that,* you give up everything else'. This was 'a great satisfaction' to Palmer, who was 'sensible how much charity and long-suffering, as well as deep affection' lay in his father's words. He knew he was unlikely to find '*entire* satisfaction in any Church of those now on earth. All that I can hope and work for will be to fix my future position with more satisfaction to myself'. He was aware that 'It requires no great wisdom to see that my present Ecclesiastical views and position are most unsatisfactory, and probably incapable of being maintained long [...].'

He had been forced to exclude from his definition of the Visible Church the Lutherans and Calvinists, the Episcopal Lutherans of Sweden, 'the Eastern heretical Churches' and finally, the Anglican Church. 'Well; this too I must give up. The last [...] was the subversion of my own position, and the giving up of everything which I valued, and to which I was attached, in the world [...] it is inconvenient to be deprived of one's standing-ground, without having as yet any other to step onto'.

> [...] it would perhaps have been better for me [...] if I had done in the first instance that, and only that, which you would have wished me to do as belonging to my present position [...] as it was, I entered upon Ecclesiastical studies without well knowing what I was doing, and certainly without having fitted myself for such studies as I ought to have fitted myself. The results have been contrary to all my anticipations, and in many respects painful.[52]

His father generously consoled him:

> If you have already, or shall hereafter attain to the knowledge of saving Truth, what more could you have done? You can have no reason, in that case, to regret for your own sake [...] any accident that may have separated us in the ordinary occupations of life now [...] I would not, therefore, that you should now "*sigh*" for *anything you might have been*; but endeavour only to do well as you are, and better if you may. I feel indeed that there are many things in you worthy of all imitation [...].[53]

As to where his son's studies had led him, 'I will frankly confess that I consider your confession honest and true. I do think you were disposed to be guilty of the error of hastily giving your sentiments as a young man, and in a confident manner upon subjects for the consideration of which you could not be properly prepared'. Even now, Palmer had declared that he could not '*decline the consequences and duties which have come, or may come, from (what I regard as) truth*'; 'Pray consider how this reads [...] what are likely to be the fruits of error, tho' you call them "consequences and duties", but error still'.[54]

His father's last letter on ecclesiastical matters discussed the nature and scope of papal authority, before concluding that the Church of Rome was '*one* of *others*. It cannot, therefore, be *the* Church, exclusively and alone'.[55] However, he agreed with Palmer that we should hold a sincere desire to be set right where we may be wrong, 'and to be found still advancing and progressing in the knowledge of TRUTH'.[56]

In September Edwin wrote from Finmere that: 'we have lost our father. A very bad night on Monday, and a similar day on Tuesday, left no doubt; and he died painlessly and tranquilly about half past one this morning'.[57] So passed the man who played by far the greatest rôle in Palmer's life. In Palmer's youth, driving, encouraging, gently reproaching; in Palmer's ecclesiastical controversies, a formidable opponent, and spokesman for all that was good and decent in Anglicanism; and when his son began to look at the course he had taken with misgiving and dismay, reassuring. Even when Palmer pursued a course with which he strongly disagreed, he never abandoned his son; quintessentially English though he was, he was never afraid to express his love for him. With his departure, Palmer's life seems diminished; an impression confirmed by Lord Selborne, who described his father as 'a rare union of all that a husband and a parent ought to be [...] consistent always, regardless of self, attentive to every demand of love and duty'. With his death 'we were to have experience of [...] the burden of walking alone, without the guide under whose shadow we had grown up. And yet, to myself, – I should suppose, to us all – years were to pass before that could be quite realised'.[58]

15 In Limbo

1. ATHENS

Palmer remained in Athens until May 1852. A letter to his sister Emma describes a typical day there:

> I get up about 7 or a little before and enjoy cold water or *tepid* water, for it is not cold by any means, only cooler than the surrounding atmosphere – look at my tongue, and dress: a boy from the Printer commonly comes about 8 am to take away the work he left me to correct the night before – at 9 I breakfast at the table d'hôte – my breakfast used when the thermometer was under 80 degrees to consist of ricemilk bread and café au lait; but since the thermometer has been nearer 90 degrees I breakfast on *Yaourt*, a light and subacid basin of fresh milk curds, and weak tea. All the day I remain in my room, keeping the light out, and wiping my face; at 5 or whenever it pleases fortune and the Cook (for the innkeepers have no clock, and their lodgers [...] no idea of hours) we dine, and about 7 it becomes tolerably pleasant to go out, and if there is a moon, as there is now you may stay out as long as you please – at least 9. But I seldom go out to walk except 10 minutes or so: for the Printer's boy commonly brings me the work done by them in the day about 7 pm that I may correct it against the next morning; – and then if it is the first correction of the sheet, or if I have a little headache as I sometimes have after an unusually hot day I stay at home and correct for the press – as this operation has often taken till midnight or one o'clock in the morning: and if it is the second and still more if it is the third correction or if, as happens too often from one cause or another, there is no work brought from the Printer – I go out [...] and spend an hour or an hour and a half at one or other of three or four houses (of the Hills, the Wenigs [...]) They are all near to my hotel.[1]

Sometimes this eremitic routine was interrupted by a public occasion, such as the funeral of the Bishop of Kynouria, on 3 February (N. S.) 1852. Palmer went with Mr. Hill to the Church of St. Irene, where they found

> soldiers at the door, & Misael in the pulpit just beginning the funeral sermon. The Church was thronged with men & boys, & the galleries above with women: the Iconostasion was all

uncovered, and the H[oly] Doors open & at them within a crowd of Ecclesiastics: the raised Quoir also was thronged & I saw some helmets of Officers, & a good many Frankish hats among the sea of Fezzes. The deceased Bp sat in a chair looking Westwards at the West end of the raised Quoir in the middle, in full robes, with the mitre on his head, & staff in his hand. After the sermon, they began to sing while many thronged up to kiss the deceased Bp's hand, as I did but was carried backwards & forwards by the Press at the top of the steps [...].

Before Palmer could get close enough, the procession moved off to 'the Monastery of the Asomati a mile from the city where all Bishops are buried'. Palmer walked up and down the esplanade in front of the palace with the Russian Archimandrite until the procession appeared again:

the Procession came up from Hermes St., preceded by soldiers, then a band playing as at a military funeral then the Cross between the Flabella & the Lanterns, & then three Court Domestics in Livery: then about 30 Priests in shabby Phenolia [sic] & Epitrachelia of various dirty looking shades: then some Deacons & the deceased Bp in the Chair [...] the road was muddy, and the wind cold & sky threatening, & the procession did not keep well together [...] At the entry to the Monastery the Soldiers halted, I and the Deacon of the Metropolitan with whom I walked went in & found the grave a rudely made squarish hole looking not six feet deep [...].

What followed was a classic piece of Greek disorganisation, drily recorded by Palmer:

We stood on the heap of earth to the South; & when the chair was brought in, it was first taken into the Church where it remained a very long time, I should think ¾ of an hour, persons crying out now & then, measuring the depth of the hole, & going back. The hole was not deep enough, and they sawed off in the Church the tops & bottoms of the Chair. And I believe changed part of the robes of the Deceased. At length the Chair was brought out & set on the N. side of the grave, & with much delay, shouting to one another, & much difficulty was lowered into the grave, the mitre being now absent, & those about it having much ado to keep the body especially the head, in a tolerable posture. Just before they lowered it, as it stood on the brink the Bp read rapidly standing at the E. end of the grave Westwards some prayers, but after it was lowered, all the clergy went away, & I heard & saw the men calling for & handing – plain, small deal boards, seemingly to cover over the Chair in the hole, before filling it in with earth. The conduct of the crowd was idle & rather riotous – even the Deacon with whom I was threw some earth by way of a joke into the neck of a clerk who was in the grave.

When I came out of the Monastery it was near 5 o' clock pm the sun shone between the clouds: Hymettus shewed solidly: the sea beyond was a clear slate sheet with the fine outline of the Mountains & islands beyond. Before me was the Acropolis, on the right Lycabettos where they were quarrying as usual: the people returning homewards mixed with clergy: one or two carriages: and these things will meet the eyes of the deceased Bishop no more.[2]

Palmer may have abandoned any hope – or intention – of becoming Orthodox, but his Orthodox friends were keen to persuade him otherwise:

> The Admiral & Mouravieff both press me to leave Athens & come to St. Petersburg where they fancy I may be of use to certain parties who they say have been addressing some questions & making some application to the Synod.[3]

Hopes had been raised by the projected submission to the Russian Synod of the 'Memorial' about possible reunification composed by various Scottish and English clergymen, which in the event proved abortive.[4] Admiral Poutiatine had written that if Palmer were to come to St. Petersburg, it

> might through God's blessing, serve to further the ends of a project now in contemplation amongst some of your friends in England. I[t] will really be a happy day, if so many good persons, wearied with the unsettled state of things in matters which ought not to be so, would unite themselves to our Apostolic Church. Such an event would give us a new impulse, and excite us to be more zealous as well for the conversion of others as for our own salvation.[5]

Mouravieff was impatient with Palmer's contention that he had been rebuffed by an unfeeling Orthodox Church:

> You say that you have knocked in vain on the doors of the Orthodox Church in Russia and in the East, and that everywhere you have been turned away, despite professing the doctrines of this Church; one of your friends has then advised you to abandon this ungrateful Church, and throw yourself into the arms of Rome. Let's see if that is how it was! You came twice to Russia, that is true, but without yet being Orthodox, for you disagreed with two fundamental doctrines, the Procession of the Holy Spirit, and Transubstantiation; but you demanded that the Russian Church accept you without condition, and moreover, as representing the Anglican Church, which did not acknowledge your opinions as its own. It was pretty difficult to please you. Later, after having thoroughly studied doctrinal questions in your country, you became completely Orthodox in spirit and you went to the East, where you found the doors closed because a second baptism was unjustly demanded of you. You did well not to go along with that, but you did badly in raising a thorny question between the Churches of the East, a question that would have fallen of itself, [...] you came into the fold of this Church through the Northern door which is always open to you, you could have been hugely useful to her and brought many proselytes by your example, instead of throwing yourself, contrary to your convictions, into the arms of Rome, without putting to her the conditions which you put to the Church of the East.
>
> You ask me, what is there left for you to do to set your mind at rest? You should knock again at the doors of the Russian Church, in that spirit of Orthodoxy that animates you now, by which you will be better understood and will better understand others. You have already done a great good in clarifying the question and making your Church better known; finish what you have begun so well, and see if you have more success now.[6]

Mouravieff wrote again in May, urging Palmer not to despair of a happy issue to the question of rebaptism, but warning him that it would take time to resolve the question definitively. The opinion of the Easterners [i.e., the Greeks] on the subject had been shaken; he was not to throw himself into the arms of Rome without awaiting the outcome of the affair. 'We hope constantly for the reunion of yourself and orthodox Anglicans to true Orthodoxy. I ask God to enlighten you'.[7]

Had he still entertained any real desire to become Orthodox, Palmer could have seized the opportunity he was given in May of 1852, when he called at Corfu on his way home to England. There he discovered from the Archbishop of Corfu that the custom was to receive converts by chrismation and not rebaptism, the standard practice for receiving Latins when the island had been part of the Venetian Republic.[8] Palmer declined, on the basis that the practice had more to do with fear of the authorities than theological conviction, and because it left unresolved his doubts over the claims of the Orthodox Church raised by the discrepancy in practice.[9] A 'moderate' Roman Catholic, Mr. Loughman, gave Palmer 'something like a scolding for *studying* so long, recommended me to give up study altogether & trust only to prayer & to go back to Oxford & say nothing against the Anglican Church till I had made up my mind in favour of another, saying that it had many good things about it, and I might be very useful in it, even if I remained in it altogether, having a Catholic intention of heart'.[10]

2. EGYPT

From November 1852 until March 1853 Palmer was incapacitated by gout. July saw him at his last college meeting; his fellowship would lapse on his conversion to Roman Catholicism.[11] As he was 'suffering more and more from the gout', Palmer decided to postpone Rome in favour of Egypt. He travelled to Cairo, hoping to read a manuscript of the trial of the Patriarch Nicon,[12] with a view to writing a life 'of this great and holy man', but found that the manuscript had been sent by the Patriarch to his friend Mouravieff.

In Egypt he 'went up the Nile as far as the first cataracts', and 'became immensely interested' in the inscriptions here, making a study of 'Egyptian history and chronology' that lasted for the rest of his life. He eventually published 'an elaborate work, entitled *Egyptian Chronicles*',[13] of which Lord Selborne remarks that 'he was led to conclusions as to the earlier dynasties widely different from those of most modern writers'.[14]

In Negadeh, where there was 'a large town, & a large Coptic Convent, as well as a R.C. Convent', they met Edward Lear[15]: 'He shewed us his sketches which were very complete, so that he will carry away with him the whole river'. Palmer went on to Luxor, Thebes, and the Valley of the Kings, and visited the 'Convent of Sinai', which he 'Left at 8am having been let down in a rope bag by the windlass which did not keep me quite clear of the wall'. Shortly afterwards, he had one of the most dramatic encounters of his life. Letting down a rope to draw water from a well at the walls of Beersheba, he was accosted by 'a rascally Arab with a spear', who demanded money on the basis that '"the water belonged to his tribe", and I should not measure it to take it away from them: I regarding this as nonsense went on, and offered him some of the water to drink [...]. I was ready to go on to the other well when he absolutely insisted on my not going'. A bargain of five piastres was struck between the Arab and Palmer's dragoman and paid, albeit contrary to Palmer's instructions. However, the Arab demanded more, and

> as I was told afterwards, said he would kill one of us, & on the dragoman's offering to pay him what he wanted out of his money he refused saying "No, I do not want to take it from you – I want to take it from the Frank [...] But you see replied the Dragoman that the Frank does not want to let you have it. At length when the Arab had once seized me by the coat he produced the money; was going to give it as from me to the Arab – but I stopped him & told him I would certainly never repay him if he did – and I made signs to the Arab that if he was not content like an honest man to be paid what he had bargained for – he had his spear, and we were unarmed, he could *take* the money if he liked – he understood enough of this (by word & gesture) to be angry and make a menacing thrust with his spear towards my breast; but my Arab going close up to him, & saying some word in a pacifying tone ended with Soria! Soria! Begone! Begone! & pushed him away & he rode off: but afterwards I found that the Arab & the Dragoman had one or the other of them actually given him either the whole or some part of the additional five piastres: But as I kept to my intention of not repaying any money so given I asked no questions. The villain said that if I had not had a Tish man with me he would assuredly have killed one of us or rather the Frank.

Palmer noted coolly, 'If I had had time to think about the picturesque just then – he was a most picturesque subject for a painter at the moment at which he struck his lance at my breast – a more cut-throat looking villain could not have been imagined. His name was Djala and that of his tribe Abou-Hamed'.[16]

Palmer went on to Jerusalem, hoping to return to Egypt after travelling to 'Georgia and Southern Russia and then up the Volga', to see the manuscript possessed by Mouravieff as well as other documents relating to Nicon; but the Crimean War intervened. In Jerusalem he stayed, 'notwithstanding the war', with the Russian Archimandrite. He again attended the Miracle of the Holy Fire on 'Easter Eve', passing, as he came into the Rotunda, 'through a sort of dance of people moving round the Holy Sepulchre, and an Arab near me was screaming "Christ died for us & is risen again: the world rejoices; the Jews are sad". At the moment of the fire (as I supposed) there as a deep roar of the distant crowd mixed with a wild discord of clatter & confusion, the striking of metal sounding boards (for Vespers) like the ringing of small tinkling & cheerful & bells, & confused cries'. The noise provoked Palmer to mystical reflection:

> It was a mixture of sounds such as might well give one an idea of the last resurrection, the old things which have passed away for ever, the confusion of nature & the flood of fire being represented by the wilder & heavier tumult & the light sharp tinkling which pierced through it all representing the new feelings of certainty as to the new & abiding life & lightsomeness & blitheness mixed with solemnity at the liberation for ever from all that was depressing before.[17]

At the Latin Convent within the Church of the Holy Sepulchre, he was privileged to be shown 'in the Sacristy behind the Latin Church the sword & spurs of Godfrey de Bouillon'.

3. THE 'DISSERTATIONS'

From Jerusalem Palmer returned to Athens. He wrote to Dr. Routh that even the heat of Egypt had not freed him from gout, and that

> What brought me here was to print in Greek some Theological Dissertations added after I left Athens in 1852 to those which I had printed here before – especially some additional documents relating to the Greek practise of rebaptising Western proselytes.[18]

If this account was less than frank, no doubt that it was because he wished to spare the President any pain by alluding to a possible conversion. Dr. Routh, meanwhile, was protecting Palmer for the last time in his long life. The *Dissertations* had attracted attention, in England as elsewhere, and the Vice-Chancellor of Oxford[19] had as a result been prompted to speak to Dr. Routh, 'with a view to some academical censure'. An account of the resulting interview was sent to Palmer by his eighty-six year old Aunt Mary[20], 'in a strain remarkable for its vivacity at her great age'. The Vice-Chancellor[21] called on Dr. Routh, and suggested that

> the same notice ought to be taken as fell upon Mr. Ward[22] some time back – *i.e.* that Mr. Palmer should be deprived of his fellowship and his degrees [...] the President [...] only answered, 'A very good man, sir; not the same with Mr. Ward.' Then something like a dialogue took place; the President, in reply, only saying at every stop, 'A very good man, sir'; 'a learned man, sir'; 'an excellent man, sir.' And when the Vice-Chancellor appeared to pause, Dr. Routh:– 'Well, sir, have you anything more to say?' On the Vice-Chancellor saying he had not, Dr. Routh replied, 'Then, sir, I wish you good-morning'; attended him to the door, and bowed him out of the room. This story the President told himself at a dinner-party he had the same day; and Edwin heard it, I believe, from one of the party. You will, I hope, be as well pleased with it as we were.[23]

The reaction to the *Dissertations* was mixed. The Anglican writer of a review in *The Christian Observer* angrily drew his readers' attention to it 'as *a specimen of the state of mind of some, who, so far as outward profession and emoluments are concerned, belong to the Church of England*'. He cited one passage ('enough to show the sentiments of the writer') about '*the evil spirit which prompted* [...] the so-called Reformation', before quoting with astonishment Palmer's proposals for missionaries to be established 'in the West in relation to the Anglican Church' to suggest corrections to ritual to be approved by 'the authorities of the Orthodox [i.e. the Greek] Church'. Worse, Palmer, 'openly admitting that the Greek Church holds the doctrine of Transubstantiation", [sic] "the necessity of confession to a Priest", "the septenary number of the sacraments", "the invocation and worship of the saints, and especially of the Blessed Virgin", and "the worship or veneration of Icons and relics", [...] defends these doctrines against "the Protestants"'.[24] The author later noted Palmer's bold suggestion that the 'under Christ the *Head*, the Blessed Virgin is, as it were, the *Neck* of the Church'; so that it was 'for such as have this belief [...] *in point of form better*' to ask for anything of or through her, than to ask it directly of Christ [...] a form beginning "Our Lady, which art in heaven," &c., [might] be preferred for general use to the original form of the Lord's Prayer" [...] We will not trust ourselves to make any comment on these facts'. Ironically highlighting the very lack of authority in Anglicanism that Palmer so despised, the author deplored the way 'such books as these' were permitted 'to go forth without even the slightest protest on the part of the authorities under whom such writers are placed in our Church'. It was clear that 'Mr. Palmer' had 'much at heart' the object of obtaining proselytes 'to the Greek Church'.

Remarking on the 'strange leaning in some quarters towards the Russian Church from the time of Mr. Palmer's first attempt to be admitted into communion with it', the author quoted Palmer's prophecy that 'the "destinies" of the old Greek Church "may be said to be practically wrapped up with those of the Slavonic race, and so again with *those of the Russian Empire*. And we may affirm it to be probable, that in the course of time it will, THROUGH THE RUSSIAN POWER, *regain the whole of those countries which formerly constituted the Graeco-Eastern Empire; and not only so, but that it will cover the whole of Asia to the uttermost shores of the Eastern and Southern Ocean*". (p.7) Such are the triumphs anticipated for "*the Russian Power*", and such is the result, which it is clear Mr. Palmer warmly desires to see'.

This romantic fantasy of the restoration of the Byzantine Empire, so beloved of many Orthodox, both Greek and Russian, might have been passed over with an indulgent smile at any other time; but on the eve of the outbreak of the Crimean War it must have appeared dangerously unpatriotic. The *Observer* closed with a pious disclaimer of any pleasure in dwelling upon 'the errors ' of the Greek Church, and expressed an Evangelical wish to labour for the restoration of 'as many as possible of its members, to that primitive faith from which it has so widely departed'.[25]

The Anglo-Catholic *Christian Remembrancer,* on the other hand, was full of praise for ' the masterly way [...] in which every point relating to the Orthodox Communion' had been handled; 'the ability and extensive information of the author leave nothing to be supplied'. It thought, however, that the restoration of communion between East and West without any acknowledgement of papal supremacy, or requirement of oaths of obedience to Rome from the East, was unlikely; 'it is the tendency of Rome ever to tighten the discipline, and rather to invent new claims than to relax an iota of old ones [...] we cannot but fear that Mr. Palmer's anticipations are destined to be disappointed, and his theory to fail'. Any reunification with Eastern Churches was not expected or desired, save as 'a case of influencing others rather than of surrendering ourselves'.[26] Nevertheless in 'this remarkable work' its author 'has done great and probably lasting service to the Church at large'. If the only result of the work was to harmonise the practice of the Russian and Greek Churches with regard to the reception of converts, his efforts would not have been wasted. However, like George Spencer before him, the reviewer wondered

> what the Author's real position can be in his own mind; he appears to be a realization – if there ever were such – of a spectator *ab extra* [...] he appears to us, from his own principles, to be, in fact, isolated from all communions, and to stand quite alone. He treats the Church as if consisted solely and exclusively of the Roman Catholics and the Orthodox Easterns, yet he himself belongs to neither of those branches. He scarcely touches at any point at issue between the Churches of Rome and England without giving his readers to see that his convictions and sympathies are with not with the latter.

There was also the strong possibility that 'when an individual, with whatever personal qualifications or attainments, takes upon himself to exercise the office, now of dictator, now of judge of the doctrines and customs of Churches [...] whatever error really does exist, may be found, at last, to lie at the door of the individual critic'. Having said that, 'if the blessing of Unity is ever to be given to the Church again, and that by the labours of an individual, there is probably no one living so likely to be the instrument of its restoration as Mr. Palmer [...] no one has examined the questions of which he treats with more care, or has possessed more opportunities of thoroughly sifting the various disputed points on which he touches'. The 'only serious want' of the book was the failure 'to have spoken more plainly', and 'extended [...] his comparison of the East and West' to 'the Church of England [...] of which he still continues a nominal member'.[27]

Fr. Gagarin[28], writing in the French Roman Catholic publication *L'Univers,* found the *Dissertations* 'a very curious work', which though written with the most benevolent of intentions, had produced entirely the opposite effect on 'the schismatics', who had evinced 'the most lively irritation'. The chapter on sending missionaries to the West was 'full of original and fruitful ideas, which would do great good to the Russian Church, if she would or could adopt them [...] Mr. Palmer has redirected their programme better than they probably would have done themselves, because anti-catholic prejudices have less of a hold upon him, and because there is more connection and precision in his ideas'. Gagarin hoped that the serious studies which Palmer had pursued with such perseverance, and the sincerity he had put into his search for the True Church would 'open his eyes more fully to the light, and prepare him to receive the graces which he needed to see the truth'. Like his English counterparts, Gagarin asked if it was not 'a curious thing to see a Protestant recommending frequent communion, the monastic life, wanting to confine missionary work to religious orders, and going as far if not further than some Catholics?'[29]

The Russian chaplain in London, Fr. Popov, wondered what the response to the publication of the book would be, and wrote that a scholar with whom he had discussed it thought it 'a most able book, but far too Latinising [...] here and there, he keeps back evidence a little, when it would tell against him – especially about indulgences'. Although the anonymous scholar prophesied that 'the Author will soon find himself in Rome', Popov believed that Palmer would not follow Newman. 'The spirit of unrest that he has developed after undergoing his trip to Greece would be settled by a true ideal. I wonder if Rome as it is or was can fulfil that ideal. At least in December he told me the following: "If I don't have enough time to be able to come to terms with some of the unclear and puzzling things about the Roman Catholic Church, then I would definitely go to Athos," which has impressed not only Palmer, but many other English travellers'.[30]

When Palmer eventually returned to Constantinople, he met with 'a most vehement condemnation of my former Dissertations' from the theologian Constantin Oeconomos:

> he inveighed against my audacity & contemptuous & hostile tone in representing the Greeks as unlearned, as inconsistent on the subject of Latin Baptism, and as being guilty of formalism (σωσυδοτυπία) a ridiculous word of my own coinage, whereas no such thing exists in their Church; That I wanted to destroy miracles; what could I mean by printing such things? Did I think that they would listen to me, or that I would get them to change their custom, or even read my books? Why should I so attack and insult a whole nation, so ancient & which had suffered so much? Did I think that the way to bring about a union of the churches? Never etc. etc. I laughed, and said that evidently my Dissertations were not calculated to be of any benefit to *him*.[31]

As for those who remained loyal to the Church of England, Palmer saw 'no reason to quarrel with Anglicans for remaining Anglicans even though they may belong to any of the higher shades or parties of their Church, & so [...] more capable of perceiving the difficulties of its position', even if they were ordained. It was different if 'in this or that particular case a man was professing to believe & [...] teach what he could not in any good sense be said to believe'.[32] It was not good to remain blind to the errors of an erring Church, but

> if any one [...] sins against that reverence which is due to truth by seeking it too intellectually [...] the truth [...] has within itself the means of punishing him. This has been the case with me. I had an ignorant & presumptuous confidence in the strength of that Anglicanism which I had inherited & after my first study of the Classics during my Undergraduateship gradually took to the study of Ecclesiastical truth in a state of unfitness & in a tone of intellectual confidence, & irreverence of which I can now only repent [...].[33]

The tone of regret had become noticeably keener.

3. PHILADELPHIA

Despite his protestations that he had done with any attempt to be admitted to the communion of the Eastern Church, in September 1854 Palmer set off to see the Churches of Smyrna and Philadelphia, a decision prompted by the verses in Revelation cited on the cover of his journal.[34] The two Churches 'out of the seven of the Apocalypse [...] alone received praise and promises from our Saviour without any admixture of blame or warning', and were 'the only ones [...] preserved down to the present time amidst the ruins of the five others'.[35] Palmer's interview with the Metropolitan of Smyrna was, however, inconclusive; his reception in Philadelphia altogether less friendly.

The Crimean War was everywhere in evidence as Palmer returned to Constantinople: 'Left the Piraeus by the direct French Steamer for CP with some Officers & 150 French cavalry troopers on board [...] found a room in a new Hotel de Belle Vue, where were one or two sick officers', he recorded on 12 October, and four days later, 'Go to Mr. Hanson's & to Mr. Grace to arrange for shipping two Portmanteaux per British Queen screw steamer to Liverpool. Their office piled up high to the ceiling with portmanteaux &c. &c. for Officers &c. in the Crimea'.[36]

In Constantinople he stayed with the ex-Patriarch Constantius, and on the way back from Antigone

> as the steamer passed near Scutari I got the Capt'n to hail a boat & put me ashore at the corner of the great White Hospital which stands on the projecting cliff just S. of the town, & which is now occupied by the wounded English [...] the place is very large, but ill-drained, & the stench was very offensive: the corridors were still half filled with wounded men on their beds but many

> beds being rolled up shewed that their occupants were on their legs again. I saw several Officers who had been with Lord Ch[ewton][37] when he lay there [...] We walked across the open space to the S. (on which the British tent were pitched before leaving for Varna) to graves of those who have died from their wounds immediately on the brow of the cliff under the Red Hospital. The view from the Hospital, & from the space between is magnificent, & seen from hence about sunset the Golden Horn shews how it obtained or at any rate deserves its name. Went into the room where Lord Ch[ewton] lay, and died. There was still a great black stain on the floor from the blood.[38]

One of Palmer's fellow-passengers on board the 'Luqsor' from Galata to Smyrna had gruesome souvenirs of the fighting:

> A connection of some of the owners or managers of the P. & O.S.P.C. who had been up to Sebastopol had with him a broken Russian musket, a silver cross made to open & containing, he said, a bit of flannel soaked in blood, taken from the body of a Russian Colonel killed in the battle of the Alma.

Palmer made a last futile application to the Patriarch of Constantinople and his Synod, who 'pretended to be ignorant of the custom of the Russian Church [...] of receiving Latins [...] without rebaptizing them' before setting off for Smyrna and Philadelphia. He was warned in Constantinople of the danger of robbers and 'advised for perfect security to go with the Caravan', but found on setting out that

> I was in truth myself the caravan, when Theodore pointing to three mules laden seemingly with rags & a superfluous packsaddle (that of my own rawbacked horse, for which I had hired an old European saddle) exclaimed triumphantly "Voila Monsieur la Caravane!" [39]

With them was the 'Caravanjee', 'mounted on the skeleton of a grey horse which fell at least 6 or 7 times a day', and was then 'beaten most savagely' to get it back on its feet; and the Caravanjee's man, a stout barelegged redfaced Turk, quaintlooking, & dressed like his superior in sadcoloured partycoloured [sic] rags. He was mounted, though he oftener walked, on a rather respectable donkey on which he was perched very high looking like an evil genius or incubus oppressing the poor little beast.

The party stayed in 'khans', or inns, in primitive conditions. Palmer describes one in a village with the lanes 'running .. with deep black mud', and the upstairs room in which they were to sleep up a ladder and with five 'window holes without any frames [...] we were close under the mountain with the wind setting right down right into our room very cold'. They spread mats over the empty windows and the cracks in the floor, but

> We were soon obliged to open two of the window holes again by having our room filled with charcoal smoke which came up through the chinks of the floor. It seemed that there was a charcoal fire burning beneath, probably for the preparation of coffee & also for the warming of a noisy party of Turks smoking their pipes & drinking it half under roof half al fresco. This lasted not indeed very long after dark, but much longer than suited us & our room.[40]

Palmer made himself a bed on the floor

> as follows [...] the saddlebags were spread to serve as mattress: a small hand carpet bag was the pillow; a small air cushion slightly inflated saved the hip bone from grinding on the floor; the saddle set at my feet kept off the wind from them: a Scotch plaid & pair of easy cloth shoes made the bed.

Suspended from the wall were all 'the little necessaries' of his camping equipment:

> a small tin drinking cup hung by a string to the knapsack; a tinbox of Lucifers; a Cairo pocket lantern & candle; toothbrush, two other brushes & comb: small tin box with small sponge & soap: a leather dressing case or roll with razor & strop, shaving brush, knife & fork, dessert & tea spoon, towel, & several small bags, one of which contained a lump of bread to be eaten on horseback in the morning, for we did not breakfast before starting; (saving that we took the usual Turkish thimbleful of coffee grounds without sugar).

It was a far cry from the comforts of Magdalen High Table. Since they lay down 'as early as 8 o'clock', they passed 'tremendously long nights, and I learned to distinguish between first second & third cockcrowing as I had never done before'. Rising with the light, they dressed and packed, Palmer festooning himself with a knapsack, a leather strap 'from which was hung by a string loop my umbrella, the whip (kowbatch) being suspended by a similar string from the wrist of my right hand, and the hat (a wideawake) being secured by a shoeribbon to the top buttonhole of my upper coat'. The 'Khanjee' was rewarded with backshish as appropriate ('I commonly gave 6 piastres i.e. a shilling'), and the caravan was on its way.

When they arrived in Philadelphia, Palmer's Greek servant, Theodore, tried to get into the ruins of the old Church of the Transfiguration, 'but was repulsed with such a volley of billinsgate [sic] by the old Turkish women within the precinct'. The bishop was hardly more polite. They called on him to compliment him on his Name's day,[41] and Palmer attempted to give him a copy of the *Dissertations* in Greek

> but he making a repulsive gesture with his left hand declined to receive it, saying I do not wish to receive it: We do not want *such* books: We have our own books which we read & do not want books from strangers. I said "*Such books* as what? Your πανιερότως [sic][42] as yet can scarcely know what the – enough - the Great Church has expressly enjoined us not to receive books from strangers. We are content with our own.

Palmer asked if he would receive an Englishman 'desiring to confess his sin and receive spiritual counsel'; the bishop said he would not. They received only the confessions of their own people. Palmer asked again if an Englishman came professing the doctrines of Orthodoxy whether he could be received? 'No, he said – I know something of your business – Nothing of the kind can ever be done'. The Protodiaconos added 'For such questions there need Councils & decisions of Patriarchs & Synods – We baptise all: but we here receive nobody – we have an order from the Great Church to receive nobody – we receive neither by Baptism nor by Chrism – we have no Chrism [...] We receive not even Jews – nor English. We desire to meddle with nobody and to be left alone ourselves – That is all we wish'.[43]

Palmer pointed out that in the Apocalypse Christ commended the Church of Philadelphia, and said that 'there is here an open door – It seems then that this open door is now shut? "Since it is shut" replied the bishop "we keep it shut"'. Palmer responded that it was not written that when even unbelievers came and bowed down at the feet of this Church she shall kick them away. After some discussion about whether or not the English were unbelievers, the bishop relented slightly:

> I have heard a good report of you – there are many people – many nowadays - who will give money, and go about: But what you seek cannot be done – why should you want to confess & be received here are there no Bishops or Priests to be found elsewhere – Have you not been or cannot you go to Smyrna – to Constantinople, to Corfou – At any rate we have the orders of the Great Church to receive nobody.
>
> I thanked the Bishop for his plainspokenness which I preferred to a hypocritical civility, and said that as he had anticipated the conversation I had desired to have with him in private, and had given me such clear and positive answers by anticipation as rendered all the questions I had to ask unnecessary I would now take my leave & return to Smyrna. "A good journey to you" he said, and so we parted. He seemed to have as little disposition to see more of me or hear more of my business as any of the Scotch Bishops had in 1846 or 1847.[44]

When they called on the Protodiaconos Philotheos, he explained that they were 'now under the [Turkish] yoke & can do nothing – Not even a Synod can meet or do anything now, as there is no Emperor etc. I replied that nevertheless now & then when they please they have done & still do something'. The local schoolmaster too was apologetic: 'these are ignorant unlearned men – the reason was that he was afraid of you: but certainly he acted amiss; he should have received the book'. The bishop should also have considered that the experience might be written up, and to his discredit; but it was true that there was 'an order of the Great Church against the publications of foreign missionaries and travellers attacking our religion'. The bishop had twice been deceived by bogus 'converts', and 'again, if we received you, the English Government might take umbrage'.

Constitutionally unable to let matters lie, Palmer composed a paper to the bishop, which he left on the floor of the church. It suggested that the proselyte who could not in conscience accept rebaptism should be given guidance as to how to be admitted to the communion of the Orthodox Church, which 'might perhaps be done' by chrismation or conditional baptism. Whether or not the bishop ever read it, history does not relate. As Palmer rode back to Smyrna, a 'Doctor Constantine' told him how shocked he had been by the bishop's words and manner, and complimented him on his 'upolomg (patience) during that interview'. 'He observed by way of explanation that this See being poor & out of the way they send here whom they please, any one whom they have a reason for raising to the Episcopate; & all are equally accepted; whereas at other places [...] they will not receive an illiterate or unqualified Bishop'. Palmer shrugged it off:

> I laughed & replied that as for that I was not inclined to quarrel with the Bishop – the style of his reception was certainly rare if not unique in the Levant, but I prefer even tough straightforwardness to hypocritical courtesy & evasiveness: and I had served a good apprenticeship in England & Scotland, & knew how people who ride principles too hard to consequences or put troublesome questions must expect to be treated. Besides which [...] it is quite true that there are now many strangers Americans & others who go about with their tracts & books expressly to disseminate their own corrupt traditions[45]: And if he even had a strong prejudice against all Englishmen it was no great wonder when one knows that he was Protosyncellus under the Patriarch Gregory whom the English Ambassador thrust out from the Patriarchate.[46]

On their way back they slept in 'the great Khan' at Cassaba, where they ate 'an excellent green-fleshed melon of which Theodore had reserved a large section for his breakfast; but in the night the mice so mangled & dirtied it that I think he could eat little of it. I felt their clammy little feet running over my face during the night, & my plaid smelt strongly of them in the morning'.

16 Rome at Last

1. CONVERSION

Palmer's journey to Rome was prefaced by news of death; on 21 November, he 'read in the papers the account of the battle of Inkerman on the 5th Nov. Also saw that Adm. Korniloff,[1] who had planned the recently erected defences of Sebastopol & had taken out for them the guns from the ship, has been killed'. On 2 January, a laconic diary entry reads: 'At English Reading Room saw in the Times an article mentioning "the late President of Magdalen College", and so learn Dr. Routh's death'. The father figures who had watched over him with such concern and loyalty were gone; he could now act as he chose.

Palmer arrived in Rome in January 1855. His theological discussions with the Jesuit Fr. Passaglia[2] caused him both dismay and irritation. Passaglia had never read Zoernikaff on the *filioque*; when Palmer showed him a passage from Gregory of Nyssa in which 'the sense of the context clearly required the absence of the πţ', thinking that Passaglia 'might be trusted to fill up the lacuna with the true reading', Passaglia 'immediately inserted the clause *with* the πţ, admitting none of the reasons urged against it, and insisting on the certainty of the text'. Palmer expressed 'astonishment & disappointment, with an increased sense (not small nor recently acquired before) of the prodigious bias given by an overwhelming idea of authority to the most acute and learned & candid & liberal minds'. Passaglia offered to call in Fr. Schor, 'a German of a different cast, & habit of mind; perhaps I should be better inclined to respect his opinion'. Palmer bluntly refused: 'this would be quite needless; I had no doubt after what he had shown me in his own person, that they would be all alike'.[3] It seemed unlikely that Palmer's wish to be brought round to the Roman point of view would be fulfilled after this unpromising start.

Palmer was at least able to enjoy the splendour of the pontifical services. On 18 January, he attended High Mass in St. Leo's, 'the Pope assisting Pontifically'. Palmer went with the students of the Academia into the 'temporary Quarter of the High Altar', from where he watched the entry of the procession,

> led up from the Great E. Doors by the boys, after whom walked Clergy Bishops & Cardinals (of the latter above 24): the Pope himself was borne aloft on his Portatory seat (as a Greek Bishop in the Levant is borne, when dead, to his grave) with two enormous & very handsome Fans (like those borne before Egyptian Kings). On the 4 great days that he not only assists Pontifically, but Pontificates, a baldaquin also is carried over his head. At his entry the Singers (without any organ) from a gold-latticed lodge struck up "Tu Es Petrus" &c.

Accustomed as Palmer now was to Orthodox practice, some things appeared incongruous,

> The position of his attendants sitting dos a dos on the steps of his platform, also that of the three junior Clerks of the Celebrant's assistants seated on the first step of the High Altar with their backs to it looked barbarous & comical, or at least not Ecclesiastical to a *Greek* eye.

others 'quaint'. Palmer's friends

> pointed out to me the "Prince" or Patrician on the steps of the Papal Chair, in a quaint dress of some three centuries ago (the dress of the Swiss barbarian guard is also most grotesque but the Roman Guardia Nobile looked well, and made one feel that the spiritual Fisherman was now a Temporal Prince even in his Pontifical Functions) also they shewed me "the [Latintitular] Patriarch of Constantinople"; and "a Greek Archbishop" in Greek robes & mitre, a tame elephant, really a very handsome man, who lives at the Church of S. Athanasius dei Greci where he officiates according to the Greek-United Rite[4] twice or thrice a year and represents "the Greek Church" on state occasions.

Despite the formality of the occasion – 'All the ladies & the gentlemen admitted within the line formed by the Guard are required to be in black evening dress, the ladies with veils' – the behaviour of those attending, clerical or lay, was casual to the point of irreverence:

> Dogs are not admitted to S. Peters, but the Protestant English & American ladies, it is said, sometimes leave chicken bones behind them, & spitting, talking & moving about proceeds as a thing of course among the Italian multitude at these great Functions, much as it might do [...] in a civic festival or gala in the piazza. Clergy, who have said their own Masses of course if Priests, look on, read their Office or some other good book if it so happens, chat a little, take snuff, &c. all except those whose duty or privileged places force them to see the whole out come in or go out as it best suits them: nor can any idea be more utterly out of place than that of a religious Anglican or even of a Russian who expects the whole assembly to exhibit throughout a reverent attitude to & participation in the most solemn act of congregational worship.[5]

Nonetheless, Rome had had 'nothing but brilliant Triduos going on ever since the 8th of Dec. as manifestations in every Church of spiritual rejoicing & thanksgiving. "Rome", I read in a French Paper, "est *ivre* de joie"'. Palmer reflected that although there were 'plenty of vicious worldly people' in Rome, which 'would be [in] immediate danger of a revolution' but for the French garrison, 'if one thinks of the religious side, imagine Manchester, or London intoxicated with religious joy'.[6]

Palmer was now put under pressure[7] by his English convert friends, such as Wynne and Coleridge[8] to go on a retreat arranged by them at the Jesuit Collegio Romano. He reluctantly agreed ('I was disinclined on account of the loss of 10 days'), and entered the Collegio on 21 February, Ash Wednesday. He found that the very priest he had dismissed with impatience, Fr. Passaglia, was to take the retreat. The retreat was an Ignatian one, and Palmer was given to meditate on the rules for choosing one Communion or another. He quoted part of them to his mother:

> 1. To think of the end for which you were created and try to be indifferent to everything else: To ask God for grace to help you to choose aright: To consider the pros and cons: To offer the choice when made to God and make it a subject of further prayer: To ask yourself what or which course would you think of with most satisfaction if you were on your deathbed – or at the day of judgement: To ask yourself whether any inclination you feel for this or that course is purely for God's sake: To suppose the case were that of some other person, and ask yourself, what would you, as his well-wisher, wish for him or advise.[9]

Passaglia had suggested that as Palmer was 'plainly an unsound member of the Anglican Church, and [...] ready to quit it', he ought to choose another, if he believed in the existence of the Church as a visible body. Palmer responded that until he could come to believe personally in the Roman Catholic definition of the Church, he did not see how he could properly profess a belief in it, nor build on such a foundation; although he was willing enough to sacrifice his personal opinions. This was Passaglia's opportunity. He assured Palmer that he could convert with his personal opinions unchanged, 'if I were really willing to sacrifice all egotism connected with them, only holding them as it were in abeyance – leaving the result to God'. Palmer should suspend his private judgement, and simply refrain from affirming anything 'contrary to the known dogmas of the Roman Church'. Passaglia 'exclaimed "My soul for yours!" assuring me that when once I had taken the step all intellectual difficulties would before long thaw and melt away'.[10] Palmer was all too aware that he was alienated from the Anglican Church, but belonged to no other; that he was consequently cut off from the Sacraments, 'which I had no intelligible *right* to receive in the English, nor any power to receive, in any other Communion', and that he could not spend the rest of his life 'in studying, and even to some extent *judging*, all Churches, without belonging in God's sight to any one of them'. His thoughts and meditations had been deliberately focused on 'last things', and judgement; he was exhausted by trying to satisfy himself intellectually of the existence of the ideal Church. He could see the 'great happiness' of his English friends who had converted, and was moved by 'the warm and touching zeal they showed for the souls of others'. All of this determined him 'to become as it were a child, and, setting aside all notions of my own, repeat such words as were dictated to me by the first Teacher on earth rather than those which hitherto I had repeated from the mouth of Queen Elizabeth and her Bishops'. Therefore on 26 February he put himself into the hands of Fr. Passaglia, who obtained 'the procured the necessary permission or Faculty from the Pope', and on the Tuesday

> in the presence of the Superior & some thirty or more of the Fathers and Lay- brothers I made my adherence to the Profession of Faith of Pope Pius IV, and was absolved from the Papal Excommunication under which Henry VIII and Queen Elizabeth brought our ancestors. Father Passaglia sobbed like a child, and they all embraced me afterwards from the first to the last with a warmth which was quite moving, though for me (so far as the intellect was concerned) the act (apart from a Psalm and Prayer which accompanied it) was a passive form much like that of signing the XXXIX Articles at Oxford.[11]

The next day he made his confession, and on the Thursday was anointed with Chrism and received the Communion from Bishop Brown of Newport,[12] Wynne being his godfather. 'God's grace', exulted *L' Univers*, 'had silently wrought the miracle learned controversies had failed to accomplish'.[13]

Was this, then, the greatest piece of intellectual hypocrisy of Palmer's life? Until now he had been unbendingly logical in his approach to religious questions, and yet here he was, fully convinced of Orthodox doctrine, becoming Roman Catholic. He admitted to Roundell Palmer immediately afterwards that his action was

> very open to criticism, and until Fr. Passaglia's prediction and assurances have been justified by the event, and my understanding brought into harmony with my present position, it would be difficult or impossible for me to attempt any intellectual justification of it.

Writing to his friends in Russia three years later to explain himself, he recalled, in a faintly sardonic way, how his

> Roman Catholic friends, proselytes for the most part, predicted to me in a tone of absolute assurance that my singular partiality for the Russian and Eastern Church would cease all in a moment, when once I should become a Catholic, and that my understanding would be fully enlightened, so as to know and recognise the true orthodoxy upon all points.

In the event, 'I am very glad [...] that I never allowed myself to be carried away by their promises, and accordingly I have not been disappointed. I have obtained from the step which I resolved upon a real peace and religious position which I am able to defend; but as for my intellectual position, it has remained almost without change'.[14]

Whenever he was asked about his conversion, this remained his answer. When Canon Meyrick asked him, 'some years later', if he was now satisfied of the truth of the Roman Church, he replied 'No; intellectually I am exactly in the same position as before; but I am more comfortable in my present communion'.[15] In 1856 he told Fr. Popov that he still had sympathy for the Eastern Church, 'not only on the liturgical side of our Church but also as regards dogma. '"As far as he is guided by his own private judgement" he is still on our side and finally submitted to the power of the Roman Church "after having suspended his intellect". It reminds me of a phrase of the Metropolitan of Moscow [Philaret]: 'His soul is not ambivalent, but his mind is [...] Here we are not talking about Communion, but enslavement'.[16] '[...] as he submitted to Rome, he must sacrifice himself to it. A whole sacrifice, an absolute sacrifice, "suspenso intellectu"'.[17] It is remarkable that in the 'Confession of Faith' that Palmer wrote for his friends in 1855, having listed all the difficulties he faced and the factors that persuaded him to submit to Rome, he should go so far as to say that the form in which he submitted contained 'some things inconsistent with his own private judgement not only on certain particular doctrines *but even respecting the Definition of the Church*, on which they depend'.[18]

It might be argued in his favour that he had never made any secret of his personal preference for Rome, and had 'dreaded rather than wished for success' when he 'thought himself obliged to seek admission to the Communion of the Greek or Eastern Church',[19] as his panic on being turned away by the Scottish bishops demonstrated. To become Orthodox would have been 'strange and irrational to everybody besides myself', 'more eccentric than praiseworthy or intelligible'. It was after all a fact that the Russians and the Greeks differed fundamentally on the manner of reception of converts, and for it to be contended that the Catholic Church was 'a visible society and yet divided into two conflicting Communions' was indeed 'paradoxical and difficult to maintain',[20] particularly when Rome, 'the greatest and most puissant of all the Churches', made the same claims, and spoke with one voice. It was a fact, too, that Palmer simply could not go on as he was; all his friends who had abandoned Anglicanism had gone to Rome, which as he had told the Russians was more logical from a cultural perspective, and although in the event the assurances he was given turned out to be nonsense, yet he could be forgiven for putting his intellect to one side and trusting them:

> You [...] will be able to understand that an individual conscious to himself of many sins, conscious too of having gained in the eyes of others with more or less reason a character for

> singularity and self-confidence, finding himself after many years in a position more or less isolated and untenable, should think it at last safer to risk the commission of an intellectual error in deference to the highest Ecclesiastical authority, than persist in maintaining a position which *might* perhaps be connected with some moral or spiritual fault in himself.[21]

If it is asked, 'Why then did he not convert to Orthodoxy later on, when he found himself still convinced, though a Catholic, of Eastern doctrine?', the answer would be that the cultural difficulties remained, and he was comfortable where he was. He had no wish to lose the 'great gain' of being 'under the chief ecclesiastical authority instead of contending against it; and to have certain sacraments instead of disputed, and positive doctrine on certain points on which the Anglican Church cannot, strictly speaking, be said to have a doctrine at all'.[22]

2. CONSEQUENCES

Nonetheless, this left Palmer at a disadvantage in a number of ways. Most obviously, he had, by becoming Catholic, ostracised himself from English society. As has been memorably said of Cardinal Newman, he had voluntarily exiled himself from 'that other Eden of the Establishment, from the golden world of the Anglican episcopal palace and deanery and public school [...] to become a Roman Catholic was still a sort of living death'.[23] Unlike Newman, he could not, because of his lasting conviction of the truth of Eastern doctrine, become a spokesman for Roman Catholicism, either as a lay controversialist or as a priest. This was clear to him from the day of his conversion, and his position never changed. He wrote to his mother that he 'by no means' looked forward 'to becoming an Ecclesiastic in the Roman Communion (supposing such an idea to be suggested)', and to Roundell that 'for the present [...] I banish from my mind as much as possible all intellectual questions of a controversial nature'.

This was a considerable disappointment to his Catholic friends, and those in the Catholic establishment who had anticipated showing off a new 'tame elephant'. The *Civilta Cattolica* praised Palmer's

> sincere and constant zeal for discovering the truth, the genius and knowledge which distinguish him, make every good Catholic hope that the divine intention is to use him as an instrument for great works. Such a man can do a great deal for the glory of God and the salvation of a great number, especially among his compatriots and among the Greek schismatics, whose dogmas and errors he knows so well.[24]

His adherence to precisely those dogmas made the Profession of Faith he had composed unpublishable by the Roman authorities. When Passaglia proposed to write another, to be vetted and revised by Palmer if he wished, Palmer 'declined'.[25] In

August 1859 Sir John (later Lord) Acton[26] wrote to Newman after being visited by Palmer that 'his religious views certainly seem very unsatisfactory':

> As I had never heard Palmer speak on religious matters before I cannot compare anything he said to me the other day with anything he may have said formerly, but I had not imagined that he was in so unsatisfactory a state as I found him. I almost thought he cherished his peculiar view about the Procession of the Holy Ghost and Transubstantiation, and, whilst he admitted that they would prevent his becoming a priest, he seemed unwilling to follow out the train of argument which has presented itself to him as a possible solution of his difficulties.[27]

Had he either changed or concealed his 'peculiar views', Palmer could without doubt have achieved eminence in the Catholic Church. In 1837 he told Count Tolstoy that he had been visited by 'Djunkovsky,[28] now "prêfet apostolic des regions arctiques"', who lived 'somewhere near the North Cape, and seems to have need of all the cold of those regions to keep his natural vivacity within bounds [...] He wanted to take me away with him and offered me I think any of the five (extinct) bishoprics within his territories, – in Greenland or Seeland.' Palmer among the Eskimo as a bishop is a piquant picture.

3. THE EASTERN REACTION

Among Palmer's Orthodox friends, the effect of his conversion produced 'no diminution of affection and respect, but a very keen feeling of disappointment'.[29] The Metropolitan Philaret 'sorrowfully expressed' to the Rev. George Williams his feeling that Palmer's 'secession to the Latin Communion [...] was [...] an injurious slight to the Church which he had studied so deeply and was supposed to sympathise with so entirely', which seemed to stultify 'his former professions with reference to the Orthodox Communion [...] and could not but counteract in great measure the good effects of his former labours'.[30] Others, such as Khomiakoff, were angry with the Orthodox hierarchy and the Patriarchs for putting difficulties in Palmer's way, and losing him to Orthodoxy as a result:

> Although he has recently fallen into the error of Rome, we dare to hope that his mistake will be forgiven him for the long, hard struggle that he had sustained. As for those (however highly placed they may be) who shut the door of the Church in his face, and caused his defection, all that we can say of them is that we hope that God judges them in his mercy; for they are culpable enough. That soul so pure and avid for truth, now thrown into the very centre of a constant and wilful lie, can expect no rest on earth, unless there is a return home which is impossible to forecast.[31]

Palmer's declaration to Popov and other Orthodox friends of his continued belief in Orthodox dogma meant that they continued to hold out the hope that he would one day convert to Orthodoxy, although initially there appear to have been recriminations, even stormy ones. Popov wrote to Tolstoy in 1856, 'The meeting was peaceful and without arguments,' and two years later, 'the way he thinks now is more calm and impartial'.[32] By 1861 his 'ultra-montanism' was 'peaceful and quiet'. In 1858 Popov told Count Tolstoy 'Palmer speaks with particular love about you and Khomiakov', and a few days later, 'he likes to boast his sympathy to us, and particularly to you. To confirm the success of this affair, it is necessary for Count Poutiatine to influence him. "He loves him as a brother"'.[33]

The 'affair' Popov referred to was the attempt by the Russians to obtain copies of a work by Palmer, 'published in 1853–54'[34], in which he judged that custodianship of the Holy Places was rightly invested in 'the Greeks', i.e. in the Orthodox Church. Tolstoy wrote that 'The matter of the Holy Places is investigated with Palmer's 'scholarship and judicial strictness, and the strictly fair decision was given to the Orthodox by this wonderful writer newly acquired by the Latin Church'.

> I never lost hope of Palmer joining the Orthodox Church. He tried so hard – too hard – to find it – seeking too hard for God to reject him from his revelation and enlightenment and to leave him forever in those contradictions of mind which his Orthodox friends with grief find in his confession written in Rome. Please pass from all his friends Khomiakov, Mde Potemkin, Muraviev and many other Orthodox that we cannot get used to the thought of eternal spiritual separation from him, and we pray to the Lord 'that with one heart and with one mind we may confess: Father, Son and Holy Spirit, Trinity consubstantial and undivided'.
>
> Isn't it wonderful that he is great friends with you. Oh if God would make your hopes about him come true, sooner or later. He is alien to the usual habits of his brethren; he never alienated himself from the Universal Truth which he once saw in holy and immovable Orthodoxy. I carefully preserved my friendship with him, and sent him Khomiakov's last book.

Palmer's friendship with Count Poutiatine might provide 'other reasons and motives to keep in himself in one form or another faithfulness to his former views', but 'everything happens according to inscrutable providence'. He consoled himself with the thought that it might

> Be to the benefit of the Holy Orthodox Church that amongst those who struggle against it, there will be a man who knows its truth and is not hostile to it. Maybe he is destined to introduce to debates that have gone on for centuries a spirit of impartiality.[35]

When Popov heard that Palmer was to revisit St. Petersburg in the 1860s, he wondered optimistically whether 'Having encountered his old impressions, will his first love not return to him? In any case [...] the traces of his sympathetic attitudes to us have not disappeared'.[36] The continued affection of the Russians for Palmer is shown by Popov's proposal to Tolstoy that Palmer be given an honorary degree,

'Magister Theologiae', by the University of Moscow 'for his work in spreading information about Russian writing [...] his knowledge of Russian literature goes far back to ancient Russian literature'.[37]

17 Life in Rome

Before settling in Rome, Palmer returned 'after Easter' to England. He mentions for the first and only time a mysterious 'Miss C W', whom he followed to the Isle of Wight and later London '(when she was removed thither)'. He then went to 'Oxford (to pack & remove books etc.)'. In the autumn he left England and set out to Rome, taking in on the way

> the Beguines at Ghent, Aix la Chapelle, St. Alban's relics at Cologne, Nuremberg, Emp'r Henry's relics, S. Willibrord & St. Walpurga at Eichstadt, New Churches & Prof. Döllinger & Card. M. Reisach at Munich, Salzburgh, Isoll (?), Passau, Scotch College at Ratisbon – Trent, Venice, Bologna, Padua, Ancona, Ravenna, Loretto, Terumi [...]. [1]

Initially, 'during the winter of 1855-6', he lived 'with R. Wilberforce[2] in the Via Gregoriana'. In 1857 he moved to lodgings at 13 Dietro la Tribuna di Tor di Specchi. Rome was

> a bad and dear place in the winter for those who have need of a *small* apartment – dear indeed for all Drawbacks, the rooms being low and (for reading and writing in winter) rather dark, with a blank wall of a convent immediately opposite to them across a narrow street, and in a region where the air is not so good as in the English quarter. They are also immediately under the roof which makes them colder in winter, and hotter in spring and summer.

After Easter the rent dropped from 18 scudi, or about £4, per month to six scudi, 'about £1.7s a month; so that living is extremely economical'.

Palmer was never in danger of going hungry for lack of funds, but he had no ready source of income. His books did not sell well; he said of his *Dissertations* that it 'had lain dead from the time that it was born'.[3] He was fortunate in the generosity of his brother. Roundell had written to him after his conversion that 'you will never be forgotten, either in my heart or in my prayers', and gave practical proof of this by sending him, in November 1855, his own share of their Aunt Mary's bequest.

Palmer replied that what he now had was 'sufficient to enable me to meet any such expenses as an occasional short illness, or an occasional journey, whether to England or elsewhere, may involve[...]', but that he 'should be in want of some assistance' if he had anything ready for publication. In 1868 Roundell covertly transferred to Palmer's account at Coutts his share of their parents' marriage settlement. When he found out, Palmer hardly knew whether 'to scold or thank' him for this 'act of affectionate prodigality'. He revealed that although he 'had for my own personal wants all and more than all that I had any right to deserve, I could not well have travelled backwards & forwards between England & Rome every summer to see my mother as I wished', which Roundell's previous gift had enabled him to do, and mentioned again the 'unsaleable publications' to which he could now devote money if he pleased.[4]

Palmer's ultimate home was an apartment in the Palazzo Capuzzuchi, on the Piazza Campitelli:

> His life, solitary as far as intimate companionship was concerned, was passed amongst his books in the suite of rooms he occupied, first as a lodger, then as the proprietor, on the third floor [...] He lived there with his only servant, 'Liberata', a bustling, active, honest, shrill-tongued Italian – a Countess too, for the old Count, to whom the rooms belonged, the last of a long line that had fallen at length from wealth and position into extreme poverty, on the death of his first wife had married this woman, who made him a faithful and devoted nurse in his old age.[5]

To help the Count, Palmer 'became the proprietor of all, and gave him a shelter till his death'. Fr. Morris evokes the Gothic atmosphere of the house at night:

> Far away from the Piazza di Spagna and the gay quarter[6] occupied by visitors to Rome, this old house on the confines of the Ghetto, seemed to belong completely to the past. Who that has entered it with Mr. Palmer at night can forget the scene:– the change from the moonlit streets to the darkness and gloom of the quadrangle, until Mr. Palmer had found his matchbox and lit the tiny light, by whose feeble ray the broad flight of seventy stone stairs that led up to his rooms was dimly visible. Yet the rooms were bright enough by day, and the sun shone in gaily upon them.[7]

Palmer was comfortable enough in his rooms, although extreme weather revealed their shortcomings. In 1871 Palmer noted a 'Very disagreeable day rain, or rather melted snow falling, and impossible to keep oneself warm in the house – wear cloke [sic]', and in 1877

> we had a scirocco & dark rainy days – enough (if the wind had not been favourable) to have caused an inundata. The ceiling of this room, in which I live, leaked in 5 or 6 places, and I have been keeping 2 large splashing tins, 3 or 4 foot-baths and 3 or 4 basins all at once (near together) under the places that drip or run; and they keep up a curious kind of music.[8]

In the salon were set out 'a small collection of Russian icons'; near his bed, 'a palm, and a little plaster of Paris representation of the Virgin and Child'. Hanging 'conspicuously in his [...] working room' was 'a small if indifferently executed copy of Fra Angelico's "Annunciation"'.[9] Elsewhere the visitor would have seen a great many books, and a leather desk, perhaps with Palmer's magnifying glass and 'manifold blotter' upon it.[10]

Although he had stated in his explanatory letter of 1858 to Count Tolstoy the intention to pass the rest of his life in studying a 'way of reconciling and uniting the two formulas of the Greeks and Latins [on the Procession] which seem to contradict each other', this ambition seems to have quietly faded away. He spent his winters in Rome, and in the summer returned to England to see his mother.[11] He indulged his interest in Egyptian chronology and archaeology with regular excursions to Egypt, and was planning one just before his death. In Rome he lived a life somewhere between that of an English gentleman of leisure and a monk. He went out to Mass 'every morning before breakfast'[12], and his diaries are peppered with notes of regular papal audiences and receptions.[13] This access to the Pope gave him the opportunity, of which he took full advantage, to defend Newman against the machinations of 'the English Manning faction' in Rome, and help Ambrose St. John when he travelled to Rome on Newman's behalf.[14]

The Catacombs of Rome provided a ready focus for Palmer's antiquarian and archaeological interests. The Roman Catholic archaeologist Count Giovanni Battista de Rossi[15] had begun a thorough exploration and study of the Catacombs in 1841, under the guidance of the Jesuit Fr. Marchi, his researches being published in three volumes between 1864 and 1877 under the title *La Roma Sotterranea Cristiana*. When Palmer returned to Rome in December 1855 he too made a 'selection of paintings from the Catacombs', that later formed the subject of a book, *An Introduction to Early Christian Symbolism*, published in 1859.[16] Between 1850 and 1870 de Rossi 'conducted many strangers, often of high rank, through the catacombs'[17], and Palmer again followed his lead by acting as unofficial guide to those English tourists passing through Rome who could claim an acquaintance with him. Newman described him as 'the most able, authoritative, and patient of lionizers'.[18] It even became something of an irritation: 'Now, I fear I must lay aside my Egyptian studies, and live a life of interruptions', he wrote in 1858. 'People who have heard of them [the catacomb pictures] are constantly asking me to show them; and as the sight of them can sometimes be beneficial [...] it is difficult to refuse to show them, when there is a sufficient previous acquaintance to justify the request'.[19] Although he was 'most good-natured' in showing J. B. Mozley[20] about Rome, he told him it was 'an office he has had to do for so many, he might as well turn cicerone and charge his scudi'. Mozley was impressed by his typical thoroughness: 'He has got up

Rome in a way that only a Palmer could – exhausting every fact, speculation, and conjecture – Basilicas, Forum, Catacombs, everything.'[21] Other visitors to Rome assumed Palmer was engaged on some unspecified research in the Vatican archives: 'Sometimes I have been accosted by strangers just introduced to me as if I probably spent a good deal of time in the Vatican Library. Others have asked me whether I have made any new discoveries recently?'[22]

Fr. Morris described Palmer in Rome as 'living for God and for the sake of all whom he could in any way whatsoever help, advise, console, or enlighten', and the best example of this was his care for Sister Henrietta Kerr. She was the eldest daughter of Lord Henry Kerr,[23] an Anglican clergyman who was received into the Roman Catholic Church after the Gorham case in 1852. Sr. Henrietta became a Sacred Heart nun in France in 1863, and between 1865 and 1872 was at the convent of the Trinità dei Monti in Rome, escorted there by Palmer.[24] Palmer ensured, by dint of visits 'paid in the most business- like way', that Sr. Henrietta was well, and that her parents were kept informed of her welfare. 'Was there ever such a thoughtful friend?' she wrote of him to her mother in 1868. In 1872 she was unexpectedly let down by her escort on a journey from Rome to Lyons; 'when Mr. Palmer [...] heard this, without a muscle of his face showing surprise, he immediately observed that he intended accompanying me'. Sister Henrietta protested 'strongly' to him about 'all the drawbacks, the long tiring journey, probable cold, possible gout, his own expense [...] but he *wouldn't* hear of it, and I do believe he enjoys it'. Even before he knew he would be required to step in as her escort, 'that incomparable Mr. Palmer' had prepared for Sister Henrietta

> Passports, little packets of Pontifical, Italian, and French money all ready for each ticket-taking. Estimates of expenses everywhere, boxes all ready labelled and directed, hand-bag, writing-desk, two warm shawls, in short, no minutest detail forgotten.[25]

She in her turn attempted to mitigate Palmer's self-imposed austerities: 'I hope you are taking proper care of yourself – not living on cold weak tea for instance – and that you do not expose yourself to this damp chilly air'.[26]

1. EXCITEMENTS

In June 1860 Palmer returned by ship to Russia, and St. Petersburg. He sailed from Hull on the 'Emperor', in company with Fr. Popov's daughter and clerk. The ship was a veritable Noah's Ark:

> with more passengers than were convenient, a vessel of Artizans' wives & screaming children (in the state cabins) the upper deck quite encumbered & built up with goods & cargo, over which one passed at top by planks, & below in single file with difficulty & with a whole menagerie on

> board – 10 horses – one pony – 2 cows – 2 sheep – 1 pig – about a dozen monkeys – above 40 dogs of different kinds, bull dogs – foxhounds – greyhounds – Scotch terriers – King Charles' breed – lapdogs – poodles & minute spaniels [...]

One of these dogs got loose and bit one of the monkeys so that it died; a subscription was raised by a Mrs. Morgan[27] to reimburse the Italian boy who owned it. Palmer

> was deputed, malgré moi, to make a speech to the boy on the deck in the presence of all the subscribers to express our sympathy & to give him the money. Having thus been chosen to be spokesman, I was made to perform again in English after the last dinner of the voyage by proposing the Captain's health & expressing our obligations to him. A quantity of Champagne bottles & cherry brandy made their appearance on deck, and a ring having been formed & the Captain placed opposite to me [...] Mrs. Morgan's brother instructed me that the speech was not to last less than ¼ of an hour. I in vain pleaded that I avoided wine & especially Champagne – and not only had to drink a glass of Champagne, but as a further consequence had to smoke a cigar – a thing which I had not done for thirty years, I think; but the Captain's gratitude would not otherwise be satisfied.[28]

It does not, fortunately, seem to have occurred to Palmer to reflect that the talent that might have been devoted to making speeches at a Gaudy in Magdalen or preaching homilies from a cathedral pulpit was now employed in consoling an Italian boy on the loss of a monkey.

When they arrived in St. Petersburg, Palmer found the ships lying off Cronstadt much as they had been twenty years before, but 'the handsome stone & iron bridge of 8 arches across the Neva, & the huge gold domes of the Isaac Church were striking novelties'. He heard from a sailor how during the Crimean War 'the English ships approached; and how the Russians practised feints to draw them within the fire of the forts – how the deep channel on the other side had been blocked up, & how on one occasion they were very nearly cutting off & taking the Grand Duke – and what alarm there was in St. Petersburgh when the English were here'. Palmer also found 'The distances & the dust are as they used to be – but the state of the paving of the streets whether stone or wood seemed to have become worse than anything I could remember – holes or rather pits where the whole had given way – [...] such as might demolish at once both horse & droshky, & fling out the passenger who has very little to hold to'.[29]

In 1868 Palmer, travelling 'to Vienna from Frascati where the Pope had been saying a Mass for troops at the Campo d' Annibale', was involved in a train crash, whose effects he noted with typical phlegm: 'I was woken by a strange jumping & clattering of the carriage, which threw one of the people in the compartment off the seat, & shook off my spectacles'.[30] In 1870 Palmer was caught up in the Italian revolution. Arriving at Civita Vecchia from Leghorn 'by a Fraissinet steamer' on the night of 16-17 September, he was imprisoned until the 22nd, when he succeeded in reaching Rome towards night.[31] The Jesuits had been thrown out by Garibaldi's forces '& their house near Frascati plundered [...] I was only just in time to recover some books which I had lent to one or two Jesuits, [...] and to remove all my Russian books from the Collegio Romano. I found a great English flag hung out from my windows, and Liberata & the old Count hailed my arrival, as if I had been a security in my own person.'[32]

2. THE PATRIARCH & THE TSAR

During his last twenty-five years in Rome, Palmer also researched and wrote his epic six volume work, *The Patriarch & the Tsar*. To write the story of the downfall of the Patriarch Nicon had been his ambition since early 1853 at least;[33] the Russian Church's gradual slide into apostasy, and Nicon's opposition to it, was something little known in the West. The first volume was published in 1871, the second and third in 1873, and volumes IV to VI in 1876. Palmer was working on a seventh volume at the time of his death. Anyone who begins to read *The Patriarch & the Tsar* expecting a sequential historical narrative will be disappointed. It is, rather, a mass of undigested primary sources, collected with extraordinary thoroughness from Russian archives, presented in no particular order. Palmer takes the part of defence counsel for Nicon,[34] peppering the sources with pungent and sardonic comments that point up the hypocrisy and illogicality of the charges brought against him by the Tsar and the boyars. Palmer then exchanges the barrister's gown for the prophet's mantle, seeing in the history of Peter the Great the spiritual consequences of the sins of Tsar Alexis against Nicon. The dedication gives the Tsar's attack on Nicon a cosmic dimension:

> The Patriarch against the Tsar, the Church against the World; Smyrna and Philadelphia against Pergamus and Laodicea, Patience and Charity against Violence and Iniquity; The Resurrection (Voskresensk) and the New Jerusalem (Novi Ierusalim) against Babylon and Antichrist.[35]

He enlarged on his theme in the Preface: Anglicans might 'owe to the State their very existence', but 'the assumption of a state supremacy has ever been condemned by the Catholic Church as antichristian, as productive of scepticism and immorality [...] that the king should delegate a commission of his own to govern the Church [...] is altogether inadmissible.' The consequence of this apostasy was that the Russian Government, far from going back, would 'go on – to destruction.' As 'Henry VIII and Elizabeth' had 'led a nation into captivity', and their successor Charles I was beheaded as a consequence, 'so will it yet be, we fear, in Russia.' It is striking to the contemporary reader how Palmer's prophecies were fulfilled by the Russian Revolution, only forty-two years away as he wrote.

There are clearings of colour in the monochrome jungle of primary sources. Many are in the second volume, which contains the journal of Archdeacon Paul of Aleppo, son of the Patriarch Macarius of Antioch,[36] one of the two foreign patriarchs[37] in Russia seeking alms, and pressed into service by the Tsar to sit in judgement on Nicon. Its observations of the often brutal world of seventeenth-century Russia are rightly described by Palmer as 'a sort of word- photograph of all that he saw and heard, set off with oriental vivacity, humour, and exaggeration, but accurate for contemporary events'.[38] To enter Russia as a foreigner at the time was to gamble with one's life; 'offending foreigners' were no longer merely repatriated, but

> in the frequent case of rambling Greek monks, who come among them and perpetrate all sorts of impurities and enormities, getting drunk and drawing daggers on each other – they now [...] have taken to this special method of correcting them, that is, they send them into darkness: and for the special crime of drinking tobacco-smoke they even put them to death.[39]

These perils did not seem to have deterred the English, 'the richest of all the Franks', who came 'in thousands to the port of Archangel'. Equally savage treatment was meted out to defeated 'heretics and infidels'. In the course of the Tsar's campaigns against the Poles, his officers killed 'God only knows how many Jews, Armenians and Poles [...] throwing their children, packed in barrels, into the great river Dneiper without mercy'. Treason, murder, sacrilege and rape were capital offences: 'Persons guilty of these crimes never escape being shown round the city with the lash at their backs, and many of them die under it. We saw some whose heads they beat off with maces, not cutting them off with swords'. As for homosexuality, 'they burn the sodomite without mercy'.[40]

Here and there, Palmer indulges in dry humour. We are told, for example, of the Tsar's maternal uncle, the boyar Simeon Streshneff, who incurred the curse of the Patriarch for teaching his dog, whom he called Nicon, to sit up and raise its fore-paws as if giving a blessing. Nicon's accuser, the venal Metropolitan of Gaza, Paisius Ligarides[41], solemnly comments: 'If a mouse eats the host, it does not communicate. So neither is a dog's blessing really a blessing'.[42] After all, as Palmer says elsewhere in a dreadful pun, 'boyars would still be boyars'.[43]

In his later years in Rome, Palmer took to wearing a beard, as appears in the only known representation of him.[44] Perhaps he was influenced by the words he records of one of Nicon's former monks, Joachim, who became Patriarch in 1674. Joachim noted in 1681 that 'the heathenish, lewd, foul, foreign custom of shaving the beard, in years past many times forbidden, and in the days of the tsar Alexis entirely extirpated, has now again, by the insolence of young men, begun to deface the image given by God to man'.[45] He excommunicated those who shaved. Joachim's successor, Adrian, the bishop of Kazan, felt equally strongly on the subject. He declaimed in ringing terms against shaving in a pastoral of 1690:

> [...] Put away from you the custom of shaving and clipping your beards. God has forbidden it, and the holy Apostles have forbidden it, saying: It is not fit to mar the hairs of the beard, nor to change the image of the man; for God has made this comely for women. [...] Our Saviour Christ himself had a beard [...]
>
> O extreme transgressors! Have ye now come to think it an adornment to shave off your beards, and to leave only moustaches? Such is the fashion given by God the Creator not to men, but to cats and dogs. [...] Look at the icon of the terrible Judgement: see ye not on the right hand of Christ the righteous adorned with their beards, but on the left the Mahometans, the Lutherans, the Poles, and other shavers of the beard, with only moustaches, like cats and dogs? See to what your imaginary adornment is bringing you!
>
> To shave the beard is not only a disfigurement and a dishonour, but it is a mortal sin. For this lewd insanity has been anathematised by the former most holy patriarchs [...] O Orthodox people! Receive not this criminal badge, but loathe it as an abomination. For the shavers of the beard, unless they repent, according to the decree of the synod, the door of the Church is forbidden; and they are deprived of the communion of the holy mysteries.[46]

The book failed entirely to find a readership. After Palmer's death the copyrights of his books were left, with his papers, to Cardinal Newman at the Birmingham Oratory. Edwin Palmer wrote to him of *The Patriarch & the Tsar* 'This book is still on sale, but its sale has been exceedingly small. Present unsold stock of 2,421 vols – these may fairly be valued at £60.10.6d. The copyright, as the book will never be reprinted, has no pecuniary value'.[47] He wrote again in November 1879 that 'in my judgement *The Patriarch & the Tsar* is a book which cannot be galvanised into any considerable sale'.[48] In 1883 he advised Newman to 'find depositaries [...] for the complete sets which are bound; & to dispose of the sheets (& odd volumes) *as so much waste paper*. This is pretty much what William himself did when they were thrown back upon him by the publishers'.[49] Newman was told that 'the best paper goes to the butterman and the grocer'; which it did, for £17.17s.[50]

No doubt Palmer would have been better advised to swallow his scruples and write a conventional 'Life' of Nicon; but his efforts were not entirely wasted. Edwin James Palmer[51] told his nephew

> I have found that my uncle William's book 'The Patriarch & the Tsar' is much valued by learned Russians of the generation younger than myself. One of them told me that it was better than any Russian book which has been written about the Church affairs of Russia in the latter half of the 17th century [...].[52]

Meyendorff describes Palmer's work as 'the chief study in the West on Nikon';[53] but despite this accolade, and the extraordinary labour expended upon its six volumes by Palmer, the indigestible nature of the work seems to have attracted few in the West either to read it, follow its lead, or even to mine it for useful material. Palmer would have faced this indifference with complete equanimity. He recognized that his literary efforts were 'unsaleable publications':[54] 'I have never found that what struck my own mind as important [...] struck the minds of other people in the same light'.[55]

3. REGRETS

Although his life in Rome was agreeable enough, apart from increasingly bad health, and although his conversion undoubtedly brought him a measure of peace and certainty, yet Palmer regularly sounded in his letters a note of regret and failure. He had 'deliberately renounced what the world calls success, and never sought human praise',[56] but he was nonetheless haunted by the suspicion that he had squandered his opportunities and talents. He most often unburdened himself to Roundell: 'For myself, having spent above 20 years of my life [...] in a sincere, active and unflinching pursuit of intellectual truth, [...] yet having totally failed in all these efforts to attain to anything satisfactory to myself or to others – and feeling now that I might have spent not 20 only but 100 years or the life of a Methuselah without attaining [...].'[57] 'I feel more and more that I have no time to lose,[58] and yet that I have been all my life losing time, and am doing so still. I can see dimly what might have been the purpose of God for me if I had been a good boy, a good youth, a good son and a good brother; – I feel with a painful though insufficient contrition and desire ever to acknowledge how much I have been wanting in all respects & to all [...].'[59] In 1872 he told Roundell how he felt the difference between 'the appearance of some good qualities and the reality [...] I may have *appeared* to you or to others to be singleminded in some particular respects – but the very thing itself – which I ought to have had, and which alone could have enabled me to be really profitable to others as well as to myself – I have *not* had'.[60]

Palmer's regrets only intensified with age. Looking back, he felt his 'unworthiness from the very earliest time of my remembrance – would that I had been a better son & a better brother! But when one comes to be old, it is easier to see & lament one's early blindness & selfishness & sin, than to amend even in one's self'.[61] Eugene Poutiatine wrote to him 'You say in your letter that you often look back with regret to the abuse & loss of opportunities of your younger days; this, I think, many must do [...].'[62]

18 Death in Rome

Palmer suffered very much from gout, so much so that Sister Henrietta Kerr described him in 1872 as 'looking very feeble, and philosophical about his ailments. I fear his feet are permanently damaged'.[1] In 1875 he had been confined to his bed with gout, and had 'had to take sick communion at Easter'. He made a joke of it, sending 'a kiss from their gouty Uncle' to his nephews and nieces, but by 1878 his health had worsened enough for him to write, if not post, the following letter to Edwin:

> Dear Eddie, I have had such strange pains in my heart today – especially after even slight walking or other exertion (I have had similar aches or pains at times after walking with any haste even very moderate distances during this year 1878, but not to the same extent as today.)
>
> Fri 11.15 am In the train for Turin Bologna & Venice – The pain has returned, & is bad.
>
> Rome Sat 9th Nov At Turin on the 26th Oct the pain had ceased – but there was much nausea, faintness & distress.[2]

In October 1878, as he slept fitfully in a railway carriage, he had a lucid dream of his father. In it he imagined that his father was feeling aggrieved at not having been introduced to Cardinal Manning, an Oxford contemporary of Palmer's. In the dream Palmer expressed his surprise:

> "My dear F., you never told me you were a Catholic" "Nor am I" he replied. I continued "You always showed such apprehension & aversion on that subject". "I did not think that you" he replied "had a right to make me a Catholic" "Nor had I" I said. "Out of your very great affection, & your unwillingness to think of an absolute severance between us you would go *very* far in seeming to assent to what I said or wrote. Nothing struck or disgusted me more than the accidental discovery of this apparent assent & sympathy; and of the very different way in which you communicated on subjects with your eldest & your younger son – straining yourself out of your great affection to agree more than you did with me, and then reverting in communicating with R[oundell] to that Protestantism which was really natural to you.

The dream ended on a note of horror: 'Here the dream broke off but I dreamed that my Father though stouter fuller in face & less aged than I should have expected, in fact more like a man of 45 – was shaven & had the yellow complexion of death'.[3]

Whether or not the dream was an omen for Palmer himself, his health steadily worsened. In December he had an 'ache or pain in breast very bad – retchings, but do not vomit. After some time it goes off'. When John Wordsworth visited him that same month, he found Palmer feeling pain in his chest under the left lung, which came on after walking, and gout in his hand. Palmer's doctor, Dr. Erhardt, told him on 21 December that he had '"a very slight gouty deposit on the outer coating of the heart not interfering with its functions" (at present) but he said or implied that the tendency of the deposit would be to increase as time went on, & to become dangerous'.[4] His diary for January 1879 is a litany of pain:

> 9 Jan 'Pain came on while dressing – bad'
> 11 Jan 'Pain came on while dressing – bad'
> 12 Jan 'Ache [*etc. as above*]'
> 13 Jan *as above*
> 17 Jan 'Pain came on while dressing – bad & more or less at times'[5]

In addition to the pain, he had begun to suffer from insomnia – 'I wake pretty often, & at times not formerly usual, & sometimes I remain awake some time [...] I almost always wake now for the first time within an hour of going to sleep; and therewith a queer sensation as if there was something wrong in the circulation'.[6] The conflicting medical opinions he was being given did not, he told Edwin, 'tend to create or increase confidence in the art'. In February Dr. Erhardt found his heart 'still ailing';[7] the pain continued through March:

> March
> 24 'much the same – ; and plenty of pain in feet at night. Keep my bed.' 25 'a good deal of pain'
> 29 'Very bad (but gout mending)'
> 30 'Scarcely sleep at all – much distress'
> 31 'Sleepless night – much distress – no appetite.'

About ten days before his death, Palmer was forced to take to his bed. John Hoskyns visited him, and found him 'in bed but quite up to conversation and [...] busy correcting the sheets of some work he was engaged in [...] he said he knew his time was drawing to an end and that he was making all preparation'.[8] The last two entries in Palmer's diary, for 1 and 2 April, make harrowing reading. The writing is jagged and spiky, scrawled across the page, although his symptoms are noted with typical detachment:

> I am really very ill with the cold which after two days or three of tickling in the throat has settled on the lungs: little & then laborious expectoration (light chocolate colour) but very great ἀπορία & difficulty of breathing, & of finding a posture to suit; no appetite whatever for solids.

He sent for Dr. Erhardt on 2 April ('the distress even greater'), feeling

> himself ailing in a different way and seriously [...] the reason of his sending was an attack which was clearly not gout but something in the chest, and he felt himself beyond his own treatment, if not beyond a doctor's. Dr. Erhardt perceived at once that it was pneumonia on the right side, and that the weakness of his heart and his general debility made it highly dangerous.[9]

Edwin Palmer had been 'telegraphed for', and set out for Rome, arriving at 6.20 am on Sunday 6 April, but it was too late. He was met by Palmer's servant Antonina[10] and a Sister of Charity, who told him that Palmer had died peacefully at 9.55 the previous night. Palmer had not been strong enough to fight the pneumonia, and 'sank in three days'. Knowing that his brother was coming, Palmer had had a room prepared for him: 'he wished much to see me, and had a great deal to tell me'. Lady Herbert of Lea[11] had been with Palmer as late as nine o'clock, and described his death as 'a saintly one'. Cardinal Manning and Cardinal Howard had also both visited Palmer the previous day, and his confessor, Fr. Armellini, had given him the last rites. The *Tablet* pronounced that

> The death of Mr. Palmer produces a sad void in English society in Rome. He was modest and unassuming in his manner, notwithstanding his great learning, and endeared himself to his many friends by his amiability and kindness. Protestants, as well as Catholics, admired and respected him. His piety was deep and fervent. He was in the habit of going to confession every week, and was a frequent communicant.
>
> He resided in the Piazza di Sta. Maria in Campitelli, and in the Church of that parish his funeral was celebrated on Tuesday, the 8th of April, the officiating clergyman being Dr. Campbell,[12] Rector of the Scots' College.[13]

Dr. Campbell himself wrote this description of the funeral:

> On Monday evening the body was removed to the parish Church of Sancta Maria in Campitelli. As is usual in Rome, it was accompanied by the parish priest and a large number of clergy, bearing lighted candles, and chanting the *Miserere* and other psalms. On reaching the Church, the coffin, covered by a pall, was placed on a bier in the centre of the nave, where it remained surrounded by lighted candles. Next morning, after the office of the dead had been recited by the clergy of the Church, a high mass of *Requiem* was sung by the Rector of the English College, the students of the Scots' College assisting at the altar. At the conclusion of the mass the celebrant, divesting himself of the black chasuble, assumed a cope of the same colour; the subdeacon, attended by two acolytes and bearing the processional cross, proceeded to the bier, at the head of which he took his station. The clergy followed with lighted tapers, and arranged themselves on the two sides, and lastly, the celebrant and deacon, who took their places at the

> foot. When the celebrant had said the prayer *Non intres in judicium*, the responsorium *Libera nos Domine* was sung by the choir. The celebrant then passed round the bier, sprinkling the coffin with holy water, and afterwards incensing it in the same manner. The absolution was concluded by the prayer *Deus cujus proprium*. The service of the interment now began with the anthem *In paradisum*. The *Benedictus* was then sung, and the anthem repeated: the final prayer chanted by the priest, the coffin again sprinkled, and two cantors sang the last *Requiescat in pace*. The coffin was now transferred to the hearse in waiting to remove it to the Cemetery of San Lorenzo. Thither it was followed by the parish priest, his curate, and the cross-bearer. Outside the Cemetery chapel the coffin was placed on a trestle, the parish priest recited alternately with those present the *Benedictus*, and repeated the prayer of the Burial Service already said in the Church; he then made the sign of the cross with the asperges over the body, which was then carried to the vault.[14]

Edwin Palmer thought the funeral 'long, not unsolemn, but in respect of the service less impressive (at least to an unaccustomed person) than our short funeral service. The General Cemetery of Rome now is outside the Porta S. Lorenzo about 2 miles from this house. A good many English friends followed, both ladies and gentlemen [...] William was evidently much loved, as he deserved to be'.[15] John Hoskyns was among those whose lot it was 'to follow our old fellow Collegian William Palmer to his last resting place in the Cemetery at S. Lorenzo this morning [...] a good many English residents attended, and the service was very long but very impressive *in the Church*. I could not help contrasting our beautiful and simple services at the side of the grave with what I witnessed today'.[16] Palmer was eventually buried in the Campo Santo[17], 'at the left corner of the first part of the ground as you enter the Campo Santo, quite close to the entrance, & in a bright sunny spot, under a tall & fine cypress'.[18] The grave was marked by 'a plain round pillar of grey marble, surmounted by a white marble cross'; on it, in red letters, was a Latin inscription composed by Edwin Palmer:

> Hic est situm corpus/Guilelmi Palmer/Angli/Collegii S. Mariae Magdalenae apud Oxonienses olim Socii/In Roma obdomivit in Christo/Mensis Aprilibus/Anno Salutis MDCCCLXXIX/ Aetatis suae sexagesimo octavo/RIP. [19]

Epilogue

Benjamin Jowett,[1] the Master of Balliol, told Edwin James Palmer 'Don't be like your Uncle William. He was the ablest of the brothers, but he wasted his life, he wasted his life'.[2] Frederick Meyrick also thought that Palmer was 'lost [...] to the name and fame that might have been his', a view Palmer himself appeared to share, judging by his letters from Rome. In terms of objective worldly success, this was undoubtedly true. The copyrights in the books that Palmer left to Newman were worthless; the remaining unbound copies of Palmer's monumental work *The Patriarch and the Tsar* went to 'the butterman and the grocer'[3] '*as so much waste paper*'.[4] Palmer was a man of remarkable gifts; of assimilation of information, of analysis, of written expression, of argument. With these abilities, he could have achieved success in almost any sphere he chose. He could have been a classical scholar, an outstanding advocate, or judge. His travel journals show a talent for descriptive writing that a professional travel writer would envy; he would have adorned the hierarchy of the Anglican, the Roman Catholic, or indeed the Orthodox Church. 'He was one of the very ablest and best men the College had',[5] 'the ablest of all our contemporaries at Oxford'.[6]

To have achieved conventional success, however, he would have had to be an entirely different man. The obstacle was his character, logical and stubborn. 'There was indeed, only one thing that William Palmer lacked, and that was the common-sense which looks at a thing all round and makes allowance for conflicting principles. Not having this, he became an ecclesiastical Don Quixote'. He was unable 'to reconcile himself to the conditions of imperfect humanity and human institutions, untaught by the wisdom of Butler'.[7] For some, such as Francis Faber, Palmer's refusal to compromise was admirable: 'William never thinks of practicability; and in that consists, *me judice*, his great superiority of character. Whatever, in his opinion, ought to be, in his opinion *can* be: and he rejects all οἰκονομία, all management, entirely'.[8]

However the danger for the man who refuses to compromise, and is convinced that he is right and everyone else wrong, is that in a world that depends on pragmatism and accommodation he will end as a party of one.[9] Such was Palmer's fate.

> His choice of objects and his choice of means to attain them were both uncommon, if not singular; as was his perseverance in the course which he had chalked out for himself [...] like energy & tenacity of purpose might have produced far greater results if they had been employed in connexion with and under the direction of an organised community, and not on enterprises which he undertook as an individual and which were beyond the sphere of individual effort. But there was as little vanity as self-interest in his isolated work.[10]

The organised community with which Palmer was connected was the Church of England; but as self-appointed advocate for its catholicity, Palmer found himself alienated from its mainstream, and in direct opposition to the head of its hierarchy, seeking support from its obscurer offspring in Scotland and America. The 'peculiar genius of the Church of England' was after all precisely 'those elements of compromise and comprehension that characterise'[11] it, and for that reason the inflexible Palmer was a highly unsuitable spokesman for Anglicanism. His inflexibility also led him to unwise extremes in his pursuit of the Princess Galitsin, 'in which he showed himself more Russian than the Russians'.[12] What began as a mission of mercy turned by degrees into harassment in the cause of ecclesiastical theory, giving the impression of instability and fanaticism, the 'monomania' described by the Scottish bishops.

That he should be so much his own worst enemy was a source of frustration to those, friends or family, who admired and loved him. For he had great personal qualities: Meyrick thought him 'a man of noble soul, unselfish, honest, true, lovable'. Newman paid tribute to Palmer's 'many and winning virtues; to his simplicity, to his unselfishness, to his gentleness and patience, to his singular meekness, to his zeal for the Truth, and his honesty whether in seeking or defending it; and to his calmness and cheerfulness in pain, perplexity and disappointment'.[13] When Palmer died, he felt he had lost one of his 'dearest, oldest and truest friends'.[14] Lord Blachford responded to Newman's tribute with one of his own: 'What you say of him is most deeply and touchingly true. His kindness, patience, generosity, industry and singleheartedness besides what lies deeper still, one can never forget'.[15] It is hard, if not impossible, to see what his friends or family could have done to divert his course. His father struggled manfully, but in vain, to argue him out of it; Francis Faber tried to make him see 'the injustice of leading the Russian theologians to suppose that the Scottish Church is not orthodox, merely because the Bishops refuse to hold a Synod at the wish of an English deacon. [...] But *nihil valui*'.[16]

From time to time Palmer would listen. He was careful to address the SPCK 'calmly and without excitement'; he allowed his 'Memorial' on the Jerusalem Bishopric to be re-written by Roundell so as to moderate its tone, and refrained from publishing his subsequent Protest at Dr. Routh's behest. It may be that if Dr. Routh had been less indulgent towards Palmer in allowing him excessive amounts of leave, and had insisted on his confining himself to his collegiate duties, some of Palmer's more extravagant actions and writings might have been avoided, and a more conventional career gradually adopted; but Palmer was so headstrong, and determined to work out in his own way the question of the existence and identity of the True Church, that such speculation is perhaps misguided.

Palmer did besides achieve much: he was a gadfly to the Churches, stinging them by words and writings out of their lethargy on the question of unity, reassessing with acuity and thoroughness the obstacles and objections to unity, and what weight was to be given to each. He was even-handed in his criticism. He upbraided the Church of England for its pusillanimity and double-mindedness, and the Russian Church for its inconsistency over the standing of the Roman Catholic Church, and its inward-looking ethos. Although ultimately he submitted to its authority, he never really accepted without question what the Roman Catholic Church said, just because she said it. His ecclesiological writings are excellent and thorough analyses of the situation of the Eastern and Western Churches as they stood in his day, as his contemporaries acknowledged:

> His learned Dissertations on the Eastern Communion, which have done so much to clear up misunderstandings, and to vindicate the position of the Orthodox Church in her controversy with the West, still remain to us, and have taken a place in the literature of the subject second to none in importance for their permanent bearing upon the momentous issues of the question.[17]

If the Churches subject of his *Dissertations* received them not with interest and gratitude, but rather with 'much irritation', this was because 'error is by its own nature at once the most inconsistent and the most intolerant thing in the world',[18] something Palmer learned the hard way.

Palmer had 'the honour of being the first Englishmen for many years who was seriously and honestly interested in the Orthodox Church, and really studied its views and practice'.[19] *The Patriarch and the Tsar*, ignored in England, was 'much valued by learned Russians'.[20] The opportunity Palmer gave to the Scottish Episcopal Church to open negotiations with the Orthodox Church could be compared by his contemporaries only to the overtures of the Nonjurors in the eighteenth century.

He deserves credit too for what he achieved by his visits to Russia. It was not simply a question of 'having gained much goodwill [...] and many friends', as Lord Selborne supposed, although that was true; he had, as Newman perceived, introduced among the Russians 'the idea and the desirableness of Unity, and made them understand that the action of the Anglican establishment was not the measure of the Catholic religious feeling in this country'.[21] This in the face of extraordinary difficulties, which impressed Newman as he worked on *Notes of a Visit to the Russian Church*:

> I wonder at his spirit. He was certainly most kindly received [...] but his lodgings and fare, the climate, his gout, his wearisome use of two languages not his own, and that in difficult controversy, and his great patience [...] make me think of him with great admiration.[22]

His visit also led to the practical result of the appointment of the popular Fr. Evgeny Popov as the Russian chaplain in London, and made the Russian Church better known in England.

Newman suggested that Palmer's Russian adventures should be seen in another context: 'labours such as his, so Christian in their aim, so disinterested and self-sacrificing in their circumstances, are, in a religious point of view, never wasted, never lost'.[23] Bishop Wordsworth of St. Andrews, quoting Bishop Hamilton's assessment of Palmer as 'the ablest of all our contemporaries at Oxford', added

> No less good than able. Surely there was also something mysterious, of which we shall know more in another world, that so much ability and so much goodness does not seem to have made its full mark, or found its worthy and proper place in this present life.[24]

Palmer himself may best explain that mystery:

> [...] in spiritual matters that which seems expedient to a worldly eye is often precisely the reverse; and that which seems most inexpedient and desperate to flesh and blood, is really the most expedient. They who love or seek their life shall lose it, and they who risk even their life for the truth's sake shall find it.[25]

Abbreviations

AC	Venn, J. A., *Alumni Cantabrigienses* (Cambridge: CUP, 1922- 54), Part II.
AM	William Palmer's Aunt Mary.
AO	Foster, J., *Alumni Oxonienses* (London: Foster, 1888).
ASC	William Palmer, *An Appeal to the Scottish Church* (Edinburgh: Laurie, 1849).
ATR	William Palmer, *Aids to Reflection on the Seemingly Double Character of the Established Church* (Oxford: Parker, 1841).
BL	British Library.
BO	Birmingham Oratory.
CB	Cokayne, G. E., *Complete Baronetage* (Gloucester: Sutton, 1983).
CCD	*Crockfords Clerical Directory* (London: Horace Cox, 1876).
CP	Cokayne, G. E., *The Complete Peerage of England, Scotland, Ireland and the United Kingdom* The Hon. Vicary Gibbs (ed.) 13 vols. (London: St. Catherine Press, 1913).
CTR	Gorman, W. Gordon, *Converts to Rome* (London: Sands & Co., 1901).
CW	Charles Wordsworth, Bishop of St. Andrews.
DNB	Stephen, Leslie, and Lee, Sidney (eds.), *The Dictionary of National Biography* (London: Smith, Elder & Co., 1885-1900).
DP	Dorothea Palmer, mother of William Palmer.
DUC	Vapereau, G., *Dictionnaire Universel des Contemporains* (Paris: Lahure, 1858).
EA	William Palmer, *Examination of an Announcement Made in the Prussian State Gazette* (Oxford: Parker, 1842).
Ed P	Edwin Palmer, Archdeacon of Oxford, brother of William Palmer.
Em P	Emma Palmer, sister of William Palmer.
ES	Brockgauz & Ephron, *Encyclopedeskii Slovar*, 82 vols. (St. Petersburg, 1890-1902).
FT	Thomson, Francis, 'William Palmer and the Orthodox Church' (Ph.D. thesis, Cambridge University, 1964).
GHP	George Horsley Palmer, brother of William Palmer.

L&D Dessain, Charles Stephen, et al., *The Letters & Diaries of John Henry Newman, 1801-1890* (London: Nelson).

LP Lambeth Palace Library.

MAG MSS at Magdalen College, Oxford.

MCR Bloxam, J. R., *A register of the presidents, fellows, demies … and other members of Saint Mary Magdalen College in the University of Oxford* (Oxford: Graham, 1853-85).

MEB Boase, Frederic, *Modern English Biography* (London: Cass & Co., 1897).

MFP Palmer, Roundell, Earl of Selborne, *Memorials Family and Personal*, vols. I & II (London: Macmillan, 1896).

MID Middleton, R. D., *Magdalen Studies* (London: SPCK, 1936).

NBG Didot, F., and Hoefer, J. C. F., *Nouvelle Biographie Générale*, 46 vols. (Paris: Didot, 1860-66).

NV Newman, John Henry, *Notes of a Visit to the Russian Church* (London: Kegan Paul Trench, 1882).

ODNB Matthew, H. C. G., and Harrison B. (eds.), *The Oxford Dictionary of National Biography* (Oxford: OUP, 2004).

RBS *Russkii Biograficheskii Slovar*, 8 vols. (New York: Kraus, 1962).

RBSI *Russkii Biograficheskii Slovar Index* (Vaduz: Kraus, 1963).

RGIA Rossiiskii Gosudarstvennyi Istoricheskii Arkhiv, St. Petersburg.

ROM Macray, W. D., *A Register of the Members of St. Mary Magdalen College, Oxford, from the foundation of the college* (New series) (London: Frowde, 1894-1915).

RP Roundell Palmer, later Earl of Selborne, brother of William Palmer.

RWB The Rev. R. W. Blackmore, chaplain at Cronstadt.

SEC Bertie, David. M., *Scottish Episcopal Clergy, 1689-2000* (Edinburgh: T & T Clark, 2000).

TLC Thomas Legh Claughton, Bishop of St. Albans.

WEG William Ewart Gladstone.

WJP Rev. William Jocelyn Palmer, father of William Palmer.

WP Deacon William Palmer of Magdalen.

Z Zernov, Nicholas, 'William Palmer', unpublished MS, in the possession of the author.

Notes

Introduction

1 P. E. Shaw, *The Early Tractarians and the Eastern Church* (hereafter Shaw) (London: Mowbray, 1930), p. 176.

2 John Lawrence, 'William Palmer of Magdalen and the Russian Orthodox Church', *Sobornost* vol. 2:1 (1980), pp. 80–2.

3 Frederick Meyrick (1827–1906), deacon 1850, priest 1852, Principal of Codrington College, Barbados, 1886. DNB.

4 Frederick Meyrick, *Memories of Life at Oxford* (hereafter Meyrick) (London: John Murray, 1905), p. 79.

5 W. J. Birkbeck, Russia *and the English Church* (London: Rivington, Percival, 1895), p. 152.

6 BO MS v. 49, f. 163.

7 LP MS 2823, f. 125.

8 NV, p. xvi.

9 Ibid., p. xvii.

10 Roundell Palmer (1812–1895), first Earl of Selborne, barrister Lincoln's Inn 1837, Q.C. 1849. M.P. Plymouth 1847–52 and 1853–7, for Richmond 1861–72, Solicitor-General 1861–3, knighted 1861, Attorney-General 1863–6, Lord Chancellor 1872–4 and 1880–5, created Baron Selborne 1872, Earl Selborne and Viscount Wolmer 1883. DNB, AO. Roundell Palmer was the second of six brothers. The third, Tom, died in infancy (see n. 27), the fourth, Henry Palmer, was lost at sea in 1835. The fifth, George Horsley Palmer, succeeded his father as rector of Mixbury, and the youngest, Edwin, became Archdeacon of Oxford. He also had sisters, Dorothea, Eleanor, Emily and Emma. DNB, and MFP vol. II, pp. 154–5.

11 11 MID, p. 124.

Chapter One: Childhood, Rugby and Oxford

1 MFP vol. 1, p. 64.

2 LP MS 2497, f. 25.

3 William Palmer senior was presented to the parish of Beachampton by his father after Bishop Horsley's death in 1806. He exchanged it for Finmere in 1814. MFP vol. 1, p. 38.

4 LP MS 2497, f. 25.

5 MFP, vol. 1, p. 5.

6 bid., p. 37.

7 Ibid.

8 Bishop Samuel Horsley (1733–1806), Fellow of the Royal Society 1767, Archdeacon of St. Albans 1781, Bishop of St. David's 1788, Bishop of Rochester 1793, translated to St. Asaph's June 1802. DNB.

9 MFP, vol. 1, p. 59.

10 Ibid., p. 57.

11 Ibid., p. 58.

12 Ibid., p. 63.

13 Ibid., p. 147.

14 William Tuckwell, '"chirurgus", privilegiatus, 10 November 1808' AO, p. 1445.

15 MFP, vol. 1, p. 148.

16 As a result of hydrocephalus, after receiving 'some accidental hurt on his head, during some of our games. [...] The hearts of my Father and Mother were all but broken. My Mother's cheerfulness did not return for years; my Father's health suffered so much that [...] he was very seriously ill'. (MFP, vol. 1, p. 69).The episode may lie behind Palmer's dream of the angry mujik whose son he had killed (BO MS v. 25, vol. 2, f. 17).

17 MFP, vol. 1, p. 147.

18 LP MS 2834, f. 48.

19 LP MS 2834, f. 50.

20 LP MS 2457, f. 250.

21 MFP, vol. 1, p. 66.

22 LP MS 2457, f. 1.

23 Ibid.

24 MFP, vol. 1, pp. 66–7.

25 Ibid., p. 64.

26 Ibid.

27 Ibid., pp. 64–5.

28 Ibid., p. 77.

29 Ibid.

30 Ibid., p. 149.

31 Ibid., p. 58.

32 Ibid., p. 74.

33 John Chandos, *Boys Together: English Public Schools 1800–1814* (hereafter Chandos) (London: Hutchinson, 1984), p. 25.

34 Brian Gardner, *The Public Schools* (London: Hamish Hamilton, 1973), p. 101.

35 Ibid., pp. 101–2.

36 Ibid., p. 102.

37 Chandos, p. 133.

38 Ibid., p. 139.

39 MFP, vol. 1, pp. 76–7.
40 Rev. William Lucas Collins, *The Public Schools* (1867), cited in Chandos, p. 221.
41 'Running the gauntlet of two lines of the upper remove armed with knotted handkerchiefs up and down the great schoolroom' Chandos, p. 255.
42 'hoisting a boy in a chair and pinching him in the "most sensitive parts of his body"' Chandos, p. 255.
43 'pelting (of novitiates in the fifth form) with hard balls of dried slime from a pool' Chandos, p. 255.
44 Matthew Holbeache Bloxam, *Rugby, the School and its Neighbourhood* (1889, 1923 edition), cited in Chandos, p. 255.
45 MFP, vol. 1, p. 77.
46 MFP, vol. 1, p. 76.
47 The Hon. & Rev. George Spencer (1799–1864), son of the second Earl Spencer, Rector of Brighton, and chaplain to Bishop Blomfield the Bishop of London, converted to Roman Catholicism 1830, later Superior of the Passionist Order. CTR, p. 255.
48 BO MS v. 17 ff. 243–4.
49 WP to parents, Aug. 1823, LP MS 2457, f. 1.
50 Ibid.
51 LP MS 1878, f. 1.
52 MFP, vol. 1, p. 78.
53 LP MS 1894 f. 2.
54 LP MS 1894, f. 1.
55 Moor to W J P, 9 Dec. 1823, MFP, vol. 1, p. 75.
56 Ibid., p. 79.
57 LP MS 2457, f. 6.
58 LP MS 1894, f. 5.
59 WP to W J P, 15 June 1825, LP MS 2457, f. 9
60 Frederick Bulley, President of Magdalen after Dr. Routh, matriculated at age fourteen ('a mere boy in a round jacket') as Routh himself had done. Middleton, p. 83, quoting, 'In Memoriam: the President of Magdalen College', *The Oxford Magazine*, 21 Oct. 1885.
61 MFP, vol. 1, p. 252.
62 Ibid.
63 Ibid.
64 Ibid
65 WP to W J P, 5 Nov. 1826, LP MS 2834, f. 1.
66 Ibid.
67 LP MS 2457, f. 15.
68 WP to W J P, 1829 (undated, probably Nov.), LP MS 2834, f. 3.
69 Ibid.

70 W J P to WP, 18 Nov. 1829, LP MS 2834, f. 5.
71 Ibid.
72 In MAG MS 827 (ii) (unfoliated).
73 In fact Palmer won the Latin essay prize three years later, in 1833.
74 ROM MS 827 (ii).
75 Edward Whateley (post Pyddoke) (1808–1894), Called to Bar Nov. 1835. deacon 1843, priest 1846. Took the name of Pyddoke, 1847. Curate of Bisley 1847–55 & 1857–75. SPG Chaplain to the forces in the Crimea, 1855–6. m. Oct. 1862. AC p. 421.
76 Edward Whately to WP, 21 Nov. 1831, LP MSS 2457, ff. 25–6, and 2837, ff. 136–7
77 Martin Joseph Routh (1755–1854), internationally renowned classical and patristic scholar. Matriculated Queens College Oxford May 1770, age 14, demy of Magdalen College 1771–5, MA 1776, deacon 1777, Proctor 1785, Bursar 1786, President 1791–1854, ordained priest 1810 on institution as Rector of Tilehurst, nr. Reading. DNB.
78 Charles Wordsworth (1806–1892), Master of Winchester College 1835–45, Warden of Trinity College Glenalmond 1847–54, Bishop of St. Andrews, Dunkeld and Dunblane 1853. AO, p. 1609.
79 Thomas Legh Claughton (1808–1892), Professor of Poetry at Oxford 1852–58, ordained 1834, Bishop of Rochester 1867, first Bishop of St. Albans, 1877. DNB.
80 MFP, vol. 1, p. 115. 'Roundell Palmer matriculated as a commoner of Christ Church, Oxford, in May 1830, but was elected a scholar of Trinity College almost immediately afterwards.' (MID, p. 128.) By 'my own College' he therefore means Trinity.
81 Entry 26 Nov. 1831, LP MS 2458, f. 3.
82 T L C to WP, 23 July 1833 LP MS 2837, f. 23.
83 T L C to WP, 11 Dec. 1833, LP MS 2837, f. 28.
84 Ibid., pp. 120–121.
85 T L C to WP, 5 March 1835, LP MS 2837, f. 36.
86 T L C to WP, 1 Nov. 1838, LP MS 2837, f. 46.
87 Ibid.
88 T L C to WP, 21 Nov. 1838, Ibid., f. 48.
89 T L C to WP, 19 April 1837, Ibid., f. 40
90 W J P to WP, 18 Nov. 1829, LP MS 2834, f. 6.
91 WP to W J P (undated), Ibid., f. 8.
92 W J P to WP, 11 Nov. 1831, LP MS 1894, f. 13.
93 WP to W J P, 9 Dec. 1831, Ibid., f. 14.
94 WP to W J P, 18 Dec. 1831, LP MS 2834, f. 17.

Chapter Two: France and Durham

1 Charles Thorp (1783–1862), Rector of Ryton 1807, Archdeacon of Durham 1831. 'A man of singular disinterestedness and liberality.' DNB.

2 LP MS 2837, f. 127.
3 W J P to WP, Jan./Feb. 1832, LP MS 1894, f. 15.
4 W J P to WP, 19 March 1832, LP MS 2834, f. 22.
5 Ibid., f. 26.
6 W J P to WP, 18 Nov 1829, Ibid., f. 5.
7 W J P to WP, 26 Jun 1832, Ibid., f. 30.
8 LP MS 2458, Diary from Nov. 1831–Jun. 1832. A 'Petersham' was a heavy overcoat
9 Ibid.
10 Entry 24 Jun 1832, LP MS 2460.
11 LP MS 2457, ff. 26–7.
12 WP to C W, (undated), LP MS 1824, f. 69. The letter mentions the prospect of going to Durham, and must therefore have been written in 1833.
13 Entry 26 July 1833, LP MS 2457, f. 33.
14 Ibid., f. 47.
15 RP to WP, 20 Nov. 1833, LP MS 2836, f. 205.
16 WP to RP, 5 Nov. 1833, LP MS 1878, f. 164.
17 T L C to WP, 7 Nov. 1833, LP MS 2837, f. 25.
18 T L C to WP, 11 Dec. 1833, Ibid., f. 28.
19 Entry 21 Jan. 1834, BO MS v.52, f. 21.
20 Ibid., f. 25.
21 LP MS 2457, f. 88.
22 Entry 27 Oct. 1834, Ibid. [Also in LP MS 2457, f. 84.]
23 WP to RP, 10 Nov. 1834, LP MS 1878, f. 170.
24 Whiting, p. 57.
25 Entry 19 Jan. 1834, BO MS v.52, f. 22.
26 Entry 30 April 1834, BO MS v. 48.
27 Entry 15 May 1834, Ibid.
28 Entry 24 April 1834, Ibid.
29 Entry 20 Oct. 1834, Ibid.
30 Entry 27 April 1834, Ibid.
31 Entry 'June 1834 ?', Ibid.
32 Entry 5 Feb. 1834, LP MS 2457, f. 60.
33 Ibid.
34 LP MS 2457, f. 62.
35 Ibid., f. 60.
36 BO MS v. 52 f. 34.
37 Entry 29 April 1834, LP MS 2457, f. 88.
38 WP to C W, May 1835, LP MS 2141, f. 9.
39 W J P to WP, 5 March 1834, Ibid., f. 50.

40 WP to RP, 26 Nov. 1834, Ibid., f. 171.

41 LP MS 2457, f. 35f.

42 Ibid.

43 Conversation with a Mr. O' Ryan in 1838, LP MS 2818, f. 18.

44 Ibid.

45 FT, p. 2.

46 LP MS 2814, f. 1.

47 Benjamin Harrison (1808–1887), wrote several of the 'Tracts for the Times,' domestic chaplain to Archbishop Howley 1838–48, Canon of Canterbury and Archdeacon of Maidstone, 1845–1887. DNB.

48 The abbé Jean-Nicolas Jager (1790–1868), Professor of Ecclesiastical History in the Faculty of Theology of the University of Paris. Engaged in a controversial correspondence with Benjamin Harrison and with Newman in *'L' Univers'* August 1834–March 1835. Louis Allen, *John Henry Newman & the Abbé Jager* (London: OUP, 1975), pp. 4 ff., 184.

49 William Howley (1766–1848), Regius Professor of Divinity 1809, Bishop of London October 1803, Archbishop of Canterbury July 1828. DNB.

50 Michael Henry Thornhill Luscombe (1776–1846), Master of the East India Company's school at Hertford, 1806-1819, consecrated to a continental bishopric by bishops of the Scottish episcopal church 20 March 1825, chaplain at Paris. DNB.

51 LP MS 2457, f. 87.

52 BO MS v.57 (travel diary) part I, f. 44.

53 On 2 September 1834, LP MS 2457, f. 78.

54 The abbé Jean-François Robert, b. 1797, honorary Canon of Tours, author of works of piety and *Souvenirs d'Angleterre et Considérations sur l'Eglise Anglicane.* (Louis Allen, unpublished MS (hereafter Allen), p. 598, and DUC (1st Ed'n, Paris, 1858) p. 1478.

55 Entry 16 July 1834, LP MS 2814, f. 1.

56 MFP, vol. 1, p. 254.

57 LP MS 2814, f. 19.

58 Ibid., f. 21.

59 Ibid., f. 30.

60 Ibid., f. 40. Compare Cardinal Newman's determination, in the context of papal infallibility, to drink 'to Conscience first, and to the Pope afterwards.' S. W. Gilley, *Newman and his Age* [hereafter Gilley] (London: Darton, Longman and Todd, 1990), p. 376.

61 Charles Whately (1815–c.1878), Rector of Burnham, 1865, Rural Dean of the Deanery of Burnham, 1855–73. AO, p. 1532, and CCD.

62 LP MS 2814, f. 7.

63 Entry 14 Aug., Ibid.

64 Ibid., f. 54.

65 Ibid. f. 55.

66 Ibid., f. 58.
67 Edward Whately to WP, 1 Nov. 1834, LP MS 2837, f. 144.
68 B/O MS v.48 f. 2.
69 LP MS 2815, f. 37.
70 Adolphe Monod (1802–1856), renowned moralist, preacher and author. Ordained pastor 1824, professor of Dogma, Hebrew and Exegesis in the 'Faculté de Montauban' from 1836 to 1852, Moderator of the French Calvinist Church. DUC (1858 ed'n.), p. 1237, and FT, p. 3.
71 LP MS 2141, f. 9.
72 W J P to WP, 27 Jan. 1835, LP MS 2834, f. 59.
73 LP MS 2837, f. 130.
74 LP MS 2834, f. 70.
75 W J P to WP, 21 May 1835, Ibid., f. 72.
76 RP to WP, 26 Jan. 1836, LP MS 2836, f. 217.
77 W J P to WP, Feb. 1836, LP MS 2834, f. f. 79.
78 WP to Aunt Eleanor, 28 May 1836, LP MS 2836, f. 271.
79 Ibid.
80 Ibid.
81 LP MS 2457, f. 93.
82 Entry 6 May 1836, Ibid.
83 W J P to WP, 30 May 1836, LP MS 2834, f. 83.
84 W J P to WP, Feb. 1836, Ibid., f. 80.
85 Ibid., f. 83.
86 RP to WP, 3 June 1836, LP MS 2836, f. 221.
87 W J P to WP, 8 June 1836, LP MS 2834, f. 86.
88 MFP, vol. I, p. 256.
89 WP to W J P, 28 Aug. 1836, LP MS 2834, f. 89.
90 MFP, vol. 1, p. 256.
91 LP MS 2457, f. 91.
92 Entry 26 June 1836, BO MS v.48 sect. 3 f. 4 ff.
93 Ibid., f. 21. What the 'crime' or the 'dereglements' [sic] were is obscure. Palmer's personal and religious standards were far stricter than today's. If they were of a sexual nature, which the reference to the 'Catholiques pieuses' might suggest, then it is a great rarity in his papers, as there is virtually no entry suggestive of love or sexual interest to be found in them.
94 BO MS v. 48 sect. 3, f. 23.
95 In French in the BO MS v.47 f. 97, translated by Palmer in LP MS 2457 ff. 27–8.
96 LP MS 2457, f. 97.
97 BO MS v. 48 ff. 27–8.
98 W J P to WP, 10 Aug. 1836, LP MS 2834, f. 87.

99 Entry 11 Aug. 1836, LP MS 2457, f. 99.

100 Entry 10 Aug. 1836, Ibid., f. 100.

101 Entry 28 Sept. 1836, LP MS 2816, f. 119.

102 Despite Palmer's spelling, probably the daughter of the Rev. Sir Harry Trelawny, 7th Baronet (1756–1834), Prebendary of Exeter and Vicar of St. Austell and Egloshayle, who became a Roman Catholic. CB, vol. II, p. 45.

103 LP MS 2457, f. 99.

104 LP MS 2816, f. 1.

105 Ibid., f. 16.

106 Ibid., f. 21.

107 LP MS 2816, f. 121.

108 Ibid., f. 125.

109 Ibid., f. 129.

110 LP MS 2834, f. 93.

111 LP MS 2816, f. 95.

112 Undated entry, LP MS 2818, f. 18.

113 WP to RP, 17 Oct. 1836, LP MS 2457, f. 109.

114 Ibid., f. 113

Chapter Three: Return to Oxford

1 WP to R P, 24 Nov. 1836, LP MS 1878, f. 181.

2 Ibid., f. 187.

3 Edward Bouverie Pusey (1800–1882), regius professor of Hebrew at Oxford 1828, author of many of the *Tracts for the Times*, spokesman and apologist for the Tractarians. The Oxford Movement became known as 'Puseyism' after him. ODNB.

4 MFP, vol. 1, p. 258.

5 Ibid.: Lord Selborne agrees, judging that it was not until 2 years later, with the publication of Froude's *Remains*, that a turning towards Rome and against the English and Continental Reformation became apparent. MFP, vol. I, p. 259.

6 Francis Atkinson Faber (1805–1876), Bursar 1836, Vice-President 1841, Dean of Divinity 1843. AO, p. 443.

7 LP MS 1878, f. 187.

8 LP MS 2457, f. 113.

9 Ibid., ff. 183, 187.

10 Ibid., f. 118

11 W J P to WP, 20 Feb. 1837, LP MS 2834, f. 95.

12 WP to Aunt Eleanor, 31 March 1837, LP MS 2836, f. 273.

13 LP MS 2457, f. 118.

14 WP to Aunt Eleanor, 31 March 1837, LP MS 2836, f. 273.

15 Entry 11 Jan. 1837, LP MS 2457, f. 119.
16 Entry 17 Jan. 1837, Ibid.
17 Entry 7 March 1837, Ibid., f. 164.
18 Entry 3 April 1837, Ibid., f. 165.
19 Entry 14 April 1837, Ibid., f. 127.
20 Entry 13 May 1837, Ibid., f. 132.
21 Ibid., f. 131.
22 'If there be any of you, who [...] cannot quiet his own conscience herein, but requireth further comfort or counsel, let him come to me [...] and open his grief.'
23 'Our Lord Jesus Christ, who hath left power to his Church to absolve all sinners who truly repent and believe in him, of his great mercy forgive thee thine offences: And by his authority committed to me, I absolve thee from all thy sins, in the Name of the Father, and of the Son, and of the Holy Ghost. Amen.'
24 LP MS 2457, f. 169.
25 T L C to WP, 20 July 1837, LP MS 2837, f. 42.
26 LP MS 2816, f.140.
27 Ibid., ff. 150–151.
28 Ibid., f. 158.
29 Ibid., f. 166.
30 Ibid., f.170.
31 Ibid., f. 189–90.
32 MFP, vol. 1, p. 262.
33 Ibid.
34 LP MS 2836, f. 275.
35 WP to C R, (undated), LP MS 2819, f. 229.
36 MFP, vol. 1. p. 264.
37 LP MS 2457, f. 151.
38 MFP, vol. 1, p. 260. This appears to be the first time that Pusey and Palmer had met, see FT p. 6.
39 LP MS 2457, f. 151.
40 W J P to WP, 26 Oct. 1837, LP MS 2834, f. 102.
41 MFP, vol. 1, p. 260.
42 W J P to WP, 26 Oct. 1837, LP MS 2834, f. 102
43 MFP, vol. 1, p. 261.
44 Ibid., pp. 260–1.
45 Ibid., p. 260.
46 W J P to WP, 26 Oct. 1837, LP MS 2457, f. 150.
47 Ibid.
48 Ibid.

49 WP to C R, 17 May 1840, LP MS 2821, f. 41.
50 T L C to WP, 2 Jan. 1840, LP MS 2837, f. 54.
51 MFP, vol. 1, p. 265.
52 LP MS 2836, f. 275.
53 LP MS 2834, f. 110.
54 Ibid., ff. 110–11.
55 Entry 7 March 1838, LP MS 2468 [no folio numbers].
56 Entry 18 August 1838, LP MS 2457, f. 175.
57 LP MS 2468.
58 LP MS 2457, f. 193.
59 NV, pp. 1–3.
60 Ibid.
61 Goldwin Smith (1823–1910), 'controversialist,' of Christ Church Oxford, Regius professor of modern history 1858–66, professor of English and constitutional history Cornell University 1868–71, also barrister and author. A friend of Roundell Palmer, although 'his views on political and religious questions were [...] pronouncedly liberal'. He 'was impatient of the Oxford Movement and scornful of all clerical influences'. DNB, AO, p. 1314. He seems, however, to have respected Palmer, describing him in 1895 as 'a man of genius and a most interesting person'. MFP vol. II, p. 59.
62 *The Oxford Magazine*, 11 Nov. 1885.
63 MFP, vol. 1, pp. 264–5.
64 Ibid.
65 George Horsley Palmer (1822–c.1890), deacon 1850, priest 1852, Rector of Mixbury 1852–1881. AO, p. 1060, & CCD (1850), p. 1852.
66 Ibid., p. 267.
67 Edwin Palmer (1824–1895), deacon 1854, priest 1868, Archdeacon of Oxford & Canon of Christchurch 1878 to death, Corpus Professor of Latin literature 1870–78. MEB, pp. 1316–17, and CCD (1887), p. 926.
68 LP MS 2457, f. 199.
69 Entry 25 Jun 1839, LP MS 2820, f. 20.
70 Ibid., f. 28.
71 Ibid., f. 82.
72 WP to W J P, 12 July 1839, LP MS 2834, f. 130 ff. 73 LP MS 2820, f. 161.
74 Ibid., f. 201.
75 Ibid., f. 208.
76 Ibid., f. 90.
77 Ibid., f. 49.
78 Ibid., f. 86.
79 Ibid., f. 47.

80 Ibid., ff. 20–1.
81 Ibid., f. 47.
82 Ibid., f. 157.
83 Ibid., f. 48.
84 LP MS 2834, f. 134
85 LP MS 2820, f. 27.
86 Ibid., f. 113.
87 Ibid., f. 41.
88 Ibid., f. 222.
89 LP MS 2834, f. 143; also in MS 2457 f. 230, where the last sin is described as 'impurity'.
90 LP MS 2834, f. 147.
91 LP MS 1894, f. 24.
92 LP MS 2457, f. 230.
93 Entry 8 April, 1840, Ibid., f. 259.
94 See n. 58 (above).
95 MFP, vol. 1, p. 269.
96 Dated 20 Oct 1839, Ibid.
97 BO MS v.17 f. 13.
98 Ibid., f. 20.
99 Ibid., f. 106.
100 Ibid., f. 135-6.
101 This is confirmed by Newman in the context of Spencer's visit to Oxford. Newman was invited by Palmer to dine with Spencer, but refused, considering him 'in loco apostatae'. He remarked: 'Palmer was annoyed. Poor fellow! he has put himself in a false position. People will assume he is one of us, and come to him for introductions to us; and he does not know even a number of us, and does not know the feelings, etc., of those he does know. So he has been hard pressed to entertain the said Mr. S.'.
L & D, vol. VII p. 205.
102 MFP, vol. 1, p. 271.
103 Ibid.
104 MCR, vol. VII, pp. 299–300.
105 Entry 17 Nov. 1839, LP MS 2457, f. 235.
106 MFP, vol. 1, p. 270.
107 Ibid., f. 153.
108 LP MS 2457 f. 246.
109 WP to GS, 15 Feb. 1840, Ibid., f. 290.
110 Ibid., f. 317.
111 Ibid., f. 261.
112 Ibid., f. 266 ff.

113 L & D, vol. VII p. 206.
114 BO MS v.17 f. 261.
115 Ibid., f. 296.
116 Ibid., f. 308.
117 Ibid.
118 Ibid., f. 317.
119 '1. To get up at once. 2. To get on with business.'
120 '4. To [deal] more patiently with mother.'
121 Entry 21 Jan. 1840, LP MS 2457, f. 250.
122 Ibid., f. 259.
123 Ibid., f. 257: '1. I cannot get up early; 2. I waste almost the whole day in doing nothing; 3. I read newspapers; 4. I do very little pressing business; 5. Impatient of the cold I sit by the fire.'
124 Entry 15/27 March, LP MS 2470
125 MFP, vol. 1, p. 277.
126 W J P to RP, 16 June 1838, LP MS 1878 f. 47, quoted in MFP, vol. 1 p.278.
127 James 1:20, MFP, vol. 1 pp. 277–8.
128 MFP, vol. 1, p. 277.
129 RP to WP, 7 April 1840, Ibid., p. 279.
130 Ibid., p. 280.
131 Ibid.
132 Ibid., pp. 279–80.
133 LP MS 2836, f. 246.
134 WP to RP, 9 Apr 1840, LP MS 1878, f. 206.
135 Rev. John Russell (1787–1863), ordained 1810, Headmaster of Charterhouse 1811, President of Sion College 1845 & 1846, Treasurer of the SPG. DNB.
136 MFP, vol. 1, p. 281.
137 LP MS 1878, f. 62.
138 Ibid.
139 Rev. John William Cunningham (1780–1861), Vicar of Harrow 1811 to death, editor of *The Christian Observer* 1850–1858, and author of *The Velvet Cushion*, a popular novel. DNB.
140 Ibid.
141 MFP, vol. 1, p. 282.
142 LP MS 1878, ff. 63–4.
143 MFP, vol. 1, p. 282.
144 Ibid., p. 283.
145 Ibid., p. 284.

146 w (1782-1854), Bishop of Oxford 1829–1845. 'Modest, retiring and nervous', he supported Newman and Pusey until Tract 90 strained his relationship with the Tractarians. On his translation to Bath and Wells in 1845 had a total nervous collapse. ODNB.

147 LP MS 2837, f. 3.

148 MFP, vol. 1 p. 284.

149 Rev. Richard White Blackmore (1791–1882), chaplain to the Russia Company 1819–47, Rector of Donhead St. Mary near Salisbury from 1847 to his death, author of the *History of the Church of Russia* (1842), and *The Doctrine of the Russian Church* (1845). MEB, vol. 1 p. 298.

150 Blackmore outlived Palmer, and wrote after his death to his brother Edwin Palmer that: 'He was one of my oldest and most esteemed friends – I always had more pleasure in his company than of any one I know and learned far more from him than any one I ever conversed with [...] I think I may say that in our long acquaintance never an angry word passed between us'. R W B to E P, 12 May 1879, BO MS.

151 WP to R W B, 15 June 1840, BO MS v. G.37 f. 90.

152 The clause in the Creed stating that the Holy Spirit 'proceeds from the Father and the Son.'

153 BO MS v. G.37 f. 90.

154 Ibid., f. 93.

155 Williams, p. 16.

156 Rouse & Neill, p. 192.

157 NV, pp. v–vii.

158 LP MS 2457, f. 283.

159 NV, p. 10.

160 Richard Waldo Sibthorp (1792–1879), ordained Anglican priest 1815, received as a Roman Catholic 1841, ordained RC priest 1842, returned to the Church of England October 1843, readmitted as an Anglican minister 1857, but returned to the Church of Rome January 1865. The Anglican burial service was read over his grave. DNB.

161 NV, p. 12.

162 NV, pp. 13–4.

163 Ibid., p. 14.

164 Ulick John de Burgh, Earl of Clanricarde (1802–1874), created Marquess of Clanricarde 1825, Baron Somerhill 1826, Under-Secretary for Foreign Affairs, 1826–7, Ambassador to St. Petersburg 1838–41, Postmaster-General 1846–52. CP, vol. III, pp. 237–8.

165 LP MS 2457, f. 277.

166 Pratasoff, Count Nicolai Alexandrovich (1798–1855), Officer of the Life Guard Hussar Regiment, 1817, fought in the Turkish War 1828. Ober-Prokuror of the Holy Synod 1835, Lt-General 1848, member of the State Council 1853. RBS, pp. 81–4.

167 'The Holy Governing Synod was formed in 1721 by Peter the Great as an alternative to the Moscow patriarchate. It was composed of the three metropolitans (of Kiev, Moscow, and St. Petersburg) and of other bishops appointed for fixed periods by the Tsar. In 1722 Peter

created the office of Chief Procurator [Ober-Prokuror], who was to be a lay official, with a large bureaucracy under him, reaching down to the full-time lay secretaries of the episcopal consistories. See H. Seton-Watson, *The Russian Empire, 1801–1917* (Oxford, 1967), p. 34.' Leon Litvack, *John Mason Neale and the Quest for Sobornost* (Oxford: Clarendon, 1994), p. 46, n. 25.

168 Amable-Guillaume-Prosper, Baron de Brugière (1782–1866), Prefect of the Vendée 1809, Prefect of Nantes 1813, on the return of Louis XVIII, made Councillor of State and Secretary General of Ministry of the Interior, after the July Revolution Ambassador to the Court of Sardinia, and to the Court of Russia 1835–48. DUC, (1st Ed'n., 1858), pp. 99–100.

169 NV, p. 14.

170 RGIA, fond 797, opis 87, delo 64.

171 LP MS 2457, f. 287. I assume the delay was due to quarantine regulations - no other reason is given.

172 BO MS Book 2 p. 7 ff.

173 Ibid., p. 24.

174 B H to WP, 7 Sept., Ibid., p. 26.

175 Ibid., p. 33.

176 When they met 'at a ball in honour of the Queen Dowager', FT, p. 24.

177 NV, p. 19.

178 WP to W J P, Jan. 1/13 1841, B/O MS 11.1. (2)/G.37 Bk. II ff. 90–1.

Chapter Four: Russia, 1840-1841

1 Entry Saturday 15 August 1840, LP MS 2457, f. 287.

2 The Russians at this time still adhered to the Old Style (O. S.) or Julian Calendar, then twelve days behind the New Style (N. S.) or Gregorian Calendar used in the West. Hence the alternative dates in Palmer's correspondence from Russia.

3 NV, p. 25.

4 Ibid., pp. 26–7.

5 Ibid., p. 29.

6 BO MS 11.1. (2)/G.37 Bk. II ff. 47–8

7 NV, p. 35.

8 Ibid., p. 36.

9 Ibid., p. 41.

10 Ibid., pp. 41–2.

11 Ibid., p. 51.

12 BO MS 11.1. (2)/G37 Bk. II f. 14.

13 LP MS 1894, f. 30.

14 Dimitri Obolensky, *The Byzantine Commonwealth* (New York: SVSP, 1974), p. 253.

15 BO MS 11.1. (2)/G37 Bk. II f. 14.

16 NV, p. 52.
17 BO MS 11.1. (2)/G37 Bk. II f. 14.
18 NV, p. 44.
19 Ekaterina Dimitrievna Dolgoroukaya, née Galitsin (1801–1881). RBS, vol. VI p. 497.
20 NV, pp. 398–9.
21 Ibid., p. 401.
22 BO MS 11.1.(2)/G.37 Bk. 2 f. 50
23 NV, p. 78.
24 Z, p. 59.
25 Z, p. 63. The 'Decembrist Revolution' of 1825 may also have hastened the demise of the Bible Society, FT, p. 32.
26 Dr. Pinkerton, quoted in NV, p. 516.
27 NV, pp. 519–20
28 Russian Censor.
29 NV, p. 515.
30 Ibid., p. 139.
31 Z, p. 41.
32 Writer, d. 1858. RBSI, p. 160.
33 NV, p. 307.
34 Ibid., p. 308.
35 Ibid., p. 314.
36 Tatiana Borisovna Potemkin, née the Countess Galitsin (1797–1869), dedicated her life to charity, 42 years the Chairman of the St. Petersburg Committee for Prisoners' Aid, took in the children of prisoners, paid for orphanages and homes for the weak and old, supported Orthodox mission, paid for new churches and the repair of the Sviatogorsky monastery. RBS vol. XIV, pp. 646–7.
37 NV, p. 284.
38 Ibid., p. 329.
39 1780-1850. RBSI, p. 160.
40 NV, pp. 391–2.
41 Ibid., p. 22.
42 Alexei Ivanovich Mallof, Magister, preacher. died 1855. RBSI, p. 7.
43 NV, p. 175 ff..
44 Vassily Ivanovich Koutnevich (1787–1866), teacher of mathematics, philosophy and languages at the St. Petersburg Theological Academy, and professor 1815, member of the Spiritual Consistory 1826, Over-priest of the Army and Navy 1832, member of the Synod 1849, Chief Priest of the Army and Navy 1858, expert on Synod procedure. RBS vol. IX, pp. 618–9.
45 NV, p. 269 ff.

46 Ibid.: 'A lovely sentiment to be sure, but a most pernicious doctrine.'

47 Ibid., pp. 270–1.

48 Valeri Valerivitch Skreepitsin (1799–1874), soldier and Civil Servant. Adviser to the Government of Kursk, moved to work for the Ober-Prokuror, Director of the Department of the Religious Affairs of Foreign Confessions, instrumental in reconciling the Uniats to Orthodoxy in 1839. RBS vol. XVIII, pp. 618–9.

49 NV, pp. 372–3

50 Ibid.

51 Ibid., p. 378.

52 Andrei Nikolaievitch Mouravieff (1806–1874), writer and traveller, Imperial Councillor, Unter-Prokuror of the Holy Synod. DUC p. 1257, RBSI pp. 45–6. Despite Newman's remarks at p. 130 of *Notes*, Mouravieff does not appear to have been at any time a cavalry officer. Newman may have confused him with Pratasoff who had been an officer of Hussars.

53 NV, p. 164.

54 Edward Law (1791–1868), chaplain to H. M. Embassy, St. Petersburg 1820. AO, p. 822.

55 Ibid., p. 77: Law was wrong in that Palmer did manage to live with a priest, albeit in some discomfort. Mr. Blackmore thought that even after 20 years in Russia, Law could not get out of the habit of 'speaking only from his English point of view' (NV, p. 76) which may explain his remarks.

56 NV, p. 308.

57 Ibid., p. 177.

58 Ibid., p. 206.

59 Ibid., pp. 119–20.

60 Charles-Robert Nesselrode (1780–1862), born in Lisbon & baptised an Anglican, ADC to Paul I, Counsellor of the Paris Embassy, and extravagantly rewarded for influencing the Emperor Alexander I to restore the Bourbons. After Waterloo saved France from partition and excessive financial reparations. In 1816 was in charge of foreign affairs, together with Count Capo d'Istria. He repressed revolutionary national movements, became Chief of the Russian Chancellery, but was replaced after the Treaty of Paris in 1856. DUC, pp. 771–5.

61 LP MS 1901 f. 56.

62 NV, p. 172.

63 WP to W J P from Cronstadt, 15/27 August 1840, BO MS 11.1. (2)/G.37 Bk. II f. 12.

64 LP MS 1894, f. 30.

65 Ibid., f. 13, and NV, pp. 54–5.

66 NV, p. 55.

67 Ibid., p. 61.

68 LP MS 1901, f. 57.

69 NV, p. 258.

70 Z, p. 76.

71 Ibid., pp. 76–7.
72 NV, p. 221.
73 Ibid., p. 392.
74 Z, p. 82.
75 NV, p. 222. This may simply mean that he lived quietly and respectably; or that he lived according to some religious or even monastic Rule, as Newman indicates in his footnote.
76 Z, p. 83.
77 Secular name Vassili Mikhailovitch Drozdov (1782–1867), became a monk, and Inspector & professor at the St. Petersburg Academy 1808, Archimandrite 1811, Rector of the Academy and Professor of Theology 1812, Bishop of Ravel 1817, Archbishop of Tver 1819, Archbishop of Yaroslavl 1820, Metropolitan of Moscow 1821 to his death. ES, Vol. XXXV (1902), pp. 739–40.
78 G. Florovsky, 'Aspects of Church History', in G. Florovsky *Collected Works* (Belmont, Mass.: Nordland, 1975), vol. IV, p. 219.
79 Ibid., p. 217.
80 Ibid., p. 218.
81 Ibid., p. 219.
82 WP to Aunt Mary, 25 Aug. O. S./7 Sept. N. S. 1840, BO MS 11.1.(2)/G.37 Bk. II f. 18.
83 NV, p. 167.
84 Ibid., pp. 177–8.
85 Ibid., pp. 317–8.
86 Ibid., pp. 195–6.
87 e.g. NV, p. 235.
88 Feodor Feodorovich Sidonsky (1805–73), Doctor 1864, Faculty of Philosophy of St. Petersburg University, later Professor of the Theological Faculty, forced to resign in 1833 because of his liberal views. RBSI, p. 266, FT, p. 46.
89 NV, pp. 248–9.
90 Ibid., p. 327.
91 (1780–1850), RBSI, p. 160.
92 Ibid., p. 390.
93 Ibid., pp. 249–250.
94 Ibid., p. 265.
95 Ibid., p. 277. This was not effected, however, without what Newman, quoting Fr. Theiner, calls 'systematic violence,' see NV, pp. 63–4.
96 Ibid., p. 480.
97 John Veniamineff (1797–1879), born John Popov, he later assumed the surname of Veniamineff. Married 1817, ordained 1821, missionary to the Aleutian Islands 1824. After the death of his wife in 1839 became a monk taking the name Innocent, elected first Bishop of Alaska, 1840–58, Metropolitan of Moscow 1868, canonised 6 Oct. 1977. Addressed

liturgically as 'Equal to the Apostles, Enlightener of North America.' *St. Innocent of Alaska*, Excerpt from the Desk Calendar of the Orthodox Church in America, http://www.roea.org/9703/ho00012.html, 25 May 2002.

98 NV, p. 344.

99 Ibid., p. 348.

100 Alexy, Patriarch of Moscow, 'St. Innocent', *The Orthodox Messenger*, vol. 8 (11–12), vol. 9 (1–2), 1997–8.

101 NV, p. 268.

102 Ibid., p. 387.

103 Ibid., p. 387.

104 Ibid., p. 366.

105 Conversation of 14/26 May 1843, in William Palmer, *An Appeal to the Scottish Church* (hereafter *Appeal*) (Edinburgh: Laurie, 1849), p. 263.

106 Conversation with Koutnevich on 28 August (O. S.), NV, p. 135.

107 Ibid., p. 272.

108 Ibid., p. 208.

109 Ibid., p. 353.

110 Conversation on 4/16 March 1841, LP MS 1901, ff. 59–60.

111 NV, pp. 354–5.

112 Ibid., p. 355.

113 Ibid., pp. 357–8.

114 Ibid.

115 Sofia Sergeyevna Mescherskaya (1775–1848), 'especially active in the translation and distribution of English tracts of the Religious Tract Society.' FT p. 31, & Z p. 86.

116 NV, p. 499.

117 Ibid., pp. 161 & 167.

118 Ibid., p. 216.

119 Ibid., pp. 229–30.

120 Rev. William Patrick Palmer (1803–1885), of Worcester College Oxford, writer and initially a close friend of Newman, although later fell out with him and lost influence in the Oxford Movement. Retired from controversy between 1846 and 1869; claimed the baronetcy of Wingham, Kent, but this was not recognised. ODNB.

121 *A Treatise on the Church of Christ* (2 vols.) (London: Rivington, 1838).

122 NV, pp. 364–5.

123 Ibid., p. 545.

124 Ibid., p. 350.

125 MFP, vol. 1, p. 271.

126 NV p. 214.

127 Ibid., p. 162.

128 Ibid., p. 366.
129 Ibid., p. 368.
130 Mikhail Mikhailovitch Galitsin (1793–1856), Lt-General, writer. RBSI, p. 162.
131 NV, p. 394.
132 This interview appears in abbreviated form at NV pp. 406–7, dated by Newman at 21 March.
133 LP MS 1901, f. 31.
134 Ibid., f. 32.
135 Ibid., f. 31.
136 Ibid., f. 30.
137 NV, p. 158.
138 Ibid., p. 213.
139 Ibid., p. 351
140 Ibid., p. 218
141 Ibid., pp. 261 & 273.
142 Ibid., p. 216.
143 Ibid., p. 334.
144 Ibid., p. 514.
145 Ibid., p. 508.
146 Ibid., p. 414.
147 Ibid., p. 157.
148 Ibid., p. 208.
149 Ibid., p. 356.
150 Ibid., p. 406.
151 Ibid., pp. 165–6.
152 bid., p. 230.
153 Ibid., p. 234.
154 Ibid., p. 386.
155 WP to Routh, 30 Nov O. S./12 Dec N. S. 1840, MAG MS 485 No. 2 f. 1.
156 Ibid.
157 NV, p. 360.
158 LP MS 1901, f. 50.
159 NV, p. 74.
160 Ibid., p. 132.
161 Ibid., p. 164.
162 Ibid., p. 396.
163 LP MS 1901, f. 52.
164 WP to AM, 25 Aug./7 Sept., BO MS 11.1. (2)/G.37 Bk. II f. 17.
165 WP to DP, 12 Oct. 1840, Ibid., f. 52.
166 WP to W J P, 19/31 Jan. 1841, LP MS 1878, f. 210.

167 LP MS 1903, f. 143.
168 BO MS 11.1. (2)/G.37 Bk. II f. 17.
169 NV, p. 286.
170 WP to DP, 12 Oct. 1840, BO MS 11.1. (2)/G.37 Bk. II f. 48.
171 NV, p. 287.
172 BO MS 11.1. (2)/G.37 Bk. II f. 49.
173 BO MS 11.1. (2)/G.37 Bk. IV f. 35.
174 Ibid., ff. 35–6.
175 BO MS 11.1. (2)/G.37 Bk. II f. 49.
176 Ibid.
177 NV, p. 288.
178 WP to W J P, 8 Oct. 1840, LP MS 1894, f. 38.
179 BO MS 11.1. (2)/G.37 Bk. II f. 50.
180 BO MS v. 25 Bk. II, f. 17.
181 BO MS 11.1. (2)/G.37 Bk. II f. 51.
182 LP MS 1901, f. 68.
183 WP to DP, 18/30 April 1841, BO MS 11.1. (2)/Bk. IV f. 36.
184 Ibid
185 Ibid., f. 34.
186 LP MS 1894, ff. 74–5.
187 WP to W J P, 8 Oct. 1840, LP MS 1894, f. 35.
188 W J P to WP, 7 Nov. 1840, Ibid., f. 40.
189 WP to DP, 18/30 April 1841, BO MS 11.1. (2)/Bk. IV f. 36–7.
190 NV, pp. 452–3.
191 It is unclear what protection a pocket handkerchief could provide.
192 LP MS 1878, f. 224.
193 NV, p. 453
194 Ibid., p. 497.
195 BO MS 11.1. (2)/Bk. II f. 69.
196 NV, pp. 223–4
197 WP to W J P, 1/13 January 1841, LP MS 1894 f. 49.
198 NV, p. 118.
199 BO MS 11.1.(2)/G.37 Bk. II f. 89.
200 George Moberly (1803–1885), the seventh son of Edward Moberly, a Russia merchant. Headmaster of Winchester 1835–1866, Bishop of Salisbury 1869. DNB.
201 LP MS 2836, f. 257.
202 WP to W J P, 19/31 Jan. 1841, LP MS 1878 f. 211.
203 Ibid
204 LP MS 1894, f. 37.

205 LP MS 2470 [unnumbered].

206 WP to W J P, 19/31 Jan. 1841, LP MS 1878, f. 211.

207 Ibid.

208 Ibid., f. 220.

209 J. F. Coakley, *The Church of the East and the Church of England* (Oxford: Clarendon, 1992), p. 35 ff.

210 BO MS 11.1. (2)/G.37 f. 17.

211 John Henry Newman, 'Remarks on Certain Passages of the Thirty Nine Articles', *The Via Media of the Anglican Church* (London: Longmans, Green & Co., 1891), vol. II, p. 271.

212 BO MS 11.1. (2)/G.37 f. 20

213 Ibid., ff. 21–3.

214 Ibid.

215 WP to W J P, 19/31 Jan. 1841, LP MS 1878, f. 212.

216 WP to RP, 5 April 1841, Ibid., f. 220.

217 BO MS 11.1.(2)/G.37 Bk. IV f. 40.

218 WP to an aunt, probably AM, 30 May 1841, Ibid., f. 83

219 Ibid., p. 439.

220 Ibid., p. 454–5.

221 Ibid., p. 461.

222 Ibid., p. 461.

223 He noted later that 'there was nothing like personal luxury', dinner being the only meal of the day, and only tea being offered once during the course of the afternoon; 'it may have been for that reason that the Archimandrite gave me such a large provision of bread after the vigil on Saturday'. NV, p. 467.

224 Ibid., p. 465.

225 LP MS 1878, f. 228.

226 NV, p. 476.

227 Ibid., p. 542.

228 Ibid., p. 545.

229 Ibid., pp. 546–8 .

230 Ibid., p. 550.

231 Ibid.

232 Evgeny Ivanovich Popov (1813–1875), taught for two years at Tver Theological Academy, ordained priest to serve in the Copenhagen Embassy 1838, posted to London 1842. RBS vol. XIV, pp. 546–7.

233 Florovsky, p. 238.

234 Leon Litvack, *J. M. Neale and the Quest for Sobornost* (hereafter Litvack) (Oxford: Clarendon, 1994) p.51 n. 39.

235 Ibid., n. 38.

236 Litvack, p.51.
237 NV, p. 552.
238 Ibid., p. 396.
239 Ibid., p. 553–4.
240 W J P to WP, 27 March 1841, LP MS 2834, f. 189.
241 LP MS 1894, f. 86.
242 NV, p. xi.
243 JHN to F. Rogers, 2 January 1841, L & D, vol. VIII, pp. 3–4. Newman was almost certainly quoting Palmer himself, as the tone and content mirror what Palmer was writing to his family at the time.
244 Underneath the text on the last half page is written at an angle 'My Dear Wordsworth'; but this may have been a greeting from another letter accidentally written on the carbon, nor does the title suggest a personal letter.
245 BO MS 11.1. (2)/G.37 Bk. V f. 36.
246 Ibid.
247 Ibid., f. 37.
248 Ibid., f. 38.
249 Ibid., f. 39.
250 Ibid., f. 40.
251 Ibid.
252 Ibid., f. 41.
253 Ibid., f. 42.
254 Ibid., f. 47.
255 Ibid., f. 48.

Chapter Five: The Cursing Deacon

1 MFP, vol. 1, p. 310, p. 314.
2 The 'waverer' was John Gooch, the Oxford bookseller, who 'appears to have become a Catholic in late 1841 or early 1842'. L & D, vol. VIII p. 623. The letter is dated 'Autumn 1841'. LP MS 1895, f. 7.
3 LP MS 1895, f. 7.
4 bid., f. 10.
5 P. J. Welch, 'Anglican Churchmen and the Establishment of the Jerusalem Bishopric', *Journal of Ecclesiastical History* 8 (1957) (hereafter Welch), p. 193.
6 Christian Carl Josias Bunsen (1791–1860), educated at Gottingen under Heine, private secretary to Niebuhr in Rome. Secretary of Legation in Rome, succeeded Niebuhr as Prussian Ambassador to the Vatican. Ambassador to the Swiss Confederacy 1839; Prussian Ambassador to the Court of St. James 1841– 54. *Men of The Time* (London: Bogue, 1856), pp. 106–7.

7 Charles James Blomfield (1786–1857), ordained 1810, Archdeacon of Colchester 1822, Bishop of Chester 1824, Bishop of London 1828–1856. DNB, AO, p. 125.

8 Gilley, p. 207.

9 MFP, vol. 1, p. 337.

10 Ibid.

11 Rev. George Williams (1814–1878), chaplain to Bp. Alexander 1840–43, chaplain at St. Petersburg 1844–5, Pro-proctor Cambridge University 1858, Vicar of Ringwood, Hants., 1869 to his death. MEB, vol. III, pp. 1363–4. Williams was a High Churchman, and was probably appointed Bishop Alexander's chaplain to placate the Tractarians. FT, p. 228.

12 Michael Solomon Alexander (1799–1845), born Jewish in Posen, West Prussia, moved to London in 1820, baptised 1825 and ordained 1827, Professor of Hebrew at King's College, London 1832, consecrated Bishop of Jerusalem

13 Williams, p. xliv.

14 Welch, p. 195.

15 William Ewart Gladstone (1809–1898), Chancellor of the Exchequer 1852–5, 1859–66, 1873–74, 1880–82, Prime Minister December 1868–February 1874, April 1880–June 1885, February–July 1886, August 1892–March 1894. MEB, vol. v, pp. 418–9.

16 Welch, p. 199.

17 MFP, vol. 1, p. 319.

18 Ibid., p. 320.

19 BO MS 11.1. (2)/G.37 ff. 64–6.

20 ASC, p. cxxiv.

21 LP MS 2834, f. 213.

22 Ibid., pp. cxxiv–v.

23 MID, p.114, n. 3.

24 EA, p. 149.

25 MFP, vol. 1, p. 320.

26 LP MS 1878, f. 76.

27 MFP, vol. 1, p. 320.

28 LP MS 1894, f. 89.

29 LP MS 1878, f. 236.

30 JHN to Keble, 17 Nov. 1841, L & D, vol. VIII p. 336.

31 LP MS 1878, f. 237.

32 LP MS 2834, ff. 219–20.

33 ASC, p. cxxvi.

34 Ibid., p. cxxxvi.

35 Ibid., pp. cxxxvi–vii.

36 Ibid., p. cxxxviii.

37 Ibid., p. cxxxix.

38 ASC, p. cxl, and MFP, vol. 1, p. 323.

39 MID, pp. 114–5.

40 ASC, cxl.

41 For example, 'To obtain for the *Evangelical* Christians of the German nation the same advantages [...] enjoyed by the Christians of the *Latin* and *Greek* Churches [...] to increase the connection of German Protestants in the East, and perhaps lead to the foundation of settlements by them [...]', ATR, pp. 9– 10.

42 LP MS 1895, f. 24.

43 Ibid.

44 MFP, vol. 1, p. 323.

45 ASC, p. cxl.

46 Ibid.

47 The comments in brackets are Palmer's, scribbled almost illegibly on the original.

48 LP MS 1895, f. 15.

49 Ibid., f. 16.

50 Ibid., f. 17.

51 Ibid., f. 18.

52 Ibid., f. 19.

53 W J P to WP, 2 Nov. 1841, MFP, vol. 1, p. 321.

54 Ibid., p. 322.

55 W J P to RP, 6 Nov. 1841, Ibid.

56 Ibid.

57 W J P to RP, 9 Nov. 1841, Ibid. p. 326.

58 LP MS 1878, f. 76.

59 Ibid.

60 ASC, p. cxl.

61 MFP, vol. 1, pp. 325–6.

62 WP to RP, 28 Nov. 1841, Ibid., p. 324.

63 Ibid.

64 ATR, p. 91.

65 Ibid., pp. 92–3.

66 Rev. Charles Portales Golightly (1807–1885), of Oriel College Oxford, 'clergyman and religious controversialist'. 1836 invited by Newman to take charge of the chapel at Littlemore. Later led an outcry against Tract 90, and defended High Church principles against what he saw as the encroachments of Romanism. A.O.

67 26 Nov. 1841.

68 MFP, vol. 1, p. 327.

69 William Palmer, *A Letter to the Rev. C. P. Golightly* (hereafter *Golightly*) (Oxford: Parker, 1841), pp. 5–6.

70 Ibid., pp. 9–10.
71 Ibid., p. 13.
72 Shaw notes that Palmer's writings 'struck even his sympathisers as violent.' Keble was the exception; in a letter to Newman Keble described a visit from Perceval, who mentioned 'another (what he termed) violent pamphlet from Palmer about the Bishop of Jerusalem. I never can understand why people call his writings violent; to me they seem particularly calm.' Shaw, p. 153.
73 See amongst others Athelstan Riley, *Birkbeck and the Russian Church*, (London: SPCK, 1917) p. v.
74 MFP, vol. 1, p. 327.
75 Ibid., pp. 334–5.
76 LP MS 1895, f. 26.
77 Ibid., f. 27.
78 Ibid., pp. 27–8.
79 Ibid., p. 29.
80 Ibid., pp. 29–30.
81 Ibid., p. 34.
82 Ibid., pp. 36–7.
83 Ibid., p. 47.
84 ATR, p. 1.
85 Ibid., pp. 37–8.
86 Ibid., p. 100.
87 Ibid., pp. 101–2.
88 Ibid., p. 110.
89 Ibid., pp. 114–5.
90 W J P to RP, 20 Dec. 1841, MFP, vol. 1, p. 334.
91 John-Albert-Frederick Eichhorn (1779–1856), Prussian statesman, Counsellor 1810, Director of the Ministry of Foreign Affairs 1831, Minister of Public Instruction 1840. NBG, vol. 15, p. 762.
92 EA, p. 8.
93 Ibid., p.13.
94 Ibid., p.21.
95 Ibid., p.30.
96 Ibid., p. 40.
97 Ibid., p. 41.
98 Ibid., p. 42.
99 Ibid., p. 48.
100 Ibid., p. 57.
101 Ibid., p. 109.

102 Ibid., p. 123.
103 Ibid., p. 146.
104 Ibid., 163
105 Ibid., p. 64.
106 Ibid., pp. 165–6.
107 Ibid., p. 170
108 Ibid., p. 176.

Chapter Six: The Galitsin Affair

1 1802–1870, née Suvorova. RBSI, p. 160.
2 NV, p. 292. From ASC, p. v, it would appear that the two younger daughters had not yet converted; Newman's text is ambiguous.
3 In ASC, p. iv, 'Evangelical Methodisme.'
4 NV, p. 293.
5 ASC Introduction, p. v.
6 Ibid., p. viii.
7 Ibid., p. xii.
8 Ibid., p. xiii.
9 Ibid., p. xix.
10 Alexander Jolly (1756–1838), ordained 1776, coadjutor to Macfarlane, Bishop of Moray and Ross, 1796, collated to sole charge of Moray 1798. DNB.
11 One of 'four short treatises [...] designed to win over from Calvinism [...] such as may read it with hearts prepared to prefer truth to worldly considerations.' ASC, p. xxi.
12 Ibid., p. xxxv.
13 FT, p. 58.
14 ASC, p. xlii.
15 Ibid., p. civ.
16 Ibid., p. lxxix.
17 Ibid., p. lxxx.
18 Ibid., p. lxxxi.
19 Ibid., p. lxxxix.
20 Ibid.
21 It was at this dinner that Lord Clanricarde made his remarks about the terrible disfigurement of the Church of England, and the slovenliness of its churches, quoted above.
22 ASC, pp. xcv–vi.
23 WP to W J P, 14/26 June, LP MS 1894, f. 81.
24 ASC, pp. xcix–c.
25 Z, p. 96.
26 Article XVIII: 'They are also to be accursed that presume to say [...].'

27 ASC, p. c; the italics are Palmer's.

28 BO MS 11.1. (2)/G. 37 Bk. V ff. 13–4.

29 ASC, p. cii.

30 Rev. William Hare, deacon 1826, priest 1828, chaplain at Geneva 1838–44, Chaplain to the Forces, Woolwich, 1860. CCD, 1860, and information from the Rev. Michael French.

31 Ibid., p. civ.

32 Lord Edward Chichester (1799–1889), fourth Marquess (and Earl) of Donegall, also Baron Fisherwick, Dean of Raphoe 1832–71. CP, vol. IV p. 394.

33 ASC, p. cx.

34 Ibid., p. cxii.

35 Ibid.

36 Ibid., p. cxiii.

37 Ibid. He did however give a report to the Prince 'after the establishment of the Jerusalem Bishopric'. When Palmer presented his 'Protest' to the Archbishop of Canterbury, he included in it a number of instances of the Church of England's abdication of its responsibilities. These included the Archbishop's refusal to sign Dr. Routh's letter, his failure to indicate whether or not he approved of Palmer's seeking the communion of the Russian Church, his failure to answer Prince Galitsin's letter, and the Bishop of London's answers to Palmer's queries. ASC, p. cxxxi.

38 ASC, p. cxiv–v.

39 Ibid., p. cxvi.

40 Charles Stuart (1779–1845), diplomat, created Baron Stuart de Rothesay of the Isle of Bute 1828, Ambassador Extraordinary & Plenipotentiary to St. Petersburg, 1841–44. The peerage became extinct on his death. CP, vol. XII (I), pp. 409–410.

41 R W B to WP, 18 Feb. 1842, ASC, p. cxvii.

42 Ibid.

43 Ibid., p. cl.

44 Ibid., p. clv.

45 Ibid., p. clvi.

46 Z, p. 103.

47 Ibid.

48 ASC, p. clxii.

49 Ibid., p. clxv.

50 Ibid., p. clxxvi–vii.

51 Ibid., p. clxxviii.

52 Ibid., p. clxxix.

53 Ibid., p. clxxx.

54 Ibid., p. cxci.

55 Ibid., p. cxciv.

56 Richard Clarke Sewell (1803-1864), Dean of Arts 1839, Bursar 1840, Vice- President 1843. AO, p.1275, & ROM, vol. vi, p.133.

57 MAG MS 485, no. 5.

58 Ibid., no. 6.

59 Ibid., no. 7.

60 Ibid., no. 9.

61 Sewell to Routh, 14 Feb. 1842, Ibid., no. 10

62 B/O MS 11.1. (2)/G.37, Bk. VI. Referred to in the *Appeal* as 'Mr. O.', he may be George Jacob Bosanquet (1791–1866), attaché at Berlin 1815, Paris 1817, and Madrid 1822–29. AO, p. 134.

63 ASC, p. ccx.

64 Ibid., p. ccxxv.

65 Ibid., p. ccxxv: 'en agissant ainsi je suis parfaitement en paix avec ma conscience devant Dieu'.

66 Ibid., p. ccxxvi.

67 Ibid., p. ccxxxi.

68 Ibid.

69 Ibid., p. ccxxxv.

70 Ibid., p. ccxxxviii–ix.

71 Ibid., p. ccxl.

72 Ibid., p. 4.

73 It stated that Palmer: 'communicated in my parish church at the feasts of Easter and Pentecost last preceding, as the canons require; and that he is free, so far as I know [...] from all bond of excommunication or other canonical hindrance to his rightly communicating either in this diocese of the Lord Bishop of Oxford or in any other diocese of other bishops'. ASC, p. 9.

74 'To whose profit?' WP to W J P, 3 /15 May 1843, LP MS 1894, f. 107.

75 MFP, vol. I, p. 404.

76 ASC, p. 9.

77 Palmer nowhere explains what precisely he understood by the post of clerk to a bishop, nor gives any historical precedent for it, as he does for e.g., Canonical Letters. He seems to take it as an amorphous combination of factotum and client, although he also describes himself as Bp. Luscombe's 'spiritual son' (ASC, p. 39). His aim was no doubt to regularize the previous anomaly of accreditation from his College Principal alone.

78 ASC, p. 11.

79 Ibid., p.12.

80 Ibid., p. 14.

81 LP MS 2834, f. 233–4.

82 ASC, p. 39.

83 Ibid., p. 44.

84 Heneage Horsley (1776–1847), s. of Rt. Rev. Samuel Horsley, Bp. of St. Asaph. Ordained 1799. Curate St. Paul's, Dundee 1807–10, Incumbent 1810–47. Dean of Brechin 1812–47. SEC, p. 303.

85 ASC, p. 45.

86 Ibid., p. 46.

87 Ibid., p. 51.

88 J. M. Neale, *The Life and Times of Patrick Torry, D. D.* (London: Masters, 1856), p. 237.

Chapter Seven: Return to Russia

1 MFP, p. 345.

2 i.e., Mr. Law's chapel.

3 ASC, p. 58.

4 Ibid., pp . 58–9.

5 Ibid., p. 61.

6 Ibid., p. 60.

7 Ibid., p. 61.

8 MFP, vol. I, pp . 403–4.

9 ASC, p. 62.

10 Ibid., p. 66

11 WP to W J P, 4/16 Sept. 1842, LP MS 2834, f. 248.

12 W J P to WP, 30 Sept. 1842, Ibid., f. 252.

13 WP to Routh, 11/23 Sept. 1842, MAG MS 485, no. 18.

14 ASC, p. 67

15 Ibid.,p.68.

16 Ibid., p.73, and BO MS v.25 Bk. II, f. 61.

17 ASC, p. 77.

18 WP to AM, 5/17 Oct. 1842, LP MS 2836, f. 141.

19 ASC, p. 78.

20 BO MS v.25, f. 139.

21 ASC, p. 80.

23 Ibid.

24 Ibid., p. 86.

25 Ibid., p. 92.

26 WP to W J P, 23 Oct. 1842, LP MS 2834, f. 258.

27 Per Lord Selborne, MFP, vol. I, p. 407.

28 Entry for 18/30 Oct. 1842, BO MS v.25, f. 156.

29 Entry for 16 Nov. 1842, LP MS 2471.

30 WP to Routh, 2/14 Jan. 1843, MAG MS 485 no. 17.

31 Although Palmer had been given the chance to look it over beforehand by its author, the Rector of the Spiritual Academy, the Bishop of Vinnitza, on 15/27 Dec. 1842. MFP, vol. I, p. 135.

32 ASC, p. 136.

33 Ibid., p. 137.

34 WP to W J P, 20 Jan. 1843, LP MS 1894, f. 96.

35 WP to W J P, 26 Jan./7 Feb. 1843, LP MS 2834, f. 274.

36 bid., f. 279. A very similar warning is given Palmer by an unnamed Russian, possibly M. Mouravieff, that 'if I left the whole thing would certainly drop, and I would run a risk if I did not take care of having it given out that I had given in a petition for a Confessor and then run off without waiting for the result'. BO MS G. 20, Bk. I, f. 39. It may refer to the same conversation.

37 ASC, p. 141.

38 Ibid.

39 BO MS G.20, Bk. I, f. 24.

40 Nikolai Stepanovich Clementievski Nicanor (1787–1856), Abbot of the Holy Trinity St. Sergius Lavra 1814, Rector of the Bethany Seminary 1818–19, Bishop of Ravel 1826–31, Bp. of Kaluga 1831–4, Bp. of Minsk 1834–40, Archbishop of Volhynia 1840-43, of Warsaw 1843–48, Metropolitan of St. Petersburg and Novgorod 1848. RBSI, p.72.

41 ASC, p. 143.

42 Ibid., p. 149.

43 Ibid., p. 255.

44 Most likely M. Rhumine, mentioned regularly in NV.

45 ASC, p. 252.

46 Ibid., p. 253.

47 Ibid., p. 256.

48 W J P to WP, 13 March 1843, LP MS 2834, ff. 281–2.

49 ASC, p. 409.

50 Ibid.

51 WP to W J P, 4 April 1843, LP MSS 1894, f. 100, and 2834, f. 285.

52 MFP, vol. I, p. 411.

53 Ibid.

54 WP to AM, 4 April 1843, LP MS 2836, f. 148.

55 W J P to WP, 22 April 1843, MFP, vol. I, pp. 412–3.

56 WP to W J P, 3/15 May 1843, LP MS 1894, f. 106.

57 Ibid., LP MS 2834, f. 296.

58 LP MS 1894, f. 107.

59 RP to W J P, 24 April 1843, ASC, p. 414.

60 i.e. with Bishop Luscombe

61 WP to RP, 18 May 1843, MFP, vol. I, p. 415.
62 Ibid., p. 417.
63 ASC, pp. 257–8.
64 Ibid., p. 259.
65 Ibid., p. 260.
66 Ibid., p. 261.
67 Ibid., p. 264.
68 BO MS G.20 Bk. II, f. 64.
69 ASC, p. 265.
70 Ibid., pp. 267–8.
71 BO MS G.20 Bk. II, ff. 64–5.
72 ASC .p. 269.
73 Ibid., p. 281.
74 Ibid., p. 282.
75 BO MS G.20 Bk. II, f. 70. No doubt there were a number of these irate exchanges, as the report to Bp. Luscombe conflated three official interviews, on 18/30 May, 2 June, and 4 June. ASC, p. 262.
76 ASC, pp. 262–3.
77 Ibid.
78 Ibid., p. 291. He notes that this condition continued for four years, and had not 'even yet entirely ceased,' i.e. by April 1849.
79 James Barmby (1823–1897), Fellow & Maths Lecturer Magdalen College Oxford 1846–60, Principal Hatfield Hall, Durham, 1859–76, Rural Dean of Easington, 1890–94. MEB, pp. 270–1.
80 LP MS 2823, ff. 124–6.
81 Ibid., f. 125.
82 'Snob' was originally an abbreviation of *sine nobilitate,* indicating, as here, someone of low class.
83 LP MS 2823, f. 126.

Chapter Eight: Struggle for a Soul

1 BO MS Bk. 3, f. 60.
2 ASC, p. 292.
3 Ibid.
4 BO MS Bk. 3, f. 59.
5 ASC, p. 302.
6 BO MS Bk. 3, f. 61. *De Processione Spiritus Sancti a Solo Patri,* by Adam Zoernikav, born in Koenigsberg in 1562, a Lutheran, studied in Oxford and London, then went to Germany,

France, Italy and finally Russia, where he became Orthodox and a priest in Kiev. The Treatise was not published until 1774–76 in Koenigsberg, in 2 volumes. FT, p. 105, n. 21.

7 MFP, p. 419. Newman was received on 8 October 1845.

8 WP to W J P, 2 March 1846, LP MS 2835, f. 23.

9 'What seems to me' is underlined by Palmer's father, and 'surely they may' [maintain their particular view etc.] written above. By 'setting up one private opinion against another' he wrote 'unquestionably.' LP MS 1894, f. 110.

10 WP to W J P, 10 March 1846, MFP, vol. I, p. 421.

11 Ibid.

12 Ibid., p. 422.

13 Ibid., p. 424. The Bull *Regnans in Excelsis* of 25 February 1570, which excommunicated and purported to depose Elizabeth I, 'was an ineffective anachronism and made matters worse for her Catholic subjects.' J. N. D. Kelly, *The Oxford Dictionary of Popes* (Oxford: OUP, 1986), p. 269.

14 W J P to WP, 23 Jan. 1846, MFP, vol. I, p. 425, also LP MS 1894, ff. 114–5.

15 Ibid., MFP, vol. I, p. 425.

16 W J P to WP, 16 February 1846, MFP, vol. I, p. 427.

17 Ibid.

18 WP to W J P, 20 Feb. 1846, LP MS 2835, f. 17.

19 Ibid., f. 18.

20 Ibid., f. 20.

21 Ibid.

22 W J P to WP, 26 Feb. 1846, LP MS 1894, f. 116. The reference to 'development' almost certainly refers to Newman, who had converted only four months before (see n. 966, supra).

23 MFP, vol. I, p. 425.

24 W J P to WP, 26 Feb. 1846, LP MS 2835, f. 21.

25 LP MS 1894, f. 117.

26 WP to W J P, 2 March 1846, MFP, vol. I, p. 429.

27 Ibid.

28 Ibid., LP MS 2835, f. 26.

29 MFP, vol. I, p. 429.

30 Ibid., LP MS 1894, f. 122.

31 Ibid., f. 123. He had written in his diary on 8 Jan., 'thought of the question of Indulgences for 10,0,000, [sic] 10,000 or 1000 years & reconciled myself more to them than ever I could before'. LP MS 2472.

32 Ibid.

33 LP MS 2835, f.23–8.

34 W J P to WP, 3 March 1846, MFP, vol. I, p. 430, also LP MSS 1894 f. 124, & 2835 f. 32.

35 Ibid.

36 W J P to WP, 3 March 1846, MFP, vol. I, p. 431.
37 W J P to WP, 6 April 1846, LP MS 2835, f. 41.
38 WP to W J P, 15 April 1846, Ibid., ff. 53–4.
39 WP to W J P, 15 April, 1846, LP MS 1894, f. 128.
40 WP to W J P, 15 April 1846, Ibid., ff. 128–9, & MFP, vol. 1, p. 432.
41 W J P to RP, 28 March 1846, MFP, vol. I, p. 433.
42 Palmer's father later told his daughter Emily that 'It is my belief, that he [Palmer] fell into the hands, many years ago, of some men of ability much older than himself, who perhaps may have been the beginning of his present opinions'. (W J P to Em P, 28 Jan. 1852, LP MS 1903, f. 49). His stress on the difference in age may indicate a reference to Newman, amongst others.
43 W J P to RP, 28 March 1846, MFP, vol. I, p. 433, & LP MS 1878, f. 98.
44 Ibid., MFP, vol. I, p. 433.
45 WP to W J P, 26 May 1846, LP MS 2835, f. 63.
46 WP to W J P, 26 May 1846, LP MS 1894, f. 136–7.
47 Armand de Mestral, a Vaudois Minister, who found himself increasingly attracted to 'les idées d'unité, d'autorité, de stabilité' represented by the Church of Rome. LP MS 2837, f. 96.
48 WP to de Mestral, 3 July 1846, LP MS 1895, f. 32 ff.
49 bid., f. 33.
50 Ibid., f. 34.
51 F W F to WP, 29 May 1846, LP MS 2837, f. 62. Frederick William Faber (1814–1863), admirer and friend of Newman, Anglican deacon 1837, priest 1839, received as a Roman Catholic in 1845, formed the 'Wilfridian' community, RC priest 1847, joined the Oratory of St. Philip Neri 1848. DNB.
52 WP to Rev. J. M. Forbes (see n. 1188), 4 July 1846, LP MS 1895, ff. 54–5.
53 Ibid., ff. 55–6.

Chapter Nine: Pearls before Swine

1 BO MS v. 49, 10.6. (3), ff. 4–5.
2 Ibid.
3 BO MS G.20 part III, f. 63.
4 William Skinner (1778–1857), ordained 1802, Bishop of Aberdeen 1816, elected Primus June 1841. DNB.
5 BO MS G.20 part III, f. 63.
6 Patrick Torry (1763–1852), ordained deacon and priest 1783, Bishop of Dunkeld 1808, and of St. Andrews in 1844, Pro-Primus of the episcopal church of Scotland 1841. DNB.
7 BO MS G.20 part III, f. 66.
8 Charles Hughes Terrot (1790–1872), deacon 1818, Dean of Edinburgh and Fife 1836, Bishop of Edinburgh and Pantonian professor 1841, Primus 1857. DNB.

9 BO MS G.20 part III, f. 66.
10 Torry to WP, 31 Aug. 1846, BO MS G.20 part III, f. 74.
11 Ibid.
12 David Moir (1777–1847), deacon & priest 1797, coadjutor of Brechin 1837, Bishop of Brechin 1840–47. SEC, p. 372.
13 Ibid., f. 67.
14 Michael Russell (1781–1848), deacon 1808, Dean of the diocese of Edinburgh 1831, Bishop of Glasgow and Galloway 1837. DNB.
15 BO MS v. 49, f. 11.
16 Ibid., f. 10, and ASC, pp. 328–9.
17 BO MS G.20 part III, f. 79.
18 BO MS v. 49, f. 13.
19 Ibid., f. 16.
20 BO MS G.20 part III, f. 80.
21 'portion of the flock.
22 ASC, p. 341.
23 Ibid., f. 81.
24 BO MS v. 49, ff. 19–20.
25 BO MS v. 49, f. 19.
26 Ibid.
27 BO MS G.20 part III, f. 84.
28 BO MS v.49, f. 20.
29 BO MS G.20 part III, f. 86.
30 Ibid., f. 89.
31 Ibid., f. 91.
32 Ibid., f. 106, and ASC, p. 334.
33 Luscombe had died of a heart attack at Lausanne on 24 August.
34 ASC, p. 335.
35 Ibid.
36 Ibid.
37 Ibid., p. 337.
38 BO MS v. 49, f. 23.
39 Ibid., f. 24.
40 ASC, p. 337.
41 Skinner to Routh, 12 Sept. 1846, MAG MS 490, f. 33.
42 ASC, p. 341.
43 Ibid., p. 342.

Chapter Ten: The Struggle Continues

1 WP to W J P, 3 Nov. 1846, MFP, vol. I, p. 436.
2 Ibid.
3 Ibid., p. 437.
4 W J P to WP, 5 Nov. 1846, LP MS 1894, f. 135.
5 Ibid., MFP, vol. I, p. 437.
6 Ibid., LP MS 1894, f. 135.
7 W J P to RP, 27 Feb. 1847, LP MS 1878, f. 109.
8 Ibid., f. 110.
9 Mrs. G. P to W J P, 3 July 1847, BO MS 10.6. (3) C, f. 70.
10 ASC, pp. 363–4.
11 Ibid., p. 366. Zernov believes these punishments were fictitious. Z, p. 103
12 ASC, p. 366.
13 Ibid., p. 367.
14 Mrs. G. Palmer to WP, 15 Aug. 1847, BO MS 10.6. (3) C, f. 70.
15 Ibid., f. 72.
16 Ibid., f. 73.
17 See ASC, pp. 401–2.
18 Ibid.
19 LP MS 1895, f. 170.
20 Referred to as 'Count N. N.' in *Appeal*, p. 404 ff. Count Alexander Petrovich Tolstoy (1801–1873), Soldier and diplomat. 1826 Joined Ministry of Foreign Affairs staff. 1828 Joined the Cavalry Guard Regiment, 1828–9 fought against the Turks, decorated. 1829 ADC to Emperor Nicholas I. 1830 Retired from military service, First Secretary of mission to Greece. 1831 Chamberlain & director of the Dept. of Economics. 1834 Civil Governor of Tver. 1837 Military Governor of Odessa as Maj-Gen. until 1840. 1856–62, Ober-Prokuror of the Holy Synod. RBS, pp. 33–4.
21 Most likely James Frederick Skinner Gordon (1821–1904) ordained priest 1844, incumbent of St. Andrews Glasgow 1844–91, author. SEC, p. 273.
22 BO MS v. 49, f. 89.
23 ASC, pp. 404–5.
24 Ibid., p. 405.
25 ASC, p. 414.
26 Ibid., p. 417–8.
27 Quasimodo and Esmerelda perhaps? BO MS 10.6. (3) C, ff. 97–8.
28 Ibid., p. 419 ff.
29 Although the Princess does complain of 'some unfairness' ASC, p. 421.
30 BO MS v. 49, f. 112 ff.

31 WP to AM, 1 Nov. 1847, LP MS 1895, f. 150.

32 BO MS 10.6. (3) C, f. 119. 'Chatelaine: an ornamental appendage worn by ladies at their waist, having short chains attached for keys, scissors, penknife, thimble-case, etc.' *Shorter Oxford English Dictionary*, 3rd Ed'n (OUP, 1968), p. 296.

33 AM to W J P, 12 Dec. 1847, BO MS 10.6. (3) C, f. 119.

34 Mrs. George Palmer - see LP MS 2835, f. 133.

35 Ibid., f. 168.

36 Ibid., ff. 169-170.

37 Ibid.

38 Ibid., f. 171.

Chapter Eleven: Passing into Oblivion

1 BO MS v. 49, f. 159.

2 WP to AM, 21 Nov. 1848, LP MS 1895, f. 171.

3 'Mrs. Gentleman's Lodgings, 93 Princes St.' WP to GHP, undated, LP MS 1903, f. 79.

4 Ibid.

5 Torry to WP, 15 Dec. 1848, BO MS v. 49, f. 193, and ASC, pp. 447–8.

6 WP to Torry, 17 Dec. 1848, BO MS v. 49, f. 194.

7 ASC, p. 448.

8 W J P to W J P, 31 Jan. 1849, LP MS 1894, f. 146.

9 Ibid., f. 148.

10 W J P to WP, 4 Feb. 1849, Ibid., f. 149.

11 WP to W J P, 2 May 1849, Ibid., f. 154.

12 MFP, vol. II, p. 55.

13 Ibid., p. 56.

14 WP to AM, 12 July 1849, LP MS 1895, f. 173.

15 MFP, vol. II, p. 57.

16 Ibid., p. 58.

17 WP to W J P, 1 March 1849, Ibid., f. 150.

18 John Torry (1800–1879), Minister of St. Ann's Coupar Angus 1821 to death, dean of united diocese of St. Andrew's, Dunkeld & Dunblane, 1824 to death. MEB, vol. III, p. 993.

19 ASC, p. 491.

20 W E G to WP, 1 April 1849, LP MS 2823, f. 53.

21 W P to W E G, 7 April 1849, BL MS 44368 f. 138.

22 ASC, pp. 503–4.

23 Skinner to W E G, 4 April 1849, BL Gladstone Papers, MS Add. 44300, f. 174.

24 Alexander Forbes (1817–1875), of the Hon. East India Company, 1836-40, ordained 1844, Bishop of Brechin 1847–75, supporter of the Scottish Liturgy and only episcopal

representative of the Oxford Movement in Scotland, prolific author. SEC, pp. 258–9, and Rowan Strong, *Alexander Forbes of Brechin* (Oxford: Clarendon, 1995).

25 Walter John Trower (1804–1877), deacon 1829, priest 1832, Bishop of Glasgow and Galloway 1848–59, Bishop of Gibraltar 1863. SEC, p. 466.

26 David Low (1768–1855), deacon 1787, priest 1789, Bishop of Ross and Argyll 1819-38, of Moray, Ross and Argyll, 1838–46, Moray and Ross, 1846–50. SEC, pp. 337–8.

27 LP MS 2823, f. 8

28 Ibid., f. 77.

29 Ibid., f. 87.

30 Ibid., ff. 83–4.

31 Samuel Hood (1782–1872), ordained 1826, Dean of Argyll and the Isles 1848– 72, Canon of Cumbrae 1853–72, DD 1870. SEC, p. 301.

32 ASC, p. 527.

33 Ibid., pp. 527–8.

34 LP MS 2823, f. 93.

35 Ibid.

36 See ASC, pp. 531–2.

37 Ibid., pp. 529–30.

38 WP to Routh, 14 July 1849, MAG MS 485, no./f. 21.

39 WP to Torry, 8 Sept. 1849, LP MS 2823, f. 108.

40 Palmer's Oxford contemporary, Charles Wordsworth.

41 LP MS 2823, f. 114.

42 Torry to WP, 14 Sept. 1849, Ibid., ff. 115–6.

43 Torry to WP, 22 Sept. 1849, Ibid., f. 121. This was confirmed in September 1850, when Palmer heard that the Glasgow Synod also rejected the Appeal; the other Synods were silent, so 'it sufficiently appeared that these had all taken the Resolutions of the Episcopal Synod as a final Settlement of the Appeal'. Ibid., f. 238.

44 The Rev. John Murray Forbes, for 14 years Rector of St. Luke's Church, New York, became Roman Catholic 1849, returned to the Episcopal Church in 1859, became Dean of the General Theological Seminary and 'virulently anti- Roman.' J. T. Addison, *The Episcopal Church in the United States* (New York: Scribner, 1951), p. 161., and information from The Rev. Dr. Roger Ferlo, Rector of St. Luke's.

45 The Rev. Dr. Samuel Seabury (1801–1872), deacon 1826, priest 1828, Editor of *The Churchman* 1833, Professor of evidences at the General Theological Seminary N. Y. C. 1835–8, and of biblical learning 1862 to his death. Robert Bruce Mullin, in J. A. Garraty and M. C. Carnes (eds.) *American National Biography* (Oxford: OUP, 1999), vol. 19 pp. 549–50.

46 LP MS 2823, f. 224.

47 Ibid., f. 228.

48 Parks to WP, 16 July 1850, ibid., ff. 223–4.

Chapter Twelve: The Correspondence with Khomiakoff

1 ASC, p. 537.

2 Khomiakoff, Alexis Stepanovich (1804–1860), Russian philosophical theologian. Served as an army officer 1822 and 1828. Became, with Ivan Kireevsky, one of the founders of the Slavophil movement, which he sought to build on Orthodox Christianity. F. L. Cross (ed.), *Oxford Dictionary of the Christian Church* (2nd ed'n.) (Oxford: OUP, 1974), pp. 778–9.

3 REC, p. xlv.

4 Ibid., p. xlv.

5 N. Barsukov, *Zhizn' I Trudy M. P. Pogodina,* (St. Petersburg, 1894), vol. viii, p. 80, quoted in FT, p. 107.

6 Ibid., p. 67.

7 REC, p. 9.

8 Ibid., p. 20.

9 REC, p. 59.

10 Ibid., p. 6 ff.

11 Ibid., p. 40.

12 Ibid., p. 70.

13 Ibid., pp. 70–1.

14 Ibid., p. 101.

15 Khomiakoff's final verdict on Anglicanism was given in 1858, in his third *Essay upon the Western Confessions*:

England seems to make an exception to the general movement of Western confessions; but even as I try to do justice to the country, I find it useless to talk about it [...] Anglicanism itself lacks any base that could merit a serious examination [...] Gallicanism is dead; Anglicanism is terminally ill. Anglicanism has not one good reason to give, nor has it ever given one, for not being orthodox. Anglicanism is at once the purest and the most illogical of the Western confessions; thrust into the bosom of the Church by everything that makes it religious, it is everything that is most opposed to the very idea of the Church; because it is neither a tradition, nor a doctrine, but simply a national institution (an establishment), i.e. a work made by human hands. It has been judged and it is dying. [Author's translation]

L'Eglise Latin et le Protestantisme, Lausanne et Vevey, 1872, pp. 257–8, quoted in REC, p. xxxi. Birkbeck, writing in 1895, adds laconically, 'It would be interesting to know what Mr. Khomiakoff would have thought on this subject at the present day'.

16 REC, p. 102.

17 Ibid., p. 80.

18 Ibid., p. 103.

19 This is likely to refer to idea of sending a 'Memorial' to the Russian Synod by clergymen of the Scottish Church. Prof. Thomson identifies the Rev. T. G. Suther* as the prime mover

behind the idea, put into action after the Gorham judgement. The identities of the others involved remains obscure. A copy of the Memorial was given to the Russian chaplain in London, Fr. Popov, who forwarded it to Count Pratasoff. Although a commission was appointed by the Synod to examine the Memorial, the Crimean War and English suspicion of Popov's support for Stephen Hatherley's attempt to create an English Orthodox Church prevented any further progress. See F.T., pp. 175–8.

*Thomas George Spink Suther (1814–1880), Deacon and priest 1837, Bishop of Aberdeen 1857-65, Bishop of Aberdeen and Orkney, 186–583. SEC p. 454.

20 Gregory Postnikoff, d. 1860, monk 1814. Archbishop of Riazan 1829, of Tver 1831, and of Kaluga 1848. Metropolitan of Novgorod and St. Petersburg 1856. REC, pp. 112–3.

21 REC, p. 109.

22 'Living in darkness and separation from all the denominations of the West and seeing in their representatives in the East [...] the fiercest enemies of Orthodoxy, the Patriarchs began to doubt even their Christianity and to try to protect themselves from them'. *The Complete Works of A. S. Khomiakoff*, (Moscow, 1900), vol. viii, appendix, p. 32, cited in FT., p. 179.

23 FT., p. 179.

24 REC, p. 113.

25 FT., p. 180, and Francis Thomson, 'Economy', *The Journal of Theological Studies* 16:2 (1965), pp. 371–2. The Greeks were also becoming anxious. In his report of December 1852, commissioned by the Patriarch of Constantinople, Constantin Oeconomos described Palmer as having 'scattered, like the thief in the night of the Gospels, tares of scandal in the fertile field of Orthodoxy and [...] disturbed the peace of the Holy Churches.' Konstantin o ex Ikonomon, Τὰ Σωζόμενα Ἐκκλησιαστικὰ Συγγράμματα (Athens, 1961), I, p. 494., cited in 'Economy', p. 371 (ref. above). This in turn to prompted Metropolitan Philaret of Moscow to write that 'the seeds of schism are being sown'. Metropolitan Philaret, *Pis'ma Mitropolita Moskovskago k A. N. M.* (Kiev, 1869), p. 369, cited in 'Economy', p. 372 (ref. above).

26 REC, pp. 118 ff.

27 bid., p. 119.

28 Letter to A. N. Popov, 1 September 1852. Barsukov, op. cit., vol. xii p. 159, cited in F. T., p. 181.

29 REC, p. 125.

30 Ibid., p. 126.

31 Ibid., p. 130.

32 Since Mouravieff was 'very angry' with him 'for trying to bring the whole proceeding [of the Memorial] into notoriety and life', (REC, p. 30), this may refer to Metropolitan Philaret of Moscow, who told Khomiakoff that he 'highly approved all that [Palmer] had done and proposed' – Ibid., p. 96.

33 Ibid., pp. 132–3.

34 Ibid., p. 146.

35 Ibid., p. 151.

36 Ibid.

37 Ibid

Chapter Thirteen: In the Levant

1 LP MS 2823, ff. 130–1.

2 Constantin Oeconomos (1780–1857), Greek theologian and writer, nominated Exarch, then Vicar of the Salonica Archbishopric in 1817, and in charge of the Greek Gymnasium of Smyrna. 1819 Preacher-General to the Ecumenical Throne. DUC, p. 1306.

3 Theoclitos Pharmakides, theologian and Archimandrite. Ordained deacon 1802, priest 1811. Nominated Secretary of the Holy Synod and given the task of drawing up the constitution of the Greek Church. Honorary Professor of Theology at the University of Athens. DUC, p. 1326. Palmer describes Oeconomos and Pharmakides as 'mortal enemies and engaged in controversy of the bitterest kind', but united on one thing only: 'that the English are heretics and that the Greek or Eastern is the only true Church'. LP MS 2824, f. 5.

4 LP MS 2823, f. 137.

5 Alexander Mavrocordato (1791–1865), a major participant in the Greek rebellion. President of the first Greek National Assembly, 1822; President of the Government appointed by the Assembly. In 1822 in charge of the heroic defence of Missolonghi. In 1832 became Vice-President of the National Assembly, in 1844 Head of the Cabinet, and Ambassador in Munich, Berlin, London, Constantinople and Paris. In 1854 formed a Cabinet which lasted 17 months. ES (CD Rom).

6 LP MS 2824, f. 82.

7 A deacon who is also a monk.

8 EP to WJP, undated letter from Athens, LP MS 4307, f. 57.

9 Edwin Palmer was told by a Mrs. King of one reason:

'the ignorance, immorality and simoniacal practices of the higher clergy in the Greek Church [...] the Athenians had of late years much diminished in their reverence for them, e.g. the practice of kissing their hands upon meeting had almost gone out: the young Greek said it was otherwise in Smyrna.'

LP MS 2852, f. 6.

10 WP to WJP from Athens, 26 Jan. 1850, LP MS 1894, f. 160.

11 Ibid., ff. 160–1. Palmer also disliked the music of the services in Greece. In December he wrote:

Sunday of the Forefathers about 10' before 8 at the Church called Chryso- Speliotissia at the end of Aeolus St. – there were standing at each of the two Quoirs a group of boys who added their most shrill ear-splitting screams to the nasal roar of the elder singers. LP MS 4307, f. 67, Sun. Dec. 23/11.

In Constantinople the following June, he wrote of the Synodical Liturgy in the Patriarchal Church:

[...] in lengthening out the Communion Anthem Αἰνεῖτε: (or whatever they added or substituted) they sang their horrible see-saw discord (which might easily be changed to harmony) till the perspiration, for it was very hot, rolled down the fat singers' faces. LP MS 2826, f. 242, Sun June 16/4.

12 'They think that the influence of Saints is often exercised through their Icons, and, on account of some reputation for miracles, prefer one Icon to another. (praying to St. Elias for rain. Mrs. Hall (a teacher) "It is God who gives us rain, and we should pray to Him for it" – "Certainly; I knew that: but St. Elias is over that department.")' WP to WJP, 7 March 1850, Athens, LP MS 1894, f. 164.

13 Ibid., f. 165.

14 Ibid., ff. 162–3.

15 Evfimy Vassilievitch Poutiatine (1803–1883), Took part in the Battle of Navarinska in 1827. In England to order steamboats in 1841. 1842 promoted Contr. Admiral, 1851 Vice-Admiral; Made a Count in 1855, and Chief of Staff of the Kronstadt Military Government. Attached to Russian embassies in London and Paris, to report on the latest naval inventions. Commanded the Eastern Ocean Fleet, promoted to Admiral 1858, and was the Russian Naval Agent in London. In June 1861 he became Minister of People's Education. Member of the State Council. Died 16 October 1883, buried in the Kiev Caves. RBS.

Lord Selborne described Poutiatine as 'the most intimate of all William's Russian friends' (MFP, vol. II, p. 60). It is unclear, however, when this close friendship began; perhaps it was when Poutiatine was sent to London in 1841, when he might naturally be introduced to someone who had travelled in Russia, and could speak Russian.

16 LP MS 2852, ff. 36–8.

17 LP MS 2825, ff. 77–8.

18 Rich and lucky. Edwin Palmer noted 'We were told that he had *found* his money digging under his house'. LP MS 2852, f. 55.

19 Ibid., ff. 96–8.

20 LP MS 2825, f. 134–5, entry for Sunday April 21/9.

21 In LP MS 2823 f. 144, this gathering is referred to as the 'Jerusalem Synod' , but it is unclear whether or not this was an officially constituted Synod (which the number and rank of those participating would suggest), or an informal meeting of interested parties to pronounce on an important question.

22 LP MSS 2825, f. 195, & 2823, f. 144.

23 LP MS 2852, f. 88, Apr. 28/16, Fourth Sunday after Easter, Palm Sunday.

24 LP MS 2825, ff. 255–261.

25 Ibid., f. 287.

26 Ibid., f. 329.

27 LP MSS 1903, f. 27, and 4305, f. 32.

28 LP MS 2826, f. 29.

29 LP MS 2852, f. 142, 4 June/23 May.

30 WP to DP, 24 June 1850, LP MS 2835, f. 191.

31 A 'metochion' is a subsidiary establishment, or outpost, of a monastery.

32 LP MS 2826, f. 167, Thursday June 13/1.

33 The Patriarch Constantios, b. 1770 Constantinople, studied theology and literature in the university at Kiev for seven years. Archbishop of Sinai in 1805. In 1836 unanimously elected Patriarch of Constantinople. His reforms were left incomplete when false allegations made the government suspicious of him, and forced his resignation. He then retired to Khalki. DUC, p. 430. Palmer noted that Constantius but in reality because he could not endure the factions of the Nation i.e. the Greeks of the Fanar.' LP MS 2824, f. 180.

34 LP MS 2823, ff. 147–157.

35 John Gideon Millingen (1782–1862), physician and writer. Matriculated at the Ecole de Médecine; in 1802 assistant-surgeon in the British Army, ordered to Egypt. Surgeon to the forces 1814. Served in all the Peninsular campaigns under Wellington and Lord Hill, present at Waterloo as principal surgeon of cavalry, and at the surrender of Paris. Wrote libretti and farces, plays and novels. DNB.

36 LP MS 2826, ff. 267–9.

37 Not financial economy, but 'a departure from the rules of the Church , so as to assist the salvation of particular persons'. Bp. Kallistos (Timothy) Ware, *The Orthodox Church* (London: Penguin, 1993), p. 311 n. 1.

38 Alexandre Caratheodori, b. 20 July 1833 at Constantinople; educated at German universities, entered the service of Turkey as a translator. Employed by the Grand Vizier, Sarvez Pasha, as a counsellor at the conferences of Constantinople in 1877-8. Nominated Minister of Foreign Affairs in December 1878, the first Christian to be nominated to this position. In May 1885 appointed Prince of the Isles of Samos. DUC.

39 LP MS 2826, f. 324.

40 LP MS 2823, ff. 170–3.

41 Ibid., 2823, ff. 173.

42 John Henry Wynne, of Christ Church, fellow All Souls College 1841–51, RC priest. AO, p. 1622.

43 James Laird Patterson, seceded to Rome 1850. President of St. Edmunds College, Ware, 1870–80 RC Bishop of Emmaus 1880. AO, p. 1079.

44 WP to WJP, 19 June 1850, LP MS 2835, f. 88.

45 At this point only an Anglican deacon; see n. 3, supra.

46 The 9th Marquess of Lothian (1833–1900), Attaché to the Lisbon legation July 1854, Tehran November 1854. Attaché at Athens 1858, Frankfurt 1862, Madrid May 1865, and Vienna June to October 1865. Secretary for Scotland 1887– 1892. MEB vol. VI, pp. 79–80.

47 LP MS 2852, f. 241.

48 They had hoped that Meyrick and Lord Lothian would travel with them, but Lothian had also fallen ill with fever, and so both were left behind.
49 EP's journal, LP MS 2852, f. 229.
50 WP's journal (made up with Edwin, but with additions), LP MS 2827, f. 81
51 EP's journal, LP MS 2852, ff. 229–231.
52 WP's journal, LP MS 2827, ff. 89–90.
53 LP MS 2828.
54 The pleated skirt of Greek national costume, as worn by the Evzones.
55 LP MS 2852, f. 262.
56 Ibid., f. 258.
57 Ibid., f. 243.
58 Ibid., f. 289.
59 Ibid., f. 422.
60 Ibid., f. 379.
61 Ibid., f. 385.
62 Ibid., f. 412.
63 Ibid., f. 342.
64 LP MS 2827, f. 197.
65 LP MS 2852, f. 414.
66 Ibid., f. 334.
67 Ibid., f. 342

Chapter Fourteen: Leaving the East

1 LP MS 1895, ff. 69–71. Letter dated 20 September 1850.
2 Ibid., f. 72.
3 LP MS 2823, f. 211.
4 LP MS 1895, f. 75.
5 Ibid., f. 76. The Orthodox worry over a possible schism between the Russians and the Greeks is apparent in Mouravieff's rebuke.
6 Ibid., f. 79
7 Ibid., f. 80.
8 Palmer visited Vortizza, where he was told 'that there are now 70 houses of Greeks in London, 70 at Manchester, and 10 more either at Glasgow or Liverpool'. LP MS 2828, f. 129.
9 LP MS 2828, f. 117.
10 He wrote to Edwin Palmer that Father Ignatius regarded the Church of England 'as the Mother and Queen wasp of Protestantism'. Bod. MS Eng. lett. d. 432 f. 22–33.
11 LP MS 2828, f. 118.
12 *Dissertations on the Anglican Church.*
13 Ibid., f. 158.

14 Ibid., f. 182–3.

15 Ibid., f. 203, Mon. 5/23 May.

16 WP to WJP, 25 June 1851, LP MS 1894, ff. 170–1, and .MFP vol. II, pp. 113– 4.

17 MFP vol. II, p. 112.

18 Ibid., pp. 115–120.

19 Ivan Alexeivich Borisov (1899–1857), famous Russian theologian and speaker. 1841 Bishop of Vologda, and translated to Kharkov. 1848 Archbishop of Cherson and Tavrea. ES (CD Rom).

20 LP MSS 2829, f. 45, & 1903, f. 93.

21 LP MS 2829, f. 121.

22 Ibid., f. 136.

23 Ibid., ff. 51–2.

24 Mihail Karpovitch Paulofsky (1810–1898), from 1833 taught theology, philosophy and logic at the Richilieu Lyceum in Odessa. Ordained 1836. When the Lyceum became a university, he stayed on as professor until 1873, when he left to become a Cathedral Archpriest. ES (CD Rom).

25 LP MS 2829, ff. 85–7.

26 Ibid., f. 129.

27 Ibid., ff. 212–3.

28 Alexei Metrophanov, d. 1859. July 1832 visited the Holy Places; 1835 he travelled to Mount Athos and Jerusalem. 1839 became the monk Arseny, and a hierodeacon. 1841 became a hieromonk. 1844 joined the revived Sviatogorsky monastery. 1850 became an Archimandrite. Wrote about his journeys to the Holy Places. RBS.

29 LP MS 2829, f. 226.

30 Ibid., f. 145.

31 Vladimir Alexeivitch Korniloff (1806–1854), Vice-Admiral and Hero of Sebastopol. Lieutenant in 1830, in 1831 given own command. Lt-Captain 1837; 1838-42 Captain, and commander of the 'Twelve Apostles,' a 120 gun ship. 1846 sent to England to order new steamboats. 1848 returned to Sebastopol on the new steamboat 'Vladimir' as a Contr-Admiral. 1851 appointed to the Emperor's suite, 1852 made Vice-Admiral. 1853 sent to Constantinople, prepared Sebastopol for war. On 5 October the positions he had set up were stormed, his left leg was crushed by a cannon-ball, and he died of his wounds. Korniloff 'was religious to the point of mysticism'. RBS.

32 LP MS 2829, f. 233.

33 Palmer recorded his 'general impression' of Alupka as: 'Religious indifference, enjoying all that art & nature can bestow earth, air, water, sun, laws, ships, Palace, luxury, Power, wealth [...] surrounded by vines & roses, sitting between Paganised Christianity and civilised Mahometanism but a shade nearer to the latter'. LP MS 2829, f. 274.

34 Mihail Woronzoff (1782–1856), Russian general. Brought up in England, and became a soldier at 17. Took part in the campaigns of 1812, 1813 and 1814. Served with distinction, and rose to general. 1818 head of the army of occupation in France. Made Governor-General of New Russia and Bessarabia. 1844 Governor of the Caucasus. 1845 elevated to the rank of Prince for taking Dargo. Died at Odessa, 18 November 1856. BU vol. XLIII, pp. 73–4.

35 Ibid., f. 399.

36 Ibid., f. 326.

37 'Turning a blind eye, for economy.' (See n. 1223 above).

38 LP MS 2829, f. 401.

39 Ibid., f. 406, & MFP vol. II, pp. 121–2. Lord Selborne mentions (MFP, p. 122, n. 1) the peculiar interpretation put on this episode by Baron A. G. Zhomini+ in his *Diplomatic Study on the Crimean War* (London: W. H. Allen, 1882), p.451: 'It was asserted that Sir Stratford Canning* made active endeavours with the Patriarch of Constantinople to procure from him a declaration of heresy against the Russian Church. An English agent named Palmer, well versed in religious matters, had been sent to study the divergence existing in the dogmas, and to show that the Russian Church had departed from the lap of Greek Orthodoxy. Such a declaration would have had an immense moral effect, as much in the East as in Europe, and even in Russia many dissidents. [sic] The Patriarch seems to have refused with firmness'.

Stratford Canning (1786–1880), Entered the Foreign Office 1807, became a famous diplomatist, styled 'the Great Elchi'. Ambassador at Constantinople, and negotiated the Treaty of Bucharest between Napoleon and Turkey 1812. Envoy to Washington 1820–24. MP for Old Sarum, 1828-30; for Stockbridge, 1830; Kings Lynn, 1835–41. Created Viscount Stratford de Redcliffe of Somerset, 1852. AC, p. 506.

+ Baron Aleksandr Genrikhovich Zhomini (1814–1888), Russian diplomat and Senior Counsellor in the Ministry for Foreign Affairs. 1875 took temporary charge of the Ministry of Foreign Affairs. 1879–1880 Assistant to the Minister of Foreign Affairs. Wrote *Diplomatic Study on the Crimean War*, published anonymously in France in 1874, although written in 1863; it appeared under his name in Russia in 1878. ES (CD Rom).

40 MFP vol. II, p. 122–3.

41 RP to Eleanor Palmer, 18 August 1851, LP MS 1879, f. 111.

42 WJP to WP, 27 October 1851, LP MS 1894, f. 174.

43 EP to WP, 2 November 1851, LP MS 1895, f. 98.

44 MFP, p. 122, n. 2.

45 WP to EP, 14 December 1851, Bod. MS Eng. lett. d. 432, f. 20. He expected these efforts to have been brought to a close 'by the end of January'. WP to WJP, 7 December 1851, LP MS 1894, f. 176.

46 WP to EP, 14 December 1851, Bod. MS Eng. lett. d. 432, f. 20.

47 MFP vol. II, p. 123.

48 If Palmer refers to his own case here, he may have in mind Hugh James Rose, 'the most eminent person of his generation as a divine' (Dean Church, *The Oxford Movement* (Chicago: University of Chicago Press), p.16), the convenor and presider over the 'Hadleigh Conference', one of the formative events of the Oxford Movement. Rose was Professor of Divinity at Durham from 1833 to 1834, delivering three lectures in that capacity before retiring from ill-health; Charles Miller believes that Rose was 'friend and mentor' to Palmer, whose Tractarian views 'strongly affected Palmer's theological disposition'. Charles Miller, *Toward a Fuller Vision* (Wilton: Morehouse Barlow, 1984), pp. 63–4.

49 WP to WJP, 26 December 1851, MFP vol. II, p. 125.

50 WP to WJP, Athens, 17 January 1852, LP MS 1894, f. 180.

51 WJP to EmP, 28 January 1852, LP MS 1903, f. 49

52 WP to WJP, Athens, 6 March 1852, LP MS 1894, f. 190.

53 WJP to WP, Mixbury, 23 April 1852, Ibid., f. 195.

54 WJP to WP, Mixbury, 23 (?) April 1852, LP MS 2835, f. 260.

55 WJP to WP, 5 January, 1853, LP MS 1894, f. 205.

56 The same letter, in MFP vol. II, pp 153–4.

57 EP to WP, 23 September 1853, LP MS 2836, f. 86

58 MFP vol. II, p. 165.

Chapter Fifteen: In Limbo

1 WP to EmP, undated, LP MS 2826, f. 118. As Palmer was in Athens working on Greek translations of *Dissertations on the Anglican Church*, and *Dissertations on the Eastern Church*, published in 1851 and 52 respectively, it seems likely that this account was written in one of those two years.

2 Journal entry for 3 February/22 January, LP MS 2830, f. 227.

3 WP to EP, 6 December, Bod. MS Eng. lett. d. 432.

4 See n. 1168, supra.

5 Poutiatine to WP, 18/30 October, LP MS 2830, f. 142.

6 Mouravieff to WP, 20 March 1852, St. Petersburg, LP MS 1895, ff. 102–3.

7 Mouravieff to WP, 6 May 1852, St. Petersburg, LP MS 1895, ff. 103–5.

8 FT, p. 175.

9 Ibid.

10 LP MS 2830, f. 326.

11 His name was 'per errorem e tabulis Collegi erasum', but restored to the College books on 25 November 1858. ROM, vol. vi, p. 93.

12 Nicon (1605–81), Patriarch of Moscow. Originally a married priest, he separated from his wife and became a monk of the Solovetski monastery. He moved to the Kozheozerski monastery of which he became hegoumen in 1643. In 1647 appointed archimandrite of the Novospassky monastery, and in 1649, Metropolitan of Novgorod, by Tsar Alexis. In 1652

elected Patriarch of Moscow by order of the Tsar. Carried out major reforms, particularly of the liturgy, which gave rise to the opposition and eventual schism of the 'Old Believers'. Fell from favour with Tsar in 1658, probably for insisting on the independence of the Church. He retired to his 'New Jerusalem' monastery, and failed to regain his position. Degraded and deposed in 1667. Alexis' successor Theodore recalled him to Moscow, but he died on the way, and was buried with patriarchal honours. All decrees against him were revoked at the order of the Tsar. Elizabeth A. Livingstone (ed.), *The Oxford Dictionary of the Christian Church* (2nd ed'n) (Oxford: OUP, 2000), pp. 1155–6.

13 '*Egyptian Chronicles* 2 vols. This book had no sale – In 1865 or 1866 the publishers declined to keep it in stock any longer, and returned the stock to the author, who disposed of much of it by gift to public libraries etc., of some as waste paper'. EP to JHN, BO MS.

14 MFP vol. II, pp. 173–4.

15 Edward Lear (1812–1888). Artist and writer of nonsense verse. DNB.

16 LP MS 2832, f. 34–7

17 Journal entry for Saturday 22 April, Ibid f. 70.

18 WP to Routh, Athens, 21 June 1853, MAG 485, no. 23.

19 Dr. Cotton, Provost of Worcester College. [details]

20 In a letter dated 14 March 1854. She died on 18 September the same year. (MFP vol. II, pp. 174 & 177).

21 The Rev. Richard Lynch Cotton (1794–1880), Vicar of Dentworth nr. Wantage 1823-39. Vice-Chancellor of the University of Oxford 1852-7. MEB.

22 William George Ward (1812-1882), Scholar of Lincoln Coll. Oxford 1833–4, mathematical and logic lecturer, senior bursar 1842. Prominent in the Tractarian movement, and author of *Ideal of a Christian Church*, 1844, for which he was condemned in Convocation in 1845 and deprived of his MA. Received as a Roman Catholic in 1845. Lecturer in moral philosophy at St. Edmund's College, Ware 1851, professor of dogmatic theology 1852–8. Edited *The Dublin Review* from 1863–78. AO, p. 1499, & MEB, p. 1196.

23 MFP vol. II, pp. 174–5.

24 Anon., 'The Eastern Churches', *The Christian Observer* (1854, Jan), pp. 42–3.

25 Ibid., p. 68.

26 Anon, 'Palmer's Dissertations', *The Christian Remembrancer*, vol. XXVI (1853, July–Dec.), p. 91

27 Ibid., p. 98.

28 Fr. Ivan Gagarin, b. 1814, Russian ecclesiastical writer. Initially a diplomat, and secretary in the Vienna embassy in 1837, then in Paris. Left to become a Roman Catholic and a Jesuit 1842. Zealous propagandist for the Catholic Church, wrote *La Russie, Sera-t'elle Catholique?* (1856) and many other controversial works. DUC.

29 *L' Univers*, 24 April 1853.

30 Popov to Serbinovich*, 3 February 1853, in *Kristianskoe Chtenie* (1904, June), p. 883.

* Konstantin Stepanovich Serbinovich (1797–1874), 1833-6 editor of the Journal of the Ministry of People's Education; 1859 Director of the Chancellery of the Ober-Prokuror of the Holy Synod, and member of the Commission for Petitions and Requests. ES (CD Rom).

31 Journal entry for 7 July 1854, LP MS 2832, f. 167.

32 WP to EP, 14 July 1854, Bod. MS Eng. lett. d. 432, f. 57 ff.

33 Ibid.

34 Rev. I: 8, 9, 10, 11; Rev. iii: 7-14. LP MS 2833. The Church in Smyrna would receive, if it was 'faithful unto death [...] the crown of life'; the Church of Philadelphia had set before it 'an open door, which no one is able to shut'.

35 REC, p. 185.

36 LP MS 2833, f. 1 ff.

37 William Frederick Waldegrave, Viscount Chewton (1816–1854), son of Earl Waldegrave. Fought French-Canadian rebels in 1837; Served in the Sikh War at the battle of Sobraon, Feb. 1846. Styled Viscount Chewton from 1846. Lieut. And Capt., Scots Fus. Guards, 1848, with whom he served in the Crimea. Died at Scutari of wounds received at the Battle of the Alma 20 Sept. 1854. CP vol. XII, part ii, pp. 314–5.

38 Ibid., 21 Oct. 1854. The Scutari hospital was where Florence Nightingale was later to nurse, arriving two weeks after Palmer's visit on 4 November 1854. One of her first actions was to flush out the sewers under the hospital that responsible for the stench that Palmer noted. Lytton Strachey, *Eminent Victorians* (London: Chatto & Windus, 1918), pp. 123–5.

39 LP MS 2833, f. 7.

40 Ibid., f. 8.

41 The feast of the saint after whom he was named, celebrated like a birthday in the Orthodox Church.

42 Should be πανιερώτατος, 'most holy', the correct mode of address to a Metropolitan.

43 LP MS 2833, f. 85–6.

44 Ibid., f. 87.

45 No doubt the bishop was referring to such when he spoke of people 'who will give money, and go about'.

46 LP MS 2833, f. 99.

Chapter Sixteen: Rome at Last

1 The same Admiral who had looked after Palmer so assiduously after his carriage accident. Korniloff's greatcoat, shredded down the left side by the shell that killed him, can be seen in the State History Museum in Moscow.

2 The Abbé Carlo Passaglia (1812–1887), took orders and entered the Society of Jesus 1827. 1845 Professor of Theology at the Gregorian University. 1861 published a Latin pamphlet, *Pro Causa Italica*, advising the Pope to abandon his temporal state and power in obedience to the voice of united Italy. Placed on the *Index Expurgatorius*, and soon afterwards fled from

Rome. Appointed a professor of moral philosophy at the University of Turin at the instance of King Victor Emmanuel. Elected a member of the Italian Parliament 1863. Thompson Cooper, *Men of the Time* (London: Routledge, 1872), pp. 752–3, and *The Catholic Encyclopaedia* (Caxton: London, 1911), vol. XI, pp. 518–9.

3 BO MSS v. 19, f. 33, see also FT, p. 193.

4 Another Uniat, the theologian Pitsipios, made an impression on Palmer by telling him that he had been received into the Uniat Church simply by accepting the Council of Florence 'without any other demands'. FT, pp. 193–4.

5 BO MSS v. 19, ff. 74–8.

6 bid., f. 87.

7 He told his mother that 'Wynne & Coleridge half-forced upon me this Retreat' Bod. MS Eng. lett. d. 432, f. 61, and Roundell that they were 'zealous in pressing it upon me', LP MS 1878, f. 254.

8 Henry James Coleridge, fellow Oriel College 1845–52. RC priest and Jesuit, formerly Rector of Farm St. Church, Berkeley Sq., AO, p. 276.

9 WP to DP, 1 March 1855, Bod. MS Eng. lett. d. 432, f. 63.

10 WP to RP, 4 March 1855, LP MS 1878, f. 255. '"When such a good man as Passaglia made such an offer", said Palmer afterwards in his half-humorous way, "it was not to be despised"'. Meyrick, *Memories of Life at Oxford* (London: John Murray, 1905), p. 78.

11 WP to DP, 1 March 1855, Bod. MS Eng. lett. d. 432, f. 61.

12 The Rt. Rev. James Brown (1812–1881), 1857 ordained priest. Professor of studies at Old & New Oscott. 1851 Bishop of Shrewsbury. DNB.

13 J. R. Bloxam, *Magdalen College Register*, (hereafter Bloxam) vol. VII, p. 306.

14 REC pp. 186–7.

15 Meyrick, op. cit., p. 78–9.

16 Popov to Tolstoy, 18 December 1856, *Kristianskoe Chtenie* (June 1905), p. 891. In the same letter Popov mentions that the Pope told Palmer 'a time would come when his "Greek sympathies" would no longer have to be sacrificed' to be Catholic. Palmer met the Pope, Pius IX, on 18 March 1855; the Pope had been informed of Palmer's views as set out in his Profession of Faith. FT. p. 196.

17 RGIA, fond 1661, op. 1, delo 593. This appears to be an addition to, or clarification of, the remarks in n. 1451 above; the date is the same.

18 REC, p. 180, italics Palmer's own.

19 Ibid.

20 Ibid.

21 LP MS 1878, f. 255.

22 Ibid.

23 S. W. Gilley, *Newman and His Age* (London: Darton, Longman & Todd, 1990), pp. 222 & 237.

24 *Civilta Cattolica* vol. cxx (1855) p. 692, quoted in FT p. 19, and Jules Gondon, *De La Réunion de L' Eglise D' Angleterre Protestante a L' Eglise Catholique* (Paris: Wattelier, 1867) (hereafter Gondon), p. 106.

25 'They wanted me to read and revise a notice with compliments and facts to be concocted by themselves, which I declined doing'. Diary entry for 8 March 1855, Palmer MSS, in FT, p. 195.

26 Sir John Emmerich Edward Acton, later Lord Acton (1834–1902), 1859 MP for an Irish constituency, from 1859 Editor of *The Rambler* (from 1862 *The Home and Foreign Review*), whose ultra-liberal tone offended the authorities; publication was suspended April 1864. Recommended for a peerage by Gladstone in 1869. The decree of papal infallibility embittered Acton towards Roman authority. 1895 offered the Oxford Professorship of Modern History by Lord Rosebery; conceived and organised the Cambridge Modern History. *The Catholic Encyclopaedia* (London: Caxton, 1907), vol. 1. p. 114.

27 *L & D*, vol. XIX, p. 199.

28 Stepan Stepanovich Djunkovsky (1820–1870), went abroad to spread Orthodoxy, but on going to Rome became Roman Catholic and a Jesuit. Studied theology for five years and became a priest. In 1853 left the Order, went to Paris and became founder of 'Mission' in the suburbs of Paris. Returned to Rome 1853 with a project for reforming Roman Catholicism and abandoning celibacy, & was exiled. In Westphalia he re-established ancient Catholic dioceses, 1855 in charge of the mission among the Eskimo. Established seven RC Eskimo parishes, re-established seven Catholic dioceses in Scandinavia defunct at the Reformation. Left the Roman Church and married an Englishwoman, whom he shortly afterwards divorced; received back as an Orthodox layman by the Archpriest Bazaroff. ES (CD Rom).

29 Henry Parry Liddon* to EP, 27 Dec 1878, Bod. MS Eng. lett. d. 432, f. 127. * Henry Parry Liddon (1829–90), noted preacher and lecturer, Canon of St. Paul's Cathedral 1870–90, chancellor of the cathedral 1886, Vice-Principal of Cuddesdon Theological College 1854–9. Prebendary of Salisbury 1864–70. Dean Ireland professor of exegesis at Oxford 1870–82. Used his influence to advance the High Church Movement in the Church of England. AO p. 851, & *Columbia Electronic Encyclopedia*, 2000, http://www.infoplease.com/ce6/people/A0829708.html., (25 Feb 2003).

30 Williams, p. xlv.

31 L & D, vol. XXX, p. 72. The passage originally appeared in Khomiakoff's *Encore Quelques Mots d'un Chrétien Orthodoxe sur les Confessions Occidentales* (Leipzig, 1858), p. 62, and later in *L'Eglise Latine et la Protestantisme* (Lausanne, 1872), p. 258. Newman commented that 'Mr. Khomiakoff is so little himself, that he finds fault with his Supreme Synod, because they acted towards William as only they could consistently act'. *L & D*, vol. XXX, p. 72. Edwin Palmer suspected that the words 'quelque haut placés qu'ils soient' probably alluded 'rather to the Patriarch of Constantinople & his Synod'. BO MSS, EP to JHN, 23 March 1882.

32 Popov to Tolstoy, 14 Nov. 1858, *Kristianskoe Chtenie* (Sept. 1905), p. 120.

33 Popov to Tolstoy, 12 Nov. 1858, *Kristianskoe Chtenie* XIV, pp. 118–9.

34 'The title of the brochure he published is "Remarks on the Turkish Question"', which was published in 1853, not, as Newman says (NV p. 572), in 1858.

35 Tolstoy to Popov, 8 January 1859, *Kristianskoe Chtenie* XV p. 121.

36 Popov to Tolstoy, 20 March 1861, Ibid., p. 396.

37 Popov to Tolstoy, 31 October 1859, RGIA, fond 797, op. 29, delo 237. Tolstoy forwarded to General Isakov* for the Tsar's approval what appears to be a modified proposal that Palmer be given the honorary title of Honorary Member of the University of Moscow, Ibid., 14 Nov. 1859. Nothing appears to have come of either proposal; it is never mentioned by either Palmer himself or Lord Selborne in MFP. Perhaps Palmer's defection to Roman Catholicism was a fundamental obstacle.

* Nicholas Vasilievitch Isakov (1821–91), General of Infantry. Involved in the expeditions to the Caucasus, the Hungary campaign, and the defence of Sebastopol. Worked in the Ministry of Home Affairs, 1858 Trustee of Moscow District, 1863 Chief of Military Academic Institutions, 1881 Member of the State Council. ES (CD Rom).

Chapter Seventeen: Life in Rome

1 LP MS 2832, f. 170.

2 Robert Isaac Wilberforce (1802–1857), archdeacon of the East Riding & prebendary canon of York 1841–47. Seceded to Rome 1856. AO 1551.

3 WP to EP, Rome 22 Dec. 1876, Bod. Eng. lett. d. 432, f. 126.

4 WP to RP, Rome 24 April 1868, LP MS 1878, f. 270.

5 Fr. John Morris S. J., *The Life of Mother Henrietta Kerr* (hereafter Morris) (Roehampton, 1887), p. 150.

6 *Not* in the modern sense.

7 Morris, p. 150. The Rev. John Hoskyns*, writing to John Rigaud about Palmer's funeral, remarked that the rooms strongly reminded him 'of those large *outer* rooms in the New Buildings at Magdalen'. LP MS 1895, f. 173. * Sir John Leigh Hoskyns (Bt.), deacon 1840, priest 1842. Hon. Canon of Christ Church 1880, rector of Aston Tyrrold, Berks., from 1845, & rural dean. AO p. 696, CCD.

8 WP to EP, 8 Dec 1877, Bod. MS Eng. lett. d. 432, f. 145. An 'inundata' is a flood. Another drawback was that the 'padrone', or landlord (presumably the old Count) had 'a way of locking up & letting no-one in.' John Wordsworth had to kick the door 'like Hercules in the Frogs' to get him to open in December 1878, Ibid., f. 167.

9 EP to RP, 18 April 1879, LP MS 1879, ff. 74–5. The Fra Angelico Annunciation 'looked so unlike the other pictures that I think he must have been bought it or someone must have given it to him.' (Ibid.)

10 From Palmer's will, Bodleian Library MSS Selborne NRA 17810 Palmer 225, 'papers of his brother Edwin as his executor'.

11 Palmer's mother moved to Bath in 1855, and died on 1 December 1867. MFP, p. 177.

12 John Wordsworth* to EP, 19 December 1878, Bod. MS Eng. lett. d. 432 f. 167.
*John Wordsworth of New College Oxford, Librarian and junior dean 1872–82, chaplain 1882-5, proctor 1874. Fellow Oriel Coll. 1883–5. AO p. 1609.

13 At one of these, on 15 January 1867, the Pope came to Palmer, 'put his hand on my shoulder, and said "I have a commission for you – to reconvert Passaglia" at which those who were with him laughed.' LP MS 2842. [See n. 1438 (above)]. Palmer's nephew, the Rt. Rev, Edwin James Palmer, wrote a short 'Personal Memoire' of his uncle in which he says that 'He became a Papal Chamberlain' (LP MS 4321, f. 77.); but despite enquiries of a number of Vatican institutions, I can find nothing to substantiate this assertion. There is certainly no mention of it by Palmer himself, or Lord Selborne in MFP.

14 See L & D, vol. XXIII pp. 209, 213. Ambrose St. John wrote to Newman from Rome that 'I think the Italians think us all; Manning, Talbot, you, Ward etc. a lot of queer quarrelsome Inglesi,' ibid., p. 209.

15 Giovanni Battista de Rossi (1822–1894), 'the modern founder of the science of Christian archaeology'. From 1838 to 1840 De Rossi studied philosophy, and from 1840–44 jurisprudence, at the Roman University (Sapienza). Appointed *scriptor* at the Vatican Library. Travelled extensively in Europe to visit museums, galleries, libraries and archives, and was a close friend of many European scholars. *The Catholic Encylopedia, vol. IV* (New York: Appleton, 1908), http://www.newadvent.org/cathen/04739c.htm (10 April 2003).

16 'This was intended to form a letterpress to a series of photographic representations of paintings in the Roman catacombs, but the design fell through. The book, in consequence, had no sale, and the remnant was returned to the author.' EP to JHN, B/O MSS, unnumbered.

17 *The Catholic Encyclopaedia*, ref. as at n. 1491 above, p. 4.

18 L & D, vol. XXIV, p. 218. By 'lionizer' Newman means tourist guide.

19 WP to Laura Palmer, 5 January 1858, LP MS 1895, f. 167. Palmer continued to impart his knowledge about the catacombs to visitors in his rooms even when he had only months to live: John Wordsworth 'heard something of Egyptian chronology & the catacombs' when he called on Palmer in December 1878 (Bod. MS Eng. lett. d. 432, f. 167), and in the same year John Hoskyns and his family were given 'a regular lecture in his rooms on the Catacombs [...] on our first arrival in Rome at Christmas'. Despite being ill and in bed, Palmer 'went through a very elaborate description of them without any difficulty', LP MS 1895 f.173.

20 James Bowling Mozley (1813–1878), deacon 1838, priest 1844, fellow Magdalen Coll. 1840–56, bursar 1843, Vice-President 1849. Dean of Divinity 1852, Regius professor of Divinity and canon of Christ Church 1871–8, canon of Worcester 1869–71. Vicar of Old Shoreham, Sussex, 1856 to his death. Took an active part in the Oxford Movement, & for about 10 years co-editor of *The Christian Remembrancer*. AO p. 995, CCD.

21 *Letters of J. B. Mozley*, edited by his sister, p. 276, cited in MID, p. 122.

22 WP to EP, Rome 17 January 1871, Bod. MS Eng. lett. d. 432, f. 104.

23 Lord Henry Kerr, second son of the 6th Marquis of Lothian, Rector of Dittisham, Devon 1830. Influenced by the Oxford Movement; visited Newman at Littlemore, and heard him preach at St. Mary's in 1843. Resigned his living in 1852 after the Gorham case, received as a Roman Catholic August 1852. L & D, vol. XXI, p. 550.

24 LHK, p. 220.

25 Ibid., p. 221.

26 Sr. Henrietta Kerr to WP, '1871?', B/O MSS misc. letters.

27 Wife of a Bank 'Director', who when they had lived at Archangel had nearly been killed 'by a bear which he thought he had shot.' When 'the man who had stood by with a spear ran away', Mr. Morgan 'plunged into the snow all but his head which the bear fairly scalped, drawing the scalp down over his eyes'. Mr. Morgan had to be led, first to Ladoga ('where was a doctor who could do nothing') and on to Archangel, where he eventually received treatment. One eyelid was destroyed; Palmer ends bathetically 'he has ever since been obliged to wear spectacles'. B/O MSS, v. 59 (unfoliated), 4th page.

28 Ibid., 3rd page.

29 Ibid., 5th–8th pages.

30 WP to EP, 27 July 1868, Bod. MS Eng. misc. d. 998, f. 50.

31 LHK, p. 192.

32 WP to EP, 25 September 1870, Bod. MSS Eng. lett. d. 432, ff. 96–7.

33 Palmer travelled in early 1853 to Cairo, in the hope of reading and translating the Greek MS of Nicon's trial written by Paisius Ligarides. However, the original MS had been sent to his friend Mouravieff in Moscow by the Patriarch. REC, pp. 183–4. It was not until 1862 that Palmer 'obtained from the late Metropolitan Philaret at Moscow facilities for translating the original MS, which had then become the property of the Synodal Library'. William Palmer, *The Patriarch & the Tsar* vol. II (London: Trübner, 1871), (hereafter PT) pp. lxviii–ix.

34 His plan was 'to exhibit a cause like that of St. John Chrysostom or St. Thomas of Canterbury – a controversy between an emperor and a primate'. PT, vol. III, p. lxviii.

35 Ibid., p. iv.

36 Macarius of Antioch, an Arab from Aleppo, ordained Metropolitan of Aleppo 1636, and in 1648 Patriarch of Antioch. ES, CD Rom.

37 The other being Paisius, Patriarch of Alexandria.

38 PT, p.xlvii.

39 Ibid., p. 64.

40 bid., p. 164.

41 Paisius Ligarides (1610–1678), Metropolitan of Gaza. Studied at the Greek College, Rome 1623–35, made a doctor of theology, possibly also ordained a Roman Catholic priest. In 1651 he went to Jerusalem, and was expelled for immorality. After Nicon's deposition came under suspicion for promoting papal views, and died at Kiev having lost his influence at Moscow. He was 'indifferent to faith and morality.' ES, CD Rom.

42 PT, p. xxxix.
43 Ibid., vol. IV, p. 864.
44 At the front of '*Notes of A Visit*.'
45 PT, p. 1535.
46 Ibid., pp. 1554–5.
47 BO MS, unnumbered.
48 EP to JHN, 10 November 1879, BO MS.
49 EP to JHN, 15 August 1883, BO MS.
50 Letters from William Neville to JHN, 21 August and 3 October 1883, BO MS.
51 The Rt. Rev. Edwin James Palmer, s. of Edwin Palmer, deacon 1896, priest 1898. Fellow of Balliol 1891–1908. Ld. Bp. of Bombay 1908, resigned 1929. Asst. Bp. of Gloucs. & Commissary of Bombay from 1929. CCD.
52 Rt. Rev. Edwin James Palmer to H. G. Palmer, 20 June 1946, LP MS 4321, f. 77.
53 P. Meyendorff, *Russia, Ritual and Reform: the Liturgical Reforms of Nikon in the Seventeenth Century* (Crestwood: New York, 1991), p. 34, n. 3.
54 WP to RP, 24 April 1868, LP MS 1878, f. 270. cf his comments about his *Dissertations*, n. 1357 (supra).
55 Ibid., f. 123.
56 Lord Selborne, MFP vol. 1, p. 443.
57 WP to RP, Rome, 6 November 1855. LP MS 1878, f. 268.
58 In the margin at this point is the grim comment by Lord Selborne 'Fear of wasted life.' WP to RP, Rome, 24 April 1868, LP MS 1878, f. 270.
59 Ibid.
60 WP to RP, Rome, 5 October 1872, Ibid., f. 275.
61 WP to RP, Rome, 10 April 1874, Ibid., f. 276.
62 Eugene Poutiatine to WP, 1 /12 May 1875, BO MSS v. G. 37.

Chapter Eighteen: Death in Rome

1 LHK, p. 217.
2 WP to EP, Hotel de la Gare, Boulogne sur Mer, Bod. MS Eng. lett. d. 432, ff. 166–7. Edwin Palmer noted 'Letter never dispatched, & found by me in his desk at Rome after his death'.
3 LP MS 2493, diary entry 31 October 1878.
4 WP to EP, Rome, 21 December 1878, Bod. MS Eng. lett. D. 432, f. 171.
5 LP MS 2494, 1879 diary.
6 WP to EP, Rome, 29 January 1879, Bod. MS Eng. lett. d. 432 f. 176.
7 'Dr. Erhardt listened at my breast & said there is something wrong: he did not say worse or better: but he seemed to assent to me when I said that I had not much expectation of his removing it – but as to probable development he said it might go on nearly in the same state for years'. Ibid.

8 John Hoskyns to John Rigaud, Rome, 8 April 1879, LP MS 1895, f. 173.

9 EP to RP, Rome, 6 April 1879, LP MS 1879, f. 68.

10 Antonina Raggi. Liberata had died some two years previously.

11 Wife of Sidney Herbert, first Baron Herbert of Lea, and daughter of General Ashe A' Court. DNB.

12 James Campbell (1841–1902), ordained 1865. Vice-Rector of the Scots College 1866; briefly kidnapped by brigands October 1868. Rector 1878, resigned 1897 because of ill-health. Lampooned by Frederick Rolfe, Baron Corvo, in *Hadrian VII*. Left the College 97,000 lire in debt, having become 'pastorally stale and financially reckless'. Raymond McCluskey (ed.), *The Scots College Rome 1600-2000* (Edinburgh: John Donald, 2000), pp. 87–92.

13 Bloxam, p. 314.

14 Ibid., p. 317.

15 EP to RP, Rome, 9 April 1879, LP MS 1879, f. 70.

16 Rev. John L. Hoskyns to Rev. John Rigaud, Rome, 8 April 1879, LP MS 1895, f. 173.

17 Thirty seven years before, in 1842, Cardinal Wiseman reviewed Palmer's *Letter to Mr. Golightly*, and general arguments for the Church of England, in *The Dublin Review*. Rejecting the 'vaunting rival' of Catholicism, Wiseman ended: 'No; let us be laid in our shroud, with that cross, at which evil spirits tremble, grasped in our hands, let the poor brethren of some pious guild bear us, with psalms of penance mournfully sung as for a brother, to our common place of rest, "the holy Field" ("Il Campo Santo"), consecrated by most solemn rites [...].' Nicholas Wiseman, 'The Anglican System', *The Dublin Review* vol. XII (1842), p. 249.

18 Willy Wolmer* to his mother, Rome, February 1884, Bod. MS Eng. lett. e. 152, f. 37. * William Waldegrave Palmer, eldest son of Lord Selborne, MP for East Hampshire from 1885. AO, p. 1062.

There is a sketch of the location of the grave in LP MS 2497, f. 17.

19 Bodleian Library, MSS Selborne & NRA 17810 Palmer, MS 225.

Epilogue

1 Benjamin Jowett (1817–93), scholar of Balliol Coll., Oxford 1835–38, resident there 1836 to death. Deacon 1842, priest 1845. Regius professor of Greek 1855 to death. Fellow 1838–70, tutor 1842–70, Master 1870–93, Vice Chancellor of University of Oxford 1882. Prolific author. MEB p. 797.

2 LP MS 4321, f. 77.

3 William p. Neville to JHN, 21 August 1883, BO MSS.

4 EP to JHN, 15 August 1883, Ibid.

5 Rev. John Rigaud* quoted in MID, p.124. *Rev. John Rigaud (1821–1888), deacon 1847, priest 1851. Fellow of Magdalen 1849 to death, senior dean of arts 1850, bursar 1852, Vice-Principal 1857. Dean of divinity 1860. CCD, MEB vol. VI, p. 471–2.

6 Bishop Walter Hamilton of Salisbury*, MID p. 124. *Walter Hamilton (1807– 1869), fellow Merton Coll. 1832–42, dean 1837, bursar 1838, Bp. of Salisbury 1845 to death. AO, p. 595.
7 Meyrick, op. cit., p. 79.
8 F F to RP, 21 Aug. 1849, MFP, vol. II, p. 59.
9 Something acknowledged by his own family – see n. 275, supra.
10 EP to JHN, Christ Church Oxford, 10 October 1881, B/O MSS.
11 Shaw, p. 175.
12 Ibid.
13 NV, p. xvi.
14 L & D, vol. VI p. 19, & vol. XXIX p. 99.
15 Lord Blachford* to JHN, 14 November 1882, L & D, vol. XXX, p. 151. *Frederic Rogers, Lord Blachford (1811–89), fellow of Oriel 1833–45. Barrister-at-law, Lincoln's Inn 1837, colonial land and immigration commissioner 1847–60, under-secretary for the colonies 1870–71. Created Lord Blachford 1871. Newman was his tutor, and Blachford was an adherent of the Oxford Movement and Newman's most intimate friend until a breach in 1843 over religious differences. In 1863 Blachford visited Newman at Birmingham and the old friendship was renewed. AO, p. 1219, DNB.
16 'I could do nothing'.
17 Williams, op.. cit., pp. xlv–vi.
18 Gondon, p. 100, and cited as article in *L' Univers*, Bloxam, p. 305.
19 Ibid.
20 LP MS 4321, f. 77.
21 L & D, vol. XXX, p. 6.
22 Ibid.
23 *Notes*, p. xi.
24 MID, p. 124.
25 ASC, p. 540.

Bibliography

Primary Sources

A. Lambeth Palace Library

Papers of Roundell Palmer, First Earl of Selborne

a. MS 1878 Family correspondence of Lord Selborne.
b. MS 1879 Family and general correspondence of Lord Selborne.
c. MS 1894 Correspondence between William Palmer and his father.
d. MS 1895 Correspondence and papers of William Palmer.
e. MS 1896 Documents relating to the history of the Russian Orthodox Church, written partly by William Palmer and partly by Emma Palmer.
f. MS 1897 Copies by William Palmer of documents relating to the history and liturgy of the Russian Orthodox Church.
g. MS 1898 Copies by William Palmer of documents relating to the liturgy of the Russian Orthodox Church.
h. MSS 1899-1900 Notebooks of William Palmer describing the liturgy of the Russian Orthodox Church, compiled during his visit to Russia in 1841.
i. MS 1901 Journal of William Palmer's visit to Russia, covering the period February – 2 May 1841. At ff. 65(v) - 8(v) are brief autobiographical notes.
j. MS 1902 Miscellaneous papers.
k. MS 1903 Correspondence of the sons and daughters of the Rev. William Jocelyn Palmer, father of William Palmer.

Selborne Papers

a. MS 2457 Autobiographical notes by William Palmer, 1823-1840.
b. MS 24548-94 Diaries and travel journals of William Palmer, 1831-1879.
c. MS 2495 Extracts by William Palmer from his diaries (essentially lists of contents, and largely illegible or in a personal shorthand).
d. MS 2496 Notes by William Palmer on Egyptian hieroglyphics.
e. MS 2497 Miscellaneous papers, including review articles in *L' Univers* of William Palmer's Dissertations; sketch of site of William Palmer's grave; biographical and other notes by Roundell Palmer.

Papers of William Palmer

a. MS 2814 Journal of a visit to France 3 July-19 September 1834.

b. MS 2815 Journal in French containing: (i) 'Conversations with members of the Church of France at Tours, 1834' (ff. 1-36(v)); (ii) 'Conversations with members of the Eglise Reformée (and others) at Paris, 1835' (ff. 37-53); (iii) 'Conversations en France, la Suisse, et l'Italie, 1836' (ff. 54-121).

c. MS 2816 Journal in French of a visit to the Vaudois Church, August-September 1836 (pp. 1-135), and to northern France, September 1837 (pp. 138-210). Copy of a letter to the Revd. William Stephen Gilly, 15 November 1839, concerning the Vaudois (pp. 212-22).

d. MS 2817 Conversations between Palmer and Christian Rassam about the Nestorian Church in Chaldea and Kurdistan [1837]. Correspondence between Palmer and Rassam (pp. 69-70, 159- 224). Includes an imaginary conversation between a Nestorian Christian and a converted Turk (pp. 73-158), and a summary of Anglican doctrine by Palmer (pp. 192-224).

e. MS 2818 Journal of conversations in France (in 1838?) expressing Palmer's views of the Church of England, and extracts from a letter by the abbé Robert of 25 September 1839.

f. MS 2819 Notebook by Palmer on the Nestorian Church, and correspondence with Christian Rassam, which at p. 242 includes a statement of Palmer's view of the Church of England and the Reformation. Also a letter from Palmer to the Revd. George Percy Badger, Rassam's brother-in-law, (pp. 266-361).

g. MS 2820 Journal of conversations about the relative merits of the Church of England and the Roman Catholic Church during a visit to Jersey and France, June - September 1839.

h. MS 2821 Notebook about the Nestorian Church, and correspondence with Christian Rassam.

i. MS 2823 Journal by Palmer of visits to the Scottish Episcopal Church and to the Greek Orthodox Church in connection with his Appeal to the Scottish Episcopal Church, 4 June 1849-June 1852.

j. MSS 2824-7 Journal of a visit to Greece, Smyrna, Beirut, the Holy Land, Alexandria, Constantinople and Mount Athos, 20 November 1849-11 August 1850.

k. MS 2828 Copy by Palmer of his brother Edwin's journal of a visit with him to Greece, 19 July-8 August 1850 and copies of official documents relating to the independence of the Greek Orthodox Church, 1850. Also a journal of a visit to Greece and the monastery of Megaspelion near Athens, 4 April-3 July 1851.

l. MS 2829 Journal of a visit to Constantinople, southern Russia, and the Crimea, 20 July-4 October 1851.

m. MS 2830 Journal of a visit to Greece, 18 October 1851-1 June 1852. At pp. 1-87 are notes of the *Russian Account of the Holy Places of Kieff*.

n. MSS 2831-33 Journal of a visit to Egypt and the Holy Land, 10 November 1853-8 December 1854. MS 2833 concerns his final attempt to be admitted to the Orthodox Church, in Philadelphia.

o. MSS 2834-5 Correspondence between Palmer and his father.

p. MS 2836 Family correspondence; also an 'answer to queries on devotional reference to the BVM', 26 February 1851 (ff. 310-315 (v)), and a paper on Palmer's proposed admission to the Orthodox Church [1851], ff. 316-320 (v).

q. MS 2837 Miscellaneous correspondence.
r. MS 2838 32 colour illustrations for the Paris edition of Early Christian Symbolism (1861).

Palmer Papers, MSS 4302- 4321

Miscellaneous family papers, incl. at ff. 33-37 of MS 4321 'Personal Memoires' [sic] of William Palmer by his nephew, The Rt. Rev. Edwin James Palmer, Bishop of Bombay.

Wordsworth Papers, MSS 2140-2151

Papers of Christopher Wordsworth (1807-1885), Bishop of Lincoln, son of Christopher Wordsworth (1774-1846) Master of Trinity College, and of other members of the family.

Whately Papers, MS 2164

Papers of Richard Whately, Archbishop of Dublin, 1810-62.

Miscellaneous Letters & Papers

MSS 1812 Letter from Newman, ff. 72-2.
MSS 1804-11 Correspondence of the Rev. C. P. Golightly, f. 204.

Eeles Collection (The Russian Church in the Nineteenth Century), MS 1550

Incl. letter from Rev. R. W. Blackmore to William Palmer from Kronstadt, 1843, f. 241.

Wordsworth Correspondence MS 1822

Papers of Christopher Wordsworth, Master of Trinity 1803-45.

Letters and Papers of William Hodge Mill MS 1491

Papers of William Hodge Mill (1792-1853), Regius Professor of Hebrew at Cambridge and Rector of Brasted, Kent, 1846-53.

Wordsworth Correspondence, MS 1824

Papers of Charles Wordsworth, Bishop of St. Andrews 1831-91.

B. The Birmingham Oratory

Note: The journals and diaries held at the Oratory are those sent back directly to Cardinal Newman from Palmer's apartment in Rome. They include: 1. v 49/10.6.(3). C
Miscellaneous correspondence, with, amongst others, the Scottish bishops, the Archpriest Koutnevich, the Editor of The Churchman, Mrs. George Palmer and the Princess Galitsin, M. Mouravieff, the Bishop of St. Andrews, Mr. Lygon, Admiral Poutiatine and Archdeacon Manning. Also accounts of dreams, Palmer's journal in Scotland, a list of events in Oct. 1847, a description of problems with the 'non-united congregation at Perth,' and Palmer's 'imaginary project' for dealing with them, correspondence about Nestoria and Chaldea, draft pieces for the Appeal, the minutes of the Scottish Episcopal Synod.

2. G 20

This contains: the Answer of the Russian Synod in 1842, 'reflections on the above' and observations, a draft Latin request for a Confessor, Palmer's Russian journal, correspondence with Bishop Luscombe, Roundell Palmer, and Palmer's Aunt Mary, Russian Liturgical Offices, a discussion of the Swedish Church, accounts of Swedish services, a Latin document concerning the Swedish Church, Palmer's meetings with the Danish Lutheran theologian and hymn-writer Dr. Nikolaj Frederik Severin Grundtvig (1783-1872), and with the Rev. Nicholas Wade, the continuation of Palmer's Scottish journal, and writings on the Lutheran (?) Church.

3. v 25 ('vol. 2')

This contains: A conversation with Mr. Blackmore at Cronstadt about 'Invocation of Saints', and 'Images,' a dream about an angry 'mujik,' correspondence with Mr. Blackmore, an extract from the Office 'In Exitu Anima', notes about the Swedish Church.

4. Book II

This contains: Russian journal (1842), corresponding to pp. 79-136 approx. of the Appeal, but in greater detail.

5. v 48

This contains (i) (at the back) notes from Durham in 1834 (ii) 3 sections concerning visits to France between 1834 and 1836.

6. v 17/11.2.(3)

Correspondence between Palmer and the Rev. George Spencer, 1839- 40.

7. G 37/11.1.(2)

Six books of carbon-copy letters (approx. 64) by Palmer; also Palmer's draft Petition to the Archbishop of Canterbury about the Jerusalem bishopric, Palmer's Protest about the same, and Roundell Palmer's redrafted Petition.

8. v 52

This contains notes made at Durham in 1834, about possible livings, local to Durham and elsewhere, character sketches of friends and acquaintances, and remarks about the low quality of the Durham students and their social impact on Durham.

9. v 2

This contains correspondence with Dr. Routh, with Rev. Benjamin Harrison (domestic chaplain to Archbishop Howley), Canon XXXIII of the Apostolic Canons, Palmer's Letters of Orders as Deacon, his Leave of Absence from the College in 1840, writing on Zoernikaff ('abridged by Theophanes Procopovich'), writing on 'Cyril Lucar', accounts of interviews with the Metropolitan of Moscow, the OberProkuror Count Pratasoff, with M. Mouravieff, an interview at which Palmer presented a Letter to the Metropolitan, the Letter itself in Latin, and the Metropolitan's Answer.

10. *Short Poems and Hymns* dedicated to Khomiakoff, Oxford 1845.

These are loose in a box with a proof copy of Notes of a Visit to the Russian Church, and Newman's annotation thereon.

11. Miscellaneous letters

From Palmer's time in Rome, largely with the Poutiatine family about visits and illnesses, but also from Mother Henrietta Kerr, Sophia Mary Leeves (including a picture of herself as a cow), A. Bitchkoff, J. M. Latham, Emma Palmer, Roundell Palmer, Edwin Palmer, also notes by Palmer on monuments and churches.

12. Letters from Edwin Palmer

Mostly to Newman after Palmer's death, about Palmer's papers left to Newman, the disposal of left-over copies of Palmer's books, and providing information to assist Newman in writing Notes of a Visit. There are also assessments in some of the letters by Edwin Palmer of Palmer's life, his approach to dealings with the Eastern Church, his relationship with his publishers (quarrelsome) and the information that 'he was never painted,' and that the engraving in Notes of a Visit was taken from a photograph taken at Rome two years before Palmer's death. There is also a letter from the Rev. R. W. Blackmore paying tribute to Palmer.

13. v 16 '1849-50 Athens'

Written in modern Greek.

14. v 19

Italian travel diary, beginning Dec. 17 1854. Travels to Herculaneum, Pompeii, and Rome. Includes Palmer's discovery of Dr. Routh's death in The Times in Jan. 1855, an account of his irritation with Fr. Passaglia over a disputed text of Gregory of Nyssa, and an account of a Pontifical Mass at St. Leo's in Rome.

15. v 61 (?) Notes for 'The Patriach and the Tsar.'

16. Account books for 1838 and 1842

These contain notes of charitable donations in 1838; the 1842 book is more taken up with travel expenses.

17. Journal entries and letters forming the material for Palmer's Appeal to the Scottish Church.

18. Sermons, 1840-42.

19. Philosophy lectures, 1836-41.

Approx. 8 lectures, or drafts for lectures, on 'Moral Philosophy' and 'Socrates.'

C. Magdalen College, Oxford

1. Palmer's *Introduction to the 39 Articles,* transcribed by J. M. Neale from a copy belonging to Cardinal Newman.
2. J. R. Bloxham's *Magdalen College Register*. This includes a number of Palmer's obituary notices.
3. W. D. Macray's companion volume, *Register of the Members of St. Mary Magdalen College, Oxford.*
4. MS 490 Bp. Skinner to Dr. Routh, 12 Sept. 1846, about Palmer's acting the part of a 'crazy person.'
5. MS 827 Macray's scrapbook. Includes (i) a letter from E. Coffin to J. Rigaud asking if Palmer's conversion is likely to influence him, and Rigaud's reply. (ii) The Rock, dated 18 April 1897, with a letter from a contemporary of Palmer's at Magdalen describing his memories of Palmer, both as an undergraduate and later when the writer returned to take his MA degree and was 'presented' by Palmer.
6. MS 485 Miscellaneous letters, including:
   - (i) Palmer to Routh in Sept. 1840 just before leaving for Russia, and from Russia in Dec. 1840.
   - (ii) Correspondence between Sewell, Routh, and the Bishop of Oxford.
   - (iii) Notes from Palmer (and in Jan. 1843, his father) to Routh in late 1842 about his delayed return to England from Russia.
   - (iv) Palmer to Routh in Sept. 1842 reporting on his lack ofprogress in Russia.
   - (v) Palmer to Routh in Jan. 1843 resigning his tutorship.
   - (vi) Palmer to Routh in May 1845 reporting a dispute with the Dean of Divinity about not wearing his surplice to 'surplice prayers' in College Chapel on the eve of St. Mark's Day.
   - (vii) Palmer to Routh in July 1849 about the possibility of becoming ordained by Bp. Torry.
   - (viii) Palmer to Routh in Jan. 1854 from Athens, conspicuously failing to mention his petition to the Patriarch of Constantinople about conditional (re)baptism.

D. The Bodleian Library, Oxford

1. Papers of Archdeacon Edwin Palmer, Bodleian Special Collections & Western MSS [Refs: MSS Selborne add; Eng. Hist. a 23-4, b 231-6, c 97-1031, d 442-80, f 27-9, g 25-27; Eng. Lett. C 454-56, d 422-33, e 152; Eng. Misc. c 685-91, d 997-98. NRA 22802 Palmer.]
2. Papers of Edwin Palmer as executor of William Palmer: Bodleian Special Collections & Western MSS. Ref: MSS Selborne NRA 17810 Palmer. The MSS include in MS Selborne 225 Palmer's will; in MS Eng. Lett. D 432, ff. 60-65, a letter to his mother explaining his conversion to Roman Catholicism. At ff. 96-7 is an account of Palmer's difficulties in returning to Rome during Garibaldi's Nationalist revolution of 1870. At ff. 166-7 are

letters to his brother Edwin about the effects of his illness, written towards the end of 1878, and at ff. 171 and 176 letters to Edwin about his doctor's diagnosis of his symptoms, written Dec. 1878 – Jan. 1879.

3. *The Oxford Magazine* for 11 Nov. 1885, with a letter by Goldwin Smith about Magdalen, with facetious comments about Palmer; and for 2 Dec. 1885, with a reply defending Palmer's memory by 'N. D.'
4. Prize verses and essay: Bodleian, Special Collections & Western MSS. Ref. MSS Don d 73, 75.

E. The British Library

1. Gladstone Papers, Add. MSS 44359-527.

a. MS 44366 Palmer to Gladstone, about the unexpected visit of Count Alexander Tolstoy, asking if Gladstone will meet him.
b. MS 44368 Palmer to Gladstone, about the St. Andrews Diocesan Synod, the attitude of the Russian Church towards possible reunion, and the advisability of any overtures from the Scottish Church.
c. MS 44300 Bishop Skinner to Gladstone, about Palmer's'strange book' and his 'Monomania.'

F. Review Articles

1. Wiseman, Nicholas, 'The Anglican System', *The Dublin Review* vol. XXII (1842), 233-249.
2. Anon, 'Palmer's Dissertations', *The Christian Remembrancer*, vol. XXVI (1853), 64-98.
3. Anon, 'The Eastern Churches,' *The Christian Observer*, January 1854, 42-69.

G. Books and pamphlets by William Palmer

William Palmer, *Aids to Reflection on the Seemingly Double Character of the Established Church* (Oxford: Parker, 1841).

——, *A Letter to a Protestant-Catholic* (Oxford: Parker, 1842).

——, *A Letter to the Rev. C. P. Golightly* (Oxford: Parker, 1841).

——, *An Appeal to the Scottish Church* (Edinburgh: Laurie, 1849).

——, *Examination of an Announcement Made in the Prussian State Gazette* (Oxford: Parker, 1842).

——, *Early Christian Symbolism* (London: Longman, Green, Longman, and Roberts, 1859).

——, *Dissertations on Subjects Relating to the 'Orthodox' or 'Eastern Catholic' Communion* (London: Joseph Masters, 1853).

——, *The Patriarch & the Tsar* (7 vols.) (London: Trübner, 1871-76).

Secondary Sources

Books

1. Pre-1900

Birkbeck, W. J., *Russia and the English Church* (London: Rivington, Percival, 1895).

Browne, Edward George Kirwan, *Annals of the Tractarian Movement*

(3rd edition, 1861, 'To be had of the Author only').

Morris, John, (ed.), *The Life of Mother Henrietta Kerr* (Roehampton, 1887).

Mozley, Rev. T., *Reminiscences chiefly of Oriel and the Oxford Movement*, 2 vols. (2nd edition, London, 1882).

Neale, J. M., *The Life and Times of Patrick Torry, D. D.* (London: Masters, 1856).

Newman, John Henry, *Notes of a Visit to the Russian Church* (London: Kegan Paul Trench, 1882).

Newman, John Henry, *The Via Media of the Anglican Church*, 2 vols. (London: Longmans, Green & Co., 1891).

Palmer, Roundell, Earl of Selborne, *Memorials Family and Personal*, vols. I & II (London: Macmillan, 1896).

Williams, The Rev'd. George, *The Orthodox Church of the East in the Eighteenth Century* (London: Rivingtons, 1868).

Zhomini, Baron Aleksandr Genrikhovich, *A Diplomatic Study on the Crimean War* (Russian Official Publication) (Glasgow: W. H. Allen, 1882).

2. Post-1900

Addison, James Thayer, *The Episcopal Church in the United States* (New York: Scribner, 1951).

Allen, Louis, *John Henry Newman & the Abbé Jager* (London: OUP, 1975).

Allen, Louis, 'French Catholics and the Oxford Movement', unpublished MS.

Chandos, John, *Boys Together: English Public Schools 1800-1814* (London: Hutchinson, 1984).

Coakley, J. F., *The Church of the East and the Church of England* (Oxford: Clarendon, 1992).

Dessain, Charles Stephen, et al., *The Letters & Diaries of John Henry Newman*, 1801-1890 (London: Nelson).

Florovsky, G., *Collected Works* (Belmont, Mass.: Nordland, 1975). Gardner, Brian, *The Public Schools* (London: Hamish Hamilton, 1973).

Gilley, S. W., *Newman and his Age* (London: Darton, Longman and Todd, 1990).

Gorman, W. Gordon, *Converts to Rome* (London: Sands & Co., 1901). Litvack, Leon, *J. M. Neale and the Quest for Sobornost* (Oxford: Clarendon, 1994).

Luscombe, Edward, *Matthew Luscombe* (Dundee: Burns & Harris, 1992).

Meyrick, Frederick, *Memories of Life at Oxford* (London: John Murray, 1905).

Middleton, R. D., *Magdalen Studies* (London: SPCK, 1936).

Miller, E. C., Jr., *Towards a Fuller Vision* (Wilton: Morehouse Barlow, 1984).

Obolensky, Dimitri, *The Byzantine Commonwealth* (New York: SVSP, 1974).

Riley, Athelstan, *Birkbeck and the Russian Church*, (London: SPCK, 1917).

Rouse, Ruth, and Neill, S. C., *A History of the Ecumenical Movement 1517-1948* (London: SPCK, 1954).

Shaw, P. E., *The Early Tractarians and the Eastern Church* (London: Mowbray, 1930).

Strong, Rowan, *Alexander Forbes of Brechin* (Oxford: Clarendon, 1995).

Strong, Rowan, *Episcopalianism in Nineteenth Century Scotland* (Oxford: OUP, 2002).

Sykes, Norman, *Old Priest, New Presbyter* (Cambridge: Cambridge University Press, 1957).

Thomson, Francis, 'William Palmer and the Orthodox Church' (Ph.D. thesis, Cambridge University, 1964).

Ware, Timothy [Kallistos], *Eustratios Argenti: A Study of the Greek Church under Turkish Rule* (Oxford: Clarendon, 1964).

Whiting, C. E., *The University of Durham* (London: The Sheldon Press, 1932).

Zernov, Nicholas, *The Russians and Their Church* (London: SPCK, 1945).

Zernov, Nicholas, 'William Palmer', unpublished MS.

Articles

Knight, Christopher, 'Anglican or Orthodox? The Scottish Dimension of the Palmer Affair,' *Sobornost* 7:1 (1985), 25-43.

Lawrence, John, 'William Palmer of Magdalen and the Russian Orthodox Church,' *Sobornost* 2:1 (1980), 80-82.

Soloviova, Tatiana, 'Anglo-Orthodox Dialogue in the 19th Century, and Gladstone's Interest in the Reunion of Christendom,' in Peter Francis (ed.), *The Gladstone Umbrella* (Monad, 2001), 50-72.

Thomson, Francis J., 'Economy,' *The Journal of Theological Studies* 16:2 (1965), 368-420.

Woolfenden, Fr. Gregory, 'Some Reflections on Orthodox and Anglican Ecclesiologies and Approaches to "Intercommunion",' *Sourozh* no. 81 (2000), 32-45.

Welch, P. J., 'Anglican Churchmen and the Establishment of the Jerusalem Bishopric,' *Journal of Ecclesiastical History* no. 8 (1957), 193-204.

Reference works

American National Biography (Oxford: OUP, 1999).

Bertie, David. M., *Scottish Episcopal Clergy*, 1689-2000 (Edinburgh: T & T Clark, 2000).

Bill, E. G. W., *A Catalogue of Manuscripts in the Lambeth Palace Library: MSS 1222-1860* (Oxford: Clarendon, 1972).

Bill, E. G. W., *A Catalogue of Manuscripts in the Lambeth Palace Library: MSS 1907-2340* (Oxford: Clarendon, 1976).

Bill, E. G. W., *A Catalogue of Manuscripts in the Lambeth Palace Library: MSS 2341-3119* (Oxford: OUP, 1983).

Boase, Frederic, *Modern English Biography* (London: Cass & Co., 1897).

Bloxam, J. R., *A register of the presidents, fellows, demies, instructors in grammar and in music, chaplains, clerks, choristers, and other members of Saint Mary Magdalen College in the University of Oxford, from the foundation of the College to the present time* (Oxford: Graham, 1853-85).

Brockgauz & Ephron, *Encyclopedeskii Slovar*, 82 vols. (St. Petersburg, 1890-1902).

Cokayne, G. E., *Complete Baronetage* (Gloucester: Sutton, 1983).

Cokayne, G. E., *The Complete Peerage of England*, Scotland, Ireland and the United Kingdom The Hon. Vicary Gibbs (ed.) 13 vols. (London: St. Catherine Press, 1913).

Crockfords Clerical Directory (London: Horace Cox, 1876).

Didot, F., and Hoefer, J. C. F., *Nouvelle Biographie Générale*, 46 vols. (Paris: Didot, 1860-66).

Foster, J., *Alumni* Oxonienses (London: Foster, 1888).

Kelly, J. N. D., *The Oxford Dictionary of Popes* (Oxford: OUP, 1986). Macray, W. D., *A Register of the Members of St. Mary Magdalen College, Oxford, from the foundation of the college* (New series) (London: Frowde, 1894-1915).

Russkii Biograficheskii Slovar, 8 vols. (New York: Kraus, 1962).

Russkii Biograficheskii Slovar Index (Vaduz: Kraus, 1963).

Stephen, Leslie, and Lee, Sidney (eds.), *The Dictionary of National Biography* (London: Smith, Elder & Co., 1885-1900).

Vapereau, G., *Dictionnaire Universel des Contemporains* (Paris: Lahure, 1858).

Acknowledgements

First and foremost I would like to thank Dr. Sheridan Gilley of Durham University for his guidance and support. I would like to thank the staffs of the libraries of Durham, Edinburgh, and Leeds Universities, of the British Library, the John Rylands Library, Manchester, the Bodleian, and in particular of Lambeth Palace Library for their help and interest. I am especially grateful to Dr. Robin Darwall-Smith, Archivist of Magdalen College, for his friendly interest and advice. I am grateful to the late Gerard Tracey, Librarian of the Birmingham Oratory for his assistance, and to Professor Francis Thomson for permission to quote from his 1963 thesis on Palmer.

I would also like to thank the underpaid and overworked staff of the Senate and Synod Archives, St. Petersburg, and Ms. Daria Yudina for her patient translation of both archives and menus. I am most grateful to Archishop Konstantin, Rector of the Spiritual Academy of St. Petersburg, for allowing me to share the life of the Academy for three weeks, and for the assistance and kindness of the Academy staff, Father Kyrill, Father Methodi, Father Vladislav, and Nadja.

I would also like to thank the following for their very generous hospitality: Father Andrey Kordochkin and his wife Alix in St. Petersburg, H. H. District Judge Margaret Brown (retired) and Martha Wailes in London, the Queen's Foundation in Birmingham, and Sister Brigitta Hoegemann and her fellow Sisters of the Work at Littlemore, Oxford.

Index

HOLY TRINITY PUBLICATIONS
JORDANVILLE, NEW YORK

PRINTSHOP OF SAINT JOB OF POCHAEV

HOLY TRINITY SEMINARY PRESS

The Making of Holy Russia

The Orthodox Church and Russian Nationalism before the Revolution

By John Strickland

A critical study of the interaction between the Russian Church and society in the late nineteenth and early twentieth century. This work introduces the reader to a wide range of "conservative" opinions that strove for spiritual renewal and the spread of the Gospel. Illuminates current issues of Church-state relations and national identity in Eastern Europe.

ISBN: 9781942699279

Embassy, Emigrants, and Englishmen

The Three-Hundred-Year History of a Russian Orthodox Church in London

By Christopher Birchall

A fascinating look at the Russian Orthodox Church abroad through the lens of one imperial embassy church turned self-supporting parish. This history offers perspectives on modern English and European history from the vantage point of a little known minority community, supported by translations of primary sources not found elsewhere.

ISBN: 9780884653363

Arab Orthodox Christians Under the Ottomans, 1516-1831

By Constantin Panchenko

This work fills a major lacuna in the scholarship of Christian history. The author draws on archaeological evidence and previously unpublished primary sources uncovered in Russian archives and Middle Eastern monastic libraries to present a vivid and compelling account of this vital but little-known spiritual and political culture.

ISBN: 9781942699088